FREEDOM'S SWORD

FREEDOM'S SWORD

Peter Traquair

ROBERTS

RINEHART

Published by Roberts Rinehart Publishers
6309 Monarch Park Place
Niwot, Colorado 80503
Tel. 303.652.2685
Fax. 303.652.2689
Visit our web site www.robertsrinehart.com

Distributed to the trade by Publishers Group West

First published by HarperCollins *Publishers*, London, 1998

© 1998 Peter Traquair

International Standard Book Number 1-57098-247-3

Library of Congress Catalog Card Number 98-85591

Maps: Peter Harper

Printed in Great Britain by Clays

10 9 8 7 6 5 4 3 2 1

CONTENTS

Introduction   7

1.   A land without a king   15
2.   To the frontier of our realm   42
3.   I have brought you to the ring,
        now dance if you can.   60
4.   An end to the business   86
5.   The making of a king   126
6.   For the Kingdom of Scotland   150
7.   Bannockburn   177
8.   Robert Bruce and the north of England   196
9.   The shameful peace   232
10. For new motive, new war   256
11. David II's captivity   300

Notes   310
Bibliography   327
Index   338

INTRODUCTION

Scotland has effectively voted for independence. As the campaign for a referendum gathered pace, most British political parties played the tartan card. John Major returned the stone of Scone in a piece of political theatre unmatched in modern Scottish political life; John Prescott retraced the steps of the English army defeated at the battle of Stirling Bridge (1297); and the Scottish National Party used the film *Braveheart* to launch a recruitment drive, standing outside cinemas to hand out leaflets. On one hand this has been all good fun, but appalling liberties have been taken with the historical facts.

When I started work on this book, the Wars of Independence attracted little attention even within the academic world. The version of history framed by John of Fordun 600 years ago had remained largely unchallenged. A few academics, mostly but not exclusively Scottish, had recently embarked on a re-examination of the sources, generating a scholarly, if low-profile, debate that produced a better understanding of the wars.

The popular view of the wars is based on the work of Scottish historians, Bruce partisans to a man writing several generations after Bruce's reign: John of Fordun's and Walter Bower's *Scotichronicon*, Andrew Wyntoun's *Orygynale Cronykil of Scotland*, and Blind Harry's *Wallace*. It is history from the point of view of the victor, written in terms of nationality and patriotism that were current at the time of writing but meant little to the actual combatants. These sources contain rich material but are framed by propagandists writing from a particular point of view, one that would have been challenged by many Scots, let alone Englishmen.

The attention these chroniclers pay the wars is not balanced by English chronicle sources apart from the Lanercost writer and Walter of Guisborough, and they are apologists for the aggressive English regime. The wars were central to English political life for a few short periods, and were often overshadowed by events in England or Europe. Modern

English historians have done little to redress this balance. There is still no adequate study of the life of Edward II. The action shifted to the continent in the mid-1330s, and the glamour of the wars in France has proved as seductive to modern writers as it did to Edward III's contemporaries. Only Edward I's policies in Scotland have been studied in detail, and then only as part of the patchwork that made up this overwhelming man.

It is a remarkable fact that the most recent history of the wars was Evan Barron's *The Scottish War of Independence*, written shortly before the First World War. Barron presents us with several problems. Medieval men did not name their wars and the 'Scottish War of Independence' is a modern invention. Coined for convenience, it does nothing to convey the many strands of the wars, of conquest, rebellion and civil war. Neither was this a single war, but a series of related conflicts. Barron ended his narrative in 1314, the year of Bannockburn. But the wars lasted on and off far longer than this, and only really came to an end in the 1560s. This book ends with the first treaty of Berwick in 1357, after which English monarchs would no longer make a sustained effort to conquer Scotland. By then there had been three discrete wars: the first, Edward I's conquest, lasted from 1296-1305; the second, when Robert Bruce rebelled, lasted from 1306-29; the third, when Edward III attempted to repeat the conquest from 1333-57.

Identifying a date that fixes the start of the descent into war is more contentious. It is perhaps best to begin from the beginning. One answer to that notorious question, 'what did the Romans ever give us?'— is that they gave us a border. The Romans landed in AD43, and although it was another 30 years before they appeared north of the Tees, Roman soldiers got as far as the Scottish highlands before renewed fighting on the Rhine and Danube curtailed operations in Britain. Hadrian ascended the imperial throne in 117, and created a formal border with the wall that still bears his name. It was imposed over the existing patterns of settlement, slicing in two several tribes that lived in the area. It formed the northern frontier of the empire for most, but not all, of the Roman period. Hadrian's successor Antoninus Pius advanced into southern Scotland and a new, shorter frontier wall was built between the Firth of Forth and the Firth of Clyde. The Romans fell back to Hadrian's wall in 161, but the emperor Septimus Severus returned nearly 50 years later in a determined effort to conquer the rest of the island, a definitive solution to the frontier problem that was only frustrated by his death in 211.

The collapse of the western Roman empire in the fifth century led to a short-lived Celtic revival in Britain, but these small kingdoms were soon overwhelmed by invaders from across the North Sea. By the seventh century, Britain was dominated by the Anglo-Saxon kingdoms of which Northumbria was once the greatest. Under the leadership of King Edwin (616-32) Northumbrian rule extended as far west as Anglesey and the Isle of Man, and from the Humber to the Clyde, including Edinburgh. But it was the southern kingdom of Wessex that proved the most enduring, surviving the Viking raids and invasions that ultimately overwhelmed the other Anglo-Saxon states.

The Vikings also destroyed the Pictish kingdom of Fortriu. The most important northern realm to survive the Viking onslaught was that of Kenneth MacAlpine, king of Dalriada. Formed in the fifth century by an Irish tribe, called *Scotti* by the Romans, Dalriada absorbed the surviving Picts to create the kingdom of Alba. This bore no resemblance to modern, or even medieval Scotland. Its boundaries were marked by the Forth to the south, the Dee and the kingdom of Moray to the north. To the west was Strathclyde, a British kingdom that revived as Northumbria weakened. As the Norse threat subsided Alba and Wessex were well placed to expand. These two powers emerged as the cradles of English and Scottish identities. Held in the north by the kingdom of Moray, the Scoto-Picts began to expand south, a process only temporarily halted in 927, when Constantine and an alliance of northern kings recognised king Athelstan of Wessex as their overlord.

The Scots had crossed the Forth by the second half of the tenth century, capturing Edinburgh in 962, but it was not until the reign of Malcolm II that the real territorial breakthrough occurred. In 1016 he forced Northumbria to cede Lothian, and two years later absorbed Strathclyde too. Malcolm's ultimate ambitions lay further south still, to the Tees and the ancient kingdom of Bernicia, the northern one of the two kingdoms that made up Northumbria.

The re-emergence of Wessex under Canute thwarted any further advance south. Canute marched into Scotland where Malcolm may have recognised his superiority in 1027. Malcolm II died in 1034. His successor Duncan later besieged Durham, but was defeated. For a short time the last of the great Northumbrian earls, Siward, re-established Northumbria's borders from the Humber to the Forth. He led invasions of Scotland in 1045-6, placing Duncan's brother on the throne, and conquered Cumberland. In a second invasion in 1054, with Malcolm III (known as 'Canmore — big-headed'), he defeated Macbeth.

The saga of raid and counter raid between rival noble houses in Scotland and Northumbria may have continued, with strong Scottish kings slowly eating into Northumbrian territory, had not a new presence entered the land in 1066. At first, William the Conqueror preserved Northumbria's semi-independent status, but in 1070 he imposed his authority in typically ruthless fashion. Malcolm Canmore's protection of English refugees, and cross-border incursions drew the wrath of the Normans. Malcolm managed to avoid engaging the superior Norman army but was forced to submit at Abernethy in 1072, recognising William as his overlord. The old Wessex claim of Scottish client status formed the basis for William the Conqueror's title, 'prince of the Normans and king of the Saxons and Britons and the Scots.'

It was with military support from the conqueror's son, William Rufus, that Duncan II and Edgar (the sons of Malcolm III) deposed Donald Ban to retrieve the Scottish throne. In one of the earliest surviving Scottish charters, dated 1095, Edgar recognised that he held Lothian and Scotland 'by gift of King William', 'by paternal inheritance'. William Rufus established the division of Cumbria between English (south of the Solway) and Scottish lands by seizing Carlisle in 1092. It served as a northern outpost to match the earlier New Castle built by his brother, Robert Curthose, on the Tyne. Only then did the border between England and Scotland became recognisable along its modern lines.

The anarchy during Stephen's reign (1135-54) offered the chance to reunite the Cumbrian and Northumbrian kingdoms under Scottish rule. David I conquered English Cumbria in 1136. He might have taken Northumbria too had he not been defeated at the battle of the Standard in 1138. Yet Stephen was in no position to follow up the victory and ceded the earldom of Northumberland and honour of Huntingdon to David's son. During Stephen's reign David held Scotland completely free of any obligation to an English king.

This shift of the border south did not outlast Stephen's reign. His successor, the altogether more formidable Henry II, promised to leave Cumbria and Northumberland under Scottish rule in return for David's support. But when he came to the throne in 1157 he reneged on the deal and absorbed the northern counties back into England. Scottish pursuit of their claim to Northumberland and Cumbria would bedevil relations between the two countries for two centuries. An attempt by William the Lion to secure the counties failed spectacularly when he was ambushed in thick fog near Alnwick and captured. He was sent to Falaise where he gained his release by recognising complete English superiority, surrendering the castles at Edinburgh, Roxburgh and Berwick.

The treaty of Falaise lasted just 15 years. At Canterbury in 1189 Richard I sold his English inheritance to fund his crusade, releasing William from English overlordship for 10,000 marks. This is often read as the key English recognition of Scotland as an independent state, but it is not: it merely returned the relationship to that which pertained prior to Falaise (although this was hardly clear). At the start of the thirteenth century William began conspiring with King John's enemies in England, but John took a large army north and intimidated William into submission. William gave up both his daughters, a sign of feudal dependence, as hostages to be married to English barons. In 1215-16 Alexander II allied himself with the English rebels, secured homage from the northern barons, and invaded England in support of prince Louis of France. John's timely death rallied support around the young Henry III. Alexander paid homage to the new king, though it is unlikely that was anything more than homage for his lands in England. For much of the thirteenth century the close relationship between the two royal families diluted English assertions of overlordship: the English pressed their claim, the Scots skilfully maintained that it never had any validity. The relationship was cemented with marriage alliances, the bedrock of medieval diplomacy. William the Lion married Ermengarde de Beaumont, a great granddaughter of Henry I, Alexander II married Joan, a daughter of king John, Alexander III married a daughter of Henry III.

The long reigns of Alexander II (1214-1249) and Alexander III (1249-86) became known as Scotland's 'Golden Age'. This is a romantic exaggeration, but Anglo-Scottish relations had never been better. Alexander II's attempt to gain the northern counties was silenced by his marriage to Joan, sister of the English king, and finally resolved by an apparently one-sided settlement at York in 1237, when he gave up his goal in exchange for estates in Tynedale and Penrith. By 1296 Scotland had established regnal authority and a settled border. Yet there was no fixed point of reference to determine the rights and responsibilities of the kingdoms, such as the 1259 treaty of Paris which governed relations between English and French kings. It has been convenient for many (mainly Scottish) historians to reflect on the peace between 1216 and 1296 as an end to the uneasy relationship between Scotland and England. It is not how Edward I saw the matter. Peace was but a temporary respite, one that depended on the distraction of Scottish and English kings by more pressing matters elsewhere or by close family ties.

There was nothing inevitable in the island of Britain dividing into two kingdoms. And when it became so, the boundary between these states was by no means pre-determined. The idea, fashionable in modern times, that nations had a permanent union with the soil is nothing but poor history and nationalist mythology. For a time it seemed likely that the island would divide into one country north of the Humber, with York as capital, and a southern kingdom based around Wessex. The division that emerged by the end of the thirteenth century was only one of many permutations arising from the historical process. Medieval England and Scotland were hybrid kingdoms, dividing between them the land belonging to the Votadini and Northumbria in the east, to the Britons and Strathclyde in the west. Scotland in the thirteenth century was a new country still trying to absorb the presence of Scandinavians in the north and the Isles, Britons in the West, the Scoto-Picts and the Angles and Normans in the South. The Norwegians were not expelled from the Western Isles until the battle of Largs in 1263. The northern earldoms, Caithness and Sutherland were still part of the North Sea world, and Orkney remained Norwegian territory for another 200 years. Galloway preserved a level of particularism that was only finally extinguished during the Wars of Independence.

It was only with hindsight that we can see the process of state formation coming to an end in the fourteenth century — largely thanks to the determined effort of Scottish leaders. Their undertaking can only be truly measured against the backcloth of a continent where few borders had yet found their 'natural' line. Older and more established kingdoms than Scotland fell, and others were yet to rise.

From a twentieth century viewpoint it is dangerously easy to see the wars in terms of nationalism, but this is to read history backwards. Nationalism of a sort played a part in the events of the 1290s, but the wars did not begin as the wars of nations. This was a feudal conflict fought to determine the rights of property, the right of one party or another to govern. They stemmed from medieval mens' obsession with legality and hereditary right, not the struggle of a nation for independence. Nationalism did not figure large in the actions of the ruling aristocracy. We only need look at the behaviour of the future king, Robert Bruce, who had himself been fighting for Edward I: when he joined the revolt and raised the banner of rebellion in his family's ancestral lands in Annandale, the men of the region sent him away with a flea in his ear. They owed their loyalty not to him, but to his father, their tenant-in-chief.

The world in which these barons lived was changing fast. The conflict was interlinked with the breakdown of feudal society and the emergence of nation states. Contemporaries were not conscious of this change, it was only identified by historians centuries later. When the war the began it was assumed that the defeat of the Scottish nobility by the English nobility ended the matter. However, feudalism had failed to accommodate the lower lords or the emerging classes in the expanding burghs. It soon became clear that in Scotland at least, the nobility were no longer the only class that mattered. If it was not a war fought in national interests, the revolts of Wallace and Murray only a year into Edward I's Scottish regime show that a common sense of identity had already been forged. The leading men responded more slowly than their tenants to the changing ambitions and culture of Scotland. It would become stronger as the suffering of the Scots, of high taxation, oppression and the demands of military service, became identified with the English occupation. Nationalism as a force that could influence events was the result, not the cause of the wars. *Freedom's Sword* is neither a Scottish history of the wars, nor is it an English apology: this is a history of an island at war.

Chapter 1

A LAND WITHOUT A KING

A land without a king lay in as much perplexity as a vessel in the midst
of the waves of the ocean without oarsman or helmsman
Walter Comyn, earl of Menteith[1]

It was the unsure footing of Alexander III's horse that began a course of
events which would eventually lead to war with England. Rumour
circulated that the night of 18 March 1286 would bring judgement on
the king—a raging storm served only to compound foolish
superstitions. Alexander held a council in Edinburgh castle. At a
banquet afterwards the king joked about the rumours. His barons urged
him to wait until the storm abated before setting out. At the river bank
the ferrymaster tried to persuade him not to go on with his journey. But
Alexander, impatient to be with his bride at Kinghorn in Fife, crossed the
Forth with three esquires. On the far bank he was parted from his guides
in the darkness and lost. Next morning he was found dead on the wrong
path, thrown from his horse, his neck broken.

The long and stable reigns of Alexander and his father would be
looked back on as a golden age. After 80 years of peace with England,
Scotland was becoming a player in mainstream Europe. The battle of
Largs (1263) had removed Norwegian influence in all but Orkney and
Shetland, and the semi-independent Galloway had been pacified. The
burghs burst into life with the growth from the wool trade and areas
under cultivation.[2] It looked as if Scotland would settle into the
inoffensive security of a small nation on the edge of Europe. Yet for all
the good of Alexander's reign it closed with the ultimate failing of
medieval kingship: he left no male heir to succeed him. On or around his
twentieth birthday Alexander's eldest son died of the catch-all medieval
illness, slow ague.

For Edward I, king of England, this was a family tragedy: the death of
his nephew, the son of his sister. 'We are united together perpetually,
God willing', he wrote, 'by a link of indissoluble love.' It is one of 'the
many kindnesses we have received' from his 'dearest brother' Alexander

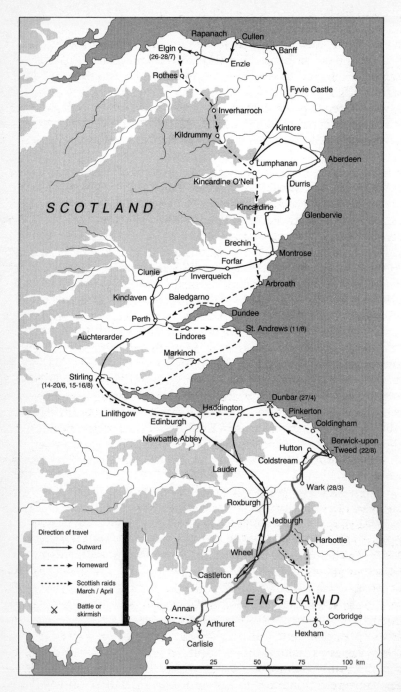

Edward I's invasion of Scotland, 1297

replied to his brother-in-law's touching note, 'much good may come to pass yet through your kinswoman, the daughter of your niece ... who is now our heir-apparent'. The letters go beyond diplomatic niceties, reflecting the warmth in family and national relations. The kinswoman Alexander referred to was his granddaughter. His daughter Margaret married Eric II, king of Norway in 1281. She died after two unhappy years in Bergen, a place she thought rough and cold (and that compared to thirteenth century Scotland). A daughter, yet another Margaret, survived her. This little girl, known as the Maid of Norway, was now heir.

Two weeks after his son's death Alexander gathered a meeting of the Scottish prelates and nobility at Scone. Here, he issued at *tailzie* or entail that confirmed the Maid, the last of the Canmores, as his successor. This was a meagre substitute for a male heir but Alexander was still only forty-three and in good health, there was plenty of time to remarry. In an effort to restore the direct male line a search began for a suitable bride. At Jedburgh, on 14 October 1285, he married Yolande, daughter of the count of Dreux—one of Edward I's Gascon vassals. With luck, there would soon be a male heir. Five months later he was dead.

Little is known about Scotland's new queen. Even her age is uncertain. So many children died young that chroniclers tended to ignore the birth of a daughter, even a royal one. In 1286 the Maid must have been no more than three or four years old. At this point there seemed little chance of her inheriting the throne peacefully. The entail that Alexander issued two years earlier carried no legal weight. A king's authority did not stretch beyond the grave, it only showed what Alexander thought should happen and was not binding on his successors. Besides, much weighed against the Maid: she was an infant, a foreigner, a woman, she was not present to press her claim, and there were other, assertive, candidates.[1]

Such a power struggle would normally be determined by the principal magnates in civil war, unless an outside ruler intervened. The only foreign rulers who could have become involved were Edward I of England and Eric II of Norway, and Eric was diverted by a threat from Denmark. The magnates who gathered for Alexander's funeral held a parliament at Scone to consider the succession. Two Dominican friars sent with the news of Alexander's death, and details of the settlement reached at the parliament, found Edward preparing for a journey to Gascony.

Edward's problems in France were more pressing than any opportunities presented in Scotland; in May he set sail for Gascony where he would remain for the next three years. In August a further delegation went to treat with Edward, finding him at Saintes. There is no evidence of this mission's remit, but no doubt they sought Edward's peaceful intentions and dealt with more mundane matters affecting both realms.

It was left to the magnates to resolve the succession. The two men nearest in blood to the throne were Robert Bruce lord of Annandale and John Balliol. Bruce seemed to deny the right of female inheritance, and when Balliol arrived there was 'bitter pleading' between the two men.[5] But civil war did not break out. Alexander's queen was pregnant.

Nothing could be decided until her pregnancy ran its course; to make a move for the throne now would prove treasonable if she gave birth to a boy. Besides, Balliol and Bruce were too evenly matched. Most nobles wanted to keep the peace and would have opposed the first to revolt. At the parliament the magnates swore an oath to keep the peace.

Without a king Scotland's government became the collective responsibility of the leading freemen, who styled themselves 'the community of the realm of Scotland'. This was a new idea beginning to establish itself in Europe, the community being formed by the people (the freemen) rather than a closed aristocratic elite. It would form the backbone of resistance in the difficult years until Robert Bruce seized the throne. It was the community of the realm that foreshadowed William Wallace's rebellion in 1297 and later legitimised Robert's kingship. It elected Guardians who ruled in its name for the following six years. The six new Guardians neatly reflected Scotland's political, social and geographic divisions. The Bishops of St Andrews and Glasgow represented the church, Fife and Buchan the earls, John Comyn of Badenoch and James the Steward the lords. Three represented Scotland north of the Forth, three the South. The Guardians also represented the loose alignments in Scottish political life. It should be stressed that this was not a fragile coalition waiting to burst apart, on the everyday matters of government that affected the realm the men could and did work together. In the short term Alexander's death had not turned out to be such a catastrophe.[2]

Bruce readied himself for the outcome of Yolande's pregnancy. On 20 September, in his son's castle at Turnberry, he signed a pact with the Steward, the earl of Dunbar and his own son, the Earl of Carrick. Essentially the document is a private one—they entered into an obligation with two Anglo-Irish lords, Richard de Burgh Earl of Ulster and Thomas de Clare and concerns Irish matters. Much has been read into the document, maybe it was a 'prelude to a show of force'[3], more than that it reveals Bruce's attitude to the Guardians' regime: it is inconceivable that such a pact could have been made during the reign of Alexander III. The document's final clause saved faith both to the king of England and 'to the person who, by reason of the blood of the late king Alexander, shall obtain the realm of Scotland in accordance with the ancient customs hitherto approved and applied in the realm of

Scotland.' Bruce hedged his bets, he took into account the possibilities of Yolande's pregnancy, with a nod to Edward should that pregnancy be shown to be false.

Towards the end of the year it was clear, whether through miscarriage, phantom pregnancy or deception—according to one hostile English source—she was not pregnant. Yolande should be elevated from the historical footnote where she has usually been consigned: although she is not mentioned again in the documents concerning the succession, she stole the thunder of both parties, giving the Guardians time to establish their authority in the nervous aftermath of Alexander's death.

A Bruce show of force was not slow coming. During the winter civil war seemed a very real possibility. Bruce captured Devorguilla Balliol's castle at Buittle. More disturbingly, he seized the royal castles at Dumfries and Wigtown. The Guardians reacted decisively, calling out the host, and against this determined opposition Bruce's uprising fizzled out. The Guardians' authority was not challenged over the next three years. The death of the earl of Buchan and the perplexing murder of the earl of Fife reduced their number to four; vacancies left unfilled reflecting the risk of shifting the balance of power from new appointments.

It is unknown when or even who first proposed a dynastic union between the Maid and Edward Caernarfon, heir to the English throne. The idea must have occurred to some minds by 1289, when Edward I returned to England. All three parties to the union could see its attractions. The fear of civil war compelled the Guardians and Eric II to seek a marriage alliance for the Maid that would secure her succession and minority.

There was no more powerful guarantor than Edward I, and no better example of English influence than when Henry III meddled in Scottish politics to secure the peace during the minority of his daughter Margaret and Alexander III. For Edward a union between the houses of Canmore and Plantagenet would not only secure his northern border but would extend the Plantagenet empire. He also had personal reasons—so far he had been unsuccessful in the European marriage market in finding partners for any of his six children.

The first stage in the protracted marriage negotiations took place at Salisbury in November 1289. A Norwegian embassy appointed to confer with Edward also met a Scottish delegation—the bishops Fraser of St Andrews and Wishart of Glasgow, the elder John Comyn of Badenoch and Robert Bruce—before Edward, who acted as an interested mediator. The king saw no urgency. Other matters demanded his attention, so he left the negotiations to some of his most trusted advisors: bishops Gifford of Worcester and Anthony Bek of Durham, William de Valence and the earl Warenne. The agreement reached was more important for what it did not say, the word 'marriage' does not actually appear.

The Norwegians promised to send the Maid to England or Scotland within the year free of any marriage contract. Edward received assurances that she would not be married without his sanction, and that Scotland was in a safe and peaceful state. The king's counsel and mediation would be sought on all matters affecting the welfare of the realm in which disputes arose. This last clause, pressed by the Norwegian delegation to ensure Margaret's safety and acceptance in Scotland, gave Edward his first legal right to interfere in day-to-day Scottish affairs. The two children shared common ancestry—Henry III as Caernarfon's grandfather, the Maid's great-grandfather—so the marriage required papal dispensation, which Edward sought from Pope Nicholas IV.

Negotiations resumed in the spring of 1290. At a parliament held at Birgham the Scottish nobility and church approved the Salisbury treaty. The Guardians and community sent letters to the kings of England and Norway welcoming the marriage, asking Eric to agree and promising to send representatives to England to conclude an agreement. The pivotal question regarding the relationship between the two realms after the marriage still had to be faced. Edward Caernarfon would only rule Scotland, if at all, by right of his wife. His successor would hold two crowns and Scotland feared that its larger southern neighbour would devour it much the same way as it had Wales.

The marriage could not take place until 1298 when both Edward and Margaret were old enough. In the meantime, both sides wanted custody of Margaret, and *de facto* wardship, and both sent delegations to fetch her. The Guardians appointed two Fife landholders: Michael Wemyss and Michael Scot.[4] They were unsuccessful as the Norwegians remained concerned for the Maid's safety. In early May Edward appointed his own envoys to treat with Eric II: it was a curiously low-key delegation, led by Thomas Sutton, Abbot of the premonstratensian house at Welbek who had never served the crown before. It left from Hartlepool on 9 May, reaching Bergen 17 days later. Eric was away from the capital and thedelegates did not take the initiative to find him[5].

In June Edward appointed Anthony Bek his envoy in Scotland. Negotiations now gathered pace. Wary of the dangers presented by the union, the Scots sought guarantees that the country would remain separate from England, divided from it by proper borders; that no new castles were to be built in the marches and the liberties of the church would be maintained. The Guardians needed Edward's protection for the infant queen and the marriage alliance that would deter other claims to the throne. But they were walking a tight-rope, with as much to lose as Edward had to gain. A reply to these demands prepared for Bek, but not presented, indicates English thinking. They would only tolerate a solitary condition, to keep the proper borders, they would not consent to the other terms. Nevertheless a draft treaty was on the table at Birgham in July, confirmed by Edward at Northampton on 28 August. The Scots achieved most of their demands in the treaty of Birgham-Northampton, chief amongst them that Scotland should be 'separate and divided, and free in itself, from the realm of England.' Edward regarded the necessary concessions as a price worth paying to bring Scotland within the Plantagenet family.

Despite the treaty Edward could not resist exerting the authority given him by the Salisbury agreement regarding the question of *reformatio* and *emendatio*, reform and reformation of Scotland. Edward wrote to the Guardians, saying he had appointed Anthony Bek his lieutenant in Scotland on behalf of the Maid and Caernarfon. He instructed them to be obedient to Bek and to defer to him in all matters 'which are required for the governance and peaceful state of the realm.' It is likely Bek was refused entry into the country[6]. On 4 June Edward received the Isle of Man from Richard Burgh, he sought no consultation with the Guardians over its future. Alexander III had suppressed a Manx revolt 15 years earlier, but the island had remained poorly governed. There was common relief at Edward's intervention, though this was of no comfort to the Guardians trying to preserve Scotland's integrity. Edward then granted the Scottish king's liberty of Tynedale and the honour of Penrith to Anthony Bek to recompense him for the pensions he granted to Norwegian nobles during the marriage negotiations.[7] These were the pinpricks of English superiority, pinpricks that should have caused concern in Scotland.

In late summer news arrived that Eric himself would come to complete negotiations. Anthony Bek and earl Warenne travelled north. On the Sunday after Michaelmas (29 September) the Scottish magnates assembled at Perth in a parliament to meet and hear messages from Edward. An Anglo-Scottish embassy, comprising Bek, Wishart, John Comyn, Earl Warenne and Henry Newark was set up to negotiate directly with Eric and envoys set out from the parliament to meet him. Eric did not come eventually, but sent Margaret to Orkney so that negotiations could be completed on Norwegian soil (Orkney was subject to Norway until 1452).

Fate had one last cruel trick to play on Alexander's family. The poor little queen never set foot in her realm. She died on 26 September 1290. The accounts of her death are few and inconclusive, none of the contemporary documents reveals any detail. The chroniclers, who would normally have written at tedious length on the subject of a monarch's death—especially one with such far reaching consequences—observe a hushed silence. Bishop Audfinn of Bergen gave us the only details we have, and even this is sketchy and written thirty years later. A rumour began in Norway that the Maid had been kidnapped and sold into slavery, a tale that gained currency when an impostor arrived from Germany. The pretender was put to death in Bergen in 1301, which only intensified the legend and a cult began to form around her. Audfinn wrote that pilgrimages to the place of her execution should end since the Maid 'died in the arms' of Bishop Narve of Bergen. It is not known whether from the journey or some other reason. Her body was taken back to Norway where it was shown to the king before being buried in Christ Church cathedral beside her mother[8]. The English envoys stopped at Skelbo for two nights and 'spoke with Scottish messengers.' It was probably now that they heard of her death, their journey made redundant they returned to England.

The marriage of the six-year old Caernarfon and the seven-year old Margaret was a reassuring but fragile solution to the threat of the minority: the broad hopes of two nations carried on very young shoulders. It was founded on the medieval lottery of the survival of two infants. Nobody had devised a fall back position. Whether a thirteenth century union of the English and Scottish crowns would have been successful or not will never be known, but it remains one of history's more intriguing 'might have beens'. There were no obvious parallels in Europe from which to draw similarities. Given the Scottish insistence at Birgham that the kingdoms were to remain separate, the immediate difference would have been limited. Once an heir was born there would surely have been closer ties and a convergence of political and social systems. Scotland and England were already interlocked: the border was natural only in its geography—the Tweed-Solway isthmus forming a clearer boundary than the Pennines, but which one which split in two the ancient kingdoms of Strathclyde in the west and Northumbria in the east. The countries had an interchangeable coinage, now touted as a definition of sovereignty, and a border with little cultural meaning. The aristocracy was at home in both courts. Of course, given what a hopeless monarch Edward II turned out to be, the case for a thirteenth century union cannot be taken for granted, but a union then would have been far easier to achieve than one in the eighteenth, burdened by centuries of appalling warfare.

The rumours of Margaret's death reached bishop Fraser of St Andrews at Leuchars by 7 October. The rumours reached other ears. Robert Bruce, who had shown himself the more aggressive claimant to the throne in 1286, went to Perth with a great following and an unknown objective; his supporters, the earls of Mar and Atholl, were raising the armies of their earldoms.

'Let your excellency deign, if you please,' Fraser wrote to Edward 'to approach toward the Marches for the consolation of the Scottish people and to save the shedding of blood, and set over them for king him who of right ought to have the succession.'

The bishop wrote his letter before the consequences of Margaret's death became clear. It was an understandable plea for help to the only source of relief from civil war if his worst fears were realised. Fraser also took the premature opportunity to let his own preference be known, telling Edward that he feared Bruce would take the throne before John Balliol had a chance to stake his claim and hinted that Edward should come to an accommodation with Balliol. There is no question at this stage of seeking Edward's adjudication, rather Fraser was petitioning Edward to act as a guarantor of the Scots' own king-making process. It was a cautious and pragmatic gesture for which the bishop and his ally, John Comyn of Badenoch, were undeservedly vilified.

In the power-vacuum after Margaret's death John Balliol was not slow to advance his own claim. From Gateshead he confirmed Anthony Bek's possession of the Scottish king's lands in the north, a charter issued in his name as 'heir of the kingdom of Scotland'.

The Bruce party features prominently, conjured up the 'Appeal of the Seven Earls of Scotland', a curious document published to further Bruce's claim[9]. It delved into antiquity to proclaim an ancient (and probably bogus) device giving the Seven Earls the right to crown a new king, challenging the right of the Guardians to decide who would inherit the throne. The document 'smacks of emotive propaganda' to drum up support in Scotland. Bruce already grasped his need for endorsement, if not backing, from England. The Appeal reaffirmed his allegiance to Edward: he was careful not to let Fraser steal a march on the one man who was strong enough to force a settlement on either side.

We simply do not know how Edward I became involved in the succession. Both St Andrews' letter and the Bruce Appeal nhint at calls for such a role from an early date, but in themselves are too vague to be considered an invitation. Walter of Guisborough, one of the best contemporary sources on the early stages of the wars, writes little on the subject of the succession. He points to a mission by Anthony Bek and John de Vescy, at the request of the Guardians. The English envoys advised them to submit the case to Edward's judgement. Guisborough believed it was advice they accepted and a Scottish parliament made a formal invitation to the king. He is a reliable source, but this is not corroborated by any contemporary documents. Anthony Bek went to Scotland in late January, it is possible that a verbal request was made to him then. Without this invitation it is impossible to know the basis of Edward's intervention.[10]

Edward's plans were rudely interrupted towards the end of November 1290 when his queen became seriously ill. Edward was devoted to Eleanor of Castile. He had relied upon her support and advice during difficult times—they had been married 36 years, and he was still only 52. Her death shattered the king. Inconsolable, he made no plans beyond the elaborate funeral and then retired to Ashbridge, where he spent Christmas and remained until the end of the month. All matters of state were put on hold. In the spring he began to return to his duties. By a parliament at the royal hunting lodge at Clipstone in Nottinghamshire, in March 1291, the case was in his jurisdiction.

With hindsight it is easy to see the Scottish invitation to Edward as naive, his history with the Welsh princes and his high-handed attitude to Scottish liberties during the marriage negotiations should have been some warning. The Birgham terms show that the Scots recognised the danger. But there is a less publicised side to the English king. It may seem hard to swallow now, but Edward I was known as a peacemaker in Europe. He was the continent's senior statesman and head of the secular crusading movement. In Gascony from 1286-89 he had negotiated between rival claims to the Sicilian crown. He had also never shown much interest in Scotland, visiting the country only once before, to visit his sister Margaret at Haddington in 1266 or 1267. In 1291 there was every reason to believe Edward would prevent the realm disintegrating into a bloody civil war.

Historians have named the events that followed the Great Cause.[11] It is one of the best documented, least well known and most remarkable events in British history. It is one of the most splendid legal and political achievements of medieval men. The Scottish community, in the heartfelt belief that the rule of law should prevail, determined to set the trial to the right of the crown before a foreign court. That it could take place at all was a clear indication of how close the two realms were towards the end of the thirteenth century.

If the events leading to the Great Cause are hazy because of the lack of original documents, the Cause itself is awash with documents due to Edward I's determination to place his dealings with Scotland on record. No other medieval event is so well recorded. Edward employed a public notary, John of Caen, rather than a court clerk to draw up the full record of the proceedings. Edward II ordered a second record, written by another notary, Andrew Tange. There is no equivalent Scottish record, which is a pity. We do not know what Caen missed out, items that may have been prejudicial to Edward, or how much Tange 'refined' his account in the light of subsequent events.

The court sat for six months over an eighteen month period listening to complex legal arguments. It placed a great strain on local society and on those who took part. There were few lodging places in Berwick and prices rose steeply. John Balliol had the luxury of being able to send men to his nearby English estates to gather necessary foodstuffs and imported wine and grain from Ireland, but few others would have been so lucky. Eighteen counties supplied the court with grain at a cost of £1,680 between May and August 1291 alone. Edward himself had to run two countries, as far away from the centre of English government as it was possible to be—fees paid to messengers rose four fold.[12]

The hearings took place in different locations along the river Tweed. Norham castle was the stronghold of the warrior bishops of Durham's northern lands bordering on Scotland, the now defunct Norham and Island shires. It stands on a natural defensive site, rising up above the village and overlooking the Tweed. It was in the keep built by bishop Hugh du Puiset after Henry II's seizure of Northumberland in 1157 that Edward held council meetings. For the English this was an obvious site to begin the cause, a traditional meeting place on the border. It was here that the treaties of 1209 and 1212 were completed. Many of the meetings took place in Norham church, a building which seems unsuitably majestic for this size parish, but this was Puiset's church— and he was not a man who did things in half measures. Most of the current church dates from the nineteenth century, only the chancel and south arcade survive from 1291; its current nave at 70 feet is shorter than in 1291. Today it can seat 500 people, ample room for 1291.

Further proceedings took place in the open air on a green 'in the parish of Upsettlington', on the Scottish side of the Tweed, accommodating a Scottish desire not to set a precedent by hearing the case in England. The exact location of this site is unknown, probably in a field directly across from Norham. This was the largest gathering place. No bridge stood there in 1291, the site was reached by a ford half a mile down stream. The court moved to Berwick-upon-Tweed for its final sessions. Edward would have avoided using Berwick if possible, as he hated towns, the court finally locating here to make the life of the delegates a little easier. The only section of Berwick castle standing today is the west wall that forms the boundary of the railway line, the rest destroyed in the wave of Victorian railway vandalism. The disused Dominican friary also had a church suitable for large meetings.

Edward arrived at Norham on 5 May. The following day a council of 'clergy learned in civil and canon law, many monks with their chronicles, and many bishops, including the archbishop of York, met to discuss finally the overlordship of Scotland ... who, after diligent examinations of times past ... declared individually and together, on their consciences, that the lordship belonged to the king of England, unless something contrary were found by which the chronicle evidence could be refuted.'

Two months earlier Edward wrote to the abbot of Evesham asking him to examine his chronicles, and send without delay 'everything that he finds touching in any way our realm and the rule of Scotland.'[13] It is one of 30 or so letters sent out to the religious houses in search of historical evidence of English overlordship. His clerks had already combed the royal archives and were widening the net. They had begun their search late because of the delay caused by Eleanor's death, now the monastic librarians had to work feverishly in the short time before Edward headed north; the Evesham reply came three days later. The work of some was still not complete. A few days after the first session started the sub-usher of the king's court was paid one mark for bringing a letter that provided evidence of William the Lion's homage to king John in 1212. This was the only document that appears to have been forged. There was ample scope for forgery, as so many important documents had gone missing or had been destroyed, but there does not seem to have been any systematic attempt to falsify documents. [14]

This scramble through the historical records reveals that Edward had determined that his intervention would come at a price, the formalising of the English crown's superior relationship with Scotland. For much of the thirteenth century the close relationship between the two royal families diluted English assertions of overlordship: the English pressed their claim, the Scots skilfully maintained that it never had any validity. The English had the wisdom to respect Scottish kingship, the Scots the good sense to ensure its alliances never threatened England and that the English king's rights were upheld. This meant that at the time of the Great Cause the feudal dependence had become vague, but certainly not meaningless. For medieval men there was no concept of the evolution of the state, rather the past bore witness to unchanging rights. Edward sincerely believed in the legality of his overlordship. He did not need to invent a claim.

The king needed to cross two hurdles, the first of his own making. The expedient signing of the Birgham-Northampton treaty in 1290 required him to respect the Scottish realm. Edward simply sidelined the treaty. It his first underhand dealing with the Scots and one which the future Scottish king would return to. The second hurdle, the Guardians' oath in 1286 to preserve the kingdom as it was left to them, could not be ignored so lightly.

Roger Brabazon opened the Great Cause on 10 May in Norham parish church, before a gathering of the magnates of England and Scotland with a prepared speech in French. It is not difficult to imagine the scene, the church packed with the most important men of two realms, most standing, many at the back not able to hear. There must have been a ripple of indignation as the implications of Brabazon's speech sunk into the Scottish delegation. Brabazon announced that Edward had come to keep the peace and judge the cause by virtue of his overlordship. He did not read the historical evidence to the court, but instead, Brabazon made a carefully worded challenge to those Scots present, requiring them to acknowledge Edward's overlordship.

The question expressly posed was 'can you produce any evidence to show that I am not the rightful suzerain?' Edward had neatly shifted the burden of proof. He would not continue without this admission. His justification, one not without merit, was that the case needed a judge, not an arbitrator. His experience of the Sicilian dispute, and of Louis IX's arbitration between Henry III and Simon de Montfort, had taught him that an arbitration, without the power to enforce the decision of the court, was worthless. Besides, to have acted as an arbitrator would have involved the abandonment of the English claim to homage, not something that would have appealed to any medieval king, especially one like Edward.

The English demand caught the Scottish delegates unprepared. Wishart put forward instant and vocal hostility. The church was the scene of a bitter row. Eventually Edward allowed a day's adjournment, extended next day to three weeks, so an answer could be considered.

The court resumed on the north bank of the Tweed for a session that lasted from 2-13 June. This time Edward brought an army with him.[15] In writs dated 16 April he ordered his brother, Edmund, some earls and prelates, together with the northern barons to meet in arms on 3 June at Norham, he also ordered English ships to stand by if they were needed to blockade Scottish ports.[15] In 1321 the Scots would claim that Edward used this force to intimidate the Scottish delegation.[16] It is a not a convincing accusation, and not made until Robert I was trying to persuade a European audience of the validity of his kingship by disputing the court's final judgement. It is unlikely that this was Edward's intention or its result. It was a small army, the paid troops amounted to only 650-750 archers and foot, the feudal summons mustered only 650 cavalry. This compares to the 25,000 he would have with him on his first invasion in 1296.[17] He is more likely to have assumed that the court would make its decision shortly after the resumption in June and called up the force as a precaution in case a disappointed claimant was intent on making trouble.

The Scottish answer to Edward's question did not come from the Guardians, but from the '*bone gent*' (the persons of substance), the community of the realm. In a written reply Edward was told that:

> 'They have no knowledge of your right, nor do they ever see it claimed and used by you or your ancestors; therefore they answer you ... that they have no power to reply to your statement, lacking a lord to whom the demand ought to be addressed ... for he, and not they, will have power to reply and to act in the matter.'

The community begged Edward to trust their loyalty and not to press his claim. He was invited to cross the Tweed and arbitrate as a friend. Edward believed that they had wilfully ducked his question (which they had), as 'nothing to the point' (which it was). Edward presented a claim to Scottish-overlordship that he strongly believed was his by right, but it was not the only interpretation of the Anglo-Scottish relationship. His dismissal of the community of the realm's written statement showed that he was willing to override other interpretations at a time when the Scots were unable to provide a vigorous response. The document was not registered in the official records but this does not mean that he dismissed it out of hand: his actions showed that he took careful note of the Scottish response.

Edward changed tack. The plea had a shortcoming that he ingeniously exploited. He insisted that the claimants present should submit themselves to his judgement as overlord on the basis that one of the claimants would be king, so if all submitted then he would have the reply of the lord. That record says that eight of the competitors were present. Edward's spokesman, Robert Burnell, the bishop of Bath and Wells, asked them if they were willing to accept Edward's judgement, and so, making 'a virtue of necessity,' all agreed. The record does not say how much the king pressured and probably bullied the candidates into submission during the first two weeks of June. Many were English lords who owed their position to the king. The weaker candidates knew that they had little chance of inheriting the crown, and even less if did not agree to the judgement on Edward's terms.

Once the king won over the Bruce party resistance was futile. John Balliol was missing on the day that Burnell sought the competitor's submission. In the records his representative, Thomas Randolph, apologised to the court that Balliol had mixed up the day he was meant to appear and entered a plea in his absence. This is difficult to accept. As the man most likely to inherit the throne, Balliol resisted Edward's demands to the last but was forced to fall into line after the other claimants submitted. The competitor's bestowal of the seisin of Scotland on Edward is known as the 'Award of Norham'. Robert Wishart and bishop Crambeth of Dunkeld wrung concessions from Edward: that upon the death of a Scots king nothing but homage and the rights incident of homage, that the competitors would be indemnified from future claims and that the case would be heard in Scotland. Edward did not get everything he wanted, but he got enough. It was another five years before war broke out. Despite mistakes made by both sides in the intervening period the war stemmed from this.

With the community of the realm's defence brushed aside, Edward moved on to the application of his overlordship. It was unclear how the award should be, or was, made. The Guardians acted on behalf of the

Maid as rulers, and from her death continued in their rule, yet it appears the competitors played the greater role as agents of transfer. There was likely some form of symbolic delivery. The castles presented something of a difficulty. Gilbert de Umfraville earl of Angus, an Englishman, refused to surrender Dunbar and Forfar on the grounds that 'he had not received them from the king of England, but from the people of Scotland.' The documents kept in the English records only refer to Umfraville. This once led historians to believe that his was a solitary stand, but it is now know that fourteen constables of twenty-two royal castles refused to surrender their charges. It seems that, because he was an English lord, letters addressed to Umfraville were not delivered and remained in the exchequer.[18]

A compromise was reached whereby Edward received the castles not as lord of Scotland but as one of the claimants on behalf of them all. Edward was descended from the marriage of Henry I and Matilda, daughter of Malcolm III; he never entered a formal claim but reserved his right to do so. The competitors then indemnified the commanders by letters patent issued for any damages resulting from their surrender.[19] The custody was awarded on the sworn guarantee that the realm would be returned within two months of a judgement to him 'who shall gain the right, by judgement, of royalty.' On 11 June the Guardians resigned. Two days later, in Upsettlington, they were reappointed. Edward did not make sweeping changes to Scotland's government, he gave the Guardians a free hand to run the country. He added to their number the Yorkshire baron, Brian FitzAlan of Bedale to demonstrate his seisin and to keep an eye on the Guardians—on the same basis Edward also appointed associates for the chamberlain and chancellor. The Guardians and Scottish magnates then swore allegiance to Edward as 'superior and direct' lord of Scotland.

The procedure by which the trial would take place was determined in tandem with the question of the court's authority. The court was made up of 104 auditors, 105 including Edward. The court recognised the principal claimants even at this early stage—with Robert Bruce nominating 40 auditors, Balliol and Comyn a further 40. Edward nominated the remaining 24. For most of the case Edward consulted his own auditors, referring to the 80 Scottish auditors on matters of law or to approve judgements.[29] It is possible that the court modelled itself on the Roman *judicium centumvirale*, a 105 member court used to settle property disputes. Recent historians have suggested that this is antiquarian nonsense, but although mechanisms were in place without resort to Roman law the adoption of a classical court fits in neatly with Edward's legal mind. This was an exceptional jury, to judge an exceptional case, and the coincidence of the number of members a little too close to dismiss out of hand. The 80 Scottish auditors represent the leading men of the realm. The two sets of auditors were fairly evenly matched: Bruce commanded the support of six earls and the Steward, whereas Balliol had four earls; this temporal support in Bruce's favour is matched by the ecclesiastical support for Balliol: six bishops, seven abbots and a prior to Bruce's two bishops and two priors. It would seem that Balliol had God on his side.

With the procedural question settled the court broke up, with a new location on its resumption eight weeks later. Berwick would allow better access and accommodation for the delegates. Edward toured his new realm, travelling as far as St Andrews, returning by way of Perth. At Stirling he ordered that all persons who would normally make oaths of fealty to the Scottish king to swear fealty to him. To 'save everyone the toil and expense' of travelling to the border fealties could be sworn at Perth, Ayr, Inverness, and in Galloway to the Guardians and other Scottish representatives of the king.[20]

On the resumption at Berwick twelve competitors appeared before the king and auditors and entered their submissions in writing. This headlong rush to claim the throne may appear unseemly today, and it was plain that many of the competitor's claims were frivolous. Five, Patrick of Dunbar Earl of March, William de Ros, William de Vescy, Roger de Mandeville and Patrick Golightly claimed descent from the illegitimate children of William the Lion, a man who 'did not curb to the full the impulses of the flesh' or 'subdue the assaults of sensuality' in his youth which resulted in an uncounted number of bastard progeny.[21] The Earl of Dunbar appeared as an auditor for Bruce, which was a measure of the seriousness of his claim. Nicholas de Soules claimed illegitimate descent from Alexander II. Illegitimacy was, in all circumstances, a total bar to medieval inheritance.

John Comyn of Badenoch's descent was legitimate, but from Donald Ban, why Comyn thought his claim valid when descendants from later generations were available is unknown. The claim of a thirteenth competitor, the king of Norway, seemed the most frivolous of all. He did not enter his claim, the thirteenth, until 2 June 1292. It rested on his relationship to the Maid, that of ascent rather than descent.

We should not judge these men too harshly. There were many reasons other than 'the medieval fondness for controversy and litigation, and a desire to appear in the public eye' for coming forward. Chiefly they entered their claims for the record, in case the legitimate line should fail. Some no doubt wanted to be seen as equals of the future king, some came to profitable private arrangements with other competitors. Eric II forwarded his claim to put pressure on the Guardians to settle his wife's dowry.[22]

The real issue lay five generations back, between the legitimate descendants of Henry Earl of Northumbria, the father of two Scottish kings, Malcolm IV and William the Lion. The descendants of two daughters entered claims: Florence count of Holland and Robert Pinkeny. The heir of a third sister, Humphrey Bohun earl of Hereford, decided not to put forward a claim for unknown reasons. The descendants of a third son, David Earl of Huntingdon, were one step closer to the throne. His inheritance was divided among three daughters: the eldest, Margaret (what else), grandmother of John Balliol; Isabel, mother of Robert Bruce the Competitor; and Ada, grandmother of John Hastings of Abergavenny.

John Balliol was a wealthy English lord with estates in seventeen English counties, worth rents of £500 a year, and in Picardy in France— hence the family's surname, from Bailleul in Picardy. William Rufus granted Guy de Balliol a large estate in Upper Teesdale in 1093, his son Bernard built the castle that still bears his name. Two younger brothers of Hugh de Balliol acquired estates in Scotland, but it was Hugh's son, John who brought the family's real interest in Scotland with this marriage to Devorguilla, heiress of John of Galloway. As a younger son, the competitor came into his inheritance after the deaths of his brothers during his father's lifetime. He did not inherit his mother's estates until her death in 1290 so was little known in Scotland. He was unprepared for the role thrust upon him, there is a suggestion that he was bound for the church[23], though he married well, to a daughter of the earl Warenne. His Scottish pedigree was sound, as his mother's Gaelic name suggests (dearbh-fhorghoill, 'true judgement').

When historians talk of Bruce being 'more Scottish' than Balliol it is because they discount the female line as less important than the male: which it was for medieval men. John Balliol had close links with the Comyns, for most of the thirteenth century the dominant force in Scottish politics. At this point John Comyn the elder led the senior branch, the red or Badenoch line. He married John Balliol's sister Eleanor. The cadet branch, the black, was led by another John Comyn, Earl of Buchan.

The octogenarian Robert Bruce was the son of the second Huntingdon daughter, Isabel. A contemporary chronicler thought him 'of handsome appearance, a gifted speaker, remarkable for his influence, and, what is more important, most devoted to God and the clergy. It was his custom to entertain and feast more liberally than all the other courtiers, and was most hospitable to his guests.' His age belied an energy and determination which bordered on an aggressiveness that was missing from his chief rival for the throne. In 1124 David I granted the lordship of Annandale to the Norman Robert Bruce II, who held large estates in Cleveland centred on Guisborough. This was all part of the peaceful penetration of Scotland by the Anglo-Norman aristocracy. The family's English ties remained intact. Bruce the Competitor played an important role in the politics of both kingdoms. He had fought with Edward at the battle of Lewes (1264) and at one time he had served as the governor of Carlisle castle. He married a daughter of the Earl of Gloucester, Isabel de Clare. Equally at home in the Scottish and English courts, Robert Bruce was an important member of the exclusive aristocratic elite in both countries.

Without formulated rules to decide disputes, succession, was one of the unresolved problems of the medieval state. The questions laid before the court were complex, and the court itself would set precedent over some issues. When all the side issues are set aside, the decisions facing the court could be reduced to two fundamental questions: firstly, whether primogeniture was more important than proximity; and secondly whether the kingdom of Scotland was partible like any normal barony.

Today, John Balliol's claim has a recognisable superiority— descended from Huntingdon's eldest daughter, his was the senior line. But primogeniture was not a fixed rule at this time. Three of Edward I's sons predeceased him, the eldest and heir Alphonse in 1290. With only Edward Caernarfon surviving, Edward 'ordained' that if he died without issue his daughters, in order of birth, would inherit the throne. Edward, in making a similar insurance as Alexander had in 1284, saw the dangers of the failure of the male line, and favoured primogeniture.

Bruce's claim rested on proximity, being a generation younger than Balliol and a degree closer in blood. The court could look to the English crown for a recent illustration that would favour his case. King John succeeded his brother Richard I in 1199 through proximity, although primogeniture favoured John's nephew Arthur. This English test case was not so much concerned with a point of law but one of force; nevertheless, its relevance was not lost on Bruce's supporters. Bruce's case was complicated by the claim that Alexander II designated him his heir apparent in 1238 after the death of his first wife, Joan. This issue would not detain the court long. Although not unlikely, Bruce could not find any evidence to support the claim. It was made when Bruce was nearest in line, before being superseded by the birth of Hugh Balliol, John Balliol's eldest brother.

The third of the Huntingdon descendants, John Hastings, held estates on the Welsh border. Hasting's claim was dependent on partibility, otherwise it was far weaker than those of Bruce and Balliol. Feudal law recognised that when the male line failed a barony would be divided into equal parts between the female descendants. The auditors had to decide whether to treat a realm in the same way. There was a close precedent involving the competitors themselves. When the brother of Margaret, Isabella and Ada, the earl of Huntingdon and Chester died in 1237 a similar question of partibility had arisen. Chester was not a normal barony, as a palatinate it lay somewhere between a barony and a kingdom. It was decided then that Chester was partible, and divided between the heiress. The principle, when applied to a crown, had never been tested.

In 1291 there were three possible outcomes: firstly to follow the rule of primogeniture, the kingdom goes to Balliol; secondly to follow the rule of proximity, the kingdom goes to Bruce; and thirdly to divide the kingdom between Balliol, Bruce and Huntingdon.

Before making any decision regarding the Huntingdon heirs the court had to settle the suit entered by the count of Florence. He came to Scotland claiming that earl David had resigned his rights, and those of his heirs, in return for a grant of land in Garioch. This potentially explosive claim, if substantiated, would have blown Bruce, Balliol and Hastings out of the case. But the quit-claim had been lost, and nothing could proceed without further investigation in the royal archives. The documents to the cause were sewn up in a sack and sealed by the bishops of St Andrews and Glasgow, and the earls of Buchan and Mar. Edward had business in England, while a search began for the Florence quit-claim.

When the court resumed the following year Edward decided that the various claims were so complicated it would not be possible to deal with them all at once. Instead he proposed that the court hear the merits of the Bruce and Balliol cases, take a decision in favour of one or the other, and then measure the remaining claims against the winner. Florence was not heard straight away. Earl David's quit-claim had not been found. That did not mean Florence was out of the running. Bruce, who was on better terms with Florence than was Balliol, came to an agreement with him on 14 June 1292, that if either should win they would enfeoff the other with one third of the kingdom[24]. That Bruce felt this necessary before the pleadings began was a sign of weakness in his case. We know little of the private negotiations that went on in parallel to the official business, undoubtedly there were many discreet meetings and secret arrangements since the stakes were so high. It was one of the reasons why those with weak claims were there.

From Monday 16 June to Saturday 21 Bruce and Balliol presented their claims, arguments were 'shown, heard and examined before the auditors, and finally given in writing by them and their counsel[25]. Balliol's case was shorter and to the point, that as a kingdom Scotland was indivisible, and as senior heir of earl David he should be awarded the kingdom. Both Balliol and Bruce employed some of the most distinguished European lawyers, but those representing Bruce had to work hardest. 'Not only did they expend every shot in the locker, but Bruce himself, outside the court, seems to have used every means possible to bolster his cause. Surely the only satisfactory explanation of all this ingenuity, self-contradiction and even chicanery is that Bruce knew the exasperating, tantalising truth that whereas politically he could count on powerful support, legally his case was weak'.

Rebuttal arguments took up the following week. Edward sought the advice of the auditors concerning which law the court should apply; uncertain, they threw the question back. Imperial or Roman law, in Robert Bruce's submission 'the natural law, by which kings reign', favoured proximity; common law and feudal custom favoured primogeniture. This indecision forced an adjournment, until 14 October, to gather learned opinion from abroad. Advice came from the best legal minds in Europe but it did not make the decision any clearer.

Bruce now made a notorious *volte face*. He saw that the use of common law could favour the division of the realm. As the case looked to be going against him he abandoned the use of imperial law, supporting Hasting's argument for the realm's division. It is difficult to judge him harshly for this. When it became clear that he would not gain the crown he still had the chance to compete for a third of a kingdom, and instructed his lawyers to present the best case possible.

On the resumption Edward consulted his council and asked them the specific question whether proximity or primogeniture should be favoured. All 50 of them said primogeniture. The same question, in the form of a draft judgement, was put to the adjudicators. One by one they chose Balliol over Bruce. Robert Wishart, the first of Bruce's auditors to speak, said that 'although formally he had been much impressed by the arguments and evidence for the right of Bruce [before the cause] now, having heard the judgement and the arguments on which it is founded, he agreed with it.' In all 67 out of the 80 replied. Thirty-eight of forty Balliol auditors voted against Bruce, as did 29 of his own auditors. Eleven Bruce and two Balliol auditors must have abstained or been absent.

The following day Bruce the Competitor resigned his claim to his son so that it would not be lost after his death. He left the proceedings and retired to his castle of Lochmaben in Annandale, a spent force. He died three years later in 1295. His son, earl of Carrick in honour of his wife, refused to do homage to king John for the earldom when she died. Instead he made over the patrimony to his son, Robert Bruce VIII—the future king of Scotland—a decision regularised in a parliament at Stirling in August 1293.[27] Robert Bruce VII took his daughter, Isabella, to Norway to become Eric II's second wife. He did not return until his father's death, to take possession of the family's estates in England.

Now that the decision between the principal claimants had been made the pace of the court's work quickened. Florence, asking the court's understanding of a 'stranger and a foreigner' pressed his petition. Balliol responded that as Florence 'has alleged a quit-claim, and has not shown it, it does not seem that for his [mere] statement he ought to be heard.' And then suddenly Florence withdrew his claim. There is no explanation for this other than that Balliol had bought him off, there was certainly a belief amongst the Dutch lawyers that the two men struck some sort of an agreement.[28]

The court then heard Hasting's pleas for Scotland's partition. Hastings, with Bruce's backing, argued that Scotland was not a proper kingdom: firstly, its feudal relationship with the king of England deprived it of the character of a kingdom; secondly, that kings of Scotland were neither anointed nor crowned, the obvious tests of kingship.

Balliol's rebuttal was short and its simplicity devastating: he just pointed to other kingdoms held as fiefs, other kings who ruled without anointment or coronation. Hasting's case did not impress the court, it seems to been dismissed without much attention.

On 17 November, in the Great Hall of the castle at Berwick-upon-Tweed, the court made its final judgement. Florence, Dunbar, Pinkeny, Soules, Ros, Vescy and Golightly had withdrawn already. The king of Norway, Comyn and Mandeville did not pursue their claims so gained nothing. The court declared the kingdom impartible and dismissed Hasting's and Bruce's claims. Balliol was awarded the whole realm. Brabazon declared him king with the ominous warning, inserted into the record at a later date, to rule justly 'lest Edward should have to intervene'.[29]

Now Edward had gained Scottish recognition of his overlordship he set about ensuring that it would not take the hollow form it had during the preceding century. Three days later Balliol swore fealty to Edward for the realm of Scotland in Norham castle. The Governor's seal, used since Alexander's death, was broken and the pieces taken to England as evidence of English overlordship. John's enthronement took place on St Andrew's day. Anthony Bek and John de St John, two Englishmen standing in for the young erarl of Fife, placed John on the stone of destiny at Scone.

It was no small thing that the delegates achieved in 1291-2. The state was left without a king, but it did not fall into the anarchy that was near to the surface in any medieval kingdom. That it did not was due to the desire for peace and the willingness to marshal all the forces of the realm to seek a peaceful conclusion and one that, in 1292, nobody disputed.

Had Edward plotted a course for Scottish subjugation as early as May 1291? The period between Edward's return to England in 1289 until the death of Eleanor, 'with the strenuous mingling of oblations, business and sport, were the happiest in his reign.'[30] The ambition of his closing years lay with the crusades not in Scotland. He had taken the cross as early as 1287. The papal bull of March 1291 allowed Edward to collect the crusading tenth from the religious houses in Scotland, something Edward had long argued was his. This was something of a sweetener from pope Boniface who, for his own reasons, wanted Edward's opposition to Philip of France to continue. The pope postponed a starting date of 1290 to 1292 and then 1293. In reality, the fall of Acre in 1291 put paid to the latin kingdom and the crusading ideal, athough with Wales and Gascony both secure before then, the prospects for a crusade had seldom been better. Towards the end of the cause, in June 1292, Edward wrote to the king of Hungary, who had offered troops, still insisting that he was going. Without the crusade to occupy him the king increasingly turned to matters at home.

If Scotland was his objective all along, Edward passed up several earlier opportunities for intervention: before the cause when the realm was in disarray, in the immediate aftermath of Alexander's death, or on the death of Margaret. During the case, when the court could not decide which law to apply, a Lombard lawyer suggested that all the candidates should be eliminated and the kingdom escheated to Edward, a conclusion much to Edward's advantage but one he never took seriously.[31] The king had manipulated the parties, particularly in securing the Award of Norham, when he pressured the competitors and kept a menacing force nearby. He did not manipulate the law.[31]

The circumstances had changed dramatically for Edward. Alexander III was his contemporary, cousin and friend. With his death he had seen the occasion to unite the two kingdoms with the marriage of the Maid and Caernarfon. Now he had to deal with lesser men, many of whom were his vassals. The writs for muster in early 1291 include in their number Robert Bruce and John Balliol, two of his northern tenants. Edward was making a point. With Margaret he had no such reservations. Indeed, the proposed marriage with Caernarfon had served a dual purpose, not only did it promise a future unified country, it prevented any of his barons marrying her themselves and the throne falling into their hands by default. He saw the process of the Great Cause not as a means of subjugating Scotland, but as a way of formalising the vague role of overlordship that had been left unsettled for more than a century. Edward became increasingly obsessed with legal rights and obligations, with his truculent barons, in Gascony, and in Scotland, but he never understood the irreversible damage that obsession and his reluctance to compromise was having.

The first crisis of this new relationship came soon enough, in a case that came before Edward's court with such speed that some have suggested it was engineered to force the issue. The case itself was mundane in the extreme. In October 1291 Marjorie Moigne, a Berwick widow, won a suit placed before the Guardians to recover money Roger Bartholomew owed to her. Bartholomew was something of a troublemaker. He lost two further suits, one for depriving a burgess of his property, the other for maliciously claiming that a certain Gilbert of Dunbar had poked him in the eye with a stick. Given the opportunity, he was not one to let matters lie[32]. On 7 December he appealed directly to Edward, who ordered the relevant documents brought before him. On the 22nd the king overturned one of the cases.

Edward summoned John to join him at Newcastle for an uncomfortable Christmas. On 26 December 1292, in the Dominican friary, he performed homage. Five days later the bishop of St Andrews, the earl of Buchan and two other Scottish lords objected to the homage since it clearly broke the terms of the Birgham-Northampton treaty that ensured the rights of Scots to plead or answer for offences in their own kingdom. Brabazon advised them that the situation since the treaty had changed—it was a marriage treaty between Margaret and Caernarfon, and now Margaret was dead—this new situation meant Edward felt justified in breaking its terms. Edward affirmed Brabazon's statement in a speech in his chamber before John. It was a point forcefully pressed, John was browbeaten by Edward to cancel the treaty of Birgham-Northampton. John himself later admitted his homage to Edward was made under extreme coercion.

The question of appeals gathered pace in the late winter. On 8 March 1293, John was summoned to Westminster to answer an appeal by John Mazun, a Gascon merchant who claimed Alexander III owed him money regarding an unpaid wine account. Mazun's case, complicated by his many creditors, had ticked over for years, despite efforts by Alexander and the Guardians to resolve it. Mazun died before the case came to court so his appeal was struck out. It was the third appeal that tested Anglo-Scottish relations. At John's first parliament in February 1293 Macduff of Fife was accused of using his position as Duncan of Fife's guardian during the earl's minority to take land that belonged to the king. John's parliament rejected Macduff's plea that the matter had been given in his favour by the Guardians under Edward's writ. Macduff appealed to Edward, who summoned John to an English parliament to hear the case.

John refused to attend or send attorneys to appear on his behalf. In response Edward ordered an extraordinary set of standing orders for hearing Scottish cases: John himself would have to attend the appeals personally to justify the decisions of the lesser court, he would be liable for damages for miscarriages of justice, and he was personally party to every suit brought under review. In October 1293 John relented and travelled to Westminster where he was confronted by Macduff. In court John stood his ground, steadfastly refusing to answer the case without the advice of the good men of his realm. Macduff pressed for an award by default. When offered an adjournment John told the court that he required no time to rethink, that an acceptance of an adjournment would admit English jurisdiction. With this the court had had enough. The decision was given in favour of Macduff, John was declared in contempt and ordered to hand over the three strongest Scottish castles until he purged his contempt. At this point John's resolve began to crumble, his bravura performance had merely laid the groundwork for a climb down. He renewed his homage and requested an adjournment until June 1294 when he promised to reply to the charges in the next parliament.

Edward's treatment of John at the Michaelmas parliament, when he stood in court as a common plaintiff, was intolerable. The appeals led to a sharp deterioration of Anglo-Scottish relations, but they did not lead to war. It is difficult to agree with the proposition that this was 'calculated oppression and provocation.'[33] We do not have the complete details of Edward's judicial rule in Scotland. He appointed justiciars and heard some judicial business the his council[34]. In 1291 Edward reserved the right to hear appeals against the decisions his appointees made while he was superior lord of Scotland. As such they were limited in number and term. In all there were only nine appeals to the English court, two English, a Gascon and six Scottish, the last two in August 1295. Since the Treaty of Paris in 1259,the Gascon appeals to the French parliament were a tiresome but everyday part of Edward's reign. For 35 years they had never threatened the peace or a breakdown in relations. Of course, Scotland was no Gascony, but the evidence that Edward wanted to treat Scotland as such does not exist. Edward's interference did not go beyond this, there was no attempt to influence other internal matters during John's short reign.

In the event, John never had to appear before Edward's court. In the spring of 1293 a fleet from the Cinque Ports met and defeated a Norman fleet off Brittany in an unofficial naval action. Whatever the reasons for the battle, the mariners of the Cinque Ports claimed Normans attacked them, Philip IV refused to compromise and summoned Edward to Paris to answer charges against him. It was Edmund, Edward's brother who went to Paris, where he was duped. The seisin of Gascony was made over to Philip on the secret understanding that he would return it after a suitable period for his anger to subside. John de St John, Edward's lieutenant, abandoned preparations for Gascony's defence and returned to England. The seisin was not returned, the charges not dropped. Edward refused to answer a second summons to Paris so Philip declared the duchy forfeit. With this sleight of hand Philip left Edward with no option but war.

Edward sent military writs of summons to king John and eighteen Scottish magnates for feudal service for their Scottish lands.[35] There is a suggestion that John agreed to go, he had been at Westminster shortly before the writs were issued, but not for feudal service. Edward's demands over the series of appeals were nothing to this new demand: he had pushed too far. Military service was implied in homage but it was nevertheless unexpected. It had last been performed by Malcolm IV in 1159. Military service abroad was deeply unpopular in a society that lived so close to the edge of survival. It was this issue that Robert Bruce and the baronial rebels in Scotland in 1297 claimed led them to rebel, and it was on this issue that England was brought to the brink of civil war in the same year.

Any Anglo-Scottish confrontation was put off by a rebellion in Wales and the cancellation of the Gascon campaign. In an action that must have impressed the Scots the Welsh used the arms distributed for the French campaign to rebel. The revolt was short-lived, crushed in March 1295 when the earl of Warwick caught the Welsh infantry in open countryside.

With Warwick's victory Edward could again turn his attention to Gascony. He needed allies and men to fight a war in France. Preparations for war were being made throughout Europe in 1295 and Scotland was drawn into the struggle between England and France. Edward attempted to surround France with allies, in Spain, Germany and Flanders. He expected Scotland to play a part by sending men. France defended herself likewise. Where the initial overtures for a Franco-Scottish alliance came from is unknown, but a French spy in Edward's household, Thomas Turbeville, advised the French to send an embassy to Scotland 'for if they get there, you will benefit forever.' In February 1295 Philip ordered that Scottish merchants should be treated in the same manner as the English, but in May he wrote to the count of Flanders that they were his friends and should be treated as such.

In Scotland there was a political revolution. In July a parliament at Stirling forced John to accept a twelve peer advisory council—four bishops, four earls, four barons—that mirrored the guardianship until 1292. Its role remains unclear. One English chronicler pictured John as friendless, 'a lamb amongst wolves, who dared not open his mouth.' More likely the council was constituted to stiffen his resolve, to give him the backbone he had lacked over the appeals. The bishops of St Andrews and Dunkeld with two knights, John de Soules and Ingram de Umfraville went to France to seek Philip IV's assistance.

The treaty arranged with France in Paris on 23 October 1295 was a far reaching defensive and offensive alliance. It allowed for a Scottish invasion of England if Edward threatened France. The treaty was secured with the proposed marriage of John's heir, Edward Balliol, and Jeanne of Valois, Philip's niece. Coupled with this alliance France secured a treaty with Norway, which promised to supply 100 ships for a fee of £50,000. The Norwegians promised to defer or place before

Philip any outstanding claims with the king of Scots.[36] Scotland well understood that this dangerous course had the same effect as a declaration of war.

Edward had been boxed into a corner of his own making, and he was furious. Not only could the alliance wreak his plans to secure Gascony, it struck deep into his belief of Scottish dependence. In autumn 1295, Edward appointed Bek and Warenne as custodians of the shires north of the Trent. This was the first stage in placing the north on a war footing. Warenne was made castillian of Bamburgh, Robert Bruce VII, who swore a fresh oath of fealty at the exchequer, was made castillian of Carlisle. On 16 October, Edward demanded the castles at Berwick, Roxburgh and Jedburgh as a surety for good behaviour during the war with France, and on the same day he confiscated Balliol's English estates and suspended trade. In early November Bek and Warenne summoned all the northern knights and two men from each town to York to receive instructions on defence.

If Edward had entertained any doubts about the need for a military demonstration they did not last long. In the winter of 1295-6 preparations were advancing on both sides of the borders. In Scotland the new year brought a demand for a *wapinschaw*, or weapon show. In March the host was ordered to assemble at Caddonlea. The English were ousted from Scotland and their land forfeited. It was a measure that hit hardest those nobles with cross-border holdings and divided loyalties, principally the Bruces. The Bruce lands in the west went to the Earl of Buchan. The English clergy were ejected 'less they formed a fifth column' and English merchants were killed at Berwick. When Edward heard the news he asked 'who could believe such wickedness and treachery?'[37] In December he issued writs to 200 tenants to muster at Newcastle on 1 March 1296. Writs were also sent to John and other Scottish magnates: one last chance to repent.

For much of the 13th century, Scottish political society had been characterised by a division amongst the nobility; it was not a rigid division, it was usually evenly matched, and only tended to come to the fore when tested by extraordinary events. Once he had reached his majority, Alexander III had held it in check. But by 1296 Edward had achieved what only the most capable of Scottish rulers had done before, he created a sense of Scottish national unity. There were still powerful men outside this new political order but there was no Bruce party as there had been in 1286 and 1291. That the traditional baronial polarisation, so evident after Margaret's death, had collapsed is a sign of how far the political revolution of 1295 had gone. The opposition of a third group, those who owed their loyalty to Edward, would not be tested until a call to arms was made. With this new found unity came a confidence and strength to stand up to overbearing English demands.

After 70 years of Anglo-Scottish peace, Scotland had become an ally of France. It was largely Edward's own fault and the Franco-Scottish treaty now gave the French an interest in British politics. English policy towards Scotland was framed by its attitude towards France. Gascony's vineyards were a source of great wealth, the duchy of Aquitaine supplied Edward with money and guaranteed his place in continental politics as a peer of France. Throughout the period his French subjects remained loyal to Edward. In contrast Scotland was poor, had little continental influence and little reason for loyalty to Edward. Edward could make a case for overlordship of Scotland, though not an unanswerable one. Edward's real fault lay in his inability to see the insensitivity of his actions on king John and the damage that was being done to an ally: 'practically speaking, Balliol found he had either to throw in his lot with Edward, and rely on his power to enable him to repress his own subjects, or else to throw in his lot with his subjects and defy Edward.'[38]

Chapter 2

TO THE FRONTIER OF OUR REALM

'...to the frontier of our realm in warlike array'
King John

Any hopes Edward may have held that the mere threat of force would result in a settlement faded during the early months of 1296. His blunt threats, in the shape of Warenne and Bek's war preparations in the north, were having no effect. With power now in the hands of the hardline nobility, it is unlikely that John could have accepted English interference in Scotland, even if he had wanted to. As spring came to the borders it was clear that war would follow close behind.

An anonymous diarist who accompanied the king kept a record of Edward's first expedition to Scotland.[1] The clarity of his journal is not matched by our knowledge of the army's strength. The only extant document gives a wage bill for foot soldiers for the year totalling £21,443 12s 0d.[2] This would be enough to pay around 25,000 men; but the record does not distinguish between the cost of Edward's army in the north and the one sent to Gascony, where war was being prosecuted (with far less success) under Edmund and the earl of Lincoln. Fighting on two fronts, Edward could not bring the full weight of the realm to bear on Scotland, a problem less of manpower than of overstretched taxation. On 23 January 1296 he asked his exchequer for 1,000 men-at-arms and 60,000 infantry. This is a nonsense figure, and both Edward and his exchequer would have known it. He merely signalled his desire to raise a large force.

The earl of Ulster was asked to bring 400 men-at-arms and 30,000 infantry; when his contingent arrived at Roxburgh on 13 May nobody was surprised that it only numbered 3,157. Edward could also count upon a contingent from the Durham franchise; the resourceful Bek would prove himself as useful a soldier as he was a diplomatist. Frustrated in his desire to mass a large army, in April Edward resorted to offering immunities to criminals and vagabonds.[3] He may have felt uncomfortable with the numbers in his force, though not as uncomfortable as the Scots: this was still a strong army.

On his way north Edward collected the Banner of St John of Beverly, brought to hallow the enterprise, and paid a visit to St Cuthbert's shrine on Holy Island—if not a holy war Edward certainly wanted God on his side. Marching under St John's protection the host moved north from Newcastle on 5 March and made camp at Brunton, a village near the border, where it stayed until 11 March.

Nearby, a tale of unrequited love was about to end in treachery. Wark was the stronghold of Robert Ros who had fallen in love with a Scots woman, Christine de Moubray. Robert planned to surrender his castle to the Scots, a plan he revealed to his brother, William Ros of Kendal.[4] William would have none of this treachery, telling his brother he was a fool and writing to Edward for help. The king sent an infantry company under the command of a knight; but as they camped at Preston they were ambushed by a Scottish party from Roxburgh led by Ros. Medieval warfare was confusing enough during daytime, with banners unfurled and armorial bearings to tell each side apart; an ambush, in the dark, between two sides who spoke English with a common dialect was a recipe for disaster. The Scots had a password, 'tabard', but the word was freely bandied about and the English used it to make good their escape. The Scots were not prepared to press a siege with the full English army nearby and so retired across the border.

The origins of the castle at Wark are unclear, the name itself derives from the old English, *weorc*, meaning fortification, which would suggest an early date. It is easy to see why: all that remains of the castle today are some earthworks, but a clear view extends from the central mound across the Tweed to the north and southwards to the Cheviots which would have made it a formidable strongpoint. It reveals the key to the Scottish defence in 1296, to hold a line along the border: James the Steward had taken command of the border castle at Roxburgh, William Douglas the castle at Berwick.

As for Robert Ros, his sacrifice was all in vain, Christine de Moubray 'afterwards would not deign to take him', but he escaped to Sanquhar, a castle he owned in Scotland.[5]

Edward said of the raid: 'By the blessing of God as the Scots had begun he would make an end' and celebrated Easter at Wark. There he met those Scottish magnates whose loyalty he trusted: Patrick earl of March and Gilbert Umfraville earl of Angus, together with the two Robert Bruces. On Easter day, 25 March, they did homage for their lands in Scotland.[6] Robert Bruce's loyalty to Edward, as an English baron, meant more to him than his loyalty as a Scottish baron to John. This is not to deny Bruce's 'Scottishness', although the term would have meant little to a feudal baron like Bruce. It is something that the future king's many apologists have never satisfactorily explained. He was still a young man (twenty-two), possibly under the sway of his father, but this first major decision of his political career reveals Bruce to be a man who was quite willing to fight in an English army. Edward's campaign would further the only cause Bruce believed in and was ready to fight for: his own.

On the other side of the border the Scottish host had been summoned to meet on 11 March and gathered at Caddonlea, the traditional muster point of Scottish armies four miles north of Selkirk. It is unclear what happened between then and the end of the month when a mounted force converged on the western border. *Lanercost* mentions a planned raid that had to be abandoned because of bad weather. What was clear was that John, side-lined politically in 1295, was now side-lined militarily. The army was formed around seven earls: John Comyn of Buchan, Alexander Stewart of Mentieth, Malise of Strathearn, Malcolm of Lennox, William of Ross, John Strathbogie of Atholl and Donald of Mar together with the younger Comyn of Badenoch. Even with Edward's army divided between Scotland and Gascony they were ill-equipped to hold it off in a pitched set-piece battle, and they knew it. They devised an alternative strategy, a large-scale raid into the north of England.

Buchan did not allow his army the luxury of an Easter celebration. The lordship of Annandale had passed to him when Bruce had refused to join the call to arms and had effectively been expelled earlier in the year. It was at Annandale that the Scottish army gathered, and on 26 March 1996, it advanced across the border in three divisions. Annandale had much the same function as Carlisle on the English side of the border: a crossing point and first line of defence. (In the 13th century the only route into England for a large force was over the Solway flats at low-tide, as the modern route through Gretna Green could not carry large numbers.) The raiders burnt villages right up to the suburbs of Carlisle. A contingent of archers from the city delayed them by lifting boards from the Eden bridge, but their success was short-lived, as an alternative crossing was found at Rickerby ford. The citizens of Carlisle had not been prepared, but the city had good walls and could be defended against all but the most persistent besiegers.

The Scots had sent a spy ahead of them to survey the defences, but 'being suspicious' he was arrested and taken in fetters to the city gaol. When he heard that the Scottish army approached, he escaped from the prison and set fire to the house where he had lodged. He climbed the city walls as the fire spread and called out to the raiding party to match his efforts, a foolhardy gesture which brought him to the attention of the defenders who later hanged him. Confusion in the town spread as fast as the flames until the citizens, leaving a select force on the gates, abandoned the walls to fight the fire which threatened to consume a greater part of the city. Their place on the walls was taken by the city's women, who threw stones and boiling water over the walls in a desperate defence. The raiding party carried no siege engines. Once the element of surprise had been lost, the fire doused, and their spy discovered, they had little option but to abandon the attack. They withdrew after two days, recrossing the border on 28 March.

It was an unusually busy day on the border. As the Scottish army retraced its steps on the west Edward crossed the border on the east. The bulk of the army crossed the Tweed near Coldstream where it spent its first night in Scotland as uninvited guests of the priory. From Coldstream Edward directed his attention to his first target, Berwick-upon-Tweed.

It is easy to take a superficiial look at the town as it stands today and marvel at its sleepy insignificance, but in 1296, Berwick was the wealthiest burgh in Scotland. Berwick's origins are lost in the mists of prehistory. The site was attractive to early settlers as it stands on a peninsula which overlooks a natural harbour that could be easily defended. It lay within the territory of the Celtic tribe known to the Romans as the Votadini. The growth of the modern town makes it impossible to say whether one of their villages stood here.

In 1018 the battle of Carham won for the Scots most of the Tweed basin and the Lothians. Berwick, along with many other towns (including Edinburgh) ceased to be English. King David made the town one of only four Royal burghs in 1136. Scottish burghs had thrived in the following century. As the centre of local trade and manufacturing burghs had to be near river mouths or estuaries as most trade was waterborne; alternatively, they could be centred on an important fording point, as at Stirling, or an outstanding defensive site as at Edinburgh. Berwick was alone in having all these advantages and was also the nearest port to Scotland's continental trading partners. Berwick stood at the fringe of an agriculturally rich hinterland, the Merse, which supported the great religious houses: at Melrose, Dryburgh, Coldstream, Kelso and Jedburgh. It is hardly surprising that by the 13th century the town had became pre-eminent over its rivals, and had grown into Scotland's major trading port with Europe. This was the town's golden age, 'a city so populous and of such trade that it might justly be called another Alexandria, whose riches were the sea and the water its walls.'[7] All this was to come to an end over the three centuries of Anglo-Scottish warfare that began in 1296. The constant building of fortifications, the spending power of a large garrison and the stature of Berwick as capital of English occupied Scotland failed to compensate for its severance from Scotland.

Edward sent messages to the town, 'well-meant overtures' offering safe-conduct in return for surrender, but his summons went went unanswered. On 29 March the host moved to Hatton, six miles from the town; from here Edward went up to the walls personally. His attempts to arrange a surrender were in vain. Worse, they were met with a reception which did not befit a medieval king, particularly one with such an acute sense of his own royal dignity matched with a renowned and volatile temper. With the confidence of inexperience the defenders ridiculed him, they 'bared their breeches', crude gestures complete with a rhyming couplet:

> 'King Edward wanne thu havest Berwick pike the
> Wanne thu havest geten dike the'
>
>   RISHANGER

Five hundred years later, the jibe has lost its cutting edge, but its repetition amongst the chroniclers suggest it had a profound impact on the king. Roughly translated, Edward would have to dig (pike) his way in to take the town, and defend it with new earth works (dike) in order to keep it.

The following morning the English army moved up to the walls. Before the attack Edward went through the traditional custom of dubbing new knights, including a certain Henry Percy, progenitor of the earls of Northumberland. In the mistaken belief that the raised banners and cheering from the English army meant the assault was underway, the English fleet attacked. This unsupported assault was a terrible blunder. The defenders rushed down to meet the ships as they entered the harbour. The leading ship ran aground and was set on fire after its crew had been 'cut to pieces' by the townsfolk. The vessels immediately behind were also set alight, their crews escaping in small craft. The rest of the fleet drew off.

Edward's response was swift and savage. The security of the town's defences was illusory: inadequate earthworks and a meagre six foot high palisade—no more than a stout fence of upright stakes which were rotten from years of neglect. They were easily overwhelmed by the first wave of English troops, who found an entry 'where the townsfolk had made a path along the fosse, [the English] entered pell-mell with those on horseback, whoever could get in first.'[8] The defenders never recovered from the ferocity of the assault, so stunned they could barely offer a defence and were unable to regroup to defend the streets. The only stiff resistance came from 30 Flemish merchants in the fortified Red Hall who held out until evening when the building was set alight, killing all inside. It was here that the only English loss was recorded: Richard of Cornwall, youngest son of Edward's uncle, lifted his visor during the assault on the Red Hall and was struck with a bolt shot out of the hall. The death of Edward's first cousin may have played a part in the bloody events that followed.

The castle garrison surrendered and was allowed to depart with military honour intact. The commander, William Douglas was kept captive for future use. It is unknown what happened to this troublesome lord between the storming of Berwick and his reappearance at Wallace's side in the next year. The women and children were allowed to depart. Those left behind, the men of Fife who had been hastily drawn together to garrison the town, the burghers and craftsmen of the town, now paid dearly for the insults they had hurled at Edward that morning. With an anger 'like that of a wild boar pursued by dogs'[9], he gave the order that no quarter should be given. There followed a bloodbath.

In four brutal days bodies, to use a contemporary analogy, 'fell like autumn leaves', until the dead lining the streets became a hazard and had to be thrown into wells or the sea since there was nobody left to bury them. It was only with the pleading of the clergy that the carnage came to an end. The Lanercost chronicler, an English source gives an incredible 15,000 slain, whilst the Scottish writer Fordun scales down the slaughter to an equally implausible 7,500. Guisborough provides a spuriously precise total of 11,060. However, medieval towns had small populations—and there was room within Berwick for a 40 acre pasture—while many burgage plots were vacant.[10] Only 80 burghers had performed homage before Edward in 1291. Even after adding a generous number for family, servants, craftsmen and apprentices the total, including women and children, would be no more than 500. Some of these families survived, the same names who are recorded as burgesses are mentioned during the English occupation. Some no doubt returned after 1296 to carry on with their businesses.[10] This is not to dismiss the impact of the slaughter, the chroniclers' exaggerations hardly mitigate the offence. In any case, the normal population of the town was swelled by town's garrison, that had been hurriedly mustered from Fife.

Scottish historians have judged Edward's actions harshly. Evan Barron was convinced that it 'left a stain on the memory of the English king which nothing will ever wash away.'[11] It is not an attitude shared by Edward's contemporaries. Lanercost (admittedly an Edwardian apologist) complemented him on exhibiting 'towards the dead that mercy which he proffered to the living', for burying the soldiers at the king's own expense.' Ruthless punishment following the taking of a town by siege was a convention of the age. The offer of terms to a town aimed to prevent bloodshed, both for the besieged and the besiegers.

For the rest of the campaign, Edward ordered that no one should plunder or burn, and that a fair price should be paid for all necessary supplies. The lack of combat in the following weeks must have irritated the less disciplined soldiers who had joined the campaign in the hope of plunder. The Placita Rolls of the English Army contain the details of justice dispensed to those who disobeyed: the likes of Patrick of Ireland who was hanged for housebreaking, or Thomas Dun for stealing vestments.[12] It is against these conventions, that the Berwick garrison brought their fate upon themselves, that Edward's conduct has to be judged.

The slaughter in Berwick was unnecessary, its encouragement by Edward leaves a bad taste, but it was not surprising. Its criticism is founded on misguided romantic ideas of chivalry: the noble knight as defender of the poor, which was far from medieval reality. Chivalry was a system of self-preservation and worked for so long as knights carried price-tags. Mercy never entered into it, neither did the poor, who had nothing to do with the making of the war but suffered more than any from its conduct. The description of the earlier Scottish raid, with Scots 'burning houses, slaughtering men', is no better, no worse. The war in 1296 was brutal, it was a brutal age, and the brutality was common to both sides.

The king stayed in Berwick for the next month. He aimed to keep the town. Within four days work began on new defences, with labourers trawled from throughout Northumberland. New earthworks with a fosse and ramparts were said to measure 40 feet high with an 80 foot breadth. Ever the propagandist, like a present day politician scenting a photo opportunity, Edward wheeled the first token barrow of earth himself. How better to answer the scorn of the defenders, he did indeed 'pike and dike'[13] As the principal Scottish trading town Edward had little to do to ensure that Berwick would become the capital of English-occupied Scotland. The new work on the town was supervised by a committee of town planners, summoned together in January 1297, whilst new English burgesses were imported to replace the Scots who had defied him.[14]

It was in Berwick castle, on 5 April 1296, that Edward received two Franciscan friars who brought king John's *diffidatio*, the renunciation of his homage and fealty. When Edward had sent his *diffidatio* to the king of France in 1294, he had been careful to ensure that it was dated before hostilities began so that he could not be accused of rebelling against his overlord, and would fight as Philip IV's equal. John's renunciation struck an understandably indignant, somewhat impotent, note at the treatment he had been handed:

> 'You yourself, and others of your realm ... have ...
> inflicted over and over again, by naked force, grievous
> and intolerable injuries, slights and wrongs upon us and
> the inhabitants of our realm, and indeed have caused
> harm beyond measure to the liberties of ourselves and our
> kingdom ... for instance by summoning us outside our
> realm at the mere beck and call of anybody, as your whim
> dictated, and by harassing us unjustifiably; by seizing our

castles, lands and possessions and those of our people within your realm, unjustly and without any fault on our part ... now you have come to the frontiers of our realm in warlike array.'

KING JOHN[15]

Unable to champion John's defiant stand, the Scottish earls led a second raid into the north of England. On 8 April, two columns led by the earls of Ross, Menteith and Atholl with the younger Comyn, moved from Jedburgh through Lockadale, and fought their way through Redesdale. For two days Harbottle castle held off a siege. The Scots laid waste Northumberland from between there and Hexham.

This was a bitter attack: 'they imbued their arms, hitherto unfleshed, with the blood of infirm people, old women, women in child-bed, and even children two or three years old, proving themselves apt scholars in atrocity, in so much so that they raised aloft little span-long children pierced on pikes.' Three monasteries were destroyed: Lanercost, Hexham and the nunnery at Lambley. At Hexham 'they burned about 200 little scholars who were in the school ... learning their first letters and grammar, having blocked up the doors and set fire to the building.' The unlikelihood of a school of that size at Hexham questions the scale of the atrocity, but it was real enough in English minds, used later by Edward I in an instrument to Philip IV to criticize the morality of choosing allies who murdered 'little scholars ... learning their first letters and grammar'.[16] Hexham had not recovered from the raid a year later when it was described as utterly waste and tenantless.

The Scots rested at Lanercost from 12-13 April, where they learned that an English relief force was on its way. Not wanting to face the English in battle or to abandon their considerable booty, the Scots retreated across the border. As they returned through Lothian and Teviotdale, a rearguard sealed off the upland passes. Finally the army reached the earl of March's castle at Dunbar. The earl, accompanied by his best men was still with Edward in Berwick. He had left a token garrison in the castle under the command of his wife. After plundering the town the Scottish raiders settled down to a short siege. The experience at Carlisle a month earlier had taught the Scots the value of siege weapons or a fifth column. What they lacked in the first they more than made up for in the second: the countess of March did not share her husband's loyalty to Edward, she duped the garrison and opened the gates to the Scots. The castle was placed in the capable hands of Richard Siward, a 'man renowned in war.' The leaders of the raiding party stayed in the castle.

The raid had much the same result as the first: it was cruel, wasted time and effort, and had no effect on Edward who was not distracted into a chase—he understood the folly of chasing a mobile Scottish raiding party around the northern countryside. Nor was Edward intimidated by the army that now occupied Dunbar. Earl Warenne was dispatched from Berwick to recapture the fortress, taking about a fifth of the army, together with 100 men-at-arms from bishop Bek's force. As he laid siege, the garrison requested a three day truce so that a message could be taken to John to find out on what terms they could surrender.

The messenger found John in a desperate position: he had lost Berwick and his raiding tactics had proved futile. The capture of Dunbar had been the only success of the campaign.

A desperate position called for a desperate response. King John decided to attack the English under the protection of the truce — trapping the unsuspecting Warenne between the Scottish army and the castle garrison. The Scots appeared at noon on 27 April on the hills overlooking Dunbar at Spott on the edge of the Lammermuirs. The castle garrison began taunting the English, calling them 'tailed dogs'. (It was a common medieval belief that Englishmen had tails.) The Scottish garrison now promised to amputate them. Warenne left his younger men-at-arms under the command of Humphrey Bohun to keep the garrison penned in the castle and manoeuvred his veterans towards the Scottish host.

The Spott Burn runs parallel to the Scottish position along a glacial, flat 'U'-shaped cut along the foot of the hills. The cut is about 80 metres wide, with sides that rise nearly vertically 15 metres: so steep that the burn and valley floor are hidden from the hillsides 120 metres above. It was along here that Warenne marched his veterans. From the Scottish position on the brow of the hills the already thin English numbers disappeared from view, and it appeared that they were withdrawing. With a telling lack of discipline the cry went up from the Scottish line, 'They flee! They flee!' the ranks broke, and the Scots surged forward into the valley.

As they reached the cut, they tumbled down the deep sides and came across the carefully arrayed English soldiers. They stood little chance. The Scottish cavalry fled the field, leaving the foot soldiers who turned and tried to escape from the English knights. The sheriff of Stirling, Patrick Graham, refused to run and was cut down where he stood. He fell 'applauded and lamented by his enemies.' Those who managed to clamber out of the cut were pursued into the evening as far as the forests of Selkirk.

The Earl of March and Edward's controller of the Wardrobe, John Benstead, were ordered to supervise a count of the dead. They presented Edward with a figure of 10,052, an impossibly high total, but there was no doubt that the Scottish foot had suffered heavy casualties while the English lost a 'single foolhardy knight'. Contemporaries believed that the battle was lost when the Scottish cavalry had deserted the field, 'their foot soldiers would have stood firm had not the knights showed their heels so readily'. Lanercost continues with a contemporary poem:

'For those Scots, I I rate 'em as sots, I What a sorry shower! I Whose utter lack I In the attack I Lost 'em at Dunbar

Fordun blames the cavalry's desertion on Mar and Atholl's devotion to Bruce.[17] This is a disingenuous argument, giving Bruce a degree of support at the time he was fighting for Edward. The explanation for the cavalry's flight does not need such strained arguments: the cavalry was simply a weak link in the Scottish battle formation, and would remain so throughout the wars.

The English renewed work on the mines and earthworks surrounding Dunbar castle. The defeat panicked the garrison into surrender. Edward had moved to Coldingham on 27 April and was at Dunbar itself on the 28th to take possession of the castle and the unconditional surrender of garrison. The captives remained until 16 May, when the leading men, Mentieth, Atholl, Ross, and the younger Comyn, were taken to the tower of London. Andrew Murray, the justiciar of Scotia (Scotland north of the Forth) was included in their number as one of the senior nobles of Scotland; his son, still only an esquire, was taken to Chester Castle, the closest to Scotland of the castles used for Dunbar prisoners. It was a decision which would be sorely regretted. Others were distributed to castles throughout southern England and the Midlands: they numbered 171 knights and esquires.[18]

The battle of Dunbar was a relatively minor action. Neither king was present and the English force was only a detachment from the main army. But its effect on the campaign was critical. The Scots had deployed their full host, and that only one senior Scottish noble was slain owes more to the nobility's rapid flight rather than suggestions that they were not present. The backbone of Scottish resistance, the leaders of the raid into England, had been captured. This was the end to an organised national threat, the remaining leaders were too thinly spread to provide effective opposition. Within days the Steward surrendered Roxburgh and offered Edward his fealty, and their respective garrisons surrendered Jedburgh and Dumbarton.[19] With the border secure Edward moved to Edinburgh, where he remained from 6-13 June. The castle held out for a spirited eight days or so.

Edward himself was not at the siege for long, 'On the eighth day [13 June] the king slept at Linlithgow, and left the engines under good guard throwing before the castle.' The English engineers 'heaped together a great mound of earth like a small mountain and on it put their machines, so that they could hurl carefully and accurately lumps of lead instead of stone, to the confusion of the citadel, low-lying places and even underground caves could be struck. The air was filled with an insupportable rain of metal which battered holes in the walls so that no place of safety could protect the besieged.'[20] With no sign of help from John a three day battering brought a submission from the garrison, who surrendered to Hugh Despenser.

Edinburgh surrendered to John Despenser as Edward had already left Linlithgow and then Stirling.[21] The latter was the last faint hope for the Scots, but the castle's garrison had already fled, leaving the porter to hand over the keys.

Edward had little left to do. The campaign began to take the form of a military promenade. With Anthony Bek in the lead, a day or so ahead of the king, making sure the way was clear and accepting Scots as they came forward to offer homage. The Scottish host had been defeated, its generals captured. King John still had to officially ackknowledge his defeat, but he had no options left: his support evaporated as the nobles surrendered one after another and the country's strongpoints fell into the hands of the enemy. His cause was lost. John spent the rest of the month north of the Forth on a futile tour. When Bek reached Perth, he received John's emissaries, seeking surrender terms.

King John's submission took place in a number of stages in early July. There appears to have been some sort of agreement struck between John and Anthony Bek, who had represented a sober voice in the negotiations for John's submission. With far-sighted moderation, Bek proposed that the kingdom of Scotland should be given to Edward in perpetuity, and in return John would be given an English earldom based around his large northern English estates.[22] Bek had a personal reason for presenting a conciliation, he was an old friend of the Scottish king: John had turned to Bek in 1291 when canvassing English support for his claim to the throne, and most of John's English lands were in Bek's Durham franchise.

Edward was not in a conciliatory mood; he would have none of this deal. Wholesale surrender would be matched by humiliation. John met with Bek at Kincardine Castle on 2 July where he confessed his rebellion, publicly denouncing his errors, made 'through evil counsel, and our own folly'.[23] On the 5th July Edward Balliol was given up as a hostage. John himself formerly surrendered on the 7th, at Strathcaro cemetery in the old royal castle of Kincardine, the symbolism of the location must have been all the more chilling for those Scots present, and renounced the treaty with France. The moment of formal surrender by enfeoffment in which he resigned his kingdom to his superior vassal did not take place until 8 July at Montrose. John's chancellor delivered up the Great Seal of Scotland in a little purse under John's own seal, to be broken up. He was escorted by the last of his supporters still at large, John Comyn the elder of Badenoch, the earls of Buchan and Mar and the bishop of Aberdeen, and committed into the custody of Bek and Warenne.

It was a week of high melodrama enacted not only to maximize John's humiliation in front of his nation, but that of his country, from the public denouncement of his errors, to the final ceremony when his coat of arms was stripped from his tabard. This final act was the one by which King John would be remembered in the chronicles:

> 'He haves overhipped I His typeth is typped I Hise tabard is tome.'[24]

Langtoft's rhyming chronicle presents something of an interpretative riddle: the first line is simple enough, it merely states an English belief that John had overstretched himself; the second is less clear, a tippet was a narrow strip of cloth worn as part of dress, and how it could have the tips cut off is uncertain — it could be that this act represented the penitent's ritual undressed appearance; the third line has no such ambiguity, the tabard was a loose coat often open at the sides and worn over armour. It was tome, or empty, of its fur trimmings and armorial bearings. It was a procedure that seemed in part to follow military practice for treason, though his office saved John from some of the more humiliating aspects, there is no evidence, for example, that he was paraded bare-foot; it was designed to go far beyond the limits of king John's personal humiliation in the Strathcaro churchyard, it was meant to symbolically announce Edward's conquest.[25]

Edward celebrated John's surrender with a banquet, after which he pushed north. By 12 July 'he was in the mountains', reaching Aberdeen on the 14th where he spent five days. On the 24th 'he was in tents upon the moor on the river Spey' which he crossed on the 25th. He stayed at Elgin between the 26 and 27 July when he turned back and headed south. At Rothes the force divided into three, his lieutenants, Hugh le Despenser, Sir John Hastings and Sir John Cantilupe went to subdue Badenoch; 'Durham he sent back over the mountains by another road from which he himself took.' While the main army had moved along the east coast, other contingents had gone into the west of Scotland. While at Roxburgh Edward sent the Bruces, Annandale and Carrick to secure their lands in the west. Ulster's men would be used in the mountains in the West Highlands against Alexander Macdougall, lord of Lorn. Edward was back in Berwick on 22 August, the entire campaign had taken 21 weeks.

King John would play no further part in his country's struggle. In the immediate aftermath of his surrender he was packed off by sea to England, in the custody of Edward's nephews, the Lancaster brothers Thomas and Henry.[26]. John was released to live in Hertford on a royal pension with his son, Edward Balliol. His was not a harsh imprisonment; he was even given leave to hunt in the royal forests within 20 leagues of London, given a gift of a huntsman, page and ten hounds.[78] King John was returned to the tower during William Wallace's rebellion lest he act as a focus for the rebels. After petitions from France and the papal curia he has allowed to leave England for good in 1299, under papal safeguards. He remained on his family's estates in Picardy until his death in 1315.

The burden of Scottish failure in 1296 cannot rest solely on John's shoulders. His stock has never been high amongst historians; many still refer to him by his surname rather than his title as if he were an aberration who was unfit for, and did not deserve, the throne. He was a weak king, unable to face up to the overbearing Edward I or the hopes of those Scots whose support he relied upon. As he sat in the bishop of Durham's London palace two years later he reflected on his time as king of Scotland, telling his captors that 'it was not his intention to enter or go into the realm of Scotland at any time to come, or to interfere in any way with it ... or even to have anything to do with the Scots, when he possessed and ruled the realm of Scotland as king and lord of the realm, he found in the men of that realm such malice, deceit, treason and treachery, arising from their malignity, wickedness, and stratagems, and various other execrable and detestable actions'.[28] It seems a harsh judgement at a time when many Scots were dying in his name. Of course, he may just have been telling the English what they wanted to hear. He beseeched Bek to inform the king of these things on his behalf, as the French were pressing for his release, but it in part reflected his bitterness at his loss of power in 1295.

Edward's campaign was a rude awakening. The Scottish barons were provincial men with provincial horizons and their strategy in 1296 was unimaginative. They fought a war and lost, but they knew it would make little difference to their way of life. The Comyns feared losing their power to Edward's Scottish supporters and abandoned the king once the English threatened their domains in the north of Scotland.[29] However heated or real their indignation at Edward's suppression of Scottish rights, it was not a national cause they defended, and would never be fuelled with the passionate nationalism and independent spirit that fired William Wallace. This is not enough to explain the complete failure of Scottish resistance. Robert Bruce's biographer, Geoffrey Barrow, found the reason for defeat in the long peace that preceded the war which left the Scots with nothing but the most conventional ideas on how to fight, ideas that compelled them into a pitched battle.[30]

Scotland had been at peace for many years, Alexander II's campaign in Galloway in 1235 and the battle of Largs in 1263 were fought by a different generation. But the imbalance in the abilities of the Scottish and English military elite should not be overstated. Despite his reputation as a warrior king, Edward I had only been in two battles, at

Lewes in 1264 and at Evesham in 1265 and he would only be in one more (Falkirk) in 1298. With him at Lewes were John Comyn of Badenoch, John de Balliol and Robert Bruce, the forbears of the current combatants. Lack of experience did not mean that Scottish knights were not trained in warfare, 'in medieval times, war demanded first and foremost active participation by the nobility. It was, so to speak, its occupation, almost its *raison d'etre*. This was feudal tradition.' As such they would have been taught the art of war, and understood its conventions.

When Vegetius wrote the military manual *De Re Militari*, dedicated to the emperor Valentinian in the fourth century, he laid down a military strategy that was being referred to over a thousand years later. Christine de Pisan, concerned with the Hundred Years War, used it verbatim as the first part of *the Book of fayttes of Armes and of Chyvalyre*, translated and printed by Caxton. Vegetius was required reading for knights and one of its recurring themes is an overriding need to avoid set piece battles. In early medieval battles the mounted knights were pointed in the direction of the enemy and charged. When they worked as a unit, the weight and momentum could easily sweep aside an infantry formation: the only real defence was an equal and opposite cavalry charge. This was the essence of Norman warfare, but its simplicity held substantial risks: the result of a battle was too much open to chance, all could be won or lost in the short time an engagement took place. So few battles were ever fought, Lewes and Evesham had been waged in the different circumstances of a civil war. Edward's experience, and that of his war machine, was in campaigning, in Wales and on crusade—he could form an army and hold it together in the field. His forces were well armed and he had commanders he could trust. The Scottish army did not have the experienced troops that Edward could readily rely upon from the Welsh wars, or even from Gascony, who could instil discipline and confidence in the ranks.

Edward I's biographer, Michael Prestwich, offers a contrasting view of the Scottish strategy in 1296. The Scots had flouted the rules of war: they had ambushed the English force sent to relieve Wark, at night, using a password: 'there was no question of a conventional declaration of hostilities; or use of formal battle cries.' When they did determine to meet the English, at Dunbar—which they captured by deception not by combat—it was during a truce.[31] This was an unorthodox means to a conventional end; but the Scots had also followed the advice of Vegetius: launching raids into England to avoid coming into contact with the larger English host.

Diplomacy, had failed. Although a settlement in the spring might have been possible neither side was willing give ground. When manoeuvres and diplomacy failed, Vegetius suggests a further option: taming the enemy by hunger. Feeding an army in the field was a difficult task. The Prior of Coldstream claimed £177 17s damages for the night that the English had spent in his priory when they first invaded Scotland. An English army had an almost limitless appetite: that night the soldiers ate their way through £50 of corn, 497 ewes with lambs, and 100 sheep.[32] It was shrewd strategy which later leaders would adopt with some success.

Until the battle of Dunbar the Scots had followed Vegetius's basic precept. So why abandon this strategy and fight? Firstly, desperation: the war was going badly. Secondly, to the Scottish leaders Dunbar presented a golden opportunity. They waited until the odds were stacked in their favour; the tactics were correct, but it was their application, combined with the desertion of the cavalry, which went so disastrously wrong at Dunbar.

Edward had conquered Scotland, it was now time to settle the peace and consolidate his victory. The booty captured at Edinburgh castle included the country's regalia and records. Edward sent them, together with the symbols of Scottish kingship, the stone of Scone and the Black Rood to Westminster as war trophies: he planned to humiliate the Scottish nation in the same way that he had humiliated John, stripping them of the outward signs of kingship as John's coat of arms had been stripped from his tabard. The stone of Scone, where Scottish kings had been seated in an ancient conferal of kingship, was sent to Westminster Abbey, and a wooden seat was made over it to become the English coronation chair.

Edward took personal control of Balliol's great Galloway lordship. He was aware of the importance of the west and played the local politics with finesse. In 1235, when the male line died out, the Celtic people of the province chose Thomas of Galloway, an illegitimate son of Alan of Galloway. Alexander II put down the rebellion and had Thomas imprisoned in John Balliol's castle. There he remained for the next 60 years: his case was under discussion on the day of Alexander III's death but attempts to secure his release by the current John Balliol came to nothing. Edward had him released from Balliol's stronghold, Castle Barnard in Durham. The poor octogenarian was then paraded around the lordship in an attempt to secure local support. What happened to him then is unknown, only that the lands Alan had bestowed on him were restored.

At Berwick Edward summoned a parliament that met on 28 August; its memorial is the Ragman Roll, 35 pieces of parchment which contain word-for-word copy of the homage and fealty of substantial freeholders of the country: the bishops and clergy, burgesses and lords. It was an acknowledgement of defeat, an effective delivery of the nation's loyalty in a common act of allegiance to him personally, rather than to the king of Scotland. Professor Barrow has convincingly challenged the idea that the 2,000 or so persons named on Roll actually crowded into Berwick, most had been collected by the country's sheriffs in the preceding weeks.[33] The few malcontents and die-hards who failed to swear fealty were outlawed by the justiciar, William Ormesby. In the heady aftermath of victory it is unlikely that the new administration lost much sleep over them.

Edward left no statement of his attitude to Scotland, which is strange when set against the record of his position during the great cause five years earlier which had been worded so precisely. He even doctored the official record so that the ambiquity remained. The loyalty sworn in the Berwick parliament had an unsubtle difference to that sworn in 1291, from 'Sovereign lord of Scotland' to 'Sir Edward, by the grace of God, king of England, lord of Ireland and duke of Aquitaine'.

For the time being Edward was to leave Scotland without a king, as he prepared to rule in his capacity as the king of England. Ranald Nicholson summed up the difficulty for Edward in this policy: 'By feudal law the escheat of a fief to its overlord left unaltered the rights and privileges inherent in the fief; and the escheated fief of Scotland was a kingdom.'[34] Whatever the merits of English claims to overlordship, there was never any doubt that Scotland existed as a realm. If this was his long term ambition, Scotland to be subsumed into a greater England, in much the same way as Wales and Ireland, its relegation from the status of a 'realm' to a 'land', it was ill-considered and provocative.

Using Nicholson's feudal principal Edward had three viable options open to him: to place another vassal king on the throne; a return of king John after a suitable period of repentance; or to take the throne himself. The only alternative to John, indeed the only legitimate candidate was Robert Bruce, lord of Annandale. Not only had he shown irreproachable support for Edward, but the ancient claim his family nursed for the crown had passed to him on the death of the competitor in 1295. It was certainly not an option lost on Bruce. After service in Edward's army he must have believed that the empty throne was his. He was painfully mistaken. His petition brought a curt response from Edward: 'have we nothing to do but win realms for you?'[35]

Had Bruce of Annandale become king it might have avoided 250 years of warfare, but after Bruce's involvement with Edward's invasion he would have been a divisive candidate, hastening the civil war which followed his son's seizure of the throne a decade later. Bruce of Annandale had little support in Scotland, he was not the man of his father or his son, and there were inherent dangers in building him up. Ranged against him was all the might of the Comyns, easily the most powerful family in Scotland.

The Comyns, and much of the rest of Scotland, hoped for John's rehabilitation, and would fight behind his banner over the next decade. His failure in 1296 did not bar his return, this was no meritocracy. If

Edward based his long-term plans around John's return after a suitable period of repentance, the rebellion that followed effectively closed this option. How could John return while the country was in open revolt against Edward's authority?

The third option of taking the throne for himself must have been tempting. Edward could now add right of conquest to his claim of overlordship, but he did not seem to have any ambition to become king of Scotland. Edward did not see himself as the conqueror of an independent country, but as an avenging overlord.[36] Instead he left it in limbo, waiting on events. Edward does not seem to have planned far beyond the conquest. With hindsight it is easy to see this as a stupid heavy-handed measure, Edward's 'colonial policy' making further fighting inevitable. Resistance eventually flourished in a power vacuum of his own making, but this was not so obvious when Edward basked in the victory of 1296. Where was opposition to come from? The earls of March, Angus and Annandale were still firmly in the English camp, as was the future king Robert, earl of Carrick; the earls of Mentieth, Atholl and Ross were captured at Dunbar and now languished in the tower of London with the younger Comyn and the justiciar of Scotia; Strathearn and the Steward had surrendered before Edward's military procession, and more still, Buchan, and Mar together with the elder Comyn had surrendered with their king. Duncan, earl of Fife was only twelve years-old. Those that mattered were sent to England, soon to be enlisted into Edward's campaigns in Flanders as the price for their freedom.

Edward had removed the leading tier of Scottish society, which formed the military strength of the nation. These men owned the nation's wealth, that wealth 'purchased allegiance'. It was from their estates that the common foot soldier came in loyalty not to their king or country but to their feudal overlord. It was they who supplied the army with its professional soldiers, the knights and men-at-arms, without which there could be no military operations.

The only other potential source of opposition was the church. The kirk had long held a tight grip on its Scottish identity after a long struggle to remain independent from the diocese of York. They were right to protect their independence. Edward ordered that only English priests could be presented to Glasgow benefices, an order later applied to all Scotland, a move designed to prevent a fifth column preaching from the pulpit. The church was to play a valiant role in the war for Scottish independence, from the twelve bishoprics only three bishops, the illustrious and long suffering opponent of the English, Robert Wishart of Glasgow, Henry Cheyne of Aberdeen and Thomas Dalton of Whithorn, appear on the Ragman Roll. But only one bishop, Mark, bishop of Sodor and Man was actively hostile; Fraser of St Andrews and Crambeth of Dunkeld were in France. Three bishoprics were vacant, Archibald of Moray may have signed, while the role of Laurence of Argyll is unknown.[37] One obscure bishop was hardly a rallying point for resistance.

The fealties of the estates were accepted at their word, so that as few changes as possibly were made to the country's administration: the day-to-day government would be left to Scottish officials. English wardens, with English garrisons, were placed in the main castles. John Warenne became Edward's lieutenant in Scotland, aided by the clever, ambitious and capable officials that played such a large part in Edwardian government — the 'fat and unpopular' Hugh Cressingham, was made treasurer, known to the Scots as the traitorer[38]; Walter of Amersham, Chancellor. Henry Percy was made warden of Galloway.

To Edward his actions had probably shown more than enough clemency: there were no punitive measures, the Berwick parliament had seen few estates forfeited or lives lost. When Edward left Berwick on 16th September, after three weeks organising the new government, it was in triumph; the victory had been achieved with an unexpected ease. He could now turn his attention towards his real desire, a settlement of the French question. As he recrossed the border he made the casual remark to Warenne, 'Bon besoiogne fait gy du merde se delivrer': 'it was well to be rid of shit.'

Chapter 3

I HAVE BROUGHT YOU TO THE RING, NOW DANCE IF YOU CAN.

'William Wallace lifted up his head from his den and slew the
English sheriff of Lanark, a doughty and powerful man'
John of Fordun

Scotland was left stunned by the ferocity of the English invasion. After Edward left in September 1296 opposition ceased for some months, although Bishops Fraser of St Andrews and Crambeth of Dunkeld lobbied hard in France. With the traditional leaders of society in English captivity, resistance was slow to form, but 'deserted by her nobles, Scotland discovered herself.'[1] At least a month before Edward left for the continent in August 1297 news had reached him of rebellion in the north. That he sailed away regardless shows he underestimated the scale of the opposition to his new government in Scotland, but it also reflects the English king's wider international interests. It is parochial to suggest Edward should have remained in Britain to deal with the Scottish insurgents. His problems on the continent were just as acute and required his energy as much, if not more so than Scotland. It is a pattern that would repeat itself over the centuries: English kings had far more to lose in France than they had to gain in Scotland.

Soon after his victory in Scotland Edward I faced the most difficult challenge of his reign. Edmund and Lincoln had received no reinforcements from England since they left for the continent in January 1296. Edmund had died the following June, leaving Lincoln in a command that could do no more than hold its own against a determined French invasion. In January 1297 Lincoln's army was defeated at the battle of Bellegarde, and the seneschal, John de St John, was captured. It became vital to relieve the pressure on Gascony. In February 1297 Edward signed an alliance with count Guy of Flanders. With this continental alliance in place, Edward could go on campaign. But he had no army and no money.

Coming so soon after a Scottish invasion that had produced few rewards for his nobles, the frantic effort to mount a fresh campaign in the early months of 1297 finally cracked the brittle bonds between king and state. When parliament met in Bury St Edmunds the king was voted a twelfth from the shires and an eighth from the burghs. When pressed for a fifth the clergy were unable to reach a decision. In February 1296 Boniface VIII had issued the papal bull, *Clericis laicos,* which prohibited secular authorities from taxing the clergy. The bull overstepped the traditional limits of papal jurisdiction, was opposed throughout Europe, and abandoned in July 1297 after pressure from Philip IV. But for now it had a formidable advocate in Archbishop Robert Winchelsea who refused to give permission for the clergy to pay the tax. Edward gave them until a convocation in London the following January to reconsider their stand. After eight days of heated debate the clergy declared that they could not make a grant without papal authority. In response Edward outlawed them. This drastic step meant that the clergy were denied royal protection, which the king promised to return for payment of a sum equivalent to the fifth he had sought: a medieval protection racket. Some gave way and were pardoned but the archbishop held out.

Without money, Edward was forced to rely on a feudal levy to raise an army. Again he faced opposition. Edward kept his nobility in check by personal friendship and by their inclusion in his military plans. The nobles gained from his success, from the profits of war and the reward of lordships. But the Scottish campaign, a joint effort of king and barons, had not seen a division of the spoils. Few estates had been forfeited for Edward to share out. When the call came in 1297 to form a new continental army the rewards were not great enough and the opposition latent in English government came to the surface.[2]

Edward faced a powerful coalition led by Roger Bigod earl of Norfolk, and Humphrey Bohun earl of Hereford. As respectively hereditary earl marshall and constable they were the key men in any English medieval army. The magnates refused to serve abroad. It was too much for the king. In a tense moment at the Salisbury parliament in late February, an instant that would define the spring and early summer of 1297, he lost his temper. When Bigod spoke for the opposition Edward told him: 'By God, earl, you shall either go or hang', to which the earl replied, 'By the same oath, O king, I will neither go nor will I hang' and withdrew without leave. Edward was finally forced into a humiliating reconciliation with his primate and an admission that military service overseas would be for the king's fee.

As civil war threatened in England, the government in Scotland was left to deal with the threat of armed rebellion with limited local resources. The English occupation of Scotland had been superficial. There may have been disturbances throughout the country in the winter of 1296-7. The earliest official record is dated 9 April 1297, when Edward sent orders to 'his faithful lieges of Argyll and Ross' to aid his 'chosen and faithful Alexander of the Isles', to end disorders:

'For certain malefactors and disturbers of our peace ...
who wander through divers places in these parts, and
commit murders, burnings, and other injuries against our
peace, do you seek from day to day and do not rest until
they are arrested and placed in safe custody'.[3]

This incident was probably put down to a local feud in the isolated
Western Highlands. These disturbances were followed in May by a
widespread and determined revolt that the government forces were too
thinly spread to stop.

Earl Warenne was growing old, and for a man whose estates and
interests lay in the south of England he found the Scottish climate
disagreeable. He spent much of the time out of the country, leaving the
day-to-day government to his subordinates. Hugh Cressingham, the
treasurer, had no estates to fall back on, his standing rested upon his
place as the king's officer. In 1297 he was the key man in Scotland, and
he tried to profit from it, lobbying hard to receive the church at Douglas
when it fell vacant. Fierce ambition did not cloud his judgement: he was
a capable administrator. But he was only a glorified accountant, and he
underestimated the forces ranged against him. William Ormesby, the
justiciar, tracked down those who refused to do homage to Edward with
a zeal that made him and the regime many enemies.

It is difficult to judge the cause of every disturbance: unrest was
almost inevitable in the medieval world when central government
proved weak. Some Scots concluded that the lack of English garrisons
in the north revealed the weakness of the occupation regime. Others
held grudges against local officials. Indeed, it was a personal grudge in
a local disturbance that has left its imprint on Scottish consciousness,
and did more than any other to ignite the widespread hostility of this and
later generations to English rule.

We know little of William Wallace's early years, not even his age,
although he was still young. He was 'a tall man with the body of a giant,
cheerful in appearance with agreeable features, broad-shouldered and
big-boned, with belly in proportion and lengthy flanks, pleasing in
appearance with a wild look, broad in the hips, with strong arms and
legs, a most spirited fighting-man, with all his limbs very strong and
firm.'[4] In a world of small men, Wallace stood out from the crowd. His
family came from Shropshire and moved to Scotland in the eleventh
century as followers of Walter FitzAlan, progenitor of the Stewarts. His
father held land in Elderslie as a vassal of the Steward. It is a long way
from his farcical representation as a wild and hairy highlander painted
with woad (1,000 years too late) running amok in a tartan kilt (500
years too early).

Wallace is a difficult character to appreciate. He was not a revolutionary. He fought to preserve the old order, not to sweep it away: he fought for king John's restoration and his country's freedom. Fordun described him as 'wondrously brave and bold, of goodly wien, and boundless liberality.'[5] He also had an unpublicised dark side: he was quite willing to use terror to achieve his ends. The English chronicler Walter of Guisborough says that the Scots 'took old men, priests and women of the English nation (whom they had specifically kept alive for the purpose) to bridges over the rivers; and when they had tied their hands or feet together so that they would not swim, they threw them or pushed them into the water, laughing and jeering as they struggled and went under.'[6] The fear of the anglicisation of the kirk did lead to attacks on English clergy, giving Guisborough's propaganda a veneer of credibility.

Wallace had a determination bordering on arrogance, and had no time for those in Scotland who differed from his cause. In 1305 a Scottish knight, Michael de Miggel, was called before a commission at Perth to explain his support of Wallace. Miggel told his inquisitors that 'he had been taken prisoner forcibly against his will by William Wallace, that he escaped once from William for two leagues, but was followed and brought back by some armed accomplices of William's, who was firmly resolved to kill him for his flight; that he escaped another time ... for three leagues, brought back prisoner with the greatest violence by some accomplices of Wallace.' Miggel was told that if he tried to escape again his life would be forfeit. The reader must judge the reliability of a man with obvious reasons to invent a defence, but since the court was ready to believe him this was probably not an isolated incident.[7] It was an attitude that would make Wallace enemies in Scotland, particularly amongst the lords. Wallace was never at ease with the barony, and they were uncomfortable with him and his low birth.[8] But without his single-mindedness and sense of purpose, Wallace would have remained no more than the younger son of a middling landowner.

The traditional view of William Wallace is based on Blind Harry's *Wallace*, a poetic account written in the 15th century. According to this, Wallace clashed with an English patrol, but was able to make his escape through his wife's house. The English burnt the house to the ground with his wife and servant still inside. In revenge, Wallace returned and killed William Hesilrig, the sheriff of Lanark. Blind Harry deals in stereotypes: the decent Scot betrayed by a bloodthirsty Englishman—a heavy-handed analogy to the English conquest of Scotland. His story owes more to his imagination than to history. The author of the *Scalacronica*, Thomas Grey of Heton, names a witness. His father was party to the events immediately leading up to and including Hesilrig's death. In Grey's account Hesilrig was holding a county court when a fight broke out and Wallace escaped. Later:

the said William Wallace came by night upon the said sheriff and surprised him, when Thomas Grey, who was at that time in the suite of the said sheriff, was left stripped for dead in the mêlée when the English were defending themselves. The said Thomas lay all night naked between two burning houses which the Scots had set on fire, whereof the heat kept life in him, until he was recognised at daybreak and carried off by William Lundy who caused him to be restored to good health.[9]

It is unknown what Wallace was doing at Hesilrig's court, even if he was a defendant. That he was involved in a fracas suggests that a judgement was made against him. *Lanercost* hints that he was already an outlaw; Walter of Guisborough suggests that this was as a result of his refusal to sign the Ragman Roll. Certainly his name was not on the Roll, but he might not have needed to sign— it would have been his elder brother Malcolm who owed allegiance, and his name is also missing. This version of events is less dramatic, but more easily reconcilable with the known events. How the murder of a minor royal official escalated into a widespread revolt is unclear, but: 'from that time there flocked to him all who were in bitterness of spirit, and weighed down beneath the burden of bondage under unbearable domination of English despotism; and he became their leader.'[10]

William Douglas was one of the first to join the revolt. Douglas had been released and restored to his lordship after the general amnesty in 1296. As a lord, a tenant-in-chief, he was an important recruit, giving the rebellion the respectability of noble backing. By virtue of his rank he assumed joint command with Wallace. They moved swiftly to try and capture Ormesby at Scone before news of the rebellion spread. Ormesby 'being forewarned escaped with difficulty, leaving much spoil to the enemy, which, when they had gathered, they proceeded, not now in secret as before, but openly, putting to the sword all the English they could find beyond the Scottish sea, turning themselves afterwards to the siege of castles.' The speed of the attack on Ormesby and the mobility of the guerrilla campaign could only have been achieved by mounted men: mobile, determined, and able. The outlying English garrisons and supporters had little defence against these lightning attacks.

Wallace's revolt was mirrored by remarkably similar uprisings throughout Scotland. Macduff of Fife, uncle of the young earl, led out the men of the earldom.[11] The men of Moray and burgesses of Inverness gathered around Andrew Murray's standard. Murray came from one of Scotland's leading families. His father, Andrew Murray was lord of Petty in Inverness-shire, Avoch on the Black Isle, Boharm in Banffshire and was from 1289 justiciar of Scotia (Scotland north of the Forth). His estates centred on Bothwell in Lanarkshire, one of few stone-built castles in Scotland. Father and son had been captured at the battle of Dunbar and imprisoned: Murray senior was held in the Tower of London, Murray junior in the less secure Chester. He escaped during the winter and made his way back to Scotland. When he reappeared it was at his father's castle in Avoch in rebellion.

The origins of Murray's rebellion are revealed in a letter to Edward from William Fitzwarin, the constable of Urquhart castle. It is one of a series of letters written in late July by Edward's allies trying to explain how the situation in Moray had deteriorated so badly and so quickly. For a rebellion that we have precious few details of, they are illuminating documents. But care has to be taken trusting wholly English sources that are not corroborated, especially ones from men with reason to protect their reputations.

The English garrison at Inverness, surrounded by strongholds at Urquhart, Nairn, Forres, Elgin and Lochindorb, dominated the region. News reached the guardian of Moray, Reginald le Cheyne, that 'evil disposed people' had joined Andrew Murray and Alexander Pilche at the castle of Avoch on the Black Isle in Ross.[12] That Murray chose as his lieutenant a burgess, not a lord or knight, reveals not only the popular nature of uprising, but the breaking down of the traditional barriers that separated the layers of feudal society: noble from merchant, laird from burgess. It also shows that the two principal and effective rebellions drew their support from a common pool.

In response to a deteriorating situation Cheyne called a council of war in Inverness. Fitzwarin was amongst those who attended. As he made his way home he was ambushed: he broke free and reached his castle, but not before the loss of two principal followers captured wounded, 'and a number of lesser men whose fate is not known.' On the following morning Murray and Pilche lay siege to Urquhart.

Nearby the countess of Ross had raised a large following from her husband's earldom. The Earl of Ross was still imprisoned in England, it could be that Countess Effie was concerned with gaining his release by showing her support for Edward's besieged garrison.[13] Fitzwarin could not be sure. An esquire broke through to tell him that the siege was not of her doing and offered help, although he counselled surrender. It was advice and aid Fitzwarin chose to refuse 'lest greater peril should befall him.' Hugh, the earl of Ross's son and heir, led the army closer to the castle and managed to get provisions through, but further help was again declined and Hugh retired. Emissaries sent by Murray to seek surrender were dismissed. There came next a fierce night assault in which Fitzwarin's son was killed, but its ultimate failure saw Murray's last chance to take the castle disappear. He could not risk remaining in the field with Ross's intentions unclear and his army so close and so withdrew.

Emboldened by the success of the rebellion, the Steward and bishop Wishart of Glasgow declared their support, soon followed by Robert Bruce Earl of Carrick. Bruce had received a commission from the bishop of Carlisle to raid Douglas's lands in the south-west, but he had other plans. Leading his force into Douglasdale, he attempted to raise the men of Annandale in revolt, saying: 'no man holds his own flesh and blood in hatred and I am no exception. I must join my own people and the nation in which I was born.' The men of Annandale were not convinced. Their feudal chief was not Bruce of Carrick but his father, Bruce of Annandale, the son of the competitor, whose loyalty to Edward never wavered.[14] Although supporters of king John in 1296, Wishart and the Steward were closely linked to the Bruce party. They were not members of the Comyn inner circle. When the king and his supporters had been removed from power, Bruce saw the opportunity to wrest control from the old guard. Even better, while Bruce of Annandale stayed loyal to Edward, the Bruces had a foot in both camps which would shelter the family's estates in England and his son from the full consequences of the rebellion.

The roles of the Wishart and the Steward during the Spring are mysterious. Historians have divided into two camps. Conspiracy theorists detect their hands behind the uprisings throughout Scotland in 1297. Norman Reid argues 'these risings were part of a prearranged, carefully co-ordinated campaign, masterminded by Wishart and the Steward, to rid the country of its English administration and replace it with one of their own.' The alternative camp, who might be called the romantics, see the rebellion, as 'the spontaneous act of middling and common folk who found their own leaders—Wallace and Murray, not Bruce and the Stewart.'[15]

The conspiracy theorists have the support of the chroniclers. Guisborough called Glasgow and the Steward 'the fabricators', the Lanercost chronicler accused them of conspiring 'for a new piece of insolence, yea, for a new chapter of ruin. Not daring openly to break their pledge to the king, they caused a certain bloody man, William Wallace, who had formerly been a chief of brigands in Scotland, to revolt against the king, and assemble the people in his support.' Their conspiracy remained secret for fear of bringing a more determined response from the English. These fears were justified. It was only after the barons' involvement became known that the English began taking firm action.

The case for a conspiracy does not seem proven. We should not give too much weight to the chroniclers' evidence: they were blinkered, seeing politics centred on the political classes, the barons and higher church. The idea of political action coming from the community was alien to them. It was natural as they wrote in hindsight that they should confuse the bishop and Steward's roles—men who became mixed up in the rebellion only a few months after it had begun.

The insurrection shows little sign of co-ordination, and seems more likely to have developed from local disturbances, rather than from some master-plan for rebellion. It seems improbable that these two politically experienced men should have chosen Wallace's murder of a minor royal official with which to begin a revolt. The chronicle sources describe a murder in hot blood, hardly the first act of a well-organised military rebellion. Perhaps Wallace had jumped the gun. More likely Wishart and the Steward became involved after, not before Hesilrig's murder, exploiting the opportunity that the murder presented.

Wishart's hand was behind the merger of the disparate rebel groups into a general revolt. He was able to guide, rather than dominate events, reacting rather than controlling or initiating them. Wallace sought the temporal and secular blessing of his local lords, he was a vassal of the Steward, whose lands lay in the bishop of Glasgow's province; how much further that involvement went is unclear, and certainly did not last long.

With Edward preoccupied with Europe, it fell to the local government in Scotland to deal with the rebellion themselves. Warenne was a disaster. He wrote blaming his inactivity on the failure of Anthony Bek to provide a promised force of men-at-arms. Bek had been in Scotland with 120 men-at-arms between May and June 1297 when he returned to England. Bek himself then began making his own preparations to travel to the continent. It was this force that Warenne wanted to take back to Scotland. Still, Edward kept faith with the victor of Dunbar, making him guardian of Scotland on 14 June, possibly in a bid to chide him into action.[16]

It was not until the beginning of June that a response came from London, but it underestimated the scale and popularity of the rebellion. It must have been galling for Edward. His presence on the continent was urgently needed, and he desperately wanted to go. Yet in the north, in the country he had conquered only months before, his officials were failing to stop local disturbances expanding into a full-scale revolt. On 4 June 1297 Edward issued new orders for the suppression of the revolt in Scotland: 'since there are many persons who disturb our peace and quietness of our kingdom and make divers meetings, conventicles, and conspiracies in very many parts of the land of Scotland, both within our liberties and without, and perpetrate depredations, homicides, burnings, robberies, rapines, and other evils in divers manners.'[17]

The sheriffs of Lancaster, Cumberland, and Westmoreland were commanded to send help to Henry Percy and Robert Clifford who had been appointed to 'arrest, imprison and justify all disturbers of the peace in Scotland.' It was a northern response to a northern problem. Robert Clifford from Westmoreland, Percy from Yorkshire.[18] Cressingham was ordered back to his post from Bolton in Northumberland where he had been negotiating with northern barons.[19]

There is some evidence of English success. Edward thanked his Gallovidian liege Donald MacCan and others for putting down the rebellion in their part of the country and retaking castles. Alexander Macdonald had not received the support from the men of Ross and Argyll promised in April but had still captured the Steward's castle at Glasrog and his bitter enemy, Alexander Macdougall.[20]

At Berwick Cressingham had gathered a force he estimated at 300 horse and 10,000 foot and was preparing to join Percy and Clifford.[21] The two northern captains were at Ayr by the end of June with a force made up of levies from the northern counties. At Irvine on 7 July they came across the baronial rebels. At this first sign of determined opposition the magnates in the revolt backed-down. Wishart and Steward sent envoys to the English when they were sighted. They were offered lenient terms, with the condition that they went with Edward to Flanders, and on the 9th they submitted. The nobility was humiliated and discredited. One Scottish knight, Richard Lundie, was so disgusted by the lords' climbdown that he switched sides.

A report of the agreement was sent to Edward in July. In mitigation the nobles spelled out the reasons for the insurrection:

> They were told for a certainty that the king would have seized all the middle-party of Scotland to send them beyond the Scottish sea in his army, to their great damage and destruction. They took counsel to assemble their forces to defend themselves from so great damages, until they could have a treaty and conference with such persons as had power to abate and diminish such a kind of disturbance ... when the English army entered within the land, they came to meet them, and had such a conference that all of them [came into] the peace and fealty of our lord the king.[22]

It reveals the nature of the nobles' concerns: the two principal estates, church and nobility, were looking after their own interests. They were not primarily concerned with the issue of sovereignty; they were protesting at Edward I's policies rather than his conquest. It does not take a great leap of the imagination to realise how Edward's plans for an expedition to the continent, leading to near rebellion in England, would be received in Scotland. They were of course justified in their fears. Cressingham wrote to Edward saying he was making a list of the 'good' and the 'bad', planning to send the latter to Edward for service abroad.[23]

The details of the baronial submission were still being argued in early August. Bruce, the Steward, his brother and William Douglas confessed their rebellion, placing themselves at the king's will. Wishart, James the

Steward and Alexander Lindsay became guarantors for the earl of Carrick's loyalty.[24] Lindsay and Douglas allowed themselves to be taken into captivity until Bruce surrendered his daughter, Marjorie. Lindsay made his own peace; Douglas would not. Percy and Clifford arrived with both men at Berwick. William Douglas was kept in Berwick castle in irons, where his warder found him 'savage and abusive'. He was transferred to the Tower of London where he died in 1299. His son, still only ten or eleven years-old, was placed under Bishop Lamberton's charge.

Bruce's lands were forfeited and his guarantor, Wishart, imprisoned when he failed to turn up to complete the covenant on 8 August. Wishart would remain under arrest in Roxburgh until 1299. Bruce had still not submitted on 14 November when Clifford was ordered to admit him to Edward's peace.[25] There is no official record that Bruce ever did submit, although ten years later the bishop of Carlisle 'seemed to remember' that he did.

Cressingham had only advanced as far as Roxburgh when he met Percy and Clifford returning from Irvine. It was now that he learnt of their success and was irritated that he could not share in the triumph of the victory. Irvine was followed by the capture of Macduff of Fife, defeated by Malise earl of Strathearn and captured with his two sons.[26] Edward was told the good news, but with dangerous complacency, the Scottish government took no action against Wallace. Percy and Clifford had warned him

> 'that even though peace had been made on this side, nevertheless it were well to make an incursion upon the enemies on the other side of the sea of Scotland, if they saw it was necessary; or that an attack should be made upon William Wallace, who lay there with a large company (and does so still) in the forest of Selkirk, like one who holds himself against your peace. Whereupon it was determined that no expedition should be made until the earl's arrival; and thus matters have gone to sleep, and each of us went away to his own residence.'

The English could not deal with all the different groups that made up the revolt in Scotland. The capitulation at Irvine left the other rebels more exposed, but Cressingham failed to capitalise on this success. He was being pressed on three sides: he could not take action without the earl; he was running out of money (which forced him to make short-sighted economies) and some of his lieutenants saw the Irvine submission as evidence that the whole rebellion would founder. He was exasperated by Earl Warenne's failure to take any action and began sending heavy hints south that the failure lay at the earl's feet. He reported to Edward that there was an 'abundance of ships in Berwick should the earl make a foray to the parts beyond the Scottish seas.' In another letter he complained that 'not a penny could be raised in your realm by any means until my lord the Earl Warenne shall enter your land and compel the people of the country by force.'

Edward's request for money to finance his continental adventure naturally applied to Scotland. At the end of May Cressingham had sent £5,188 6s 8d to the exchequer. The king then told him to use revenue raised in Scotland to crush the revolt. This was as unrealistic as any of Edward's demands that summer. At the beginning of June Cressingham's royal officers had been chased from the shires and could no longer raise taxes. He wrote a forceful letter describing the conditions in Scotland: 'by far the greater part of your counties of the realm of Scotland are still unprovided with keepers, as well as by death, sieges and imprisonment; and some have given up their bailiwicks, and others will not dare return; and in some counties the Scots have established and placed bailiffs and ministers, so that no county is in proper order, excepting Berwick and Roxburgh and this only lately.' Edward had to return £2,000, a subsidy with the condition that it would be repaid by the following August out of Scottish issues.[27]

On the day that Cressingham was pleading for more money and action from Warenne, the constable of Berwick wrote to Edward that 'your enemies are dispersed and dismayed, and if the peace which has been given them in your name does not please you, they shall speedily be disgraced.' Another letter told him 'that your peace progresses and improves, and we hope to have a good peace soon', one more 'that your enemies of Scotland were dispersed and frightened from their foolish enterprise.' It is difficult to understand on what basis these royal officials were writing between now and the beginning of August. The rebellions that had been rolling over the country had been impossible to subdue. Even the contrite nobles at Irvine were not coming forward to Berwick with their covenants.[28] They seem to have badly misjudged the threat, weakening Cressingham's attempts to force a response from the king.

Freed from aristocratic dominance, Wallace and Murray continued the struggle. Wallace remained in the south, using Selkirk Forest as a secure base from which to attack English strongholds south of the Forth. He had not been involved in the Irvine fiasco. His fury at the nobility's submission was very real and he attacked Wishart's palace at Ancrum, seizing not just his property but his sons. Wallace's anger and the attack on Ancrum were the result of his personal feeling of betrayal by Wishart. However, their ties were too strong for their split to last—after the battle of Stirling Bridge Wallace besieged Roxburgh in an attempt to free him.

Edward was at Ospringe in Kent when news arrived of Murray's attack on Urquhart. The messenger, Andrew Rait, a neighbour of Murray's from Rait Castle near Nairn, at last brought the scale of the revolt to Edward's attention. His report led to immediate action. During June and July Edward offered to release the Scottish barons he had captured in 1296 in return for their service in France. On 6 June John Comyn earl of Buchan, Alexander Stewart earl of Menteith, the elder Comyn of Badenoch, Alexander Comyn, Reginald Crawford, Nigel Campbell and William Bisset agreed to the conditions. Earlier on the morning of Rait's arrival on the 11 June they set out to return to Scotland to prepare for the campaign.[29]

Edward decided to use some of these men to subdue Moray. And who better than the Comyns, who knew the rebels and the land where they would be fighting. Edward sent Rait in pursuit of the barons with new orders, relieving them of their pledge to go with him to France. Rait overtook the Comyns as they returned home. He informed them of the situation in Scotland and gave them their orders: to relieve Urquhart, strengthen the castle, and subdue the rebellion. 'Do ye comport yourselves with the vigour I expect of you' wrote Edward, 'that I might rightly commend in this business your diligence and fidelity.'[30] It was a

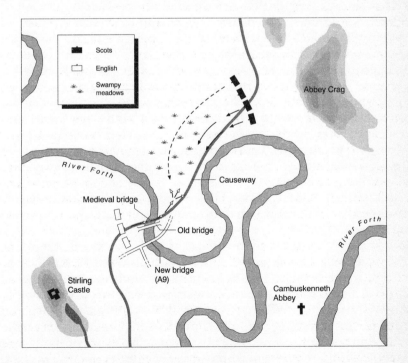

The Battle of Stirling Bridge

typically Edwardian gesture, and one that was to blow up in his face.

Edward's new recruits sent a report from Inverness on 24 and 25 July.[31] They led a foray from Aberdeen on the 12th northwards in search of Murray. The road from Aberdeen ran through Enzie, skirting the 'Bog of Gight'. It was here they found him on the 17th, 'with a large body of rogues.' Murray had not been disillusioned by his brief failure at the siege of Urquhart. He moved on to lesser targets in a vigorous guerrilla war. When he encountered Buchan he was fresh from the capture and destruction of Duffes castle, the family home of the Murrays of Duffes whose heiress had married Reginald Cheyne.

Buchan did not fall into the trap of leading his men into the bog. Andrew Rait tried to parley with Murray but was unsuccessful. A similar attempt was made in the following month, on 28 August safe conducts were issued to Hugh Ross and Murray.[32] It could be that the failure of the rebellion in Irvine led Murray to re-evaluate the chances of success in the north. Nothing came of the meeting.

The party crossed the Spey and reached Cullen castle. Next morning they pushed on early to make Elgin before nightfall. Marching in battle formation they would have been too strong for Murray who retired and was not seen again. From Elgin, to Forres, Nairn and finally Inverness where he met up with the local men on the ground—Henry Cheyne, the bishop of Aberdeen, and Gartnait, the son of the earl of Mar and brother-in-law of Robert Bruce, Reginald Cheyne, the countess of Ross, John of Aird and the constable of Urquhart.[33] This combination of Englishmen from the garrisons, pro-English Scots and those whose loyalty to Edward was at best half-hearted, began preparations for a campaign in the north-east. The letters they sent south reveal very little for fear that Rait would fall into Murray's hands. It was up to the messenger to give a verbal account to Edward. This spate of letter writing was not the most convincing attempt to subdue a rebellion. Not only were they failing to put down the revolt, they were not even holding what ground they had.

Rait arrived back in Berwick on 5 August. Cressingham was not persuaded by whatever Rait had to tell him, and in his own dispatch he told Edward that 'the peace on the other side of the Scottish sea is still in obscurity, as it is said, as to the doings of the earls who are there ... Sir Andrew de Rait is going to you with a credence, which he has shown to me, and which is false in many points and obscure, as will be shown hereafter, as I fear; and therefore, sire, if it be your pleasure, you will give little weight to it.'[34] Without Rait's verbal account the evidence for Murray's campaign is tenuous, but Cressingham's contemporary criticism must count heavily against the barons Edward sent against Murray. Nothing definite had been heard of Murray since he was at the Spey. Reginald Cheyne was singled out especially, his lands laid waste until Inverness fell and he was captured.[35] The castles at Elgin and Banff fell. It was the last news of Murray until September, when he reappeared on the far bank of the Forth. In five short weeks he took complete control of the north.

Wallace himself moved north. Blind Harry places him at Aberdeen on 31 July when he destroyed shipping and swept through Buchan. More likely this was the work of Murray. But the two men did link up, probably at the siege of Dundee in early September. It must have been a tense moment, two men of such towering personalities, one a noble, one a vassal, who could so easily have taken a dislike to each other. Instead they found a powerful bond of mutual necessity that meant they would combine their forces and lead them as equals.

The rebellion continued to spread. The earl of Mar never returned to go with Edward to Flanders, and Strathearn was refusing to send Macduff of Fife to Warenne. In late July Henry de Latham, the Lancashire-born sheriff changed sides. How he became caught up in the revolt is a mystery, he was either swept along by the rebellion or just took the opportunity to set himself up as a local tyrant. When the bishop of Aberdeen returned from Inverness he found that the Sheriff had 'thrown off allegiance.' Earl Warenne sent men to take him but had no news when he wrote to Edward on 1 August. He was not caught: in February 1298 he was still 'a rebel and adherent of the Scots' when his lands in Lancaster were seized.[36]

On 27 July Henry Percy wrote to Edward that he and Earl Warenne would be in Berwick the following day. On 1 August the earl himself wrote to Edward that he was planning an expedition against the northern insurgents ... just as soon as the bishop of Glasgow, the Earl of Carrick and the Steward arrived in Berwick to complete their covenants to Henry Percy. As the English position deteriorated, Cressingham and Edward started a dialogue on the terms that Brian FitzAlan would take on the guardianship when Warenne left with the king for Flanders. FitzAlan was quibbling over his fee that the king thought should be less than Warenne had been paid. He was appointed on 18 August, on the same basis as Warenne.[37]

Meanwhile, Philip IV had invaded Flanders and was in control of much of the region. Edward left England on 22 August, taking with him Bek, Despenser and Aymer de Valence. Twelve year old Edward Caernarfon was left as regent, under the counsel of the justiciar of Chester, Reginald Grey. The Scottish contingent amounted to a paltry ten knights and 25 esquires under Sir Edward Comyn, and even some of these slipped away to Philip IV (only to be turned back as a truce was in effect). John Strathbogie earl of Atholl went, although as he served without pay his contingent is unrecorded.[38]

Edward's Flanders campaign was a stubborn gesture. He took too few troops to fight a war that had already been lost. The earls of Hereford and Norfolk had refused to serve and were in arms outside London. On 20 August 170 loyal knights were ordered to Rochester in a defensive measure disguised as a parliament to meet on 8 September. The regency council realised their northern officials' optimism was misplaced and that Warenne could not be spared either to go to France or even to bolster the Rochester summons. On 7 September they countermanded Warenne's plans to join Edward, ordering that he remain in Scotland.

Warenne finally left Berwick and moved his forces to Stirling. When he arrived on the 10th it was to see the far bank of the Forth occupied by Wallace and Murray who had left the siege of Dundee castle to the town's burgesses, on pain of life, and moved south. A full scale pitched battle was new to both Wallace and Murray—their success to date had been based on the ability to move quickly, unhindered, with brief raids on English outposts. Success would depend on their ability to improvise. Their army was composed of the untrained foot soldiers that had gathered to Wallace in the Forest of Selkirk and Murray at Avoch. The officers appointed to collect revenues would also have been used to demand 'common service'. There was a leavening of professional soldiers, men-at-arms, who had been with Wallace when he crossed the country in August.

They established a strong defensive position at Stirling. The medieval road crossed a causeway, now largely followed by the A9, although the medieval bridge was north of the Old Bridge, itself just farther north from the New Bridge that carries the road traffic today. The flats on either side of the causeway were swampy meadows, impassable to knights on horseback. Wallace and Murray prepared to defend the causeway about a mile north of the bridge. Immediately behind them was the Abbey Crag, a volcanic plug that secured their position from a rear attack: the turns of the river protected their flanks.

The English host was not duly concerned at the rabble that faced them across the river. Cressingham was expecting another submission like that at Irvine. Ever the accountant, he had reduced his overheads by dismissing Percy and his detachment. Presumably Cressingham had the 300 hundred men-at-arms and 10,000 infantry he had raised from Northumberland in July, although the numbers from the county must be grossly exaggerated. Warenne would have brought his own retinue of men-at-arms, even if he may not have added to the infantry. This was far from the enormous English army of legend. There were only four bannerets present, the earl, Walter Huntercumbe, Marmaduke Tweng, and Cressingham himself. The demands for troops elsewhere, with the king in Flanders, accompanying the regent in Rochester or supporting the two earls outside London left precious few men available for the Scottish campaign.

James the Steward and Malcolm earl of Lennox tried to negotiate with Wallace to avoid battle. They claimed they were acting to avoid loss of life, but they may have been trying to buy time for Wallace and Murray, or even trying to take command of the army from them, reasserting their traditional place in Scottish society. They concluded by promising Warenne that they would join his army on the following day with 40 knights. Their credibility was not improved by a subsequent skirmish with English foragers returning to the camp. Lennox wounded one of the English foot who was taken before Warenne by men now seeking vengeance. The earl wisely calmed tempers and promised satisfaction next morning if they failed to bring their retinues.

Warenne's advisors warned him not to cross the Forth: the bridge at Stirling could only take two knights abreast. Richard Lundie, the Scottish knight who had come over to the English at Irvine, offered to take a party to a ford where a troop could cross 30 to 60 men wide. This force could then form a bridgehead to protect the crossing or create a diversion. Cressingham was unimpressed both by the idea of splitting the force, and of the costly delay.

The English began crossing the Forth early on the morning of 11 September. The men were recalled when it was discovered that Warenne was still in bed. Guisborough claims that they had moved 5,000 troops across as Wallace and Murray looked on. It was a blunder on both sides, the English for not securing the far bank when they had so many troops across, the Scots for not contesting the crossing. When finally stirred from his bed Warenne went through the tradition of dubbing new knights before the English attempted to cross the bridge a second time. Again, the advance was halted and the English retreated, this time on the arrival of the Steward and Lennox. They did not bring the promised troops. Warenne sent two Dominican Friars across the bridge in a last bid to secure Wallace and Murray's surrender. Wallace told them to 'tell your commander that we are not here to make peace but to do battle to defend ourselves and liberate our kingdom. Let them come on, and we shall prove this in their very beards.'

Two false starts and a derisive taunt moved Warenne to make rash decisions. The English made a third attempt to cross the Forth. When the leading elements reached the far bank Wallace ordered a flank attack from his spearmen, who charged across the causeway towards the bridge, cutting the English army in two. The English van under Marmaduke Tweng cut a swath through the Scottish host that scattered before them. But behind them, at the bridge, a slaughter was taking place as the Scottish spearmen overran those troops who had crossed the river. Tweng saw what was happening, turned, and managed to reach the far side with his nephew and an esquire before the bridge was broken. Some of the Welsh, and a knight, swam across the Forth. Few others survived. Among the slaughtered was the hated Cressingham. His body was flayed, the skin used to fashion Wallace a sword belt. Panic spread to the remainder of the army on the south bank.

Warrene rode for Berwick after a hastily-formed garrison (under Tweng and William Fitzwarin) was placed in Stirling. Instead of defending the Forth, he opened up the lowlands to the Scots. Warenne's departure had left the English wagon train barely guarded. Lennox and Steward had hidden their men in nearby woods, and they set them on the wagons. Warenne's long but undistinguished military career, under Henry III, at Lewes and Evesham and in the Welsh wars had taught him nothing of military strategy. He was an 'ordinary, stupid and arrogant feudal chief.'[39] The one battle in which he was in command before Stirling Bridge was at Dunbar, a battle he won by default. At Stirling Bridge his luck deserted him.

Andrew Murray had fought in the front-line and was fatally wounded. He lived for several weeks, dying in early November. After the battle of Stirling Bridge Murray and Wallace appear in three documents with the title, 'commanders of the army of the kingdom of Scotland', the first dated 11 October at Haddington, and two more on 7 November at Hexham. Murray's name always appears first in respect of his social standing. Then his name disappears from the documents. It is because of Murray's death that Wallace dominates histories of the period. Murray had no propagandist like Blind Harry to document his achievements. In the 20th century Evan Barron's *Scottish Wars of Independence* elevated Murray into a heroic figure, to a rightful share of Wallace's renown. But should that share be equal? Possibly, but he died too soon for us to ever really know.

By the time of Murray's death Wallace's leadership was unassailable. Guisborough may be overstating the case when he asserts that 'the common folk of the land followed him as their leader and ruler; the retainers of the great lords adhered to him; and even though the lords themselves were present with the [English] king in body, at heart they were on the opposite side.'[40] It does seem that some gave Wallace aid when they could. Many nobles did not recognise Wallace's legitimacy, they bid their time, lent support when necessary, or when forced. This was the inherent weakness in Wallace's government, he drew his support from the lower orders, but it was the nobility where much of the country's power still lay. They had been placed in an unenviable position. They had sworn loyalty to Edward in a much more personal way than Wallace. It was likely that Edward would take their rebellion as an insult to him personally. Lennox and the Steward had come out after Stirling. In the north Buchan and the Comyns supported the rebellion. What happened to the earl of Carrick is unclear.

Before news of the disaster reached Edward I, he sent fresh orders to

Warenne: 'as he understands that the disturbances in Scotland are not yet pacified, commands him to remain til the country is settled.' Too late. The earl was in full flight. The northern counties of England and the garrisons in Scotland were abandoned to deal with the Scottish rebellion by a south preoccupied with war on the continent. In the short term— and only the short term—the balance of power shifted in Scotland's favour. However, Wallace did not follow up his victory at Stirling Bridge with an immediate invasion. In not doing so he missed a golden opportunity to strike at Warenne while his army was still in disarray. Instead, he took part in the victory celebrations. When heads cleared, he followed the earl to Hutton Moor, near Berwick. There he found the English arrayed to oppose him so retired to bivouac in Duns Park.[41]

The battle of Stirling Bridge led to the near total collapse of the English occupation. Stirling castle's garrison did not last long: Tweng and Fitzwarin surrendered when supplies ran low. Minor fortresses fell, leaving only the strongholds at Edinburgh, Roxburgh and Berwick in English hands. Without siege engines or experience in siege warfare the Scots would have to rely on starving these garrisons into submission. Fordun places Wallace at Dundee after the battle, helping to complete the siege. Alexander Scrymgeour took command when the town surrendered. Henry de Haliburton captured Berwick—his task made easier as the town had no walls and the English had fled. The castle garrison could only watch the town's occupation. The besieged castle sent a messenger swimming naked across the Tweed with letters in his shoes to Norham, where Warenne promised relief. They would have to wait until the spring of 1298.[42]

The north of England panicked, people fled to the safety of castles and towns. The destruction of the army assembled by Warenne left the north undefended.[43] A nervous few weeks were spent waiting for an invasion that did not come. The Northumbrians breathed a collective sigh of relief and began to return to their homes when, towards the end of October, Wallace finally turned his attention towards the north of England.

The winter of 1297 was harsh and the crops poor. Wallace decided to let his army feed at his enemy's expense. Guisborough gives two dates for the invasion, 18 October and 11 November; they are not irreconcilable. Initial marauding parties, with help from men of the newly reoccupied Berwick, established a base in Rothbury forest. No attempt was made to take castles. These raids were the result of high-spirits after the victory and aimed at an open door. The northern English castle garrisons, particularly at Alnwick, were able to launch sallies against the raiders, but could not send them home. This sporadic activity took a new direction in early November when Wallace himself became involved, Scotland's army crossed the border through Tynedale to Bywell and then Corbridge.

On 7 November Wallace was at Hexham where two letters were written. The first gave the Abbey protection; the second gave the canons safe-conduct to approach the Scottish army. The inference must be that Wallace was demanding protection money. From Hexham the Scots travelled along the Tyne-Solway isthmus towards Carlisle.

Edward needed strongholds that could ensure the border's integrity. The Earl of Buchan's raid in 1296 had shown how vulnerable the north was. As early as May 1297 the king had expressed concerns about the city's defences: 'as we have heard a bad account of the engines which are at Carlisle, which have occasioned us much expense and annoyance.' He sent his own engineer to examine the works and hide the available timber 'for we hear that the workmen do us more harm than their work will ever be profitable to us.'[44] John Halton bishop of Carlisle replaced Robert Bruce of Annandale as garrison commander; no doubt since Irvine the English were wary of the family's loyalties. In tandem Henry Percy commanded the city's defence. Reinforcements arrived for the garrison: 14 crossbowmen and 95 foot soldiers, but Percy left before the Scottish army arrived at Carlisle and was two days ride away. His contingent threatened to join him and only stayed after the bishop bribed Percy's marshall.[45]

Wallace sent a priest ahead of him to order the city's surrender in return for safe-conduct. The defenders called Wallace's bluff, answering that they did not trust the word of a man who had caused such devastation. They then drew up their engines to show that they were prepared to withhold a siege. The northern registers date the siege from 11 November to the 8 December. This was merely the work of a large detachment left to keep the garrison cooped up so that they could not repeat the sorties that had hampered the Scots' army at Alnwick.

Wallace moved on. South of Carlisle his troops vented their frustration on the villages in Inglewood forest, Cumberland and Allerdale as far as the Derwent.[46] From Cumberland Wallace attempted to move into Durham, travelling across the Pennines at Stainmoor. Bek was not in the franchise—he had accompanied Edward to Flanders—this left the constable of Durham castle to try and improvise a defence. In the end a snow storm turned Wallace back at Bowes.[47]

The army retraced its steps along the Tyne Valley in the direction of Newcastle. At Hexham Abbey Wallace was subjected to a test of his authority remarkably similar to an event during the reign of David I. The abbey was still under Wallace's protection, a protection that had emboldened three canons to return. As Wallace prepared to celebrate mass holy articles needed for the service were stolen. When Wallace heard of the theft he ordered the thieves to sought out and executed, blaming the theft on Galwegians, who, when looking for culprits served much the same purpose as the Welsh in the English army. The search was half-hearted. David I had not been willing to suffer a similar and direct flouting of his authority. He had stationed men at the abbey; when Gallovidians had sought plunder two were summarily executed, while others escaped in terror but were hunted down and executed.

There is no question that Wallace set any different store on sacrilege than David, and it is certain that he punished those who disobeyed his authority as ruthlessly as any medieval commander. That his orders were ignored less than two weeks after they were given would suggest his hold over sections of the army was not complete; perhaps it never was. The army stayed for two days at the priory, delayed by bad weather, then marched east. As it travelled along the north bank of the Tyne 'the men of Ryton in Durham, thinking themselves safe, came out to jeer at the Scots across the swollen river; and great was the panic in the Bishopric when a party of Scots braced the torrent to burn down their village.'

On the other side of the country Newcastle was in a precarious position. So far south of the border, its defences had never received the attention of Carlisle's. In the thirteenth century the town had followed the European wall-building trend but work had been painfully slow. The sheriff of Northumberland spent £4 2s 4d on wood, iron, brass, lard, string and canvas for a springald made in the castle, the turrets were repaired, an engineer employed (from 30 September until the 2 November at 6d a day) and the wages of a smith, carpenters and millers paid. The castle itself held a garrison of six men-at-arms, 88 crossbowmen and an equal number of archers.[48] The defences were not so formidable, though: the garrison left the walls and drew up outside the town. For a second time, Wallace decided against a fight in the open, divided up the spoils and returned home.

Wallace had limited objectives after Stirling Bridge. He was riding the wave of his success and high spirits in his ranks led to the uncoordinated raids in aftermath of the battle. His aims after the battle were simply to feed his army and consolidate his hold on power. He must have recognised Stirling Bridge for what it was, a fluke, and understood the odds were not in his favour in a straight fight between his foot soldiers and well-equipped mounted knights. This would explain why he avoided battle at Berwick on ground chosen by Warenne.

Wallace approached the major northern towns but he cannot have believed he had any hope of capturing them without a formal siege, and he had no siege train. Carlisle was too well-fortified, and by the time he had reached the poorly defended Newcastle his men had been away from home too long. The harsh winter had made the campaign a difficult one, they were tired and cold, the Galwegians troublesome. Besides, they had captured a considerable weight of booty that needed to be taken back safely. The Galwegians returned through Tynedale.

Wallace himself stopped long enough to destroy Mitford castle on 25 November before recrossing the border.

During the winter of 1297 Wallace was knighted by one of the earls, although it is unknown which one. It could have been the earl of Carrick, but as likely Malcolm of Lennox or Malise of Strathearn. It was only now that he was elected as guardian of the realm. In one of few surviving documents he is styled 'William Wallace, knight, guardian of the kingdom of Scotland and commander of its armies in the name of the famous prince the Lord John, by God's grace illustrious king of Scotland, by consent of the community of that realm.' Too much can be read into that consent. The magnates remained uneasy with their unaristocratic commander.

Just as the English were mistaken as to the extent of their success in 1296, so the Scots overestimated their victory in 1297. It was believed that the road was clear for John's return and restoration. The 11 October letter was addressed to Hanseatic traders, to the mayors and communes of Lubeck and Hamburg telling them that it was safe to resume trade as Scotland was now 'recovered by war from the power of the English', the only survivor of many such letters.

Both sides underestimated the other's resolve. Stirling Bridge had seen an English army beaten not by another feudal army, but by foot-soldiers. Worse, it had led to an invasion of England. All the disputes between the king, the church and the barony were set aside to avenge this humiliating defeat.

News of Cressingham's death arrived in London by 21 September. By the 24th the news had crossed the channel and Edward ordered emergency action. Warenne was told that he was 'on no account' to leave Scotland, and that Clifford was to join him. The sheriff of York and 13 northern barons, destined to support Edward Caernarfon in the dispute with the barons in London, were diverted northwards. Warenne had already retreated as far as York by 27 September, he had abandoned not just the Forth, but the Tweed and even the Tyne. The regent called for the northern levies to respond, but there was not much that they could do. Robert Clifford managed some ineffectual raids into Annandale where he killed all the Scots he could find and burned towns but achieved little else.

Writs for a new army were issued on the 23 October. The clergy now voted money for the new campaign.[49] During the early winter preparations for the invasion gathered momentum. Warenne had been dismissed, but Edward had little option other than to reinstate him—the alternative candidates were with him in France or with Caernarfon in London. A grand council of magnates met at York in late January. Amongst those in attendance were the earls of Norfolk, Hereford, Warwick, Gloucester and Arundel, the barons Percy, Wake and Segrave.

The Scottish barons were summoned to the council, both now and again in May 1298: they 'neither came nor sent.'

Warenne was told not to wait for the Welsh contingent, but to cross into Scotland at once.[50] He relieved Roxburgh and recaptured Berwick. Without the king's experienced household to organise the day-to-day aspects of the campaign, the army was poorly supplied. The usual difficulties were compounded by a scorched earth policy operated against them and the over-ambitious attempt to campaign in winter. News then arrived that the king wanted to take personal command of the campaign so no further attempts were made to make war.

Edward's campaign in France had not been a happy one. With an insufficient force the war had ground to a stalemate. On 7 October an armistice was agreed. At Tournai, on 31 January, this was turned into a year long truce. It was clear to Edward that the failure was due to his inability to raise a large enough army because of the opposition of the barons and the diversion of resources to Scotland. It was time to resecure his northern border. While still in Flanders he began to organise a summer expedition into Scotland. With the king in command and the wardrobe organising the war effort the preparations took on greater urgency. Levies were ordered from Wales and provisions from Ireland. In March 1298 the king was back in England. On the 30th a meeting of the privy council issued writs to 155 military tenants to appear at York on Whit Sunday (25 May) and further writs were issued for Welsh levies. On 10 April a parliament was called to coincide with the host's muster. On 1 June the Law courts and Exchequer transferred to York. Edward's priority was to bring an end to Scottish resistance. By moving his government to the north, where it would remain for the next five years, he signalled his determination to finish the work he had begun in 1296.

The army finally mustered at Roxburgh in June. No official figures exist for the strength of the cavalry, but the number of men-at-arms in Edward I's armies was typically about 2,000. He also had a party of well-equipped Gascon horse. Large numbers of foot were recruited: 10,900 Welsh and 14,800 English. From Roxburgh Edward moved north. Bek took a company to take Dirleton and two unnamed smaller castles. He had no siege engines and sent John FitzMarmaduke to the king to seek instructions. Edward told FitzMarmaduke to 'Go back and tell the bishop that as bishop he is a man of Christian piety, but Christian piety has no place in what he is doing now. And as for you, you are a bloodthirsty man, I have often had to rebuke you for being too cruel. But now be off, use all your cruelty, and instead of rebuking you I shall praise you.'[51] The castles soon fell when faced with this ugly determination.

Anticipating difficulty finding supplies the main army headed for Edinburgh, where the king expected to meet his supply ships. Seaborne supplies were a highly practical method of feeding a large medieval

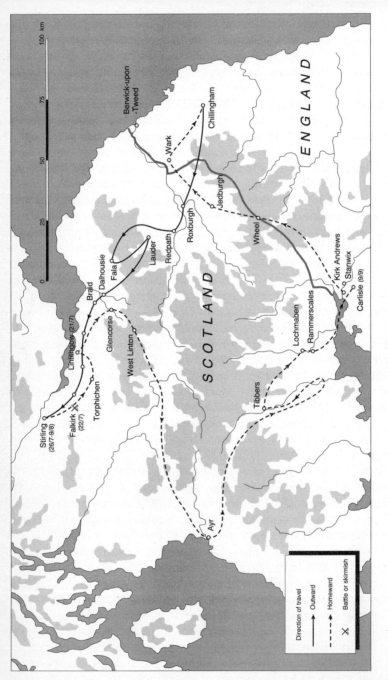

The Falkirk Campaign

army, but they were a gamble. In 1298 it did not pay off: contrary winds prevented the ships' arrival and the army began to starve. Bek's troops 'filled their bellies with pulses and beans gathered in the fields.' When some ships finally appeared they were loaded with 200 tuns of wine. The effect on empty stomachs when the cargo was distributed amongst the starving infantry was as fast as it was predictable. The resulting riots centred on the Welsh contingents. When 18 Englishmen were killed the men-at-arms were called out. They fell on the Welsh camp and left 80 dead. The campaign had reach its nadir. Edward had to consider turning home, having never met up with the enemy.

Then Edward's luck changed. Patrick Dunbar earl of March and Gilbert Umfraville earl of Angus arrived at the camp with news of Wallace: his army was barely 20 miles away at Falkirk. Wallace was aware of the English difficulties and was laying plans to hamper their retreat. He misjudged his enemy; the king was no Warenne. Edward declared that he would 'not trouble them to seek me.' That night the English camped at the Burgh Muir of Linlithgow. The men slept in their armour, with horses bitted ready for an early start. During the night an alarm was raised when Edward was trampled by his charger, freed due to the carelessness of a groom. He led his men next day with two broken ribs.

Early in the morning the army began its march towards Falkirk. At one point the spears of a Scottish party were seen in the distance on the hills of Polmont but disappeared from view as the English drew near. A halt was called near Falkirk, on the banks of the West-Quarter Burn. The tents were pitched and Edward heard mass with Bek.

Wallace had determined to stand and fight. His position had been guaranteed by his victory at Stirling Bridge, but guerrilla campaigns meant little to the nobility and their continued co-operation needed a fresh victory. He arrayed his troops into four schiltrons along the crest of a gentle slope. The schiltron was a hedgehog formation of grounded spears held together with ropes staked into the ground. Not very manoeuvrable, it was the only defence foot soldiers had against the bulldozer that was a medieval mounted charge. An unmissable target for the English bowmen, the schiltron required protection by mounted troops able to drive off enemy archers.

The front was defended by a palisade of stakes and marshy ground. Between each schiltron Wallace stationed archers from the forests of Selkirk and Ettrick. To the rear the nobility's cavalry. To the right was Falkirk church, to his left the present day Grahamstown. As the Scottish army waited for the English Wallace delivered his famous rallying call: 'I have brought you to the ring, now dance if you can'.

The English army arrived tired and hungry. Edward wanted to rest his men, but the barons disagreed, eager for action after a frustrating campaign and alert to the danger of encamping so close to the enemy.

Edward met this with pithy resignation: 'be it so then.' The van under the earls of Hereford, Norfolk and Lincoln advanced, but became bogged down in the swamp and wheeled around to the west, opposite the Scots' right wing. Behind them, Bek's second division saw what had happened and so wheeled to the east. Bek's men pushed ahead too fast, and he tried to slow down to allow the units led by Edward to catch up. His lieutenant, Ralph Basset of Drayton scorned Bek's caution, 'To thy mass, bishop, leave us to fight'.

Outflanked, the Scottish horsemen fled, leaving the infantry dangerously exposed. Deserted by the professional soldiers, Wallace was left with those knights who had dismounted to command the foot. Without support from their own men-at-arms, the Scottish archers between the schiltrons were cut down. The English could now turn towards the massed ranks of foot: The Scottish spearmen did not turn and run with the nobility, but stood their ground to face the English head-on. English archers and slingers fired into the schiltrons until a gap was created, allowing the cavalry to break in. It was a devastating combination. As the slaughter of the Scottish infantry began the Welsh, who had played no part in the battle, eagerly joined in.

Few Scots nobles died—Andrew Murray of Bothwell and Macduff of Fife who had stayed with the commons of the earldom, and James Graham of Abercorne, his name recorded by the nearby town. Most nobles fled with the cavalry, but the men on foot had little chance of escape across the open ground. Walsingham puts the death toll at 60,000, Guisborough at 56,000, numbers that vastly exceed Wallace's total forces but suggest terrible carnage. It was amongst the 'gentlemen of Fiff and Brandans of Bute' that Scottish losses were heaviest. Many drowned in the river Carron trying to escape. Wallace was able to take a remnant of his schiltron into the nearby Callander Woods. Recorded English losses were limited to two knights, Brian de Jay, master of the Temple in Scotland with another Templar who had led the chase into the woods where they were surrounded.

After the battle Edward moved to Stirling where he spent the next 15 days recovering from the injury he had received the night before the battle. Falkirk was to prove the only triumph in an otherwise fruitless campaign. Wherever Edward went, the Scots disappeared before him. Edward sent detachments to criss-cross Scotland: Clackmannan and Fife were 'clere brent'; St Andrews was found deserted and the buildings torched; Perth was destroyed by the Scots, which saved the English the trouble of doing it themselves. At Edinburgh he gave an audience to ambassadors from Philip IV. Still short of supplies the army then crossed Selkirk Forest to Ayr where Robert Bruce's castle, which had been hastily evacuated, was taken—town and castle burned on Bruce's orders. The king expected supplies from Ireland but none came. He began the journey south, on 5 September he occupied Lochmaben castle, and on the 8th he was at Carlisle. One important border fortress, Jedburgh, held out for a short time, Edward was there in early October supervising the siege.

Edward saw the need to maintain pressure after his victory and wanted to continue but problems with the barony meant he could go no farther. He did not repeat the mistake of his 1296 campaign which had produced few forfeited estates with which to reward the barons. But his award of the Isle of Arran to an Antrim magnate infuriated the earls. And Edward showed no sign of fulfilling his promise (made before the campaign began) that he would confirm the charters. Bigod and Bohun took their leave from the army. Once they had gone Edward began the distribution of estates in earnest, although few records survive. Many of the lands were still in Scottish possession, awarded 'in hope'. While still in the north writs were issued to raise levies for a muster the following summer, 'for the purpose of punishing the malice and rebellion of the Scots, and also of putting the king's lieges in seizin and possession of the lands which he had granted or intended to grant to them in Scotland.'[52] The barony now had a financial incentive to support Edwardian policy in Scotland.

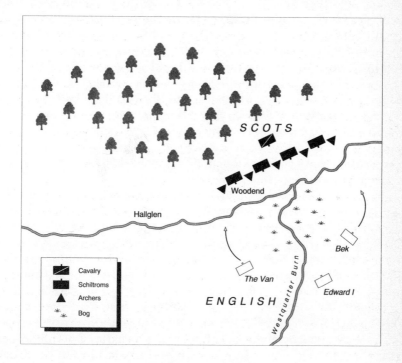

The Battle of Falkirk

Chapter 4

AN END TO THE BUSINESS

Wallace resigned the Guardianship and returned to the ranks, although whether he jumped or was pushed is not known. His support had depended on military success and his fragile standing with the nobility could not weather the defeat at Falkirk. He had no earldom or great barony which he could fall back on, and no patrons of high standing who could rally support amongst the lords.

His movements after Falkirk are not easy to piece together. He is next heard of in 1299 when he left Scotland on a freelance mission to the continent—still trying to rally support for John Balliol's kingship. Wallace and other 'knights of Scotland' remained at the French court where they received aid from Philip IV. He left towards the end of 1300 carrying letters of recommendation from Philip to the pope and Haakon of Norway. We can assume he visited at least one and probably both.

Wallace's defeat did not lead to a break-down of government in Scotland. One of the notable aspects of the Scottish resistance to Edward I is the continuity of government despite sharp setbacks. This reveals the strength of 'the community of the realm', the legitimate representation of the king's free subjects—the nearest a feudal society came to the later idea of the nation state. Modern historians have considerable emotional attachment to the 'community of the realm.' Yet after Falkirk, it was not quite as formidable an ideal as it had been in the period from 1286 to 1291, or under Wallace's guardianship. The nobility's failure to rally around Wallace's standard had revealed that their idea of the community was very different from the men and women Wallace represented. For the nobles the community could only be represented by the social hierarchy, the earls, nobles and bishops. It meant themselves. The old order still had the practical difficulty of reasserting its dominance as there was no obvious candidate to fill the role of guardian.

It is unclear what happened in Scotland after Falkirk. There may have been a power-struggle, since two political adversaries, Robert Bruce and the younger John Comyn of Badenoch, were elected as joint guardians some time between July and December of 1298. Bruce and Comyn acted as 'guardians of the kingdom of Scotland in the name of the famous prince the illustrious King John, together with the bishops, abbots, priors, earls, barons and other magnates and the whole community of the realm.'[1] This statement of their authority in a letter from Philip IV hides the real nature of Comyn-Bruce guardianship: an uneasy alliance formed out of mutual necessity. Comyn would work for King John's restoration. Bruce would not. It became fashionable to blacken the Comyn name as opponents of Bruce's kingship. This is misleading, after Wallace's defeat the Comyns, particularly the younger Comyn, were at the forefront of the independence struggle.

The conflict between the two men came to a head in August 1299. The English constable of Edinburgh, John Kingston, sent news of Scottish preparations for a raid on Roxburgh. A large force had gathered on the other side of the 'Scottish Sea', at the time of writing had crossed the Forth and moved to Glasgow. Kingston's intelligence—that they planned an attack on the borders was—remarkably accurate. The English had good sources in the Scottish camp. The bearer of Kingston's letter to Walter Langton, the English treasurer, was Simon Fraser, the commander of Selkirk Forest. Kingston did not trust Fraser, who he believed had met the Scottish lords for a conference 'and ate and drank and were on the best of terms.' Kingston's suspicions of Fraser, who was held in high regard by the king' were well founded. He went over to the Scots in the winter of 1300, something Edward found hard to forgive.

The story of the raid was taken up by another English spy, to Robert Hastangs, the constable of Roxburgh (or the same man reporting to another commander).[2] The Scots had reached Peebles on 19 August where a meeting was held. By this time Wallace had either left the country, or was planning to leave, without the permission of the Guardians. David Graham demanded his goods and lands as penalty. Wallace was defended by his brother, Malcolm, there in Bruce's party. Daggers were drawn at which point the younger Comyn 'leapt upon the earl of Carrick and seized him by the throat' and the earl of Buchan 'grappled' with bishop Lamberton. The difficult relationship between Comyn and Bruce was well known, though why Buchan went for Lamberton is unclear. He had been elected to his bishopric over William Comyn, Buchan's brother, which may have left some personal animosity.

After the fracas Lamberton was elected as senior Guardian, with Bruce and the younger Comyn as subordinates. When the relationship between Bruce and Comyn broke down Lamberton was seen as neutral, a man who could hold the guardianship together while bringing the support of the church to the political movement. The bishopric of St Andrews held an ancient 'hegemony of prestige' over all the other Scottish bishops. When William Fraser died in 1297 Wallace pressed for the election of William Lamberton, a protégé of that other staunchly nationalist bishop, Wishart of Glasgow. It was while Lamberton was at the court of Rome for his consecration that Wallace was defeated at Falkirk. He must have been involved in the lobbying of Boniface that would later culminate in the papal bull *Scimus, fili,* and was known to have been involved with John Soules in negotiations with Philip IV on his return from the curia.[3]

Lamberton's importance led to strenuous English efforts to capture him and his party on their return from the continent. The English had been warned that the Scottish envoys were at Damme waiting to depart and ships had been sent to try and intercept them. Lamberton slipped through the blockade and returned in time for the Selkirk meeting carrying letters of support from the king of France. Philip IV told Bruce and Comyn that he was 'moved to the very marrow by the evils brought on their country by hostile malignity.' He urged them to rally around the king and promised his support, as soon as he finished 'pondering' how to help. Philip would spend some time pondering. He would not abandon the Scots, as Edward did the Flemings, until 1302, but neither would he offer concrete support by way of troops or money.

The planned raid was abandoned. Roxburgh was too well fortified and an ominous report arrived from north of the Forth concerning Buchan's brother, Alexander Comyn, and Lachlan Macruarie who had been devastating the district they were in, 'attacking the people of Scotland.' Probably a local feud. The magnates then went their separate ways: Carrick to Annandale, Buchan and Comyn north of the Forth, the Steward and Menteith to Clydesdale. Robert Keith was left in the forest with 100 barbed horse and 1500 foot besides foresters and men left behind by the lords.[4]

The Comyn-Bruce guardianship was an effort to paper over the cracks. Scotland was deeply divided: a majority fought for King John's restoration; a minority could not hide their contempt of the king but for the time being saw him as the legitimate representation of an independent nation; and supporters of the English king, whether because they believed in his cause or saw him as a valuable patron. The lack of cohesive leadership may have meant that it was difficult to rally the nationalist cause, but during that time only one Scot of rank, Robert Bruce, deserted to the English who were kept penned into the south-east for much of the next five years.

This stalemate was as much a result of English inactivity as Scottish defiance. The defeat of William Wallace had not led to any political gains for Edward. Indeed, the Scottish nobility now found it easier to rally around a cause led by men of their own class and began to desert the English. Edward had his own problems which would prevent him unleashing the full force of his realm. The end of the 1298 campaign was the nadir of Edward's reign. He had shown a stubborn need to take on all-comers: his barony, the clergy, the Scots, the French, and the papacy. As a result he had faced a rebellion in Scotland, the seizure of his French lands and near civil war in England. He would not be able to return to Scotland for almost two years, which not only gave the Scots the time to recover from Falkirk, but to go on the offensive and besiege outlying castles.

* * *

We know very little of what was happening in the Scottish areas during the following years as the country became geared for war. Day-to-day administration recovered where there was no English presence, sheriffs and justices appointed, rents collected and occasional 'parliaments' held. We know more of the English occupation, and how they consolidated their hold on the south-east. In October and November 1298, after the Falkirk campaign, Edward issued instructions from Newcastle on the defence of the north. In the first instance he needed to ensure that his strongholds in Scotland were well victualled. Indentures were entered for the supplying of the garrisons. In Lothian Scottish castles were given English garrisons, sheriffs were appointed, the northern nobility recruited to the garrisons.

Berwick became the focus of English occupation, manned with 100 men-at-arms and 1,000 foot, including 100 crossbowmen.[5] English merchants were recruited into the town in a way never attempted at the other key burghs, Roxburgh or Edinburgh. As the English position in the south became more secure Berwick ceased its military role, becoming a supply point for the garrisons further north.

An indenture with Robert Clifford to hold Dumfries reveals the nature of those garrisons. The force at Dumfries was to number a total of 76 men: twelve men-at-arms, 24 foot and 26 crossbowmen. The numbers were made up by the non-combatants. The list of provisions, provided to last from 20 November to the last day of June (223 days), show that the garrison ate well, what was lacking in variety was made up in quantity: 120 quarters of wheat, ten tuns of wine, 20 quarters of beans and pease, 100 quarters of oats for the horses, 50 oxen carcasses, 10,000 herrings, 500 dried fish. Ten marks a week were allowed for expenses and as much iron and steel as was necessary. The bishop of Carlisle lent three crossbows. Clifford himself placed two springalds and four crossbows in the castle.[6]

John Kingston sent a return to the king in 1300 of the larger garrison at Edinburgh. Together with his own esquires and grooms were two Carmelite friars, Master Thomas the engineer and his boy, the sheriff's two clerks, the almoner, pantryman, the cook and his boy, the baker and his boy, two brewers, a boy keeping the swine, the miller, the cooper, the granaryman, the harper, the watchman, 'le Ewer', two carpenters, two smiths, two maltsters, two carters, a sea coal carrier, a herdsman, the bowyer and boy, Geoffrey the messenger, Elias the marshal and his shoer, a candlemaker and others. There were 67 men-at-arms, 18 crossbowmen, 60 foot. In all 347 men, with 156 horses and hackneys.[7]

The constant need for military forces in the north and the emergence of captains, mostly household knights, professional soldiers close to the king—Robert Clifford, William Latimer, the warden at Berwick, Robert Hastangs, John St. John—led to profound change. It was the beginning of a northern standing army, centred on the men of the garrisons: a military elite willing to serve long periods under contract. Patrick Dunbar was made Edward's lieutenant of Scotland south of the Forth, with orders to raid Scottish territory, supported by Robert Clifford the king's lieutenant in the Western March and Walter de Huntercombe in Northumberland.[8] In July 1302 John St John, captain in the north-west (Mersey to Roxburgh) was promoted to lieutenant in Scotland with powers over the wardens of Marches, overseeing a system of defence intended to prevent a repeat of the raid Wallace had led in 1301. John St. John died in September and was replaced by John Segrave.

Forays would become a regular event for the garrisons and nationalists alike. In December 1298 Walter Huntercombe, Simon Fraser and the warden of Berwick met to plan a raid on Stirling. Spies were sent out to bring back as much news as possible on the enemy's dispositions and their plans. A message was sent to John Kingston at Edinburgh to do the same. It would be left to him to appoint a day when they should meet at Edinburgh to undertake the foray. These forays could be on a large scale; for this the sheriff of Northumberland was asked to send 300 horse, with the northern captains and garrisons adding another 200.[9]

It is difficult to assess the degree of support the English occupation had in Scotland. There were Scottish lords who remained constant to Edward: the earls of Angus and March. Alexander Balliol kept Selkirk forest with 30 men-at-arms. Others swayed. Many more accepted English lordship until their chance came to oppose it, but few remained totally opposed to English rule. Many, like the earl of Strathearn, just disappear from the record from 1298 and 1303, when Edward forced their hands. Attitudes of ordinary men and women varied too. In Lothian, where English garrisons were thickest on the ground, there was little active opposition.

Where English garrisons were less concentrated it was a different story. John de St John had difficulty recruiting levies to take part in raids or the garrisoning of castles. In March 1300 he was granted special powers to distrain and amerce all who had disobeyed the commands of the king's 'cheventagne' and lieutenant and who had refused to assist in the defence of the marches.[10] This attitude of keeping heads well down could be expected. Sometimes the locals went further. In 1301 the warden of Lochmaben, Robert de Tilliol, was under threat from a Scottish army. He reported that the Scots were recruiting amongst those who had come into the king's peace and were threatening a raid into England.[11]

The preparations for a campaign in 1299 proved to be in vain. The Anglo-French Tournai treaty was originally intended to last for one year. Boniface attempted to turn the truce into a permanent Anglo-French peace. As neither king wanted to see a pope meddling in temporal matters he acted in a private capacity, as Benedict Gaetani. When he promulgated a reasonable settlement in June 1298, based on a return of all territory, he believed he was close to achieving peace.[12] In the spring of 1299 he pushed both sides to reach an agreement. Gaetani's plan foundered on Philip's refusal to release Gascony, and on Edward's insistence that the Scots should be excluded from the peace.

Neither France nor England were ready to return to open warfare and both made the concessions needed for a temporary truce. By a conference at Montreuil-sur-mer in June a deal had been struck. Philip agreed that Scotland would not be party to the truce, neither would the Flemings. The new truce was sealed with a marriage alliance: Edward to Margaret, sister of Philip, and more disastrously Carnarfon to Isabella, Philip's daughter.

Both junior allies, Flanders and Scotland, made late bids to be included in the peace. Count Guy Flanders lobbied the pope for protection, in November 1299 the Scottish guardians pressed Edward to submit to French arbitration. Neither party had any success. Both kings would be free to deal with their troublesome neighbours. In return Edward, under papal and French pressure, agreed to release King John. On July 11th he was taken from the tower of London to Canterbury to talk to the king on matters of business, under the revealingly small escort of a single knight. A week later he was in France, taken by the constable of Dover castle. When he was delivered into the hands of the papal nuncio Edward exacted an undertaking that the pope would not 'ordain or decide' the kingdom of Scotland to John.[13]

That Edward had shown a 'willingness to abandon the Flemings and marry the sister of man who was keeping him out of Gascony could only be explained by his desire to prosecute the war in Scotland.'[14] Edward had overstretched himself. He would never be able to take a large army to the continent while his northern border was exposed. He would deal with the easier of the two problems first.

While Edward waited in Canterbury during the spring and summer so that he could give speedy advice to his ambassadors in Montreuil, the Scottish campaign was postponed four times. Eventually it was cancelled altogether.[15] Freed for the time being from the threat of French interference, Edward determined to mount a winter campaign.

Winter campaigning was difficult and unpopular. Medieval armies depended on living off the land, virtually impossible during winter. It was especially difficult to find fodder for the horses. To mitigate the worst effects of the season Edward sanctioned an extra payment: his men 'should receive such courtesy, beyond their customary pay, that they should acknowledge themselves satisfied with his treatment of them.' The muster formed the largest contract army of Edward's reign with 22 bannerets, and 44 knights.[16]

Berwick was as far as the army went. The barons still bridled over Edward's failure carry out forest reforms and the army objected to campaigning in winter. The worst desertion came from the once dependable men of Durham, who left en masse. This refusal was a serious setback to the campaign and a considerable embarrassment to the warrior bishop of Durham. Edward complained in a letter to Bek who imprisoned many of the deserters. But the Durham men would not give way. They claimed the tradition of *Haliwerfolk*, which bound them only to defend the body of St Cuthbert in the land between the Tyne and the Tees. The open revolt of the Durham men, added to his barons reluctance to fight, meant a campaign was out of the question. There followed a flurry of activity reorganising the defences of the border, John St John being given a greater role as warden of the west of Scotland.

Edward's purpose for this unpopular and expensive campaign must have been the relief of the hard-pressed Stirling garrison, which was eventually starved into submission, surrendering to the sheriff of Stirling, Gilbert Malherbe, 'a Scottishman'. The siege itself was conducted by a kinsman, Herbert Moreham, himself captured by the English garrison at Edinburgh in 1300. John Sampson, Stirling's commander, made a claim for losses amounting to £61 13s 10d. Amongst the list for lost armour and robes was an account for two horses, eaten by the starving garrison. In a most chivalrous gesture the 90 men of the garrison were taken under escort and released at Berwick.[17]

Attention now turned to the west. Early in the year the Earl of Buchan went into Galloway to try and secure support from the independently minded Gallovidians. He was missing from a parliament held at Rutherglen in May 1300—a report of which came from John Kingston's reliable source. Bruce must have resigned the guardianship by now. This was the beginning of Bruce's alienation from the patriotic cause. The traditionally difficult relationship between the Gallovidians and the earls of Carrick may have been the cause of his resignation now. With Buchan trying to cultivate Gallovidian support, Bruce must have seen this as contrary to his own interests in the west. At the Rutherglen parliament the younger Comyn refused to be associated with Lamberton, but we do not know why. The inference must be that Comyn was a difficult young man to work with. Since Lamberton was backed by James the Steward and the earl of Atholl, two allies of Bruce, it may have been Lamberton's relationship with Bruce. Comyn gave way, remaining as guardian with Lamberton and the Balliol partisan, Ingram de Umfraville.[18]

Infuriated by his inability to save Stirling, Edward needed a new focus for a campaign in the summer of 1300. The castle at Caerlaverock had been taken in 1299 after a Scottish push in the west, probably by Robert Bruce who went on to unsuccessfully besiege Lochmaben. The two castles were key to the western approach, guarding the crossing any army would need to take across the Solway. News from the Lochmaben reached England in October 1299. In the commander's own words: 'there is a castle near here called Caerlaverock which has done and does great damages everyday to the king's castle [Lochmaben] and its people. But the Sunday next after Michaelmas we had such success that their constable's head was now set on the great tower at Lochmaben. Many are wounded on both sides; fewer of the king's than the others.'[19] Lying only ten miles apart the garrisons had become involved in their own little war, culminating in the death of Caerlaverock's constable, Robert Cunningham, a nephew of the Steward.

Edward turned to a feudal summons to form a new army. While still in Berwick, on 30 December 1299, writs of military summons for feudal service were issued. Feudal summons were already an anachronism by Edward I's reign. None more so than in the case of Hugh FitzHeyr—whose obligation consisted of serving with a bow and arrow. When he reached the border he shot the arrow at the first Scots he saw and promptly went home.[20]

Edward saw the use of a feudal muster, repeated in 1303 and 1306, as a means of raising larger numbers of cavalry. It was not a great success, John Morris calculated that the English had a total of 2,000 cavalry in 1300, a number he thought most likely to be on the generous side. This was about the total Edward had with him at the battle of Falkirk and seems to have been the average for a later Edwardian army.[21] Since this was a feudal army, muster rolls of chivalry were kept, and a list of horses used by the household knights was also drawn up before the campaign to simplify compensation claims. This makes it possible to calculate the size and structure of the army. The feudal element numbered 40 knights and 366 sergeants. More men would have been raised by contract. The largest group belonged to Edward's household: 22 bannerets and 53 knights, whose retinues brought the household element of the army up to 750 men.

The cavalry divided into four units, which was unusual although not unprecedented. One was commanded by Caernarfon, presumably created for that purpose. With him were the Lancaster brothers, Thomas and Henry and the earls of Gloucester and Arundel, with a total of seven banners. The van was led by Lincoln, Hereford as constable and Segrave acting for Norfolk as marshal with a total of 16 banners. The king's squadron was the largest with 34 banners, including the earl of Dunbar and John of Brittany. The forth unit, under Warenne, Warwick and Aymer Valence, was 14 banners strong.

The impressive cavalry force was not matched by the infantry. The writs had summoned 16,000 foot from the northern counties. Only 3,500 had arrived for the start of the campaign on 1 July. By mid-July, at Caerlaverock, late-comers had made the numbers up to 7,500. Edward had to draw upon the local 'garrisons' at Lochmaben, Roxburgh and Berwick i.e. the local population. Infantry strength peaked at 9,000, falling to 5,000 in August. The foot soldiers must have been restless during the siege, desertion was again heavy. Welsh levies were not called upon, Edward wrote that 'we have given them leave to remain at home, because of the great work which they have done in our service in the past',[22] which, after the debacle at Falkirk, reveals the king's normally well-disguised sense of humour.

The feudal demand for the service of ships was made from the Cinque Ports, whose obligation lasted for two weeks after which they were paid the king's wage. The ports sent 30 ships, with a complement of 1,106 men. Two more galleys were provided by Simon de Montagu, and a further eight ships were sent from Ireland. The navy was mainly used for bringing stores to Carlisle's port at Skinburness, and then ferrying them across to Solway.

Despite five months of planning, the midsummer deadline for the muster came and went. Urgent letters were sent to the Irish justiciar, chancellor and treasurer chasing the wheat, oats, wine and dried fish from Ireland which should by now have reached Skinburness. Further letters to hurry supplies were sent to the towns of Dublin, Waterford, Drogheda, Cork, Limerick, Kilkenny and Rosport. Supplies did come in. The Caerlaverock poet witnessed 'on every side, mountain, and valley were filled with carts and sumpter horses, stores and baggage, tents and pavilions.'[23]

The army finally set out to cross the Solway on 4 July. From Annan up the river valley to Ecclefechan, on the second day to Applegarth and then west to Lochmaben. They were at Tinwald on the 8th, Dumfries on the 9th. From here the siege of Caerlaverock could begin, a castle which Peter Langtoft dismissively described as 'a poor castlelet'.[24] Surrounded by marshes, Caerlaverock castle stood 'like a shield in shape'. It was more formidable than Langtoft suggests. The chronicler Rishanger records an offer of surrender by the garrison, on condition of free passage with possessions. Edward would not hear conditions, he was, we are told, furious, 'like a lioness whose cubs are taken from her.'

In this temper the five day siege began. Tents went up, trees were cut down to make huts, and the marshals allocated lodgings before an infantry assault on the castle. The Caerlaverock poet then describes the pointless charges of the English chivalry, each knight anxious not to be outshone by his comrades. But it was the siege engines that brought about the garrison's surrender. The trebuchets hurled vast stones into the courtyard which scattered lethal splinters of jagged stone.

When they surrendered the 60 members of the garrison were each given a new robe by the king. Or so wrote the Caerlaverock poet, short of chivalrous deeds to report. The wardrobe accounts make no mention of any such payments. The Lanercost chronicle offers a different fate, saying that some of the garrison were hanged. A record from Newcastle finds eleven of the garrison, together with the constable, imprisoned in the keep. Ten more prisoners at Appleby may also have come from the garrison. It contrasts starkly with the Scottish treatment of the English garrison who surrendered at Stirling the previous year. A contrast that was to become sharper as the wars progressed.

Edward then led the army into Galloway: 'meeting no enemy, but encountering every other kind of difficulty. The cavalry could not act and the infantry would not act; provisions were scant, and the rain incessant; the cattle, the only product of the county, had vanished with their owners.'[25] At the Bridge of Dee Edward turned south to Kirkcudbright. Here the younger Comyn of Badenoch and John Comyn earl of Buchan attempted to secure a truce. This was the second attempt at peace negotiations, the first by Thomas bishop of Whitehorn. The price of Scottish submission was the restoration of John Balliol and the redemption of confiscated estates in England. Edward was left indignant and after two days parlay the negotiations were deadlocked.

The desertion of the English foot now became more acute. At Dumfries commissioners were ordered to arrest deserters. Before he left Kirkcudbright the numbers were so depleted that Edward sent orders to the sheriffs of York and Lancaster to raise more men to muster at Carlisle, but the recruits deserted en masse before they even reached the muster.

On the last day of July Edward left Kirkcudbright, crossing the Dee to Twynholm, where he stayed a further week to receive supplies. A foraging party reached as far as the River Cree. The marishal, Robert Keith, lay on the far bank. He crossed the river but was worsted in the mêlée and captured. Keith, with another prisoner Robert Baird, was sent to the castle at Carlisle, moved further south to Nottingham and then to Bristol and Gloucester when Edward heard that they were 'among his worst enemies and of bad repute.'[26]

On 8 August, the bulk of the English army reached the Cree. The Scots were arrayed on the far bank; the horse divided into three divisions under Ingram Umfraville, Buchan and the younger Comyn. Archers from both sides exchanged shots for some hours across a ford. As the tide went out some English foot crossed without orders. Earl Warenne and the earl of Hereford went across to retrieve them. Mistaking the earl's movement the archers believed a general attack was under way and pushed forward. Caernarfon and a group of men-at-arms crossed in support.

Edward was forced to follow where his troops had led, ordering a general advance. With this the Scottish army broke up. Many of the horses were abandoned and much baggage jettisoned as the Scots scattered into the hills, in the words of a chronicler 'like hares before greyhounds.' Edward's horse could not operate in the Galloway hills, now he sorely missed the Welsh infantry—the ferrets who might have rooted out the hares.[27]

After this the campaign began to fizzle out. The only other reported engagement occurred when a Scottish spy led 200 English horse and foot into an ambush, salvaged by an English counter-attack. The desertion of the infantry continued and the magnates saw no reason to

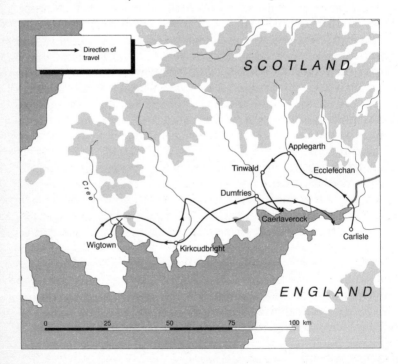

The Caerlaverock Campaign

stay and left with their retinues. The army arrived at Wigtown on 16 August, where it turned back, reaching England at the end of the month. The campaign had been a dismal failure, more like a holiday outing than a campaign. The chronicler Langtoft hinted that this was a result of Edward's own idleness, that he slept in too long in the morning.[28] Edward was left 'in very bad temper'. It was in this mood that Archbishop Winchelsea found him.

* * *

The Scottish envoys in the curia had worked hard to secure papal support. On 27 June 1299 Boniface issued a bull, known by its first two words, *Scimus, fili,* ('We know, my son') which declared Edward's occupation of Scotland illegal. This was the result of sustained lobbying, although it must be more than coincidence that David Murray's consecration as bishop of Moray took place at the papal court on the following day. Boniface urged Edward 'to set free his Scottish captives, and retire from Scotland', declaring Scotland as a fief of the holy see, 'as thou well knowest my son.' Edward knew no such thing. The claim strikes of opportunism, it is nonsense, without any historical justification and at odds with earlier papal recognition of English overlordship.

That is not to say that *Scimus, fili,* did not have merits. The pope referred to the Birgham-Northampton treaty, when Edward 'safeguarded the interests of the nobles, before they were willing to consent to this marriage [Margaret to Caernarfon] by writing that the realm should remain for ever entirely free'. Boniface accused Edward of making 'certain unaccustomed innovations ... at the time when the realm of Scotland lacked the protection of a ruler, which effect the state of the realm and the freedom which previously it enjoyed, those things have been done by the nobles of the realm, who were then without a head.'[29] This was the really biting criticism in *Scimus, fili,* made more so because it was contemporary.

Now, with an unexplained year-long delay, Robert Winchelsea had been given the onerous task of delivering the Bull. We have to pity the poor archbishop. Boniface threatened him with suspension if he refused. The journey north would be difficult and expensive. And at the end of it he would have to face Edward with news he would not want to hear. He 'groaned at the thought.' When Winchelsea reached Carlisle the latest news from Scotland was that Edward was in Kirkcudbright. No local guides could be found to take him on what would have been a dangerous passage to find the king. Winchelsea could do nothing but wait Edward's return. He remained in Carlisle for six weeks with a sufficiency rather than an abundance of food. News finally reached him that Edward had arrived at Sweetheart Abbey, not far over the border.

Winchelsea crossed the Solway and came across the army 'an unexpected and not very welcome guest.'[30] Edward was at dinner and refused to be interrupted. Two earls were eventually sent to inform the archbishop that he would be granted an audience, but not until the following day.

At noon next day Winchelsea read the bull to Edward surrounded by his magnates, first in Latin, then repeated at Edward's command in French so that all would understand. When he had finished Winchelsea added his own appeal to Edward 'for the love of Mount Zion and Jerusalem' to obey the pope. Edward had sat silently listening to the bull, but he would not remain quiet for the archbishop, cutting him short: 'By God's blood! For Zion's sake I will not be silent, and for Jerusalem's sake I will not rest, but with all my strength I will defend my right that is known to all the world. ' The bishop was dismissed, told later in the day when Edward had calmed down, that a formal response would be made only when a full parliament considered the issue.

When Edward was persuaded to abandon the campaign at the end of August the Scottish army was still in the field. He was forced to stay in the north and keep elements of his army together, though now too few to take the offensive. Amongst those receiving wages was a young Gascon knight, Piers Gaveston. It was probably then that his dangerous intimacy with Caernarfon began. The king spent much of the following two months in the bishop of Carlisle's residence at Rose Castle, or at Holme Cultrum.

On 17 October 1300 Edward set out on a tour of the Galloway defences, visiting Annan, Dumfries and Caerlaverock, before returning to Carlisle in early November. At Dumfries he met Scottish envoys. The meeting was recorded by an English chronicler. When they made offers of peace he told them 'Every one of you had done homage to me as chief lord of Scotland. Now you set aside your allegiance and make a fool of me as though I were a weakling.' With some bravado the Scottish envoys replied 'you should not laugh; we offer peace in all seriousness. Exert your strength and see if might will triumph over right or right over might.'

Edward told them not to return with the same answer; and promised them that he would waste Scotland from sea to sea.[31] But not that winter. On 31 October he yielded to a personal request from Philip to agree a truce, to last until Whit Sunday, 21 May 1301. He sent a writ to all his officials in Scotland, by name, assuring them that the truce was made at the behest of Philip as a friend not as an ally of the Scots.

No doubt Philip's intervention was welcome to both sides. The Caerlaverock campaign had been a disaster. It had been costly, an expense the English exchequer could not cover indefinitely; an army nearly as large as the one which had won victory at Falkirk had managed to capture a solitary castle. On balance the year favoured the Scots, but they did not have the season all their own way. Caerlaverock was important to the defence of Galloway, and their army had been panicked into flight in much the same way as at Dunbar and Falkirk. But they had learnt how easy it was to frustrate an English army. They had learnt to stay in the background, to deny the English supplies, to attack stragglers. It was a strategy that would be refined in the following year.

The king began the journey south on 16 November for a parliament that was called to meet at Lincoln in January. Coming after a campaign which had shown so few results the Lincoln parliament was not one of the high points of Edward's reign. The question of the confirmation of the charters which had dogged his relationship with the barons since 1297 now returned. The issues were complex, long-drawn-out and dull to all but the most committed constitutional historian, they need not detain us long, but it is the backcloth against which Edward's failure to take firm action over the past years has to be measured. It lay at the heart of his weakness in England—why the victory at Falkirk in 1298 had seen no tangible rewards and why Stirling Castle had been lost in 1299.

In October 1297, after the English defeat at Stirling Bridge, the regent had reissued Magna Carta and the Charter of the Forest, which Edward had confirmed. The barons feared that the confirmation would be declared invalid because they had been granted while Edward was abroad. At the London parliament in 1299 Norfolk and Hereford again pressed for their confirmation. The king sought delay until the following day, but slipped out of the city that night. The earls, backed by a London mob, followed him.

Edward complained that he had been forced to leave as 'the bad air of the town hath hurt our health'; he promised that an answer was being prepared by his council. The earls returned to London where the charters were sealed. When read out they included the new cause 'saving the right of the king'. With this sleight of hand the barons left discontented, with business unfinished.

After the fiasco of the 1299 winter campaign Edward decided to draw a line under the issue. At the London parliament in March 1300 the charters were confirmed and a perambulation of the forests, which would decide the forest boundaries, set in motion. The discontent between the king and barons spilled over at Lincoln. Edward saw the reports on the forest perambulation as open to discussion and examination, the opposition did not. The forests, the personal property of the king, covered a quarter of the country, Edward resented any restriction as 'an insult to his person and to his dignity', while the barony saw the confirmation as a sign of the king's goodwill. Despite his 'outrage', in the end it was the king who gave way.[32] Once he signed he reaped the political rewards.

After 1301 dissension at home declined rapidly, but he never forgave the opposition. Hereford died in 1302. His successor married the king's daughter and was literally wedded more closely to the crown. Norfolk was isolated and persuaded with a financial arrangement to abandon his hostility to the crown.

After a bruising week, Edward turned to *Scimus, fili*, as an issue which could rally support. Boniface was the most fickle of popes: his support for the Scottish patriots had more to do with his attempted rapprochement with Philip IV than it did with Anglo-Scottish politics. Edward could not afford a breach with the pope and had to tread carefully. No such restraints held back the barony who sent an answer separate from the king. The barons' letter was not independent, it was part of the government's planned rebuttal. Seven earls and 64 barons sealed an outspoken defence of the king's secular authority, they would not give way even if the king did. There is no evidence that this document was ever delivered, but it was widely circulated and probably intended to whip up popular support for English policy in Scotland.

The matter of Edward's formal answer was taken very seriously. The chancellors of Oxford and Cambridge were told to send representatives to Lincoln to advise the king while the monasteries were ordered to scour their libraries for evidence that would establish 'the right and dominion that belongs to us in the realm of Scotland, and which the kings of England, our predecessors, had in that realm in former times'. Research also took place in the royal archives.[33] The advice of William of Sardinia, a lawyer in the service of Archbishop Winchelsea, has survived. This document neatly summarises the anxieties of the English and the problems they faced in Boniface's challenge. He set out seven courses of action, ranging from acceptance of Boniface's right to arbitrate, to ignoring the bull altogether. He warned Edward that 'it would be dangerous to send according to the terms of the mandate, because in this way the pope would be admitted as superior, and as a proper judge in matters temporal', his claim that Scotland was a papal fief would be examined with the pope as judge in his own cause.[34]

In the end Edward sent his answer 'altogether extrajudicially, in order to set the mind of your holiness at rest.' The crux of *Scimus, fili*, Scottish independence from England, was founded on an historical narrative that must have been furnished by the curia's Scottish envoys. Edward's first task was to set this record straight, to justify the English occupation. His letter begins with a long mythological prologue based on Geoffrey of Monmouth's twelfth century *Historia Regnum Britanniae*, the apocryphal 'British history.' With this Edward thought he was on firm ground, 'the historical mythology of English overlordship of the British Isles had an almost immemorial resonance to it.'[35] It dates from the time when 'a certain valiant and illustrious man of the Trojan race called

Brutus, landed with many noble Trojans, upon a certain island called, at that time, Albion. It was then inhabited by giants, and after he had defeated and slain them, by his might and that of his followers, he claimed it, after his own name, Britain, and his people Britons.' Britain was divided between his three sons, to Locrine went England, to Albanact went Albany or Scotland, to the youngest Camber went Cambria or Wales, both subordinate to Locrine. The history begins in earnest with the reign of Edgar in 901. Edward stressed the submission made during the Great Cause, when the Scots 'recognised of their own certain knowledge, purely, simply, and absolutely English overlordship' and finished with the surrender of the kingdom by John Balliol and the submission of the prelates and magnates to himself as lord.[36]

It was not until 22 May 1301 that two messengers, Thomas Wale and Thomas Delilse crossed the channel with Edward's letter. We are fortunate that Edward was not in England when the envoys returned: after a round journey of 2,000 miles they were not expected to deliver their report personally to the king who was in Scotland; instead their report was written. The two knights had been granted an audience with Boniface on arrival at the papal court at Angani. Boniface waited until the following day to discuss the letter's contents. In terms that are starkly removed from *Scimus, fili,* the pope declared himself delighted with its contents and declared that he held Edward above all the crowned heads in the world. He told the envoys that he was bent on preserving the suzerainty of Scotland for the crown of England. Wale and Delisle spent a week in Angani, going through the papal registers with another English envoy, William of Gainsborough. Here they found three documents touching on Anglo-Scottish relations which they copied and brought home with them.[37]

In his letter Edward had made a pointed dig at the influence of Scottish envoys in the curia: 'beyond doubt these matters have been familiar from times long past and still are, though perchance it has been suggested otherwise to your holiness' ears by foes of peace and sons of rebellion'. Perchance it had. In the beginning of the year John Soules was appointed sole guardian of Scotland. Soules was a compromise candidate, the younger son of a leading family he was related to the Comyns but on friendly terms with Bruce, a man who could hold together the patriots. Fordun called him 'simple minded', but Soules was an able guardian, one of very few Scots who remained constant to King John, one of fewer still who refused to swear allegiance to the English king.[38]

He had some success, not only by cementing the relationship with Philip VI but also as a military leader, avoiding the pitched battles that had caused such serious reverses. In the spring Soules had appointed an embassy to the curia to press the Scottish case. Edward's formal response to *Scimus, fili* came up against the formidable ecclesiastical lawyers who gave the nationalist cause its intellectual backbone: Master Baldred Bisset, a lawyer based in Bologna, who was the brains of the outfit; with Master William of Eaglesham and Master William Frere. The documents Bisset wrote were an important stage in the formal declaration of Scottish independence and freedom, predating the Declaration of Arbroath, but written in the same terms and using similar arguments.

They had begun work on the case towards the end of May, interrupted when the English knight messengers arrived. Boniface had copies of the English letter made for the Scottish envoys. Two documents were written in response, *Instructiones* and *Processus*. The provenance of the *Instructiones*, a series of unstructured notes, is uncertain. It was possibly prepared in Scotland for the envoys use or may have been the envoys' own working notes.[39] The *Processus* is the work of Bisset. This was a pleading before the Pope, a rebuttal of Edward's letter to show that Edward 'refers to many things but proves few things.' The *Processus* contains an equally exotic and equally improbable survey of early Anglo-Scottish relations: with Scota, the daughter of pharaoh of Egypt, pitched against the Trojan Brutus. Scota 'landed in Ireland with an armed force and a very large fleet of ships. Then after taking on board some Irishmen, she sailed to Scotland, carrying with her the royal seat which this king of Scotland forcibly took away from the kingdom of Scotland to England with the insignia of Scotland. She conquered and overthrew the Picts, and took over that Kingdom.'

The Scots drew attention to Edward's descent, not from Brutus but from William the Bastard; to the fact that he had extorted Scottish fealty; and that he had fabricated Balliol's confession. They also drew attention to the quit-claim of Richard I in 1189. A report of their case was sent by an English envoy at the curia, probably William of Gainsborough. He ably summarised the Scottish counter to Edward: 'They endeavour to prove in five ways that the realm of Scotland is free in itself and in no wise subject to you: by papal privilege, by common law [that no kingdom should be subject to another], by prescription [Scotland was independent before written records], by its free status at all times, and by muniments and writings which, so they claim, they can prove authentic.'[40]

Bisset's arguments were more authoritative, the history closer to the known facts, but he was whistling in the wind. William of Sardinia had warned of the problems of sending an envoy who could 'after clever and subtle questions put by the pope, go beyond his instructions and perhaps say things which are prejudicial'. Wale and Delisle were not diplomats but middle-ranking knights. Their task was to deliver the letter, not say too much, keep their eyes open, and come home. It contrasts with the delegates Edward chose for the abortive talks with France in Canterbury during May: the earls of Surrey and Warwick, Aymer de Valence, John de St John and Hugh de Vere. For Edward this was where the business of Anglo-Scottish relations would be settled.

Edward had concluded his letter with the assertion that the 'kingdom of Scotland belongs to us *pleno jure*, by reason of *proprietas* no less than possession.' It was the clearest affirmation of Edwardian authority, its implication was clear, that it was Edward's right and duty to quell rebellious subjects.[41] Whatever comfort they achieved for the patriots at home, whatever moral victory was won, nothing the Scots did at the curia changed this. The whole thrust of the Scottish effort in the curia was to achieve papal arbitration. In this they failed.

* * *

Edward could withstand papal pressure for the time. The truce organised at Philip's request in the previous autumn expired in May 1301. Negotiations with French and Scottish envoys broke down in the spring. This was much as Edward expected and had prepared for. Plans to form a new army were well advanced and completed by the end of May. Writs of military summons had been issued in February to six earls and 76 barons for a muster at Berwick on 24 June. Bigod was growing old, excused service providing he sent a proxy to perform his duty as marshal. In May commissions of array for levying foot were sent to the sheriffs. 12,000 were called for, the bulk from Yorkshire and Northumberland.[42] The measures Edward had taken the previous year to punish deserters had little effect. Some 7,500 appeared at Berwick, by the first week in September he had 5,000 left, and by mid-November only 400.

After the failure of the 1300 Caerlaverock campaign Edward tried a fresh approach. The army he had marched around Galloway the previous year was too large for its purpose. The Scots were beginning to learn how to defeat an English invasion, by avoiding a pitched battle and waiting until the army went home and dispersed. If the Scots would not face him in the field, Edward decided he could achieve more by splitting his force into two. He would lead part of the army in the east from Berwick. His son would lead a second expedition into the west.

At the Lincoln parliament Edward had revived the title of prince of Wales for the 16-year old Caernarfon, nudging him towards a greater role in government. The barons were told that Edward expected the chief honour of taming the Scots should go to the prince. Summons were issued to Henry Lacy, the experienced earl of Lincoln whose seniority placed him in command of the division, together with Arundel, Lancaster and Gloucester and 18 barons. Hereford was later diverted from the Berwick muster with 18 more barons to strengthen the prince's battle, giving both father and son five earls apiece.

Foot were recruited from Cumberland, Westmoreland and Lancashire, together with levies from Wales, men less prone to desertion. The numbers are not specified; the sheriff's writ merely asked that he was to array 'all within his county, as well horse as foot'. The records of the pay rolls indicate that the prince had the larger of the two divisions invading Scotland: the total cost of the infantry with Edward was £4,500, with the prince £11,273.[43] Caernarfon could also count on the local knowledge of John de St John who brought with him the men of the marches, and a large contingent from Ireland. The king was anxious to have the earl of Ulster in the prince's division, but despite flattery, the promise of the pardon of debts, and wages, the earl did not come. An Irish contingent was sent with the justiciar, John Wogan, 2,200 in all.

The king's division moved along the Tweed and was at Coldstream on 21 July, crossing into central Scotland, through Kelso, Peebles and Traquair. Edward hoped to deny this wild district to the patriots. At Peebles he granted the lands of Andrew Murray to Aymer de Valance, including the barony and castle of Bothwell. He would first need to win it. Built of stone, it guarded the western route into the north of Scotland, much as Stirling guarded the east. Bothwell was one of the strongest castles in Scotland.

While detachments were sent to Edinburgh the bulk of the army headed towards Glasgow. Preparations for the siege began in late August. Carpenters built a bridge over the Clyde for the army to cross, and then began work on a moveable wooden siege tower, built with sides of leather for protection against fire. *Berefrey* took two days and 30 wagons to be moved the eight miles from Glasgow to the castle. No details of the siege survive, beyond the arrival of three balistae from the earl of Dunbar and 23 miners from the Forest of Dean.[44] Bothwell surrendered by 24 September, though as a result of the work of *Berefrey*, mining, or balistae is unknown. From here Edward abandoned plans to invest Inverkip castle as too late in the season and moved to winter headquarters in Linlithgow. Hurried preparations were made for Edward's arrival: the treasurer was ordered to send weapons, the king's chamber repaired or rebuilt.[45]

The prince's campaign in Galloway is not so easy to piece together. One school of thought has him hugging the southern coastline until he reached Loch Ryan, where records pinpoint him on 28 September, before turning back for Carlisle along the same route. Scottish activity on the edge of his division meant that he could not leave the protection of his supply fleet to travel inland. There is strong evidence to suggest that this account does a disservice to Caernarfon.

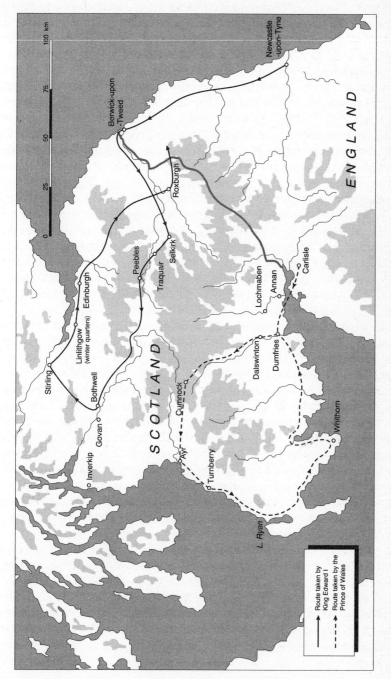

The English invasion 1301

Route taken by
King Edward I

Route taken by the
Prince of Wales

Turnberry castle was taken by the English late in August—the king
received the news on 2 September. This operation could be assigned to
a detachment from the prince's army, on 16 August a magnate
assigned to the prince's division acknowledged receipt of wine at the
nearby port of Ayr. But on 28 August it was one of the clerks in the
prince's own household who acknowledged receipt of supplies. On the
same day a Gascon knight, Montassieu de Noaillac who had joined
Caernarfon on 1 August from the Lochmaben garrison, was made
constable of Ayr, and squires from the prince's army were left to serve
in the garrisons at Ayr and Turnberry where repairs were carried out.[46]
This would have placed the prince at or around Ayr from the
beginning of September.

It seems more likely that when the prince left Carlisle he pushed into
central Galloway along the Nithsdale valley. Turnberry was captured.
Its garrison was locked up in Carlisle keep, secured by chains and fetters
bought for the purpose.[47] At Ayr the prince received the provisions from
Ireland that had been sent to the Isle of Arran. After leaving Ayr and
Turnberry he travelled south to Loch Ryan and then returned to Carlisle
along the southern coast route. He was at the river Cree on the 3rd, and
back in England by 5 October.

During the early part of the campaign the Scots remained largely out
of sight—there are no records of any serious engagements or skirmishes.
William de Durham sent a letter to the king of the retreat of an enemy
army in northern Galloway into Glencairn and Nithsdale.[48] It was a
policy which won few plaudits from English chroniclers: they 'achieved
nothing glorious or praiseworthy', that they 'would not fight with either
army, but fled as they had done the previous year. Howbeit they took
some fine spoil from the English and did much other mischief.' The
Lanercost chronicler hints at activity on the edge of one of the divisions,
probably the prince's.[49]

Suddenly, a Scottish army appeared in Galloway. The first reports
came in early September from the keeper of Lochmaben, John Tilliol. He
sent a report of John Soules and the earl of Buchan, who were at Loudon,
and Simon Fraser at Stanhouses. Tilliol sought reinforcements of 100
men-at-arms so that he could ride upon them and prevent the country
rising. Tilliol did not need to ride out, Soules came to him. On 7
September Soules and Ingram de Umfraville attacked the castle, set fire
to the town and pillaged the local countryside. Tilliol counted 14
bannerets, 240 men-at-arms, and 7,000 foot in the Scottish army. After
two days, with casualties on both sides, Soules left for Dalswinton
where he began recruiting men from Nithsdale.[50]

The English had no idea where Soules would next strike. Tilliol, the
man on the ground, thought the English Marches. Edward ordered the
march captains to strengthen the northern defences, Robert Hastangs

sent a message that lookouts had been sent to warn of the Scottish army's approach; Alexander Balliol, Walter Huntercombe, Hugh Audley, strengthened with a force from Berwick to hold Selkirk, and Richard Hastangs were ready to bring troops at a days notice. Alexander Balliol promised that 'whenever the enemy issue from Galloway, he will know two days before.' Soules did not issue from Galloway; he wrong footed the English by turning west. On 3 October he was before the castles of Ayr and Turnberry, which were only held with some difficulty.[51] The attack on the Galloway garrisons was the last that was heard of the Scots in this season.

Why did the prince not intercept Soules? Perhaps he believed his force was too small. More likely he lacked intelligence, not knowing of the attack on Ayr he feared a Scottish flanking movement and headed for the last reported sighting. The prince spent most of October in Carlisle, before setting off by way of Haltwhistle, Alnwick, Berwick, Dunbar and Edinburgh to join the king at Linlithgow on 14 November. The English army could do little from Linlithgow. The winter of 1301-2 was harsh and set in early. Fodder was unavailable for the horses, many of which died from the cold. On 18 December writs were sent to the southern counties for fresh grain supplies, Edward's plans to remain in Scotland for the rest of the season to 'annoy the enemy' were being hampered by lack of provisions for the sustenance of the host.[52]

Edward now received disturbing news from the continent. Wale and Delisle, Edward's messengers to the curia, arrived back in England on 18 August. Wale's report of the meeting with Boniface was carried to Scotland where it was intercepted and opened by a high-ranking Edwardian official. On 1 October the official wrote to Edward to inform him: 'that the agents of the king of France had taken John Balliol from the place where he was settled by the pope, to his castle of Bailleul in Picardy.' There were rumours that Philip was preparing to send an army to Scotland to reinstate Balliol on the throne.[53] Unprepared to maintain the army all winter, and facing this new threat from France, Edward ordered that the negotiations with France for a new truce should not stumble over the inclusion of the Scots. He remained at Linlithgow from 5 November until after the truce had been ratified on 26 January.

Edward did not have the funds to match the castle building program he had achieved in Wales but after his stay at Linlithgow he decided to convert the existing castle into 'a place of some strength', a royal palace. The project was confirmed at a council meeting held in Roxburgh on 12 February to discuss 'the works which the king has devised in order to make the fortress at Linlithgow.' John Kingston and the constable of Linlithgow, Archibald Livingston, were charged with looking after the project, but the building was supervised by one of the great Welsh castle builders, the Savoyard Master James of St George.

The castle stands on a promontory jutting into the Loch. Edward, who took a personal interest in the work, ordered a stone gatehouse with a stone tower on either side, with two stone towers rising from the Loch. The side of the castle was extended south, to bring the church inside the defences. A smaller, defensible, inner palisade surrounded the promontory. When the king met with Master James in April timber replaced stone. No doubt money and time were the reasons—the castle would need to be defendable at the end of the truce in November. The palisade was made with whole logs, or larger logs not split too small. The change in material meant bringing in more carpenters; 20 were already at work, and the sheriff of Northumberland was asked to send 30 more, but could only find another 20. Earth works formed a crucial part of the defences. 140 women ditchers were recruited to help the 103 men already at work, although paid a half pence less than the male rate of two pence a day. Towards the end of September the work still had some way to go, and the new constable, William of Ferrers, promised the labour of his 100 strong garrison, 'because if they were not the works would get seriously behind.' Similar work was carried out at Selkirk, with a wooden palisade and towers, and stone gateways added to the motte and bailey castle.[54]

The two castles were central to English strategy. The defensive line along the south of Scotland had slowly been pushed north. Berwick was no longer a key defensive site, but a supply base for the more exposed castles further north, at Edinburgh and Linlithgow. The castle at Selkirk was an attempt to deny the central highlands and forests to the patriots. In the west the capture of the castles at Caerlaverock and Turnberry left the other patriot safe-haven in Galloway far more exposed.

* * *

The treaty of Asnières-sur-Oise was still only a truce, to last nine months—a final Anglo-French peace treaty was proving elusive. Edward agreed that English held lands and castles taken in Scotland since the Canterbury talks in the spring of 1301 should be placed under French control until 1 November 1302. For Edward, the stumbling block for an Anglo-French peace had been the failure of the French to honour their secret agreement with Edmund to leave Gascony. As Boniface had told the English envoys: 'What the French once lay hold of they never let go, and to do with the French is to have to do with the Devil.'[55]

The treaty was an astonishing break from Edwardian policy. Was Edward preparing to give up Scotland in return for restoration of Gascony? The last article of the treaty was added by the English ambassadors. It states that although the King of France affords the title of king of Scots to John Balliol, the English maintain the contrary. If this was still unclear the English wrote an elaborate diplomatic note of the reasons why the Scots could not be allies of the king of France: that an alliance made against common-right, against sound morals, and against oaths of fidelity was invalid.

Edward's insistence that he did not regard France and Scotland as allies, nor recognise Balliol's claim to the throne, was sounding increasingly hollow. The campaign in 1301 had been as ineffectual as all those since 1296. He had not been able to raise an army to go to France since 1298. He was opposed by Philip in France, by Boniface in the curia and the residual baronial problems had infested the day-to-day running of the government. The forces ranged against Edward, the patriots in Scotland, the king of France and the pope, had a clear aim: king John's restoration. John Balliol's star had risen during the French-Anglo-Scottish truce of 1301. Acts that had been made in the name of the Guardians were now made in King John's name, and John Soules was a Balliol nominee.

Edward's fortunes improved dramatically in 1302 with the submission of Robert Bruce early in the year. Throughout 1301, and probably since 1300, Bruce had become increasingly estranged from the patriotic cause. He had spent the previous two years on his estates in Annandale, 'the silence of the sources suggest he was sulking.'[56] When news arrived of King John's release from papal custody Bruce saw that the only hope for his long-term ambition lay with Edward I. The exact date of his surrender to John de St John is not known, but it was certainly before 16 February 1302, probably before or at the confirmation of the treaty of Asnières.

The memorandum detailing Bruce's submission was only discovered in the 1950s. The document is vague, and it is possible that Edward meant it to be so, leaving his options open. It begins with a frank admission of Edwardian weakness, a recognition, 'God forbid', of the possibility of John's restoration either by French force or papal arbitration. The document then deals with Bruce's right, *le droit*, to pursue his claim if this should happen. There is a question mark over what claim the document refers to, Bruce's claim to the throne or to his lands and titles. It seems unlikely that at this early stage Edward was contemplating backing Bruce's claim to the throne, the thrust of Edwardian policy had been to change Scotland's status from a kingdom to a land. Besides, Bruce was a rebel who had only just come into Edward's peace—it would be some time before he was rehabilitated.

It may be that Edward was reserving his position should Boniface succeed in having the Great Cause reopened, so that he would have in Bruce his own candidate. More likely Bruce was concerned with his own estates in Scotland. Bruce's castle at Turnberry had been taken after May 1301, so under the terms of the Asnières treaty would be placed in French hands. Now that he had submitted to Edward, under the same treaty he was liable to loose his earldom with no guarantee of restoration. With this in mind he sought Edward's promise of support and Edward gave what guarantees he could.[57]

Edward's run of luck continued. The reconciliation between Boniface and Philip, that had secured papal support for French policy against Edward in Scotland, broke down. In April Philip held the first meeting of the Estates General to rally popular support against Boniface. Against this concerted French opposition Boniface needed English support. By August 1302 his about turn was complete. He wrote to the Scottish bishops ordering them to lead their erring flocks onto a better path, singling out Bishop Wishart as 'a stumbling stone and rock of offence.'

Boniface never recovered from this final conflict with the French, which would last until his death in October 1303. The papacy of Benedict XI was too short to exert any influence. The election of Bertrand de Got, whose reign lasted until 1314, would be no help to the Scots. He was a Gascon noble, archbishop of Bordeaux since 1299. As Clement V he was dependent on Philip and a subject of Edward. He refused to go to Rome. Crowned in Lyon, he spent the first years of his pontificate in Poitou and Gascony.

Then, with an irony which must have crushed the Scots, the Flemish allies Edward had abandoned rose up against French occupation. In May 1302 the French garrison was massacred in the 'Matins of Bruge'. The French army, the finest in Europe, was then destroyed by Flemish craftsman at the battle of Courtrai. The most decisive battle of the first stage of the Wars of Independence had taken place on the continent, and not a Scotsman nor Englishman had taken part.

* * *

As the Anglo-Scottish truce expired on 30 November 1302 the autumn parliament turned its attention to a new campaign in Scotland. Philip IV sought a personal conference with Edward to try and achieve a permanent peace, 'but by the advice of the whole realm it was decided that the king ought not to leave England at anybody's bidding or suggestion, but attack the Scottish rebels.'[58] Reports had already been received that Scottish magnates were to assemble for a parliament on 8 September, from which, after the truce had expired, they intended to 'approach the march of England. ...to destroy it if possible.'[59]

In January 1303 Segrave, now lieutenant of Scotland with John Botetort, Edward's bastard son, captain in the west, sent news that this had not been an idle threat. The Scots had broken into English held lands and seized castles, including Selkirk—an obvious target for the patriots, as Selkirk Forest had always been a valuable base. On 3 February Edward ordered the arrest of Alexander Balliol, the keeper of Selkirk; he must have feared Balliol's desertion to the patriots, or at least his incompetence. Edward's other new castle, at Linlithgow, withstood a siege. The king's chapel turned into a granary, a chapel within the church into a wine cellar for the duration of the siege.

The barony had no enthusiasm for a winter campaign. But Edward was anxious not to allow the Scots to have the season all their own way. He pressed the northern barons to supply military aid to prevent the Scots breaking into England.[60] He sent orders that Segrave should organise a large scale reconnaissance in strength as far as Kirkintilloch to report on the state of the country in preparation for a larger campaign led by the king. The force was assembled by Manton at Wark, moving north in early 1303.

The English army advanced in three divisions, which the Scots 'did their best to harass and annoy.' At night the divisions were camped several miles apart, with poor communication between them. The younger Comyn and Simon Fraser led a Scottish force on a night march out of the district between Lanark and Peebles and fell on Segrave's detachment early on Sunday morning. Segrave, his brother Nicholas and 16 knights were captured. Robert Neville's division of the English army was hearing mass some miles away. He led his men to attack the Scottish force, which he found busy over the plunder. When this new English force reached the field the Scottish leaders gave the order to kill the English prisoners, but it seems that only one English prisoner of rank, the paymaster Manton was killed. Manton had vainly sought to buy his life from Simon Fraser, 'Fraser fiercely reproached him for defrauding his king and withholding their wages from the soldiers', a 'ribald near at hand, he seized the wretched cofferer and cut off his hands and his head.' Neville managed to secure Segrave's release after a long struggle.[61]

The encounter at Roslyn was played up by the Scots and played down by the English. It was certainly a victory that gave a boost to Scottish morale and showed their continental allies that their cause was worth supporting. But it was no Stirling Bridge, no Bannockburn. It was a serious check to the English advance in Scotland, but it was a raiding force that was defeated, not an invading army.

* * *

As the Scottish position in Europe had deteriorated, the most powerful delegation that could be mustered—the Guardian John Soules, bishop Lamberton of St Andrews, bishop Crambeth of Dunkeld, the earl of Buchan and James the Steward—headed to the French court in a last bid to save the alliance and to lobby for inclusion in a final Anglo-Scottish peace. But Philip's defeat at Courtrai and the heightened tension between him and the pope meant that he could no longer afford to advocate the Scottish cause. Towards the end of the year the balance shifted still further in Edward's favour when Bordeaux rebelled and expelled the French. Only the Scottish alliance now prevented a permanent peace between England and France. Worse, Philip had a letter from John Balliol consenting that he had a free hand to prosecute his affairs in Scotland. It was the last disastrous decision of a disastrous king.[62]

The final treaty was sealed in Paris on 20 May 1303. This was an offensive and defensive alliance with the *de facto* restoration of Aquitaine confirmed. No mention was made of the Scots. The French forces that were to occupy the castles and keep the peace in accordance with Asnières never came. Philip abandoned the Scots as quietly and quickly as Edward was loudly and determinedly to crush them.

Five days later the Scottish envoys sent word of the treaty to John Comyn, the 'Warden of Scotland', presumably made so while Soules was out of the country. The envoys still held misplaced hopes that Philip had not deserted them, that he was sending an embassy to England to press their cause. But the tone of their letter saw the harsh reality that they had indeed been abandoned by both the curia and the French. For the first time since 1296, Edward was free to act with the full force of his realm in Scotland. The envoys urged Comyn to come to a reconciliation with Edward: 'But if he should harden his heart like Pharaoh, now if ever quit yourselves like men.'[63] Lamberton also wrote to William Wallace, seeking his help for the community, ordering his own servants to give Wallace fresh supplies.

Edward determined to make, in his own words, an end of the business.[64] He did not raise a large army, but he planned to keep it in the field for longer than ever before. Writs were issued to the barons in November for a muster on 26 June. By the time writs were issued to raise infantry levies, Segrave had been defeated at Roslyn and the muster brought forward to 12 May at Roxburgh. At most he had only 7,500 infantry. Numbers fell as usual, though not as fast as in previous years. Severe measures were taken against deserters and bailiffs who accepted bribes from those selected to serve. Edward would also be operating in the north of Scotland, which meant deserters would have to travel far through enemy territory to return home. Walter of Guisbourough suggested he left Stirling in Scottish hands at the rear of his operations in the north for just this reason. When he wintered at Dunfermline he still had 1,000 foot with him.[65]

The king arrived at Roxburgh in May 1303, where he stayed until the general advance began in the first week of June. He had learnt the lessons of the two previous campaigns. There would be no aimless rambling of the Scottish countryside in search of an evasive enemy this time. Edward intended a display of English military power, aimed at terrorising the Scots into submission. The king 'advanced by daily stages of moderate length taking much plunder, burning and destroying everything', 'on every side he burnt hamlets and towns, granges and granaries. So did the prince, unsparingly.'[66] His officers, Robert Bruce, the Earl of Ulster with a large Irish division, and his northern captains worked independently throughout the country so that the meagre Scottish resources could not recover.

The Scots could only snap at the edges of the English column. The normally reliable *Scalacronica* reports one such incident. Shortly after crossing the border Hugh Audley quartered with 60 men-at-arms in Melrose Abbey, away from the main army at Dryburgh which was too crowded. The younger Comyn in Ettrick Forest discovered this small contingent and led an attack on the abbey, forcing open the doors and killing or capturing those inside, including the chronicler's father.[67] The army moved north past Edinburgh and Linlithgow to the river Forth. There was no intention to force a passage past Stirling castle, or be tied down to a tedious siege.

* * *

Orders had been issued in January for the construction of three pre-fabricated pontoon bridges, built and shipped at the enormous cost of £938. They were of different sizes, *maior, medius* and *minor pons*, perhaps one was meant for horse, another for foot and the largest for the wagon train. Each was defended by brattices incorporating drawbridges, two with springalds. They were completed and ready for shipping on 23 May. The brattices were carried complete on three ships, each flying the standard of St George. A lead ship acted as guide, with 27 more ships carrying the bridge sections. When or where the convoy arrived at the Forth is unknown. The carpenters who went with the fleet to assemble the bridges were paid off on 8 June, which may have been the date of crossing.[68]

Edward reached Perth on 18 June, where he remained until 13 July, sending forays out into the countryside. News arrived of a Scottish attempt to break out of Galloway. Simon Fraser and Edmund Comyn raided around Kilbride, John Moubray and Wallace attacked English garrisons in the west. Both Scottish forces met at Annandale in June, threatening a major raid into northern England. The men of the northern marches were mustered, but nothing more was heard of the patriots.[69]

From Perth Edward moved north to Brechin, where the castle put up a spirited resistance. The siege engine *Esplante* from Jedburgh and another from Edinburgh were shipped to Montrose with timber and stones; five wagon loads of lead was stripped from Brechin church to provide counterbalances for the trebuches.[70] The castle's commander, Thomas Maule, scorned Edward's siege. Whenever the walls were hit by stones from the engines he ran out laughing with a towel in his hand to wipe the mark off the wall. His luck ran out, and he was killed by a ricochet from a shattered stone. His last words were a curse on anybody who surrendered, but the garrison lacked its commander's mettle and yielded the castle on 9 August. Urquhart and Cromarty fell shortly afterwards.

In September Edward reached Kinloss on the Moray Firth where he stayed to tighten his grip on the north and receive submissions. He then made a circuitous route through the mountains south to Dunfermline, which he made his winter headquarters. Dunfermline was one of the largest monasteries in Scotland. Its precincts stretched over three ploughlands, 360 acres, within which were 'many places almost royal in character'. It was poorly fortified, so work began on a ditch and palisade. The sheriff of Edinburgh was ordered to send sixty carpenters and 200 ditchers, only to report that none could be found since as the king still owed wages for the work at Linlithgow the workers would prefer to leave the country than work for him. Men were found locally to complete the ditch.

Edward was at Dunfermline from November until March, when he moved to St Andrews to hold a parliament. The complex was destroyed when Edward left, what could not be burnt was levelled—the chambers, palaces and walls. Only the church was spared, and some rooms for the 200 or so monks. At St Andrews he again had problems with his workmen. Six carpenters sent to make preparations for his stay went on strike for three days 'because they did not have their wages as they wished.'[71]

The prince had left the king towards the end of November, making his winter headquarters in Perth. Here, Fordun comments on a glut of food and wine.[72] Judging from the prince's household accounts Fordun was well informed. At Christmas 'there dined with the prince the earls of Lancaster, Warwick, Ulster, Atholl, Strathearn and Sir John of Brittany, Hugh Despenser, Richard Siward, Alexander Abernethy, and other magnates, both English, Irish and Scottish in the army. Eight and a quarter 'beeves', 40 lambs, 20 'Aberdeens', twelve swans, two cranes and five casks, 28 sesterces of the king's wine was taken from the king's store. In February alone there were feasts on the 2nd, 4th, 10th, 11th, and 21st.

English forces operated throughout Scotland during the winter. In January a foray led by Botetort and John St John with four bannerets, 141 men-at-arms and 2,736 foot raided into Galloway. A 'chivauchee' was launched from Dunfermline across the Forth, led by Segrave, Clifford and Latimer. This raiding party, assembled under strict secrecy in case a spy might inform the Scots, routed a Scottish force under William Wallace and Simon Fraser at Happrew, although the two

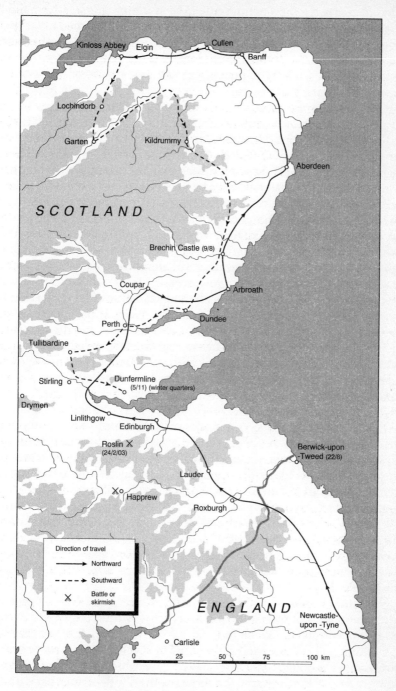

Kinloss Abbey · Elgin · Cullen · Banff
Lochindorb
Garten · Kildrummy · Aberdeen
S C O T L A N D
Brechin Castle (9/8)
Coupar · Arbroath
Perth · Dundee
Tullibardine
Stirling · Dunfermline (5/11) (winter quarters)
Drymen
Linlithgow · Edinburgh
Roslin ✕ (24/2/03) · Berwick-upon-Tweed (22/8)
Lauder
✕ Happrew
Roxburgh

Direction of travel
→ Northward
--→ Southward
✕ Battle or skirmish

E N G L A N D · Newcastle-upon-Tyne
Carlisle
0   25   50   75   100 km

The Stirling Campaign 1303

patriots escaped.[73] The younger Comyn still had an army in the field, albeit a small one. The countess of Lennox sought help when a party of 100 men-at-arms and 1,000 foot on a foray into Lennox reached as far as Dryman in early October. But Comyn was already making the first tentative moves towards peace. He sent an embassy to Aymer de Valence, Edward's lieutenant south of the Forth, on 26 September. Valence held hopes of success, but Comyn was not ready to give up altogether, perhaps he hoped the English would go home for the winter.[74]

By 22 December the patriots had made their conditions for surrender known to Valence at Perth.[75] A writer from Perth in January reported that Comyn remained 'in their lands beyond the mountains, where none … who came on horseback could go.' Some of his men made a foray across the Tay, but Comyn had not joined them. The abbot of Coupar-Angus sent news of a large enemy raid that had gone towards Strathearn but returned to Angus.[76] These were the last movements of Comyn resistance. Edward's campaign in 1303, one that would be extended in 1304 was, only for the second time threatening Comyn interests north of the Forth. Besides, Comyn had seen a slow trail of Scottish lords making their way to Edward's door: the Macdougalls in 1301, Robert Bruce in 1302, Ross in 1303 and Atholl in 1304. If the Comyn family was not to lose its foremost place in Scottish society to Edward's allies, it would have to surrender before being defeated in the field. Comyn sent a clerk to arrange a meeting. On 11 January, the earl of Ulster, Aymer de Valence and Henry Percy travelled to Kinclaven castle to meet Comyn, accompanied by 200 men-at-arms for safety.

The two sides met on the 19th. Comyn remained undefeated and felt able to present terms. It says volumes for Comyn and the dignity of the office of Guardian he represented that he would not surrender unconditionally. Comyn demanded that all those who surrendered should be allowed life, limb and liberty, an amnesty and restoration of their property. In a faint echo of the treaty of Birgham he called for the protection of the Scottish people 'in all their laws, usages, customs, and liberties'. This last clause was especially important: a tangible expression of distinctive Scottish indentity.

Comyn's proposals were forwarded to Edward at Dunfermline. The king was prepared to be lenient, to allow all who submitted by 2 February life and limb, with a guarantee that they would not face imprisonment or dishersion. The king would not allow Comyn his terms, but in a generous note told him that he would consider his terms kindly once he had surrendered.

The prince of Wales was empowered to receive all who were willing to submit. On 9 February the earl of Ulster met with the Comyn at Strathord near Perth where the terms of the Scottish submission were hammered out. The meeting began at nine in the morning, and went on until three in the afternoon. Comyn was able to secure the promise that no one who came in by the 20th would be excluded from the surrender. The prince granted life and limb, liberty and freedom from dishersion. Comyn would face exile for one year, the Steward and Soules for two, Fraser and Thomas du Bois for three. Edward ratified the terms, although adding Wishart, David Graham and Alexander Lindsay to those who would face temporary banishment. They were singled out not for rebellion but for personal betrayal of the king's trust. Wishart was added as a serial troublemaker, Graham for false dealings with the king's council, and Lindsay since he had abandoned the English after being knighted by the king's own hand.

The terms were lenient for those who were willing to submit. Individual losses were small: exile for one or two years and fines. But for Scotland all that was salvaged was a commitment that the laws, customs and privileges be observed from the days of Alexander III, not to be changed without the consent of the responsible men of the realm. Anything more would have to rely on Edward's goodwill.

* * *

John Soules could not stomach the conditions, he preferred permanent exile in France. Otherwise, all except Stirling, under William Oliphant, submitted. The terms that had been offered to William Wallace were verbally modified: 'Let him put himself at the grace and disposal of the lord King if that seems good to him'. It did not.

Nothing had been heard of Wallace, or for that matter Simon Fraser, since their defeat at Happrew. Wallace was still south of the Forth, in Selkirk Forest with a small group of now desperate men. The hunt was now on to capture him. In early March 1304, the prince of Wales sent Alexander Abernethy with 40 men-at-arms into Strathearn and Mentieth towards Drip to complete a guard already in place.[77] The king commended the prince, but also offered Abernethy reinforcements. Two days later Edward decided that if the prince or Abernethy did not request aid, he would send it anyway. He commanded the prince to reinforce Abernethy to keep the fords and passages of the Forth closed. He advised sending the young knights in the prince's company, to win their shoes or their boots.

In the letter offering support Edward responded to a request from Abernethy to clarify the terms that should be offered Wallace. He told Abernethy 'that it is not our pleasure by any means that either to him, or to any of his company, you hold out any word of peace, unless they place themselves absolutely and in all things at our will, without any exception whatever.' It is unclear why Abernethy sought this clarification. It is possible, as some chroniclers believe, that Wallace was seeking terms using Abernethy as a sympathetic intermediary.[78]

Edward was tightening his grip on Scotland. A picture emerges of the countryside bristling with troops, with the main highways denied to the few remaining patriots. Edward had sent out so many of his own men that he could not send more lest he was left 'too much alone.' The earls of Strathearn, Lennox and Mentieth were stationed to hold the fords of the Forth and deny patriot access to Stirling. Their presence at the Anglo-Scottish parliament was to be in as plain a manner as possible, with few people, so that their forces were not depleted. Abernethy and Bisset were told to go alone.

Patrick Dunbar sat out the campaign. Edward wrote to him in a fit of anger. The record of the letter is a draft, dictated by Edward to a scribe. Part of a scatological expression is half recorded by the scribe, until Edward has a change of heart and opts for a quote that loses nothing of his contempt: 'When the war was over, Andigier found his sword'. The chided earl was ordered to take up a position near Stirling to prevent supplies reaching the castle.[79]

Amidst all this activity Wallace remained at large, undetected. That he could do so could only have been as a result of support amongst the local population who risked their lives protecting him.

In early March Edward held a joint parliament of Anglo-Scottish magnates. Practically every Scot of rank attended. Even those with pressing duties guarding the Forth were told to attend at the last minute. Those who had submitted formally entered into Edward's peace. The question of their ransoms was held over until a future parliament. The king consulted three Scottish magnates, bishop Wishart of Glasgow, Robert Bruce and John Moubray on how the government of Scotland should be settled. It was they who told him that a ten strong delegation, two bishops, abbots, earls, barons, freemen, should be elected from the community of Scotland, who should represent the community at an English parliament at the king's pleasure. The irreconcilables were then outlawed: Simon Fraser, William Wallace and the Stirling garrison. At some point during the siege of Stirling castle Simon Fraser surrendered, and was treated leniently.

Nevertheless, a small group of patriots under the command of William Oliphant found the courage to defy Edward, to hold Stirling castle. There was no hope of relief (from whom?). With all serious resistance broken, the stand taken by the garrison seems pointless, even foolhardy. The *Scalacronica* offers the briefest of insights: because they held it of the 'Lion'. Oliphant's stand certainly won him admirers amongst the English chroniclers. Rishanger describes him as 'a wise and tireless soldier', Matthew of Westminster applauded him as a hero.

It was to the last legitimate representative of the 'Lion', John Soules, that Oliphant sought permission to send a messenger to see on what terms the castle could be surrendered.

Edward has been criticised for refusing this request, but it was hardly a practical proposition. Soules was in France after his refusal to accept the terms of surrender, so any exchange of messages would have taken months to sort out. In any case, Edward was not a patient man: 'If he thinks it will be better for him to defend the castle than yield it, he will see.'

Edward had a fine contingent of earls and barons, it became a 'social and military occasion', the king even had an oriel window constructed in his house in the town so that the queen and ladies of the court could watch in comfort. But sieges were not the stuff of chivalry. The taking of Stirling would be the work of engineers and the clerks who kept them supplied. Behind it all was Master James of St George, probably supervising the whole operation.

The spring of 1304 saw the greatest concentration of military hardware Britain had yet seen. The largest engines carried names, *Gloucester, Tout le Monde, Parson* ... thirteen of them were brought to Stirling. In early April Master Reginald took delivery of a siege train from Richard Bromsgrove, the keeper of the king's stores at Berwick: the timbers for two engines made at Brechin, another called *Segrave*, one called *Vernay*, one called *Robinett*, 16 beams of one called *Forster* and 18 beams of an engine from Aberdeen. Adam of Gashom was sent to Linlithgow before joining the siege with twenty-one wagon loads of parts, counterweights and ammunition. The engines used against Brechin were sent, as was *Berefrey* from Bothwell. Master Robert of Bedford came from St Andrews to take charge of *Kingston*, Master Reginald of Bedford with John Segrave's engine, *Weland*. John Kingston received a writ 'to see that Master Thomas the king's engineer takes in the wood of Neubotel all the timber he needs' for repair of the engines at Edinburgh which were shipped on the *Leugarebard* and *la Welyfare*. One ship from the Isle of Wight sailed to Inverkeithing to pick up an engine from Perth or St Andrews.[80]

When the king thought the work too slow he sent a royal clerk to the engine supply points, Inverkeithing, Blackness, Edinburgh and Linlithgow, to hurry them along. The sluggish constable at Inverkip was given a dressing down and ordered to seize all the iron and great stones in Glasgow, to be forwarded without excuse or delay. Robert Bruce sent his siege engines, but could not find wagons to send the great beam of one large engine; Edward urged him to find a means of carrying the engine, and sent John Botetort to help.

Plans began for the construction of new engines. Thomas Houghton, the senior of seven master carpenters, worked with a force of 80 to 90 carpenters and sawyers. Owen of Montgomery was in command of anywhere between 150 and 200 woodsmen, busy making wickerwork for mantlets and hurdles. The lead for counterweights was found locally, Caernarfon ordered to take it from churches around Dunblane and Perth, leaving only the altars covered.[81] The trebuchets needed constant feeding: the original supply lasted two weeks. Master Walter of Hereford supervised masons providing ammunition. On 7 March he had been assigned to choose and bring into service as many masons as he saw fit.[82] New supplies were forwarded from Linlithgow in early May. Forty quarriers worked from 9 June to 20 July 'cutting stones for the king's engines' at Stirling, shaped at Linlithgow.

Berwick-upon-Tweed became the focus for the collection of supplies which would then be sent on to Linlithgow before delivery to the siege. On 24 March Richard Bromsgrove was ordered to send all he could to Blackness, to brew beer and grind flour and malt to be sent as soon as possible. Keeping the army supplied was always a problem; at one point in June the supply of food was running low, the horses in need of oats and beans with nothing to eat but grass. In April *la Seintemariship* of Alemouth arrived with a cargo of lead, iron, crossbows and bolts, in May a receipt survives for 6,050 bolts for crossbows of two feet, 18,000 of one foot; a payment to the mayor and bailiffs of Newcastle for 336 goosewings and 360 feathers and wages for four men making arrows; another receipt for 100 picks, mauls, 155 ameraxes for masons, six gavelocks (crowbars), 200 chisels, eighty coignes (wedges) and 100 trowels.

The siege began on 22 April and lasted for three months. Supplies must have stopped reaching the castle by early April, when the earls of Strathearn, Lennox and Menteith were ordered to stop their people selling or buying provisions or having any communication with the garrison. On 17 April William Bisset seized the boats belonging to the garrison that had been their last source of supplies.

Despite the preparations, Stirling proved a difficult nut to crack. The castle occupies a superb defensive site. The trebuchets hurled giant rock projectiles that scattered lethal showers of splinters when they landed. *Ludgar*, an engine built on site, smashed down an entire wall, although a great battering ram failed because it was poorly constructed.[83] An account for the supply of a horse load of cotton thread, one load of quick sulphur and one of saltpetre, shows that Greek fire was used, loaded into earthenware pots and thrown into the castle. This was the work of the Burgundian, Jean de Lamouilly. Charcoal was the only additional ingredient needed to complete a mixture for gunpowder; since this could be found locally, explosives may have been used in the English siege operations.[84] According to Langtoft the Scots only had one engine; the rod broke early in siege and could not be repaired.[85] There was some safety for the garrison in deep caves, where supplies could be kept safe.

All that time 'the king exposed himself as freely as any of his men.' One day a quarrel pierced his armour, but without wounding him.

When the bolt was extracted the king spat on it, and showing the bolt shouted loudly that he would hang the man who had shot it. On another occasion his charger was knocked clean off his legs by a huge stone hurled from the walls. His men, hastening to the rescue, dragged the king downhill, declaring that he must take more care of himself. 'As the lord liveth,' he said, 'I will not desert you, whether ye go to life or death.' This sounds like medieval Chinese whispers and may have been a single incident embellished by successive chroniclers.

For all the fury of the bombardment, the garrison was forced to surrender when it ran out of food. A private letter casually mentions that the castle had surrendered without conditions but 'the king wills that none of his people enter till it is struck with the *Warwolf*, and that those within defend themselves from the said wolf as best they can.' Five master carpenters, 50 carpenters and five pages had worked on the new machine, and Edward would not allow an offer of surrender to prevent him from using it. The episode is comic rather than ruthless: the garrison had surrendered, there was no question of them defending the walls from an assault and they could have easily retreated to the safety of the cellars. The letter is the only source for the episode, contemporaries saw no reason to mark it in a hostile way, and neither should we.

With the king's pride and joy tested, Oliphant marched out at the head of 24 men of substance, those named in the surrender documents. Edward would not accept anything but unconditional surrender. They were allowed to make a submission to the king, in shirts, bare feet covered with ashes, when they begged humbly for pardon. Edward threatened them with disembowelling and hanging, telling them that 'You don't deserve my grace, but must surrender to my will.' As usual he put the fear of God into his captives, and then relented. One Englishman found amongst the garrison, a deserter, was hanged on the day of surrender. About 50 of the defenders were then sent south to English prisons.[86]

By the summer of 1304, all Scotland was at peace with Edward. The castles were refortified and garrisoned, a clerk supervised the return of the siege engines from Stirling to the Scottish castles. John Segrave was appointed justiciar and captain south of the Forth, the earl of Atholl north of Forth. On the day of Stirling's surrender the king asked the barons to make their requests for rewards for the campaign. The barons asked that the ordinance should wait until the next parliament. Edward then took his army home. He would never again step foot in Scotland. The royal administration, which had been based in York for the past seven years, packed its bags and returned to Westminster.

Wallace was still free, but he was now on the run and Edward no longer feared him. He told the Scots to 'bring me Wallace. If you seek favour or remission of ransom, bring me Wallace before Christmas.' James the

Steward, John Soules and Ingram Umfraville were denied safe-conduct until Wallace was captured, and the younger Comyn, Simon Fraser, Alexander Lindsay and David Graham were told to 'exert themselves until 20 days after Christmas to capture Sir William Wallace, and hand him over to the king, who will watch to see how each of them conducts themselves so that he can do most favour to whoever shall capture Wallace, with regard to exile or legal claims or expiation of past deeds.'

It has been suggested that these demands bore the mark of a 'personal vendetta' of Edward towards Wallace. This is the worst light that could be put on Edward's demands. It was important for Edward that Wallace was captured by a Scot. It is not surprising that he wanted to keep the leaders of the patriotic cause, the three men he had faced across the river Cree in 1300 and who had harried the prince of Wales in 1302, out of the country until the man who had so enflamed nationalist feeling was no longer a threat. The demand was not insisted upon, the men given safe conducts to return from France on 17 February 1305. Edward also wanted to test the loyalty of those who, in his eyes, had rebelled against his peace.

* * *

Edward did not plan to make the same mistake as he had done in 1296, when he left the government of the country in limbo. A Scottish parliament met in Perth in May 1305 to elect the delegation to the forthcoming Westminster parliament. The result was a representation of Scottish society, two bishops, St Andrews and Dunkeld; two abbots, of Coupar-Angus and Melrose; two earls, Buchan and March; two barons, John Moubray and Robert Keith; and two commoners, Adam of Gordon and John of Inchmartin. The earl of Buchan missed the meeting, replaced by the earl of Mentieth.

The Westminster parliament met in September and spent 20 days drafting an ordinance for the establishment of a Scottish administration.[87] Scotland would be ruled as a land, not a realm, under a lieutenant appointed by the English king aided by a chancellor and chamberlain. Edward appointed his cousin, the unexceptional John of Brittany earl of Richmond, who had a salary of £2,000. Four sets of justices were appointed, an Englishman and Scot for each of the main geographic regions. Most sheriffs were Scots but the key military points apart from Stirling were kept for the English. The lieutenant would have a council which was made up of the royal officers together with 22 Scots: four bishops, four abbots, five earls and nine magnates. A new legal code in accordance with 'God and reason' was planned. The lieutenant and council were instructed to review the laws of David I and the amendments of later kings. Any they wanted to change but 'dare not undertake without the king' were to be drawn up and presented at the

Easter 1306 parliament. Only the use of 'Brets and Scots' was forbidden. This Celtic form of *wergild* was a system of bloodmoney, a price set according to rank by way of compensation for homicide and wounding in lieu of punishment. It was an archaic practice that was probably dying out in Galloway and all but the furthest reaches of the realm.

In victory the king had shown statesmanlike moderation, consulting the vanquished on the new regime and expecting them to play a part in it. Edward was 'so pleased' he remitted the Scottish leaders' exile and reduced their ransoms. The king has been praised for the ordinances even by his sternest critics: 'The political wisdom of King Edward is shown by his resolve to consult Scottish leaders on the new constitution to be devised for the country and to give them some measure of responsibility for making it work ... it was no small achievement for this elderly, conventional, conservative, unimaginative man that he had learned anything at all.'[88]

As a victorious general he had shown himself willing to be a peacemaker. But nothing Edward did could hide the fact that this was the settlement of a conquered country: the key appointments, lieutenant, John of Brittany; chamberlain, John de Sandale; chancellor, William de Bevercotes and controller, Robert Heron, were all Englishmen.

William Wallace was finally captured on 3 August 1305 near Glasgow by men of John Stewart of Mentieth, a younger son of the earl of Menteith. He was taken straight to London, where he arrived on 22 August. In Scotland his life was barely and poorly chronicled; his trial and execution came under the spotlight of English records, in close and grim detail. The king refused to see or speak to him. On 23 August he was taken on horseback to Westminster Hall to be tried before a special commission appointed by the king, the senior members, the mayor of London, John Blunt, the soldier John Segrave and the justiciar of England, Peter Mallore. Wallace was forced to wear a crown of laurel, because it was believed he had claimed he would one day wear a crown in Westminster.

He had been outlawed by the St Andrews parliament, and outside the law 'there was no indictment by jury, no appeal by an individual, no accusation by the king's prosecutor but merely a statement of the crimes which the crown held Wallace to have committed, terminating with the judgement.'[89] Stress was laid on the murder of the sheriff of Lanark, of issuing writs like those of a king, of holding parliaments, assemblies and counselling the magnates of his party not to submit to the King of England. He had invaded England, burned or laid waste religious houses, killed clergy, women and children. He had sought to compass the death of the king.

There was no need to trump up an indictment, overstate the case or repeat the wilder propaganda. Wallace only spoke out on one charge, that of being a traitor since he had never sworn or owed allegiance to Edward I. Wallace and later generations certainly saw the charge in this light. As he sat alone in Westminster Hall amongst a hostile crowd he left a calling cry to later generations. As a 'Scot of Scottish birth' he owed no allegiance to any king of England. The legal case was not so simple. Wallace was not accused of breaking his allegiance, but being unmindful of it. The court recognised that he himself had not sworn an oath of allegiance, but that it was enough that a lord spoke on his tenant's behalf. When Balliol had returned to homage in 1296 his submission, and that of the tenants-in-chief in the Ragman Roll was inclusive of his subjects.

Wallace suffered an horrific death. For the crime of treason he was drawn on a door of a hall made fast to a horse's tail to his place of execution, from Westminster to the Tower of London, through Aldgate to the Elms at Smithfield. For the crime of robbery, murder and felony he was hanged until near to death, then disembowelled. For the crime of sacrilege his entrails (believed to give rise to blasphemous thoughts) were burned. For the crime of sedition his body was dismembered, the parts displayed as a deterrent. His head was impaled on a spike on London Bridge, his right arm on Newcastle bridge, the left at Berwick, his right foot at Perth, the left at Stirling. Contrary to popular belief this punishment was not devised for Wallace. During Edward's Welsh wars David ap Gryffydd had suffered a similarly barbaric death and there are similar cases which predate this.

Wallace was feared and hated in England. His public death after a show trial was an occasion for much rejoicing. The crime of treason was a personal one, against Edward himself not the state. But Wallace was not executed for this. The execution of a rebel was unusual: during the Baron's rebellion no one had been executed. Edward had shown leniency to other rebels, even to men such as Simon Fraser and William Oliphant; but although they had been outlawed, they eventually surrendered to Edward's authority. Wallace had not. Whatever the legal correctness of Wallace's trial this was a personal matter. Wallace's execution was a failure for Edward. He did not want Wallace's death, he wanted his abject submission. He wanted Wallace to lie prostrate before him and beg for mercy. Once he had been caught Wallace had no interests that could save him, no lobby to defend him. He could be executed with impunity.

History, particularly in the Romantic period imbued with the nationalism that he came to represent, has been kind to Wallace. It has painted a life of tragic heroism. He is so closely tied to the Scottish collective identity that it is difficult to distinguish the man from the legend that he became. As it turned out, this was the high point of English attempts to conquer Scotland. When the English chronicler

Walter of Guisborough wrote that Wallace 'was joined by an immense number of the Scots, for the community of the land followed him as their leader and chief. Moreover all the followers of the magnates adhered to him; and as for the magnates themselves, they were with our King in body, but their heart was far from him'.[90]

Guisborough was forecasting Wallace's lasting appeal. He fired the embers of nationalism by uniting the people in common cause. He had created a gulf between England and Scotland that no English king would ever be able to bridge.

Chapter 5

THE MAKING
OF A KING

*'We are given to understand the earl of Carrick is
attempting to seize the realm of Scotland.'*
Anonymous English Correspondent

In February 1306 the king's justices met to hold an assize in Dumfries. There was nothing extraordinary in the meeting, just another day in the business of government. Robert Bruce was nearby at his castle of Lochmaben, John Comyn of Badenoch, the Red Comyn, at his in Dalswinton. On the 10th these two political adversaries took the opportunity offered by the assizes to confer. They withdrew to a private conference in the Greyfriars kirk, where an argument broke out, swords were drawn and Comyn was killed before the high altar. That much is known. Any more has to be deciphered from later Scottish chroniclers,[1] who made a concerted effort to whitewash the episode; or to the equally biased English chroniclers, hostile to a rebel whose success was seen as an insult to the memory of a much revered king. It will never be known exactly what took place between the two men in the church.

John of Fordun wrote the principal Scottish account 70 years afterwards and it has been further embroidered by later chroniclers. According to Fordun, Bruce had offered Comyn a deal that 'with an eye to the common advantage' Comyn should assume the kingship and give Bruce all his private lands, or to allow Bruce to reign in return for his lands. A similar agreement to the one made by Bruce's grandfather and count Florence during the Great Cause. If, as seems likely, Bruce was planning to make a claim for the kingdom his cause would need either the support or elimination of John Comyn, who had been the key man in Scotland for much of the struggle with Edward. As a former guardian and nephew of king John, son of Balliol's sister Eleanor, he represented the legitimate kingship. The Balliol inheritance would rest with him should the line die out (there was a direct heir in Edward Balliol). He would bring with him the support of the patriot party.

A Bruce-Comyn covenant is plausible and is common to all sources—

disagreement surrounds its timing. Comyn was certainly not the first confident of Bruce's plans. On 11 June 1304, while the two men were bystanders at the siege of Stirling, Bruce met with Bishop Lamberton in Cambuskenneth Abbey and entered into an indenture to aid the other 'against any persons whatsoever', omitting the normal clause saving loyalty to the king of England. The unspecified arduous business the document refers to must have been the Bruce claim to the throne. It would seem likely that Bruce had sounded out other sympathetic supporters, probably Bishop Wishart of Glasgow, perhaps also some of his traditional allies.

Barbour dates the Bruce-Comyn covenant to the same period, as the two men were riding together. These sources have Comyn accepting Bruce's indenture to which both men set their seals. Comyn then secretly and treacherously revealed the covenant to Edward, who summoned Bruce to an English parliament to explain himself. The king handed Bruce the sealed indenture and asked if he recognised it. Bruce told the king that he had forgotten his seal and would return with it next day so that he could compare them.

Edward confided to Ralph Monthermer earl of Gloucester that he planned to have Bruce arrested. That night Gloucester sent a messenger to Bruce with twelve pence and a pair of spurs. Bruce was aware of the danger, he gave the messenger the pence and keeping the spurs fled that night to Scotland. We can discount the dramatic Edwardian scene. There was no English parliament held at this time, and the idea that Edward trusted Bruce until he could find firm evidence to show otherwise is a touching mockery of what we know of the English king. This effort to palliate the murder, to find just cause, has left Bruce open to the charge of premeditation, that he had invited Comyn to the church to be killed.

With a twist this line has been followed by English chroniclers where the suggestion of premeditation implicit in the Scottish sources is simply made explicit. The *Scalacronica* has Bruce sending his brothers to commit the murder, but they could not go through the deed when they found Comyn too courteous and friendly. There is no question of treachery on Comyn's part, rather he is presented as the victim: this promotion of Comyn as innocent and trusting in contrast to Bruce as furtive and deadly is common to English accounts.

So when did Comyn learn of Bruce's plans? Comyn was an old enemy. It seems unlikely that the covenant was made as early as 1304 and that Comyn sat on this valuable information for two years. The balance of probabilities, and it can be no more than this, is that when the two men met Comyn either knew nothing of Bruce's plans and was told at the church, or had only recently been told and Bruce was hearing his answer for the first time. Despite the chronicle evidence, everything points to a murder in hot blood. They had brawled in Selkirk forest five years earlier. And if Bruce was planning to murder his rival it is incredible to believe he would choose to do so before the high altar of a church, adding sacrilege to the crime. It was a reckless, spur-of-the-moment act that cast a shadow over Robert's kingship, but it was not planned.

As Badenoch fell Robert Comyn, John's uncle, attacked Bruce but was slain by Christopher Seton, Bruce's Yorkshire brother-in-law. When he left the church Bruce told his esquires that he was not sure if Comyn was dead, to which Kirkpatrick answered 'Doubt ye? I'll mak siccar' (make sure). This gruesome finale may be invention, although both Scottish and English traditions have Comyn despatched at a second attempt as he was being nursed by the friars.

Bruce had no alternative but to take the initiative. From the Greyfriars kirk he took the nearest horse, Comyn's as it happened, and rode to his castle at Lochmaben. Once prepared he returned to Dumfries where the justices had barred the doors of their hall. They surrendered when threatened that the building would be burned down around them and were allowed safe conduct to England. It was six weeks between now and Bruce's installation as king.

* * *

The story of 1306 and 1307 is that of one man, of Robert Bruce and his metamorphosis from an ally of the English to a patriot. Bruce's early career is the history of Scotland that dare not speak its name. He was an unlikely patriotic leader. By 1306 he 'seemed to have purged himself of any excessive Scottishness.'[2] His marriage to Elizabeth de Burgh, daughter of the Earl of Ulster, bound him closely to the English aristocratic elite and the court. When Robert Bruce VII lord of Annandale died in March 1304, Robert VIII became one of the wealthiest men in Britain. He was now lord of Annandale and held part of Garioch as well as the earldom of Carrick. Bruce also had vast estates in England, a house in London and the suburban manor of Tottenham.[3]

Popular historians, from John of Fordun down to the present day, have conjured up all sorts of excuses to mitigate Robert Bruce's pre-patriotic years. They present his actions as those of a young man too dominated by his father. They have given him a far greater role in the first Wars of Independence, attributing actions to him in the period before his surrender for which there is no evidence. This is unfortunate, since we do not need to be too critical of Bruce, merely recognise that his actions to date were simply those of a man of his age. Only two Scots of rank—John Soules and William Wallace—ever kept unswerving loyalty to the nationalist cause; both were younger sons who had little to lose.

In the feudal world a man owed his loyalty to his family, not his country. To press his family's claim to the throne, for his ambition to outweigh his patriotism, would have been expected of Bruce. After all, when the Comyn family's interests were threatened by the Bruce revival, they too sought help from Edward. Robert Bruce and the Comyns were thus two sides of the same coin: acting on behalf of their family, whose interests at this point were tied to the patriotic cause.

When Bruce of Annandale died, Bruce of Carrick lost a restraining Anglophile influence. As head of the family he was now the legitimate Bruce claimant to the throne: a claim denied by Edward to his father and grandfather but one that had never been abandoned. He had resented his treatment since his surrender in 1302, which had gone unrewarded. He had not taken part in the parliament that issued the Ordinances, and although he was a member of the council who advised the new lieutenant he was not pre-eminent. Bruce had never completely regained Edward's confidence and by the middle of 1305 was losing favour at the English court. The ordinances for the settlement of Scotland contain a passage referring to the earl of Carrick, that he 'be ordered to put the castle of Kildrummy in the keeping of a man for whom he himself is willing to answer.'[4] It is an enigmatic paragraph, made more so as it is sandwiched between ordinances dealing with the punishment of Alexander Lindsay and Simon Fraser. This seems more than a coincidence. It is unlikely that Edward knew Bruce was plotting against him, but his lack of confidence in the earl can only have been because 'he knew of Bruce's consuming ambition for the Scottish throne, knew that he had played Bruce false over it, and knew that Bruce now, with the collapse of the Balliol right, had an alternative—rebellion.'[5]

Bruce had become convinced that if it had any hope of escaping English domination, Scotland had to tie itself with his own ambitions to become king. By identifying his cause with that of the community of the realm he appeared less selfish, less ambitious. This theme, of the king's subjection to the community, was later developed, particularly in the Declaration of Arbroath, as a means to legitimise his kingship. The experiment with Guardians as the realm's safeguard had failed; king John had not lifted a finger to forward his cause for nearly a decade.

Convincing Bruce was one thing, convincing the community was another. It was no small thing what Bruce asked of the patriotic movement: 'A Scot who came out for Bruce in 1306 was deliberately forsaking something the Scots had been fighting for since 1296—a legitimate, constitutional kingship lawfully adjudged to John Balliol—and was, moreover, supporting a man who had slain, in church and at peace, one of the greatest of his fellow nobles, who had himself played a leading part in the Scot's struggle for freedom for some six years.'[6] Bruce was not just resuming a war of liberation—he was starting a civil war.

We have to rely on English documentary evidence for much of the Wars of Independence: Scottish records have mostly been lost, destroyed or stolen. But from now on this lack of Scottish documentary evidence is balanced by the work of John Barbour, the archdeacon of Aberdeen, who wrote a poetic account of the king's life, *The Brus,* in 1375. The book's tone is set in the first chapter, with some of the most famous lines in Scottish literature:

> Ah! Fredome is a noble thing
> Fredome mays man to haiff likin.
> Fredome all solace to man giffis,
> He levys at es that frely levys.[7]

It is the most complete history of any medieval monarch, using sources that are now lost, together with the recollections of eye-witnesses. Sometimes Barbour is frustrating—for example, he gives no year dates in the entire work which has left many areas still open to debate, especially as he is willing to telescope events to add to the romantic drama. He is prone to exaggerate, to elevate his champion to an heroic stature, and at times he verges on hagiography. And then just when his story seems to have become too extraordinary, too unbelievable, he is backed up by English records or chronicles. He is worth reading for making Bruce a man of flesh and blood who cannot be found in the dry records that are normally the stuff of medieval historians—but he should still be treated with the same caution reserved for any medieval source. It is history written by the victor at the expense of the large numbers of Scots who fought for Scottish independence, but not for Robert Bruce.

The details of Bruce's movements after the murder are contained in a newsletter written by an Englishman in Berwick shortly before his installation as king in March.[8] Within eight days of the murder, by 18 February, Bruce had moved to Glasgow where 'the wicked bishop remains as his chief advisor.' Bishop Wishart's duty as a man of the church was clear, he should have excommunicated Bruce. But we are told he absolved him from the crime. Excommunication would follow, on 18 May Clement V passed sentence of excommunication for sacrilege. Bruce sought absolution from Clement who ordered his chief penitentiary to investigate the case: to this end a commission was sent in July 1308 to the abbot of Paisley. There must be some doubt over the authenticity of this document as Bruce remained excommunicate for many years.[9] Wishart then made Bruce swear an oath that he would maintain the independence of the Scottish church.

After meeting the Bishop, Bruce received the fealty of the people and told the men of the district to be ready to be called out at 24 hours notice. This is important,only a king could issue such instructions. By claiming kingship now he could appropriate the machinery of royal authority. It

Robert Bruce's first campaign 1306-7

seems more than likely that Bruce's claim to the throne came at the patriotic bishop's shrewd counsel. As a tenant-in-chief Bruce held the right to call out the men of his lordships of Annandale and Carrick. The young earl of Mar was his ward, so Bruce could call out the men of that earldom. This would not be enough to protect himself from his enemies. By making a claim for the throne he had opened the possibility of legally demanding the service of men outside the districts he controlled. The actions he took in the first few weeks are concerned with self-preservation. He was protecting himself both from the vengeance of the Comyns and king Edward's justice.

This interpretation fits in with the reaction from the council at Berwick. By an extraordinary piece of good fortune the lieutenant, John of Brittany, had not yet taken up his post; in February Lamberton, of all people, had been made temporary warden with John de Sandale, Robert Keith and John Kingston.[10] The council ordered Bruce to surrender the king's castles and 'the towns that belonged to John Comyn and should belong to the king because of the death of John.' Had they believed that Bruce was making a claim for the throne then this demand, the council being concerned at the legal implications of Comyn's estates escheating to the king, would have been comic understatement. The newsletter reports the only contact with Bruce, a request made directly by Bruce to Edward. The actual document is lost, the only information is a second hand reference contained in the newsletter. The letter's writer informs his correspondent that Bruce 'would take castles, towns and peoples as fast as he could,' until he received an answer, and if not granted 'he would defend himself with the biggest stick that he had.' We do not know the question or the answer. The request has been taken to mean Bruce's claim to the kingdom, but this is far from clear: Bruce makes no claim to protect his nation or his country, it reads more like a request for a pardon.[11]

Bruce returned to the west and captured the royal castles at Ayr and Dumfries, and Comyn's castle at Dalswinton. Tibbers castle fell, the commander, Richard Siward, held prisoner inside. Most of the castles Bruce took in these early days of his rebellion were re-occupied shortly afterwards: Tibbers had an English garrison on 22 February, Dumfries on 3 March, Durisdeer on 1 May.[12] Bruce did not have the man-power to defend them. Instead, they were plundered to reinforce his castles at Loch Doon, in the wild central Galloway highlands, and Dunaverty, on the tip of Kintyre, which had been obtained by exchange from Malcolm McQuillan.

Bruce made war in Galloway, but the men of Galloway were Balliol loyalists who would not support his kingship easily.[13] Roger Boyd captured Rothesay and went on to besiege Inverkip, held for the Anglo-Scots by Adam of Gordon 'until help comes from the king.'[14] Orders to send half the English army's supplies to Ayr were superseded in April; the whole sent to Skinburness while the seamen were told to keep the high seas but not approach Ayr or Galloway on any account.[15] This suggests Bruce also held Ayr. Loch Doon, Ayr, Turnberry, Dunaverty and Rothesay are closely knit, they could provide mutual support and deny English access to the west of Galloway from Skinburness. They would also let Bruce bring mercenaries from Ireland and, should it be needed, provide an escape route. Bruce then crossed north of the Forth with 60 men-at-arms. This was the opening stage of the journey towards Scone, stopping at Dumbarton castle where he appealed unsuccessfully for John of Menteith to surrender.

* * *

It was important for a man who was usurping the throne that the ceremony of inauguration was modelled closely on the traditional ceremony of the kings of Scotland. This would not be easy. Edward had pilfered the stone of Scone in 1296; the 16-year old Earl Duncan of Fife who enjoyed the ancient MacDuff right of installing a Scottish king was a ward at the English court; the bishop of St Andrews was in the Scottish council at Berwick. Bruce had to make do, on 25 March the ceremony took place. There were no bishops present, Wishart had remained in the west. He had given Bruce some of the trappings of kingship: robes from his wardrobe and, in a nice touch, the lion banner of the last king of Scotland that he had hidden when Edward I was busy looting the outward signs of Scottish kingship ten years earlier.

Although the stone of Scone was in London Edward could not remove the abbey, itself the site of ancient Scottish kingship: he would try, later seeking permission of the pope to have the abbey removed to another diocese to prevent a recurrence.[16] The place of Fife was taken by his aunt, Isabel of Fife, the countess of Buchan, who slipped away from her husband, who was in his estates in Leicester. She took his horses to make sure that he could not follow. The English chroniclers explain her devotion to Bruce as the actions of a mistress. It was she who placed a gold coronet on Bruce's head. Bruce was not crowned (Scottish kings were not crowned until 1329); the coronet served to distinguish the king.[17] Lamberton left the king's council in the middle of the night, crossed the Forth and was at Scone where he performed high-mass for the new king on 27 March. Lamberton later claimed that he had merely gone to speak to Bruce, who had bullied him into holding the ceremony.

There is little chronicle evidence for the three months between the coronation and the battle of Methven. Atholl besieged Brechin. Wishart lent timber assigned to the rebuilding of his bell-tower to make siege engines to take Kirkintilloch. The bishop seized Cupar, holding it '*homme de guerre*', as ' man of war.' The king went north, to Dundee, though he took the town the castle withstood a siege. There is also evidence of damage to the castles at Forfar, Aboyne and Aberdeen. Alexander Abernethy found Forfar burned and destroyed, he made what repairs he could and believed he could hold out against an assault until relief arrived.

Bruce's support was thinly spread. His prospects seemed bleak. In Bower's words: 'not only did he raise his hand against the mighty king of England, but also devoted himself to a struggle against one and all in the kingdom of Scotland, with the exception of a very few well disposed to him.'[18] The *Scalacronica* credits him with 'a strong following through kinship and alliance.'[19] That would be the men of Annandale and Carrick together with some of his natural allies. We can include John Strathbogie earl of Atholl, Malcolm II earl of Lennox and Murdoch earl of Mentieth. As important as the support of the magnates was that of the church where a similar division existed. His two important adherents were Wishart from Glasgow and David Murray of Moray. The medieval church was a powerful ally as the only source of information for many in society and so a potent conduit for propaganda. Wishart and Murray preached from their pulpits that a war against England was as holy as one against the infidel.[20]

Amongst the country's leaders this was still a minority faction. No more than a third of the Scottish earls supported him: Bruce was actively opposed by the Earls of Strathearn, Buchan, March, Angus, and Ross. John Strathbogie's son, David, who inherited the earldom in 1307 would also be counted amongst these men. The earls of Sutherland and Caithness were minors, their earldoms falling under the earl of Ross's influence. Apart from Dunbar and Angus it would be difficult to describe this as a pro-English party. They had been at the forefront of the community of the realm that had been defying the English conquest.

Bishop Lamberton claimed he only supported Bruce under duress. He told an inquisition in Newcastle 'that on the occasion [of meeting Edward] he had utterly forgotten the confederacy' with Robert Bruce he had made in 1304 and found amongst his possessions. Lamberton could only fall back on the lame excuse that he had gone to Bruce to speak with him, adding 'that because of Robert Bruce's severe threats made against him, both in regard to his person and property, and for no other cause, he went to him to mollify his will, for which he declared he was now very sorry.' Lamberton is not a convincing witness. One of his inquisitors was John Sandale, fellow council member at Berwick. His line of questioning was straightforward, that the bishop had 'left the council secretly and by night, not under pressure, or unwittingly, but of his own free will'. Lamberton had support in the English court and made his peace with Edward in August 1308.[21]

The tactics he describes have the ring of truth about them. Strathearn told a record of inquisition that Bruce had sent a messenger demanding his homage and military service. Strathearn had replied that he would have nothing to do with Bruce. The king and Atholl combined their forces and marched on Strathearn's earldom. Robert issued safe conducts to meet the earl but cancelled them. Strathearn told a furious Atholl that his loyalty was 'as fragile as glass.' Strathearn was imprisoned on the isle of Inchmartin where the keeper, Roger Boyd, urged Bruce to put him to death; Atholl harried his lands, and Bruce warned him that he would hang if he did not submit. This intimidation brought a reluctant and short-served homage.[22]

Outside his core followers the evidence for the popularity of Bruce's rising is less tangible. Barbour reveals little of these three months, suggesting he did not know what happened, and he just makes the throwaway comment that the king 'friends and frendschip purchanesand.'[23] After the battle of Methven Edward had a list of forfeited landowners made: 135 men mainly from Perthshire, Ayrshire and Lennox, Aberdeen, Banff and Moray, where the bishop was preaching his crusade.

Strathearn was not alone in falling under Bruce's iron hand. At Dundee Bruce took six foreign merchants into his train, another three from Aberdeen, kept to ensure local obedience.[24] Bruce resorted to pressure, intimidation and force to recruit men. This is hardly surprising, he was not inviting them to a tea party. There were many in Scotland who deeply resented the way in which Scottish kingship had been broken. They resented still further English garrisons and English lords, whose presence was a constant reminder of ten years of war and defeat. But however much the Scots hated the English many would have weighed up Bruce's chances and found the odds stacked against him too great to come out in 1306. Where Bruce could not go, into Comyn territory in the country north of Inverness, or in the heavily garrisoned south-east, he had few recruits.

* * *

Despite the apparent weakness of Bruce's cause it was the English and Balliol patriots who sank into the background as the news of Bruce's kingship spread. The main garrisons received reinforcements but no offensive action was taken.[25] Edward had retired for the winter to the south coast. His health had seriously deteriorated with the illness that would eventually kill him. For much of the time he was carried on a litter, although the sickness that ate away at his body did not weaken his determination. Edward's grip on events remained as tight as ever. He was in Winchester in February when news arrived of the rebellion. At first he seems to have refused to believe that Bruce was involved. On 23 February he committed Comyn's English lands to John Moubray until the succession was settled.

The following day he sent instructions to his escheator south of the Forth, James Dalisle, to see to the peace and quite of his lieges in his district because John Comyn had been murdered '*by some people* who are doing their utmost to trouble the peace and quiet of the realm of Scotland.'[26] The news was still hazy and Bruce's guilt not yet established.

When events became clearer at the beginning of March 1306, steps were made to form a new army.[27] Bruce's lands were confiscated and awarded to Humphrey Bohun earl of Hereford and his wife Elizabeth, the king's daughter.[28] With immediate effect Aymer de Valence was made lieutenant in Lothian, Yorkshire and Northumberland with the power to muster foot at eight days notice. Valence was in his mid-thirties; he would not inherit the earldom of Pembroke until the death of his mother in April 1308 so he had no large barony to support himself. He came to the fore as one of the ablest English captains. Barbour describes him as a worthy knight. Praise indeed from a source who found few amongst the English worthy of any accolades. He was also the brother-in-law of the murdered Comyn. Henry Percy was made lieutenant in Galloway and the north-west, Valence's junior companion. The lieutenants had under their commands the now familiar and formidable northern captains, in the east Henry Grey, William Latimer, Aymer and William le Zouche, and Richard Lovel; in the west, Robert Clifford with the men of the Durham bishopric, John de St John, Thomas Payne and Robert Felton.[29]

Valence rallied the local forces and went north towards the end of May. He did not have a large army. The pay records give him 50 knights, 21 esquires, 140 arbelasters and 1,960 archers.[30] Besides the warden of Berwick, Roger Fitzroger, he had support from Comyn sympathisers: John Moubray, Ingram Umfraville, and Alexander Abernethy. They aimed at Perth where Edward had built a ditch, palisade and peel there in 1304, one of the few fortified towns in Scotland.

* * *

Valence's campaign is recorded in a series of letters between the lieutenant and king. It is easy to sense Edward's powerlessness as he chided the earl for not sending news fast enough. In the first half of June alone he wrote to Valence on the 8th, 9th 12th, and 16th (twice). His life's work seemed complete and then he saw his victory snatched from him just as it was too late to do anything about it. It was all too much for this old, dying man. He was not in a forgiving mood. In one of Barbour's most chilling passages, Valence was ordered to 'Byrn and Slay and raise dragoun'.[31] Edward had confided in the magnates, he had trusted them, included them in his plans for Scotland, they had sworn allegiance to him, and now they had rebelled. The king told Valence to receive the 'middling' men into his peace, but not the magnates.[32]

Simon Fraser's lands were to be burnt, and the same to all king's enemies on his march: 'and to burn, destroy and waste their houses, lands, and goods in such wise, that Sir Simon and others may no have refuge with them as heretofore.' Four days later he sent instructions to do the same to the lands and gardens of Michael Wemyss and Gilbert de la Hay, 'or worse if possible' as the king had done him great courtesy when he was last in London. Only Bruce, Atholl and Simon Fraser were to escape summary execution, guarded until the king's pleasure was known.[33]

The king urged Valence to 'take the utmost pains' to capture the bishops of Glasgow and St Andrews. A detachment took Wishart at Coupar by the 8 June. Edward wrote that he was 'almost as much pleased as if it had been the earl of Carrick.' Lamberton proved a little more elusive, but less of a threat. He had tried to secure an English safe-conduct which the king refused and had then written to Valence to assert his innocence. It seems likely that he gave himself up to Valence. They were sent south with the Abbot of Scone. Their episcopal rank saved their lives, if not fetters for the journey and irons in jail. Wishart was sent to Porchester castle, Lamberton to Winchester, and the abbot to Mere in Wiltshire. Edward sent money to the cardinal of St Sabina who had suffered the loss of property in a fire. He took the opportunity to press the cardinal to advance the case of William Comyn, brother of the Earl of Buchan and Geoffrey Moubray, brother of John Moubray, to the bishoprics of St Andrews and Glasgow in place of Lamberton and Wishart.[3]

Bruce approached Valence at Perth on 19 June from the mountains in the west with his force split into two divisions. This was an opportunity to defeat the English before the king arrived with the full host. It suggests Bruce's force was larger than that available to Valence. Still, the knights wore white shirts over their heraldic blazons—they may have been eager to fight but understood the consequences of their rebellion and did not want to be identified. Bruce offered battle but Valence declined. It was a Sunday and he was not prepared to take on a force already arrayed on the ground of its own choosing.

Bruce waited outside Perth until midday then retired to the forest at Methven, six miles west of the town to set up camp. His army scattered, some on a foraging party, some to find quarters. It was at this point that Valence's force fell on the Scottish camp. Bruce's cavalry mounted and although fighting was fierce, Valence had a horse killed from beneath him, and they could not hold off the English who swept through the camp. The battle soon turned into a rout. Tradition has John Haliburton seizing the reins of Bruce's horse but letting go when he recognised the king. Bruce managed to extricate much of the chivalry. The 'small folk' were left on the field. In his first battle with the English Bruce had shown poor leadership. He had divided his force, left his camp poorly defended and as a result lost some of his key supporters. He had captured the public's imagination and led them to defeat. The heart went out of Scottish resistance. Bruce's nephew, Thomas Randolph, was captured and kept in Inverkip castle by Adam Gordon.[35] He would fight for the English until his recapture by the Scots in 1309. Others would not be so fortunate.

* * *

A second English army now moved into Scotland. In May Edward rallied the knighthood of England in an event that was aimed at stirring the cult of Arthur into the country's chivalry to ensure they played a part in the new enterprise. He called all the eligible young men of the realm to London where they were knighted with the prince of Wales. Caernarfon and his close friends spent the night before in an abbey in 'quiet contemplation' that was so noisy the monks could not sleep!

Three hundred appeared, the numbers so great two knights died in the crush. Swans were brought into the evening feast, their necks draped with chains of gold. Edward rose and swore 'before God and the swans' that he would not rest until the death of Comyn and the insult to the church had been avenged after which he would never again fight Christian men. When he sat Caernarfon rose and swore never to rest two nights in the same place until Bruce had been defeated. The rest of the knights followed suit. And so the king passed on the work of invading Scotland to a new generation and guaranteed that the endless cycle of Anglo-Scottish warfare would not end with his death.

Edward was too ill to campaign and sent Caernarfon ahead. He had with him all the components of a feudal army and infantry from Wales. Added to these must have been the young men who swore to avenge Comyn's death and the magnates with an interest to win the lands Edward had confiscated from the rebels. He entered Scotland at Carlisle and immediately took Lochmaben. The garrison surrendered on the day he arrived when promised a fair trial. And there Caernarfon stopped. A letter from the prince's camp to Valence explained that he had spent all his provisions since leaving Carlisle so he would remain in the district for three to four days collecting new supplies before moving to Perth to join up with Valence's division.[36]

To have run out of supplies so soon into the campaign seems incompetent. In part it can be explained by the pope's residency in Bordeaux. The curia consumed so much of Gascony's wine that there was a general shortage in England which remained a problem until the curia settled in Avignon.[37] The breakdown in supply arrangements was due to the absence of the king's experienced wardrobe officials. In Chester the prince's men had taken all the ships so that the king's officials had no way of transporting the supplies that had been amassed in Shropshire and Staffordshire. Ten ships had to be diverted from north Wales. This confusion must have been common. The prince eventually found his supplies and headed off towards Perth. On 2 July the admirals of the two fleets were sent to Skinburness and Kirkcudbright to ferry supplies north 'as the king's magnates and others sent by him to Scotland have so far progressed against his enemies there that they have arrived at the town of St John, Perth.'[38] Like Cressingham ten years earlier the prince was none too pleased that Bruce had been defeated without him.

* * *

After Methven Bruce fled into the hills with the chivalry that had been able to disengage from the battle. Valence was close behind. The only record of a second action is a claim in the English wardrobe accounts for horses lost at Loch Tay. Robert d'Arcy and Giles d'Argentine, two knights who had the misfortune to lose destriers at Methven, lost more horses here.[39] Again, Bruce managed to withdraw with his force intact.

With his enemies closing in, Bruce's only avenue of escape lay in the south-west, to the isles or to Ireland. At Dail Righ (Dalry, 'kings meadow'), on the borders of Perthshire near Tyndrum, his route was blocked by John Macdougall of Lorn and the barons of Argyll. Macdougall was the son of Alexander Macdougall of Argyll, a kinsman of Comyn. This third battle was too much. Bruce's army was shattered. The horses were given to the ladies of the party who were sent under the earl of Atholl's protection to Kildrummy, held by Neil Bruce. The king escaped as a hunted fugitive into the hills. Barbour has his party reduced to 200 followers, amongst them Neil Campbell and Douglas. Lennox had become separated from the fugitives.

At Loch Lomond Douglas found a boat that could only carry three men. He took the king across and then began to ferry the rest of the men across. All the while Bruce sat on the far bank reading a twelfth century French romance, *Fierabras*. The Macdonalds had always been loyal supporters of Edward but they had an overriding hatred of the Macdougalls. That inter-clan hostility now came to Bruce's rescue. He was now under the protection of Angus Og Macdonald. From Loch Lomond he fled to the Isle of Bute and then to Dunaverty castle.

Henry Percy was reported at Dunaverty on 9 September. A siege had certainly begun by the 22nd when Caernarfon was asked to send miners to help John Mentieth and John Botetort. The castle surrendered to the earl of Lancaster towards the end of the month.

Bruce was no longer inside. He had feared for his safety at Dunaverty and left after only three days. He then disappears from the historical record, not to be heard of again for over four months. Hugh Bisset of the

Glens received orders from Edward in January 1307 to join John Menteith and the Somerset baron Simon Montagu with his ships to search for Bruce and 'destroy his retreat in the isles between Scotland and Ireland.' Bisset's loyalty to Edward has been questioned but a large English fleet out of Skinburness and Ayr did search for Bruce.[40] The season was too late; he could not be found. Barbour has Bruce escaping with the help of Neil Campbell and the earl of Lennox to the island of Rathlin off the Antrim coast. Fordun says that he was aided by Christiana MacRuairidh who held extensive lands in the West Highlands and Islands.[41] There is no reason to disbelieve either of them. It seems unlikely that he made the journey to the court of his sister's husband, Eric II of Norway, though he may have. We can forget the idea that he spent the time watching spiders. More likely he began to raise forces along the western seaboard, perhaps in Ireland certainly in the western isles. In November he sent his agents into Carrick to uplift rents that would help to buy mercenaries.

The adventures of Robert Bruce over the next year became legend in his own life time. Barbour retells many of them but his account does not form a coherent narrative. Many of the stories are of local or anecdotal tradition. The Scottish chronicler Fordun eschews Barbour's detail but his account is probably as close as we can get to the character of the king's flight:

> 'The king was cut off from his men, and underwent endless woes, and was tossed in dangers untold, being attended at times by three followers, at times by two, and more often he was left alone, utterly without help. Now passing a whole fortnight without any food of any kind to live upon, but raw herbs and water; now walking barefoot, when his shoes became old and worn out; now left alone in the islands; now alone, fleeing before his enemies; now slighted by his servants; he abode in utter loneliness. An outcast among the nobles, he was forsaken and the English bade him be sought for through the churches like a lost or stolen thing. And thus he became a byword and a laughing stock for all, both far and near to hiss at.'[42]

Edward treated Bruce's followers with unprecedented savagery. Two knights, David of Inchmartin and John of Cambo, the king of Scots' hereditary standard bearer, Alexander Scrymgeour, together with eleven others were hanged in Newcastle. There was no trial, no jury, no defence, merely a statement of crimes the men had committed followed by the sentence. John Seton was taken at Tibbers. He was drawn to his place of execution for his part in Comyn's murder.[43]

Christopher Seton was taken in Bruce's castle at Loch Doon about 26 August: he was hanged and drawn at Dumfries. Simon Fraser had raised a force in Selkirk Forest. He was not able to break out of the forest and was captured at the battle of Kirkencliffe near Stirling with a large number of 'knights and swains, freemen and thanes.' John de Lindsay waded into the water to drown rather than be captured.[44] Fraser was sent to London to meet the same grisly death as Wallace. His body and the gallows were burned on Edward's orders, his head stuck on a pole next to Wallace. Herbert Moreham had not been released in the general amnesty of 1304. He had been a household knight, in receipt of wages and robes from Edward, and as such his obligation to the king was greater, more personal than the other prisoners. He had rashly wagered his head that Simon Fraser would never be captured. The day after Fraser's execution the king took him, and his esquire for good measure, at his word.[45]

Caernarfon besieged Kildrummy which was taken by 13 September when a traitor set fire to the grain store. Neil Bruce was captured but Atholl and the ladies of the court had already flown. They headed north. The ultimate destination must have been Orkney and Norwegian safety but Anglo-Scottish forces were too close and the party attempted to seek sanctuary at St Duthac in Ross. It was here that they were taken by the earl of Ross. Edward's queen begged him to show mercy to Atholl who was a kinsman (his mother was the great-granddaughter of king John through an illegitimate line). Such things normally mattered to medieval men, but it cut no ice with Edward. In respect of his thin Plantagenet blood Atholl was hanged from taller gallows: the first earl to be executed in England for over 200 years. The captives from Kildrummy, including Neil Bruce, were executed at Berwick.

To his discredit Edward treated Mary Bruce and the countess of Buchan with vindictive cruelty. Specially constructed cages were built for them; the one for the countess may have been in the shape of a crown in recognition of her part in the coronation. Edward expressly ordered that they should be built in towers, but the English chroniclers are explicit that they were open to public view. This was a public punishment, in Scotland (the towers were in Roxburgh and Berwick), to deter others. That they were large, with their own privies, hardly mitigates the punishment. The countess remained in her cage for four years before being released into the custody of the Carmelite friary in Berwick; Mary Bruce remained in Roxburgh, also until 1310, when she was removed to Newcastle before her final release after Bannockburn.

A similar fate awaited Bruce's twelve year-old daughter Marjorie in the Tower of London, but on reflection the king relented and sent her to a Yorkshire nunnery. Another sister, Christina, went to a nunnery in Lincolnshire. The queen had apparently disapproved of the rebellion; she scolded Bruce for playing at kings and queens. Edward approved; besides, she was the daughter of the king's friend and supporter, the earl of Ulster. She was sent to the royal manor at Burtswick in Holderness.

Edward himself moved slowly north towards the border. He was at Newcastle in August 1306 and then began the journey across the Tyne-Solway isthmus to the West March. He arrived at the priory at Lanercost on 29 September. Apart from some repairs to the guest house there was no work on a grand scale for the king's arrival as he only intended to stay a few days. His health was rapidly deteriorating and it was clear quite soon that he would need to rest. Within a day or two of his arrival work had begun to adapt the priory to the needs of the royal household: new timber buildings were constructed to accommodate the 200 members of his personal staff.

The queen and her household moved to the castle at Carlisle where 'her soul was provided for by the construction of a chapel and her body by the installation of a bath.'[46] The king was now in the advanced stages of illness. Two surgeons were in constant attendance. During his respite £164 was paid for 2,196½ lbs of medicines, paid at the flat rate of 18d per pound. He would remain as the expensive guest of the priors for nearly six months.[47] A parliament was held in Carlisle from late January to discuss the settlement in Scotland, but the king could not attend in person so little business of importance was done.

* * *

At the beginning of 1307 Bruce returned to the offensive. In early February he had a force on Kintyre. James Douglas 'wes angry that thai so lang suld ydill ly'[48] and persuaded Robert Boyd to join a raid on the Arran castle of Brodick. The castle had been settled on John Hastings of Abergavenny, as part of the earl of Menteith's confiscated lands.[49] Douglas ambushed a squadron sent to reinforce the castle, winning valuable arms and supplies. Bruce then led his force from Kintyre to join Douglas on Arran.

Barbour interweaves his story with a biography of James Douglas, often at the expense of Bruce's senior lieutenants, his nephew Thomas Randolph and his brother Edward. James Douglas was a true child of the Wars of Independence: brave, chivalrous, bold to the point of foolhardy, he became pivotal to the Scottish military effort. We shall hear far more of him. He was the son of William Douglas who was with Wallace at the beginning of his rebellion and had died in the Tower of London in 1299. James's birth was ascribed to the year of Alexander III's death, so at the time of Bruce's rebellion he was only 20 years-old. Douglas junior had been educated first in Glasgow and then for three

The Winter Campaign 1307-8

years in Paris. This was not unusual for a man of noble birth; neither does it seem unusual that he led a student life, impious and carefree. He was at the siege of Stirling where Edward rebuffed his request to have Douglasdale, awarded to Robert Clifford, restored to him.

The documentary evidence shows a James Douglas retained as a valet in the company of Henry Sinclair and Robert Keith on 6 June 1306, just before Methven, when he received wine and grain from Piers Lubaud at Linlithgow.[50] If this is the same James Douglas (which is by no means certain) then Barbour's account of him must be dismissed as literary invention. This gives rise to an alternative sequence of events, of loyal service by a young man in search of justice in an attempt to regain his inheritance. Disappointed when it became clear that his loyalty would not be rewarded, he saw Bruce's rebellion as the route to secure his lands. He then retook his family castle by force.

The castle was taken twice, the first time on Palm Sunday when the garrison was murdered and the castle slighted in an episode known as the Douglas Larder, the second in May when the garrison was sent home. Professor Duncan has convincingly challenged this chronology. It is much more likely that Barbour has transposed these actions: the Palm Sunday massacre was in the following year, 1308.[51] Daunted by the implications of his personal rebellion Douglas 'begged' (the word used in an English report) to be received back into English peace prior to the encounter at Loudoun Hill. This request could only be contemplated while Douglas could still distance himself from the excesses of the rebellion,and certainly from the atrocity of the Douglas Larder. He only made the firm decision to support Bruce's rebellion at Loudoun Hill when he saw the English retreat.

Bruce led a division into his earldom while a second army led by two of his brothers went to Galloway. Edward I well understood the complex politics of western Scotland, and intervened there with great subtlety. In 1296 Edward personally retained John Balliol's rich lordship of Galloway. His principal tenant in the lordship was the loyal servant John de St John, and after the Caerlaverock campaign his son, also John de St John. The other key Englishman in the west was Henry Percy, the lieutenant of Galloway and sheriff of Ayr: one of Edward's most successful captains. Besides the English presence were the clan chiefs: Macdouall, MacCan and MacCulloch who could be trusted to oppose Bruce.[52]

The Galloway invaders, Thomas and the Oxford scholar Alexander Bruce, an Irish sub-king, Reginald de Crawford, and Malcolm McQuillan lord of Kintyre, commanded a strong following carried in eighteen galleys. Once landed at Loch Ryan they suffered an absolute disaster, beaten back by local partisans under Dungal Macdouall. Only two galleys escaped. Macdouall sent the heads of the Irish king and the lord of Kintyre to Edward at Lanercost. The two Bruces, together with Crawford, were taken to the king. They were dragged at the tails of horses the eight miles to Carlisle where they were hung and beheaded. Edward's now rapidly expanding collection of heads were placed on Carlisle's gates, Thomas's reserved for the keep. Macdouall was rewarded with a knighthood, a gift of 50 marks and a charger.

Bruce's own landing nearly came to a similar end. He had sent a spy to light a warning beacon if a landing was safe but mistook a local fire for the beacon and landed close to a large English detachment. Instead of ready local recruits he found Henry Percy and 300 English troops at Turnberry. The king led a night assault on the English as they bivouacked in the town, slaughtering the troops as they slept. Percy retained the castle so Bruce went to ground before an English counter attack could be organised. It was only on landing in Carrick that Bruce learnt of the fate of his supporters. He now knew that this was no chivalrous game, the price of his ambition had been the loss of all those who were close to him, killed, executed or imprisoned.

Edward constantly expected to receive reports of Robert Bruce's defeat. On 6 February 1307 he wrote to his chancellor to 'express great wonder at having no news of Sir Aymer de Valence and his forces since he went to Ayr.'[53] Five days later he wrote directly to Valence, commanding him 'to write distinctly and cleanly by the bearer, news of the parts where he is, the state of affairs there, and the doings of himself and the others hitherto, and how he and they have arranged for further proceedings. For he suspects from his silence that he had so over-cautiously conducted matters that he wishes to conceal his action.' He sent similar letters to the other English captains dispersed widely throughout the south-west, Ralph Monthermer Earl of Gloucester, Humphrey Bohun Earl of Hereford, John St John and Henry Percy.[54] The English captains had nothing to write, they simply could not find Bruce. John Botetort commanded a foray into Nithsdale. With 19 knights and 51 esquires and a small formation of footsoldiers, he was in the field from 23 February to 3 May, but could find no sign of Bruce. A larger raid went into the wild central region of Galloway along Glen Trool. John Botetort was again present but it seems that Valence had taken personal command of the foray.

It is against this foray that Barbour awards Bruce his first victory over the English. The event was marked in 1929, the 600th anniversary of Bruce's death, with a monument of Galloway granite. Glen Trool is a typical well-developed glaciated valley, U-shaped, the floor filled by Loch Trool which flows out of the base of the valley where Valence's foray would have entered. The steep sides offered Bruce ideal ambush territory against cavalry which would be unable to ride arrayed against Bruce's infantry. This is Barbour's interpretation of the episode, and for want of an alternative has been accepted until recently. But a record in the English wardrobe accounts contradicts Barbour: it merely records the loss of horses 'in the chase against Robert Bruce between Glen Trool and Glenheur.'[56] This episodes sounds more like a hit and run skirmish, a botched ambush followed by an English regrouping and a futile chase.

On 10 May Valence encountered Bruce a second time. Bruce had been in Kyle and Cunningham in Ayrshire, recruiting men. At Loudoun he chose a site to meet the English cavalry that would favour his infantry. Loudoun Hill sits in a fork of two tributaries of the Irvine. Either side of the even and dry high road lay an area of peaty ground, a 'bow-draucht' or arrow's flight wide. The bogs would restrict the English cavalry onto a front narrowed still further by three defensive dikes. Valence sent his two divisions, totalling some 1,500 men, against Bruce's 600-man schiltron. The first division could not break the schiltron and turned back onto the oncoming second rank of cavalry, the confusion turned to flight. Bruce chased Valence back to Ayr. It was only an English relief force that ended Bruce's siege of the town.

The battle of Loudoun is more interesting since it has English corroboration, not just in two chronicles but in a contemporary letter written from Carlisle. Clearly an encounter took place, Edward was furious that an English force had retreated before 'king Hobbe', but not on a scale evinced by Barbour. More likely the English encountered the Scots in a strong defensive position and decided not to press a fight. The defeat of Gloucester with a relieving force three days later is probably fiction. There was certainly no siege of Ayr which remained an open port: Bruce did not have the strength to lay siege to a town and castle the size of Ayr. It has been suggested that this siege has been transposed from an earlier date, probably 1301.[57]

Edward had been so concerned about the lack of news from his local captains that he sent his treasurer, the bishop of Chester, on a fact finding mission in advance of a summer campaign. The bishop left for Ayr on the 8 May, and on the 15th he was at Bothwell, where he ordered James Dalisle to release forty marks to Robert Leybourne, the constable of Ayr, for repairs to the gatehouse and storehouses.[58] It is likely that Bruce, desperately in need of funds, was trying to seize the treasurer and the money he carried. Despite two stunning victories, by August he was alone, hiding in the moors and being hunted by hound and horn by John Macdougall, in command at Ayr with 800 men.[59]

So why have the battles taken on such importance? An official at Forfar castle sent a report to the king five days after Loudoun in which he expressed deep concerns about the loyalty of the locals:

> 'I hear that Bruce never had the good will of his own
> followers or of the people generally so much with him as

now. It appears that God is with him, for he has destroyed king Edward's power both among English and Scots. The people believe that Bruce will carry all before him, exhorted by 'false preachers' from Bruce's army, men who have previously been charged before justices for advocating war and have been released on bail, but are now behaving worse than ever. I fully believe, as I have heard from Reginald Cheyne, Duncan of Frendraught and Gilbert of Glencarnie, who keep the peace beyond the Mounth and on this side, that if Bruce can get away in this direction or towards the parts of Ross he will find the people all ready at his will more entirely than ever, unless king Edward can send more troops for there are many people living loyally in his peace so long as the English are in power'.[60]

The real victory for Bruce lay not in the defeat of two English armies, but that he was able to survive to portray Glen Trool and Loudoun as victories. Bruce commanded little support in the country; after the battle of Methven he more than anybody realised the importance of a victory to his cause.

King Edward made a short recovery from his illness and was able to meet a papal envoy in Carlisle. The feudal host gathered in early July 1307. The grizzled old warrior set off from Carlisle on the 2nd. On the first day he could only manage two miles, two more the day after. On the third he rested. On the fourth he travelled a short distance before being forced to rest in the Cumberland village of Burgh-on-Sands from where he could see Scotland across the Solway. His massive frame could no longer keep pace with his boundless ambition. He died as his servants lifted him to take food. After so many years of firm direction his commanders were at a loss and kept his death secret until Edward Caernarfon arrived eleven days later. On the following day the new king received homage from the men of the kingdom who had gathered to form his father's army.

Edward's illness had been long and the end predictable. Late in the season, when most of the castles held by the patriots had been captured and the hunt for Bruce moved on to the western islands the young knights of the English army became bored with routine garrison duties. Caernarfon had already left for England. In mid-October Edward ordered the sheriffs of 24 counties to seize the lands and goods of 22 deserters, 'knights and other men-at-arms who have crossed to foreign parts for a tournament ... without licence, while the king is engaged in the war in Scotland.'

Queen Margaret became peacemaker and the king's temper soon eased and he pardoned sixteen of the knights. It is not until the names of the knights are read, Giles d'Argentine, Ralph Basset, Walter and William Beauchamp, Henry and Humphrey Bohun, John Chandis, Gilbert, son of Thomas Clare, Peers Gaveston, Roger Mortimer of Wigmore and Payn Tiptoft, that the significance of the episode becomes clear. These were the men who would surround Caernarfon in the early years of his reign, and three of them would be killed at Bannockburn. It must have been all too apparent to the dying king that he was not leaving the realm in mature hands.

In April Gaveston was banished, his intimacy with the prince already causing concern. All Scotsmen, whichever side they were on, had been waiting for this moment. Bower relates a story of an English knight who was terrified by visions of demons raging against the king on the night of his death.[61] The Forfar correspondent had foreseen the future:

> 'May it please God to prolong king Edward's life, for men say openly that when he is gone victory will go to Bruce. For these preachers have told the people that they have found a prophecy of Merlin, that after the death of 'le Roy Coveytous' the people of Scotland and the Welsh shall band together and have full lordship and live in peace together to the end of the world.'[62]

Edward I campaigned tirelessly but despite his battlefield victories he was unable to break the spirit of the Scots. He had no money to fortify Scotland as he had done in Wales. He had alienated the leaders of the Scottish church when he tried to anglicise the church. By his contention of overlordship Edward legitimised his claim, but in the long term this policy failed. As overlord he left in place those men who would swear him fealty: many found submission convenient during a crisis and would consequently break their oaths.

Savage cruelty Edwardian armies, as it does all armies. In 1305 proclamation was made throughout England and Aquitaine for all persons who felt in need of dispensation or absolution for offences committed during the war, directing them to bishops and abbots appointed especially for the purpose. It plainly stated the king's troops had killed many of the enemy 'in accordance with the custom of enemy against enemy'. Edward treated the Scots as rebels against legally constituted authority, and acted as any medieval overlord would when dealing with rebels. He demanded their complete submission to his will, but never exercised the full weight of justice available to him. The Scots saw themselves in quite a different light: their struggle was regarded as a fight to maintain independence against foreign aggression, which compelled them to observe the medieval laws of war.

At the end of his reign Edward was no longer able to forgive the rebels and he embarked on a brief reign of terror, which effectively forced Scots to choose between Robert Bruce or English occupation. Neutrality was no longer an option. Edward realised that he had made a terrible error. In March he wrote to Valence:

> 'As some persons, he understands, interpret his late ordinance for the settling of Scotland as too harsh and rigorous, which was not his intention, he commands him to proclaim through Scotland, that all who have been compelled by the abettors of Robert de Brus to rise against the king in war, or to reset Robert innocently by his sudden coming among then, shall be quit of all manner of punishment.'

It was too late. The mass confiscation of property and the summary execution of prisoners had done more to swell the ranks of Bruce's army than any military success.

Edward died the most revered of English kings. Edward did what medieval kings were supposed to do rather well, particularly as he was bracketed between the truly awful kings, Henry III and Edward II. In recent years historians have concentrated on his underhand treatment of the barony and his intervention in Wales and Scotland. We must not fall into the trap of trying to justify the actions of a man who has been dead for 600 years. By the standards of late twentieth-century western society, Edward I is an unpleasant man, his actions deplorable, but modern liberal attitudes were quite alien to his age. Edward was an opportunist, but one 'imbued with a fierce determination to preserve, protect and enhance his rights as king.'[63] In this respect he was in tune with the patriots in Scotland: his obsession with his rights and the extents of his jurisdiction would contribute to the formation of the nation state in England.

In the time of Elizabeth Tudor, when Edward's reputation was still at intact, the epitaph *Mallus Scottorum* was added to his tomb. Given the ultimate failure of his policy the inscription seems inappropriate. But we should not overstate his failure. At the time of his death there was nothing inevitable about English defeat. After the Ordinance of 1305 many Scots thought it sensible to submit to Edward. The actions of Valence and campaign of Caernarfon had left the new king a fugitive on an isolated island, his lieutenants swinging on the end of English ropes. As Edward lay dying Bruce was being chased around the Galloway countryside by John Macdougall and a pack of bloodhounds. If the king had been five years younger, would one last push have been enough to secure his goal? For the first time Edward had the support not just of the anglophile party but of many patios. When he died there was nothing ordained about Scotland's independence.

Chapter 6

FOR THE KINGDOM OF SCOTLAND

*'It was indeed a mighty undertaking that the king began, taking
unbearable burdens upon his shoulders, for not only did he raise his
hand against the mighty king of England and all his confederates and
flatterers, but also devoted himself to a struggle against one and all in
the kingdom of Scotland ... like a drop of water reckoned against the
waves of the sea'.*
Walter Bower, *Scotichronicon*

The death of the 'Hammer of the Scots' changed the course of the war.
His successor, Edward II, was a very different man, supremely unfitted
for the harsh challenges of medieval kingship. Edward Caernarfon was
already on his way north when news reached him of his father's death.
He hurried to Carlisle where he arrived on 19 July 1307. With an army
already gathered the first thoughts of the new king were of the campaign
in Scotland: his father's funeral and his own coronation would have to
wait. He would need to act fast if he wanted to maintain momentum and
the military ascendancy.

Robert Bruce had yet to score a significant victory but the patriots had
been waiting for this moment: Bruce knew Caernarfon, and appreciated
that he was made of different mettle than his father. Yet Caernarfon had
a powerful army and could strike hard against the patriot cause before
Bruce had time to establish his kingship. Caernarfon took his father's
body as far as York, where it was entrusted to the archbishop for the
remainder of the journey south. He then returned and led three columns
into Scotland, halting for ten days at Dumfries to receive the homage of
a large number of Scottish barons. On 12 August the army set out along
the Nith valley to Cumnock. Here he stayed until 25 August. Having
achieved little, Edward was back in Carlisle by 1 September and then left
for London. He would not return to Scotland for three years.

Towards the end of the 1307 campaign arrangements were made for
the defence of the north of England and the government of Scotland.

Aymer de Valence was appointed guardian on 28 August, but was superseded only two weeks later by Edward's cousin, John of Brittany Earl of Brittany.[1] It is unknown why Edward replaced Valence; it may have been the impulsive influence of Piers Gaveston. Valence was the ablest English commander, respected by both his enemies and his colleagues. Brittany was not; he was untested and would prove to be a mediocre candidate. Without great wealth or standing amongst the lords to push matters forward his lieutenancy could be no more than a holding operation.

Special 'conservators' of the peace were appointed in Cumberland, Westmoreland and Northumberland to 'defend the counties and punish the rebels'. The king told them 'not to be lukewarm' discharging their duties. They had the support of the local sheriffs who could call out the county 'posses'.[2] These new posts can only be explained by the need to defend the northern counties from early cattle raids. In August 1308 Patrick Lerebane, receiver of Alexander Bastenthwaite, was driving animals from Bampton Fair to Carlisle when he was robbed by 'enemies of the king of England.' This may not have been out of the ordinary but the northerners' fears of a large scale invasion were unfounded.[3] These were forces available should Brittany call upon them though Edward warned him that it was 'not the king's will that the levies shall be marched out of their respective counties, unless required by urgent necessity.'[4] In December the king wrote to his allies in Scotland urging them to keep the king's peace, promising to take counsel for the subduing of Bruce's rebellion on his return from France to do homage to Philip IV.

Bruce had retreated into the hills, but as soon as the English army left Scotland he returned to the offensive. Bruce began the recovery of Scotland by punishing the Macdoualls for their actions at Loch Ryan the year before. By late September refugees from Bruce's harrying sought protection in England where Robert Clifford allowed them to feed their flocks and herds in Inglewood forest.[5] When the news of Bruce's victories began to spread: 'Not withstanding the heavy vengeance inflicted on the Scots who took part with Robert Bruce, the multitude of those wishing to confirm him in his kingship was increased day by day.'[6]

John de St John, Dungal Macdouall and Donald MacCan had been unable to hold the district against Bruce who was 'burning and plundering, and inciting and compelling the inhabitants to rebel.' They sought help from Edward who called out the forces available from the northern counties and the Anglo-Scottish captains who were in Berwick for what must have been a council of war.[7]

Edward told Brittany to march on Galloway with his utmost power 'unless he shall think it advisable to march elsewhere, on account of more immediate danger.' Brittany was wrong-footed, though not for lack of warning. While still in Berwick he had received a messenger from

John Macdougall of Lorn with the news that Bruce had left Galloway and was approaching Argyll.[8] Galloway was too dangerous, too close to the English strongpoints. Leaving behind men to ensure the English were kept occupied Bruce had determined to eliminate his enemies in the north, beyond the interference of English garrisons in the south-east. It is this march north, along the Great Glen, that Bruce's grasp of strategy is first evident. This was the decisive moment of the campaign. Action now, in the winter, would mean the English and their allies would have difficulty finding supplies and their lines of communication vulnerable.

The evidence for the winter campaign is meagre, sometimes undated and often contradictory. The interpretation of a badly soiled letter sent to Edward from an English supporter, Duncan of Frendraught, has cleared up many of the outstanding questions surrounding the campaign, but some of its text is illegible or lost at crucial points. It was probably after Valence left Scotland from Bothwell, in the third week in September, that Bruce moved north, an action combined with a naval force sent into Loch Linnhe. This operation persuaded the Macdougalls to enter a temporary truce. Alexander was old, and his son, John of Lorn was sick in Dunstaffnage castle for much of the winter. In March 1308 he wrote to Edward that:

> 'I was confined to my bed with illness, and have been for six months past. Bruce approached these parts by land and sea with 10,000 men, they say, or 15,000. I have no more than 800 men, 500 in my own pay whom I keep continually to guard the borders of my territory. The barons of Argyll give me no aid. Yet Bruce asked for a truce, which I granted him for a short space.'[9]

With his back now protected Bruce could advance along the Great Glen. At the head of the Glen stands Comyn of Badenoch's castle at Inverlochy. In October the castle fell to Bruce through the treachery of the garrison. With the Great Glen open Bruce moved his army north. Urquhart on Loch Ness was destroyed. Frendraught says that the keeper of Inverness, Gilbert of Glencarnie the elder, could not hold the castle because of lack of water so left it abandoned. Bruce had it dismantled. Nairn was burned at night.

Bruce now turned west to face William earl of Ross. The earl takes up the story in a letter to Edward II that did not arrive at Westminster until 22 January 1308. It was either delayed by the difficulty of getting a dispatch through Bruce's lines, or because Ross was not eager to give Edward the bad news:

> 'Be it known that we heard of the coming of Robert Bruce towards the parts of Ross with a great power, so that we

had no power against him, but nevertheless we caused our men to be called out and we were stationed for a fortnight with three thousand men, at our own expense, on the borders of our earldom, and in two other earldoms, Sutherland and Caithness; and he would have destroyed them utterly if we had not made a truce with him, at the entreaty of good men, both clergy and others, until Whitsun next [2 June].'[10]

Edward II had already crossed the channel to Boulogne for his marriage to Isabella of France. With the northern earldoms knocked out until the following summer, Bruce turned eastwards towards his own estates in the Garioch, perhaps hoping for recruits and supplies, and laid siege to Elgin castle. The commander, Gilbert of Glencarnie the younger, was granted a truce that allowed Bruce to move on to Frendraught's castle at Banff. Then Bruce fell ill. He lodged for two nights at Corncarn in a manor belonging to Frendraught. John Comyn earl of Buchan, David Strathbogie earl of Atholl and John Moubray lifted the siege at Banff. The district was too exposed to keep a force, 'for there all plain was the country, and they were but a small meinie to lodge without a fortified place in the plain.'[11] He retired to Slioch, south of Huntly, where a wooded bog afforded some defence.

Bruce's condition deteriorated, his illness so severe he could only be moved on a pallet.[12] He could not eat or drink, his men could not find medicines to treat him. They feared that he was close to death, his strength wholly lost. Winter set in, snow covered the ground and it became difficult to feed the small host. It was at this point that the Earl of Buchan's army arrived. At first Buchan determined not to fight as Bruce's disposition was unclear. A skirmish of sorts took place as archers from both sides 'bickered', but neither side wanted to force a battle. It must be counted as a lost opportunity for the Comyn party—their force was probably stronger and Bruce was still on his sickbed. Buchan left in search of infantry, when he returned a week later Bruce had gone.

John Moubray sought help from the earl of Ross, who refused to break his truce with Bruce. Moubray led reprisals against Bruce adherents and then, in February, it seems he obtained a short truce. He left men in Coull castle to guard Mar and, with other barons, drove cattle into the Mearns and sought help from Brittany. The lieutenant was of little use and unprepared to send forces to the north. When Buchan and Bruce finally met up in May for the engagement that would decide the campaign he was five hundred miles away giving a personal report to the king.[13] In that time Bruce must have made a partial recovery: in March 1308 Buchan's castle at Balvenie was destroyed by fire; then Reginald Cheyne's castle at Duffes and surrounding estates were wasted. Bruce pushed west to take Alexander Comyn's castle at Tarradale in the Black Isle. The earl of Ross and his son retreated before him but Bruce did not follow them into the earldom while the truce was still in effect. A supporter, William Wiseman, sheriff of Elgin in 1305, took Skelbo that belonged to the young earl of Sutherland. On 7 April Bruce had another crack at Elgin that was relieved by Moubray who led a force across the Mounth.

Bruce may have spent some time gathering forces for when he was next heard of he was heading towards Inverurie where it would be easier to find food for his men and was ready to tempt the Earl of Buchan into an engagement. Buchan approached Bruce on the road from Oldmeldrum to Inverurie. A skirmish took place between David Brechin and some of Bruce's men—news Bruce found better than any medicine.[14] The king rose from the pallet that had been his sickbed and mounted his horse; lacking the strength to remain upright he was kept propped up in his saddle by two men. When they saw Bruce mounted Buchan's force drew back. Bruce pressed this advantage and Buchan's infantry scattered. The cavalry stayed in the field for a short time but did not engage Bruce, finally they turned in flight and were pursued twelve miles to Fyvie. Buchan and Moubray hardly stopped until they were in England. John Comyn's earldom was left undefended: it was laid waste by Bruce from end to end. All who remained loyal to Comyn were put to the sword, the earldom consumed by fire. Barbour, an Aberdonian, says that the 'Herschip' or harrying of Buchan was lamented for fifty years.[15] The district only recovered when men were planted from other districts. Bruce now took Aberdeen. The English effort relied on a blockade of Scotland, denying access to military supplies from Europe. The ports along the eastern seaboard: Leith, St Andrews, Dundee, Perth, Montrose, Arbroath, Edinburgh and Berwick were all in English hands. By capturing Aberdeen, a port with strong Flemish connections from the wool trade, Bruce opened a supply line to the continental arms trade.

While Bruce was pacifying the north James Douglas had remained in the south for the winter of 1307-8. Valence lost a destrier worth £65 pursuing him in the forests of 'Passelewe' in early September; 25 of his men, including Thomas Randolph, lost horses in the same action.[16] In November he captured Alexander Stewart and Randolph from an English company. He re-emerged after winter on Palm Sunday (7 April) to take Douglas castle from Clifford's garrison a second time. On this occasion he did not send the men home. They were caught in church and massacred. The castle was left with a solitary guard and the cook. The cook had been at work preparing a meal that Douglas and his men sat down and finished before a search was made for any supplies worth taking. What could not be carried, sacks of meal, malt, corn and flour, were taken to the cellars, ripped open and strewn across the floors.

Casks of wine were staved in to make an 'evil porridge.' Salt and the dead horses were mixed in before the prisoners were brought down to the cellars and beheaded. Their bodies were thrown into mess, an episode recorded with grim humour as 'The Douglas Larder'.

Douglas then joined Bruce's younger brother, Edward, Alexander Lindsay and Robert Boyd with forces from the outer isles in a punitive raid into Galloway.[17] The herschip of Galloway was brief and savage. Many Gallovidians were slaughtered, those that could escaped south of the border. On 29 June 1308 he defeated Donald MacCan on the banks of the Dee or Cree. MacCan was captured, the 'knight Roland' (Roland MacGachan) killed. Dungal Macdouall was driven from his lands, later to be given the command of Dumfries from where he could continue the war with Bruce. In March 1309 Edward Bruce was rewarded with the lordship of Galloway. This was something of a hollow title, an incentive for Edward Bruce to conquer the district. The great castles, of Caerlaverock, Lochmaben, Dalswinton, Ayr, Turnberry, Loch Doon, Tibbers and Dumfries stayed in English hands. It would not be until 1313 the English presence would be removed from the west.

With Buchan's patrimony devastated and Ross quaking in the north, Bruce turned west in the third week of August to face the Macdougalls of Argyll. Bruce had a month between taking Aberdeen in July and this major campaign in Argyll, time he used to recruit a large force. He advanced towards Oban through the Pass of Brander. The pass follows the river Awe that flows five miles from Loch Awe to Loch Etive. It is overshadowed by Ben Cruachan (3,695 feet) that falls away deeply into the loch. Barbour describes it as an evil place. This is where John of Lorn prepared to hold him. Lorn had evidently not recovered from his illness and watched events from a galley on Loch Awe, one of a flotilla on the loch.[18] He had stationed his men on the steep slopes of Ben Cruachan where they were hidden and could pour boulders and arrows onto the pass in an ambush. Bruce had been forewarned. He sent James Douglas with lightly armed highlanders higher up Cruachan's slopes. Douglas fell upon Lorn's men from above, as they began their assault on the main body of Bruce's army. Caught between the two divisions the men of Argyll were worsted in close combat and broke. They fled along the valley to the wooden bridge over the Awe but did not have the time to break it before Bruce's men were across and Macdougall's army scattered.

Alexander of Argyll was in Dunstaffnage, which Bruce besieged and took by September or October. John of Lorn retreated to Inchchonnell on Loch Awe. He sought authority to supply the castle from England and Ireland but could not hold out for long. Alexander performed homage to Bruce and attended his first parliament in 1309. John of Lorn escaped south.

By the end of 1308 Bruce had conquered or neutralised the centres of

Comyn and Balliol power: Buchan, Argyll, the far north and Galloway. From being a hunted fugitive Bruce, as master of Scotia, the seat of Scottish royal dignity, could now lay claim to be king of Scots by right of conquest. It is far easier to chronicle this remarkable turnaround in the winter of the rebellion than to account for it. The first factor in his success was the different nature of Scottish, as opposed to English feudal society. In their own provinces Scottish feudal chiefs were supreme and commanded loyal support as a result of their wealth, patronage and ties of feudal dependence; they had also retained the military responsibilities that had been whittled away south of the border: a public office to call out freeholders. Outside their patrimonies they held little sway. Bruce stationed himself in Moray where there was no earl to organise resistance (there had been no earl of Moray for 200 years). Here he could appeal directly to the local population.

Had the Macdonalds, the earl of Buchan and earl of Ross combined their forces and converged on Bruce then they could have overwhelmed him, but the lords did not co-operate. When Ross was forced to conclude a truce he complained that the men of Moray refused to come to his aid without the warden of Moray's permission. The warden (Reginald Cheyne) was out of the country.[21] John of Lorn had complained that he could not be sure of his neighbours in any direction. Scotland's geography compounded this failure of the local lords to support each other. Stationed in Moray Bruce divided his opponents, Buchan in the east, Ross in the north and the Macdonalds in the west. From here he could prevent his enemies from reaching each other so he could confront them one by one.

The king's core force was perhaps only 50 to 200 men. That he could force truces and take castles could only have been achieved by drawing on local manpower when and where he needed.[19] Some northern knights with their supporters came out for him. He also had support from the 'lesser folk', both in supplies and, when called for, military service. It had been the constable of Forfar castle who had prophesied growing support for Bruce. On Christmas night 1308 the local foresters of Platane crept over the castle's walls and killed the negligent garrison, the first castle to fall south of the Moray.[20] In Bruce they saw an inspired leader who not only rebelled against the hated English, but was able to defeat them. It was these supporters that John Moubray punished in the truce before Inverurie. It says much that Bruce only harried Buchan and Galloway: he was not being reconciliatory to his enemies but recognised in other regions, in the far north and north west he had received support.

The garrisons found themselves on the losing side. Instead of their castles dominating vast territories they had become virtual prisons. At Perth the garrison had not been paid for 20 weeks and their morale was at a low. Such was the antagonism between garrison and town that the commander, Edmund Hastings, begged the Scottish chamberlain to appoint an English justice to the garrison 'as it would be too much for them to be tried by a Scotsman during the war'. The castles of northern Scotland were nothing like the great southern castles, they were simple motte-and-bailey types of timber construction, perhaps with stone gatehouses. The garrisons were small: Forfar, far from being 'stuffit all with Inglis men' held only 25 men, the larger Aberdeen only 55, Dundee 38.[22] Against a cowed community they had proved an effective tool, against guerrilla warfare they could only offer transitory and isolated protection and used up limited resources. By attempting to hold the castles the English supporters in the north spread their forces too thinly. Their supply lines could not hold out—the only castles that survived Bruce's war in the north were Dundee and Perth, supplied from the sea.

The English *Vita Edwardi* had a sneaking respect for Bruce, perhaps from sympathy for the underdog. The author was tempted to sound his praises had not 'the guilt of homicide and the dark stain of treachery' kept him quiet. The temptation proved too much. On the following page he describes Bruce as another 'Æneas fleeing alone from the captivity of Troy.'[23] The author's opinion of the king, and perhaps that of the public as a whole, did not survive Bannockburn, by which time he thought of him as an arrogant traitor.

Bruce fought a guerrilla war: holding strong positions in the hills and moors, ravaging the countryside to deny the enemy resources, confining himself to ambushes and night surprise attacks. Guerrilla warfare was not new to the Scottish wars—there had been no attempt to force a pitched battle since Falkirk. It was the slighting of the castles he captured that was key to Bruce's long term success: not only did it deny English garrisons the opportunity to rule from behind strong walls, but it ensured that the two devastating invasions of the north, in 1296 and 1304, could not easily be repeated.

Bruce conducted his northern campaign with great skill. He had ensured that his Scottish enemies could no longer operate as an independent Balliol party which had been left rudderless by Comyn's murder and Buchan's defeat. From now on any action they took would be under English arms. But the north had always been hostile territory to the English and had never come under English control as the south had. This is not to suggest that the north of Scotland won Scottish independence or was somehow 'more Scottish' than the south. The idea that a Gaelic revival won Scottish independence has rightly been demolished.

Resistance was more difficult in the midst of the garrisons of southern and central Scotland. These were not the motte-and-bailey fortresses that Bruce had so easily swept aside. Stirling, Linlithgow, Edinburgh, Roxburgh, Berwick, and Bothwell were great castles with professional soldiers who co-operated with the magnates still not reconciled to Bruce's rule. It had taken Edward I's best engineers three months to capture Stirling. Bruce had neither engineers, nor Edward's formidable siege weapons, and he had no time to press home a siege before a relief force could be organised. Guerrilla warfare could not capture these strongpoints. However, even these areas of English strength were not safe from Bruce's raids and ambushes.

There was one final, overriding, factor in Bruce's success: Edward II. While King Robert was winning the civil war, legitimising his kingship, Edward II was hamstrung by internal opposition—the predictable result of his own incompetence. He would not, he could not, take major action in Scotland for three years. In that time Bruce was able to secure a strong base from which to resist an English invasion. It has become unfashionable for historians to think of history being dominated by personalities, many prefer to see personalities being swept along by the ebb and flow of events and forces out of their control—in the case of Bruce's Scotland by the rise nationalism. Fourteenth century personalities are never very tangible yet when the two men are measured against each other it is difficult to come to any other conclusion: the eventual expulsion of the English from Scotland was determined on the one hand by the strength, purpose and tenacity of Robert I, and on the other by the weakness of his English counterpart. For Edward II, the Scottish question was secondary to the power-struggles at his court and the threat from his over-mighty cousin, Lancaster.

Edward was 23-years old when he came to the throne. He shared many of the physical characteristics of his father: tall, strong and handsome. Here the resemblance ends. Although he shared his father's ambitions, he exhibited none of his energy or commitment. His interests—he loved outdoor sports, hunting of course but also swimming (in mid-winter) and rowing; as well as country pursuits, ditching and thatching—all criticised by his contemporaries as debasing the dignity of the crown.

When Edward inherited the throne there was considerable goodwill from the barons. The recall of Piers Gaveston was part of a policy to reconcile those who had been harshly treated in the last years of Edward I's reign. Within a month Anthony Bek had returned from exile to his principality, and by the end of the year Edward I's most determined opponent, archbishop Winchelsea, was reinstated. Only Walter Langton was dismissed and deprived of his lands. He had made many enemies and few would have been troubled by his going.

Opposition did not take long to form. The *Scalacronica*, not the most critical of Edward's chroniclers, says that the king 'was too familiar with his intimates, shy with strangers, and loved too exclusively a single individual.' In the early years of his reign that individual was Piers

Gaveston. The harsher critic, the *Vita Edwardi,* reported what must have been the common view of Gaveston, that 'the magnates of the land hated him, because he alone found favour in the king's eyes and lorded it over them like a second king... Almost all the land hated him too, great and small.'[24] Gaveston's promotion to the earldom strained Edward's relationship with his barons. Even at the best of times the magnates feared the inclusion of new men into their ranks. It was a dilution of their power and wealth: there had been no promotions outside the Anglo-Norman aristocracy since the reign of Stephen.[25] The earldom of Cornwall, traditionally reserved for one of the king's younger sons, was destined for one of Edward's brothers. Gaveston was also awarded the valuable marriage of the king's niece, Margaret de Clare, sister of the earl of Gloucester.

Edward spent Christmas 1308 with Gaveston before crossing the channel to marry the 12-year old Isabella, daughter of Philip IV, the marriage that had been arranged at Montreuil-sur-mer in 1299. The ceremony took place in Boulogne after Edward performed homage for his French domains. The king left Gaveston as regent while he was out of the country, a position of immense power but one that he does not appear to have exploited. Edward's coronation took place a month later. Throughout the ceremony Gaveston took a leading role, walking before the king carrying the crown sword of St Edward. The anglophile Charles of Valois had accompanied the queen from France to attend the coronation. He went home disgusted that so much attention was paid to Gaveston, so little to the young queen.

The marriage should have cemented Anglo-French relations and isolated the Scots from their ally. Instead it insulted the French king. For the magnates, Gaveston was becoming an embarrassment that they would have to deal with.

The coronation oath had remained unchanged since Richard I became king. Edward's oath followed those of his predecessors but included a new clause, that he would 'uphold and defend the laws and righteous customs that the community of the realm shall choose.' It was designed to block the manoeuvres that became familiar with Edward I, when the king passed laws under pressure which he later broke. The magnates now prepared to use this oath to get rid of Gaveston. A week after the coronation the earls made it clear that Edward would be expected to uphold a literal interpretation of the oath and agree to anything they, acting as the community of the realm, resolved. The king began to make preparations for civil war.

At the parliament in April 1309 the opposition, Lincoln, Lancaster, Warwick, Hereford, Valence and Warenne, arrived in arms demanding Gaveston's banishment. Archbishop Winchelsea, not mellowed by Edward's support for his return, declared Gaveston excommunicate should he stay. The king blinked first. Edward could no longer support his friend, and acceding to the magnates' demands Gaveston left England for Ireland, where Edward made him his lieutenant.

With an unseemly speed that irritated the opposition Edward signalled his ambition to sponsor Gaveston's return. He sent letters to the king of France to intercede with the pope to have Winchelsea's threat of excommunication lifted; Thomas of Lancaster received the hereditary stewardship to reconcile him to the king; other gifts were made to Brittany, Gloucester and Henry Percy.

By the Stamford parliament in July Edward had managed to divide the magnates and Gaveston was allowed to return. Unfortunately, neither the king nor Gaveston had learned anything. Edward was still infatuated, and Gaveston remained 'somewhat haughty and supercilious' to rile the magnates.[26] It was then that he began his foolish habit of coining pet names for the earls—Warwick he called 'Black dog', Lancaster 'the player' and Valence 'Joseph the Jew'. The great men did not take such personal insults lightly. Gaveston was greedy, but his worst crime was his indifference to the magnates whose influence he had usurped.

The earls refused to attend a parliament in February 1310 or a council in York in October while Gaveston was present, and threatened that if they were obliged to attend it would be in armour for their own safety. Gaveston was sent away so the assembly could meet. When the earls arrived it was in military array, in direct defiance of the king. Their grievances were presented in the form of a petition: the basis of their complaints was that the king, led by 'unsuitable and evil councillors' had wasted money meant for the defence of the realm and the support of the royal household which meant the king was being forced to live by extortion. Furthermore the crown had been dismembered by his failure to take action in Scotland which was as good as lost. The crown's insolvency contributed to its failure in Scotland. The king had been granted a twentieth at Northampton in October 1307 and a twenty-fifth for the mitigation of prises at Stamford in July 1309 but the war had not progressed, nor had the people relieved of the burden of prises that were being extracted even though campaigns did not take place. The *Vita* says that 'many colloquies and councils were held for the défence of the land of Scotland and the defeat of Bruce, but the effects of these were not clear nor did they issue any action.'[27] Against this sustained pressure the king was forced to appoint a commission of reform, the Lords Ordainers. Their work would not be finished until August 1311.

Many of the magnates had been endowed with Scottish lands, the fruits of their labours from Falkirk to Edward's death. Warwick had received 1,000 marks of land belonging to Geoffrey Moubray in

ve Hadrian's Wall, *an early reminder of a contested border.*

w The funeral of Alexander III from Walter Bower's Scotichronicon. *(By permission of the ter and Fellows of Corpus Christi College, Cambridge)*

Right An image, thought to be Edward I, from the Sedilia, Westminster Abbey. *(Dean and Chapter of Westminster)*

Below The Great Seal of the Guardians. The obverse shows the royal coat of arms, the reverse depicts St. Andrew on his cross, revealing that their authority derived from the community of the realm. *(From James Anderson, Selectus Diplomatum et Numismatum Scotiae Thesaurus)*

Left *Barnard Castle, ancestral home of the Balliols.*

ve Edward I creating his son
ce of Wales in 1301. (British
ary)

t The daughters of Henry,
of Huntingdon. (Courthauld
itute of Art)

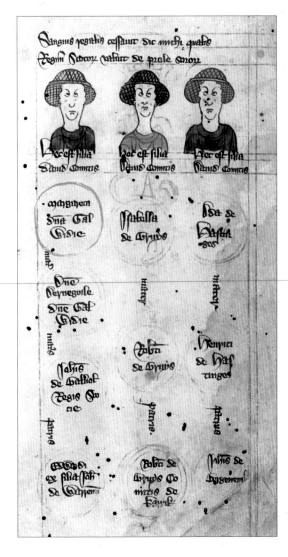

Above John Balliol pays homage to Edward I in the Black friary at Newcastle, 1292. (British Library)

Right The seal of King John. (From James Anderson, Selectus Diplomatum et Numismatum Scotiae Thesaurus)

...ham castle, stronghold of the warrior bishops of Durham.

Bothwell castle as it would have looked in the early 14th century. (Historic Scotland)

Scota · Gathelos

Above *Scota, daughter of Pharoah, with her husband Gathalos, from Walter Bower's Scotichronicon. (By permission of the Master and Fellows of Corpus Christi College, Cambridge)*

Left *The coronation chair with the Stone of Destiny in situ before its removal to Scotland in 1996. (Dean and Chapter of Westminster)*

Above Caerlaverock castle, taken by Edward I and held by the English until 1312.

Below Castle Doon, a Bruce castle taken by the English but recaptured in 1311. It was mov
when the loch was dammed in the 1950s. (George Washington Wilson Photographic Archiv

Above Glen Trool, site of Robert I's first victory against the English. (*Argyll Tourist Board and Historic Scotland*)

Left The battle of Bannockburn with Stirling castle in the background and Robert I in single combat with Humphrey de Bohun. (*By permission of the Master and Fellows of Corpus Christi College, Cambridge*)

Below The first seal of Robert Bruce, in use 1313-16. It follows the basic pattern of English seals. In 1316 Bruce had a second seal made, inspired by that of Louis X of France. (*From James Anderson,* Selectus Diplomatum et Numismatum Scotiae Thesaurus)

Left Dunstaffnage castle
it would have appeared i
the 14th century. It belon
to Robert Bruce's bitter
enemies, the Macdougall
Argyll. (Historic Scotland

Below Ben Cruachan an
Loch Awe. Robert I defe
the Macdougalls along th
steep slopes of Ben Cruac
along the Pass of Brande
(Argyll Tourist Board)

...laration of Arbroath. (By permission of the Keeper of the Records of Scotland)

Above Edward II's tomb in Gloucester Cathedral.

Left Robert I's equestrian statue on the Bore Stone designed by Pilkington Jackson after the king's second seal.

Below The siege of Carlisle from the initial letter of the Charter of 1316. The plumed knight is Andrew Harcla.

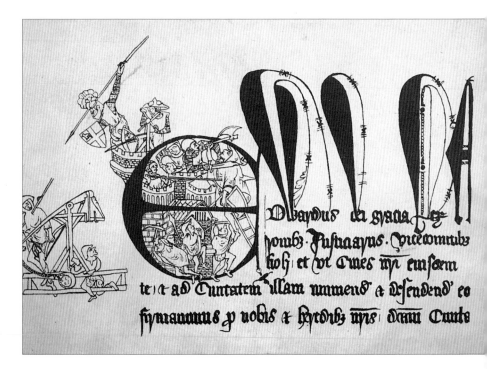

ROBERT
THE
BRUCE
KING

...aulx (above) and Byland Abbeys (below), from where Edward II barely escaped from a ...ish raiding party.

Above *Berwick-upon-Tweed, seen from Halidon Hill.*

The great Northumbrian castles at Alnwick (right), Bamburgh (below) and Dunstanburgh (below right) offered protection to their inhabitants but were worthless against the lightning guerrilla warfare used by Robert I.

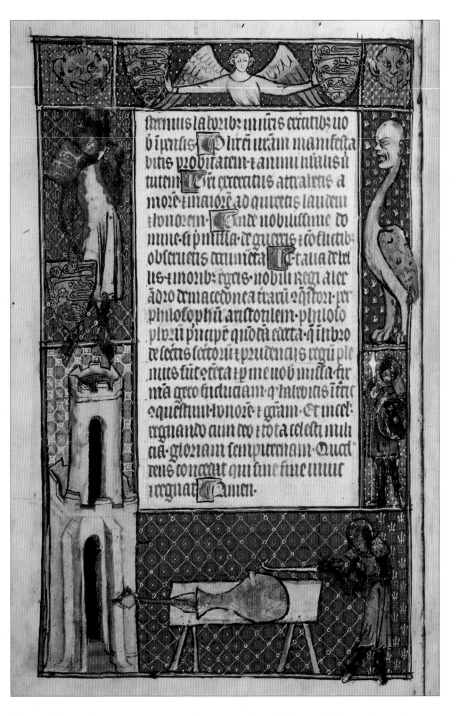

Above *The earliest known picture of a cannon from Walter of Milimete's treatise. Barbour notes the 'crakys of war' during the campaign, the earliest reference to the use of cannon in Britain. (Christ Church College, Oxford)*

Above *The battle of Neville's Cross and the capture of David II. (Bibliothèque Nationale)*

Below *Edward III of England with David II of Scotland. (British Library)*

Above *Edward III presented with lance by St. George, from a milita thesis by Walter de Milimete presented by the prince in 1327. (Christ Church College, Oxford)*

1298, and in 1307 he received John Balliol's estates centred on Barnard Castle. Valence had received lands worth £1,000 including Bothwell castle in 1303, together with the forest and castle at Selkirk. Hereford had been rewarded with Annandale and Lochmaben castle. Below them the second rank of nobles, John de St John and Henry Percy had been endowed with lands. They had invested in those estates and expected a return. On 18 October 1307 the king ordered them to proceed to Scotland after Edward I's funeral in defence of their lands there. The lands had been awarded by the king, but now Edward II expected the magnates to protect them—and they would have to do it without the greatest of the English magnates, the king himself. It is not surprising that when an opposition emerged it should include Valence, Warwick, and Hereford, the three who had benefited most from these grants.[28]

It would be wrong to think that the problems of Edward's reign were all the result of his relationship with Piers Gaveston. Gaveston was a ready scapegoat for baronial opposition that had deeper roots, sometimes beyond Edward's control. Despite an enormous burden of taxation the crown was insolvent. Towards the end of his reign Edward I had given up even trying to balance the budget, leaving the shortfall to be picked up by his Italian bankers, the Frescobaldi, who secured the debt against future customs.

In June 1308 writs of military service had been issued for a muster at Carlisle on 22 August; commissions of array were ordered for the northern counties and Wales; and a fleet from the southern ports ordered to rendezvous at Skinburness.[29] It was only after Edward's first reconciliation with the earls and Gaveston's first banishment that the campaign was cancelled: 'in consequence of some obstacles which had arisen, but which are now removed.' Proclamation was made throughout the kingdom that those persons owing military service were to remain at home.[30] The muster seems to have been organised merely to assert the primacy of the king over his barons. After this failure to mount a campaign Edward announced that although he would not take a truce himself 'the wardens of Scotland there may take such as long as possible, as they have done hitherto of their own power or commission, so that the king however may furnish his castles with men and victuals.' In other words, a truce could be agreed but only with the proviso that he could break it if he wanted to.

The same document records the English command in Scotland: Robert Umfraville Earl of Angus, Henry Beaumont and William Ros commanded the land between Berwick and the Forth, each with 40 men-at-arms; in the north, from the Forth to Orkney, Alexander Abernethy, Edmund Hastings and John FitzMarmaduke with 120 men-at-arms between them; in Galloway, Buchan, John Moubray and Ingram

Umfraville each with 40 men-at-arms.[31] Brittany was replaced by Robert Clifford as lieutenant with 100 men-at-arms, 60 of his own and 40 from the household, and 300 foot. Clifford alternated his command with John Segrave. Segrave took up the post in March 1309, Clifford returned in December, Segrave in April 1310.[32] This was a large undertaking and an expensive drain on the exchequer.

Late in 1308 the king agreed to a truce proposed by the king of France.[33] In January 1309 Gloucester and two other earls went north with papal envoys and negotiated a truce to last until the following November. Both sides agreed to retreat to their positions on the feast of James the Apostle (25 July 1308). Bruce had no intention of giving up his gains and Edward was in no position to make him. The king summoned the members of the Stamford parliament in July 1309 to advise him on how he could punish the Scots for breaking the truce. A resolution was made to reopen the conflict. A campaign organised for June had already been cancelled. Another expedition was planned to muster on 29 September. The campaign was prorogued in August until October, by September the forces called for were being slimmed down. On 23 October the king acceded to a Welsh petition to be spared on account of the approaching winter; three days later the muster was cancelled altogether. The only activity came from the earl of Gloucester, made commander of the king's army in Scotland in September 1309. Gloucester relieved Rutherglen castle but took no offensive action against the patriots. It was a temporary respite—the castle fell to Edward Bruce sometime in the same year.[34]

The earl of Ulster went on a diplomatic mission in August 1309. As Bruce's father-in-law he may have been seen as having influence. If his relationship with Bruce was not enough Burgh took with him a strong, almost intimidating, following. John Menteith and Nigel Campbell received safe-conducts to treat with him but nothing substantial was achieved.[35]

With the truce due to expire in November 1309 the king sent John Segrave to keep Berwick; the earl of Hereford, John Cromwell and Robert Clifford were sent to Carlisle. These commanders secured a truce with Bruce to last until 14 January. Clifford sought the king's agreement to extend the truce beyond this, until March, and then until the summer. The king told the commanders at the more exposed castles, at Ayr (under attack in June 1309), Perth, Dundee and Banff to make what truce they could until Whitsun (7 June 1310). He expressly prohibited the south-western castles from making similar truces. They were in the heart of territory hostile to Bruce and could easily be supplied from England. Truces here were seen in Edward's court as an unnecessary luxury.[36]

It was Bruce who made most use of the truces. He may have gone over the heads of the lords to enlist support but he was shrewd enough not to alienate the magnates. The earl of Ross, who had surrendered Bruce's queen to the English, himself surrendered in October 1308. Not only did he receive his own lands, but was awarded the burgh of Dingwall and estates in Sutherland. The earl, and his son Hugh, became life-long supporters.[37] Bruce won over James the Steward; he may have been too old to give anything but moral support but his name carried great weight. Dumbarton was surrendered by perhaps the most surprising recruit, the Steward's kinsman, John Menteith who had been awarded the title of earl of Lennox by Edward I. He exchanged this paper title for the reality of the lordships of Arran and Knapdale. Thomas Randolph was a nephew of Bruce but a knight of John Balliol. He fought with Bruce at Methven but despised guerrilla warfare and after his capture fought for the English. When he was recaptured he told Bruce that this warfare was beneath the dignity of a knight but eventually gave way and became Bruce's most important lieutenant: in 1312 he was made Earl of Moray, the creation preceding that of Carrick for Edward Bruce.

Kingship was about more than the winning of battles. Bruce needed to fix his regime on good government. In March 1309 Bruce held a parliament in the neutral city of St Andrews aimed at rallying the Bruce party. The parliament gathered to respond to a letter from Philip IV who was pressing for a crusade and the suppression of the Templars. The Scots welcomed Philip's 'special love' for Bruce and told him they would be happy to crusade but, in a nice touch of understatement, were tied up with other matters.

Philip was in a difficult position. He was now an ally of the English and had invested heavily in John Balliol: as late as April 1308 he had made a payment to Balliol as 'king of Scots'.[38] He did not want to antagonise his ally or his dependent. So his letter was addressed to Bruce as the earl of Carrick. Philip was not alone in shunning Bruce's title. Clement V issued two bulls, *Faciens misericordium* and *Regnans in celis*. The first called for an enquiry into the Templars, the second called representatives to the general council of Vienne. Clement nominated the bishops of Whitehorn, Glasgow and St Andrews: the first an English ally the other two in English custody. In part this was a matter between Clement and Edward, in nominating Wishart and Lamberton the pope was ensuring their release so that their cases could be considered under papal jurisdiction. But the bull had been addressed to every monarch in western Europe, bar Bruce.[39] It was clearly time for Bruce to pronounce his kingship beyond Scotland.

Bruce inherited (a more fitting term might be appropriated) the propaganda that had so bolstered the patriots and had culminated in the action at the curia in 1301. The propaganda had been applied to John Balliol but this dilemma, like Balliol's reign, was ignored. Acts in Robert's name referred to Alexander III as his immediate predecessor as if Balliol's kingship had never happened. The results of the parliament were declarations from the nobility, now lost, and the clergy in support of Bruce: a manifesto for the Bruce party. The declaration based Bruce's claim on the 'four pillars of inheritance, virtue, election and conquest':[40]

> 'this people, being unable any longer to endure injuries so many and so great, and more bitter than death, which were being continually inflicted on their property and their persons for lack of a captain and faithful leader, agreed, by divine prompting, on Lord Bruce who now is king.'
>   DECLARATION OF THE CLERGY[41]

This was the earliest occasion when the outcome of the Great Cause was questioned, developing the myth that Balliol had been chosen over the rights of the true heir of Alexander III, Bruce the competitor, to become an English puppet ruler. The parliament and the declaration of the clergy were the 'triumphant conclusion' to the first stage of king Robert's reign.[42]

Pope Clement V never recognised Bruce, but it was easy to sway the king of France to anything that caused the English such a headache. Later in the year French messengers carried letters still addressed to Robert earl of Carrick. This was for English consumption. Copies of the letters sewn into the messenger's belt were addressed to Robert king of Scots. Edward was not fooled by this deception and made his feelings known to Philip in August 1309.[43] Edward, of course, still had difficulty with Bruce's title. His emissaries were sent with commissions to speak with the 'the people of Scotland', not the king.

Edward did not plan to stay in London while the Ordainers were at work. His absence would hamper their work, made even more difficult by the removal of the Exchequer and Benches to York, the offices that were essential to the gathering of evidence concerning the rights of the crown and nobility. The *Vita* suspected that Edward went on campaign to avoid going to France to perform fealty to Philip. Edward certainly told the French king that he cancelled their meeting because the Scots had broken the truce.[44] It is tempting to believe that the sole reason for the campaign was so that Edward could avoid his responsibilities elsewhere, there was certainly a strong element of shallow opportunism. But his responsibilities in Scotland had been clearly set out by four loyal Scottish magnates: Alexander Abernethy, Alexander of Argyll, Ingram Umfraville and John of Lorn. They had come to London and warned Edward that nothing could be done unless the king himself went north. Their candour shook the king. He wrote to Aymer Valence earl of Pembroke that 'we should lose both the land and those who still remain faithful to us by reason of our default and our laxity.'[45]

Edward asked Valence to go to Berwick to campaign and in the meantime to go to Westminster to give council on the Scottish problem. Valence refused this personal appeal. The king tried again on 4 July 1310 without success, Valence remained in London.[46] Hereford, Lancaster, Valence and Arundel all missed a meeting arranged in Northampton in August to consider measures the king might take against Bruce, telling the king they could not attend because of business in London.[47] Only three earls obeyed the summons: Gloucester, Warenne and Cornwall. Lincoln remained in England as regent.

The force was never going to be large. Nicholas Segrave and Bartholomew Badlesmere organised the muster of the levies in Tweedmouth. Segrave, driven from court by the Ordainers as one of the king's 'evil councillors', acted as marshall (Bigod died in 1306). Badlesmere took on the role of constable. The king was particularly vexed at the non-appearance of the hereditary constable, Humphrey Bohun earl of Hereford.[48] He wrote to the earl as late as 6 September commanding him to come at once. The summons had no effect.

The earls sent their basic obligation, Lancaster owed six knights' fees and proffered four knights and four *servientes*; Warwick and Hereford sent ten *servientes*, Valence a knight and eight *servientes*. The military tenants were obligated to send a total of 236 knights' fees and sent 51 men-at-arms with two barded horses (worth one fee each) and 370 *servientes*: a total of 421 mounted men.[49] Edward's failure to mount a serious offensive in Scotland must be balanced by the refusal of the magnates to become involved when he tried.

Edward planned to bolster this modest force with a large contingent from Ireland brought by the earl of Ulster who would land in Ayr to act with the Macdougalls. On 2 August the Irish contingent was cancelled 'on account of the season'.[50] The crops had been poor leaving little fodder to feed the horses over a winter campaign. But there was another pressing factor—a threat to the Isle of Man. The earl went to Man with 500 troops to aid Simon Montagu, admiral of the fleet.[51]

The 1310 campaign, such as it was, was lamentable. Its limited objective was to strengthen and provision the garrisons. The army crossed the border at Wark on 16 September, before resting at Roxburgh. On the 21st Edward entered Selkirk forest, the only bold move on the campaign, emerging at Biggar on the 29th having found no enemy. From here the army moved west, along the Clyde valley as far as Renfrew before turning east, possibly to Stirling, reaching Linlithgow on 23 October.

By 1 November the king was back in Berwick where he remained until June 1311. The infantry returned home having completed their service. Warenne quartered at Wark, Gloucester at Norham and Gaveston at Roxburgh.[52] Throughout Edward's circuit of the defences the Scottish army remained hidden, only emerging to attack stragglers or foraging parties. The *Vita* records one such attack, the only detail of the campaign given by the chroniclers:

> 'One day, when some English and Welsh, always ready for plunder, had gone out on a raid, accompanied for protection by many horsemen from the army, Bruce's men, who had been concealed in caves and in the woodlands, made a serious attack on our men. Our horsemen, seeing that they could not help the infantry, returned to the main force with a frightening uproar; and immediately leapt to arms and hastened with one accord to the help of those who had been left amongst the enemy; but assistance came too late to prevent the slaughter of our men... Before our knights arrived, up to 300 Welsh and English had been slaughtered, and the enemy returned to their caves. From such ambushes our men suffered heavy losses.'[53]

When Edward retired to Berwick Bruce launched an audacious raid into Lothian to punish Scots loyal to the English. Edward pursued them with a small force but by the time they had mobilised Bruce had disappeared. After Christmas Gaveston led a foray to Perth. Lanercost says that this was because Bruce was marching to Galloway, and the English feared he would return across the Forth to collect troops.[54] Gaveston fortified Dundee, where he behaved so 'rudely there than was agreeable to the gentlemen of the county, so that he had to return to the king because of the opposition of the barons.'[55] While Gaveston was making a nuisance of himself in Dundee, Gloucester and Warenne made a foray into Selkirk forest. Gaveston took command at Perth until Easter, when he was relieved by Henry Percy and the earl of Angus with 200 men-at-arms 'besides the great Scottish lords.' Robert Clifford had 100 men-at-arms surveying the castles south of the Forth with instructions to 'do his best on the enemy till the 'grass' when the host may foray and get supplies for the horses.'[56]

Gloucester left the campaign shortly afterwards to replace the deceased earl of Lincoln as regent. The new earl, through his wife, was Thomas of Lancaster, already holder of the earldoms of Lancaster, Derby and Leicester. The Lacy inheritance brought two more, Lincoln and Salisbury. Lincoln had been an influential and experienced leader of the opposition whose death left Lancaster as the focus of the opposition movement. What England needed was a man who could temper Edward II's poor kingship; but in Lancaster the country had a man who was 'sulky, vindictive, self-seeking, brutal and vicious'.[57] Without Lincoln's restraint, Lancaster's opposition became ever more strident.

Lancaster approached the border to do homage for the Lincoln inheritance but refused to cross to Berwick to do homage outside the kingdom. At first there was an impasse, as Edward refused to go to Lancaster, and Lancaster threatened to return with 100 knights to enter his lands by force. Edward relented and crossed to Haggerston, just south of Berwick, where Lancaster did homage.

By Summer 1311 Edward was seriously short of money but did not want to call a parliament to raise taxes for fear of the Lords Ordainers' reforms. He raised a loan of £4,000 from Lincoln's executors that helped for a short time. Plans were made for a fresh expedition launched from Ireland, in what the king called 'one of the greatest movements of the Scottish war.'[58] Sixty-two ships were to carry an army from Ireland to Ayr, but by June a steady stream of letters was arriving from English ports explaining their failure to send vessels.[59] Sidmouth had been told to send two vessels, but had none in port, nor any money to fit one out. Weymouth and Exeter said that they had already performed their duty by sending two ships. Barnstaple offered money instead; Chester had no ships in harbour. Looe reported that local towns would not give any aid; Haverford and Shoreham that their ships and mariners had left for distant parts and not yet returned. The litany of excuses has a familiar ring from 1310 when so many ports failed to produce any vessels. Service in a Scottish war was deeply unpopular with the merchants, threatening their trade with the continent. Worse, many of the ships missing from the muster or out of port were making healthy profits smuggling with the enemy.[60]

In May Edward issued writs for a muster of foot on 24 June for one foot-soldier from each vill to serve for seven weeks, paid for at the expense of the vill. This was a novel and creative summons that extended the normal limits of military obligation. Writs were also sent to 91 barons 'as the war against the Scots is now shown to be successful; and, for the purpose of finally repressing their insolence, the king proposes to make a raid against them.'[61] The response from vills and barons alike was poor. Edward could no longer postpone calling a parliament. He travelled south in July to face the Ordainers who had now finished their work.

Edward left Gaveston in Bamburgh and travelled to Westminster to hear the worst. The Ordinances, which were only accepted when the magnates arrived in arms, placed Edward under the control of a baronial council. The king's finances were reorganised, the Frescobaldi, who bankrolled Edward I's Scottish wars, were expelled and the king was prohibited from collecting the New Customs. Edward replaced the Frescobaldi with a new banker, the Genoese Antonio Pessagno, who began supplying loans to Edward to finance the wars.

Gaveston's renewed exile was demanded and agreed, but he did not stay away for long and was back in England in November 1311. This was a direct defiance of the Ordinances that caused the earls to issue the second ordinances, seeking the removal of specified officers from Edward's administration. Edward was enraged and now openly called Gaveston to Windsor, where they kept Christmas. They then moved north. The *Vita* repeats gossip that Edward sought safety for Gaveston in Scotland.

Edward was willing to pay a high price. He offered Bruce the crown of Scotland in perpetuity. Robert replied, 'How shall the king of England keep faith with me when he does not observe the sworn promises made to his own liegemen?'[62] The political situation in England was tense, by May 1312 the opposition was in armed rebellion. In this sort of climate such rumours must have spread easily, certainly the normally well informed chronicler was forced only to speculate.

The outcome of the dispute is well known. The king and Gaveston tried to find security at Newcastle but fled the town on news of Lancaster's approach. Clifford and Percy held forces on the March, not to stop a Scottish invasion but to prevent the king or Gaveston escaping north, giving some credence to the *Vita's* rumours. From Tynemouth Gaveston made his way to Scarborough castle which was surrendered after two weeks to Valence, who made a personal pledge for Gaveston's safety. He was captured by Warwick and beheaded on Lancaster's orders.

Gaveston's death removed the one common interest uniting the earls. The opposition fragmented, with Valence, Warenne and Henry Percy returning to the king. This divide in the baronial ranks would last into the next reign, and would mean that no concerted action was taken against the Scots in the way Edward I had done between 1298 and 1304. The short periods when one side or the other gained the upper hand or when a shaky truce patched up the differences between the parties coincided with new campaigns: in 1314, 1318 and 1322.

As the threat of civil war hung over England from 1311 until Edward's reconciliation with Lancaster and Warwick in 1313, Bruce was free to pursue his policy of dislodging the English in Scotland, and began launching raids on the north of England. It was a policy much favoured by the Scottish chroniclers. 'The fruitless English nation, which had unrighteously racked many a man, was now, by God's righteous judgement, made to undergo awful scourges; and, whereas it had once been victorious, now it sank vanquished and groaning.'[63] In other words, the boot was on the other foot.

In August 1311, only two weeks after Edward left Berwick, Bruce launched a blistering raid into northern England, crossing the Solway, passing through Gilsland, Haltwhistle and Tynedale. After eight days he returned to Scotland loaded with booty and cattle. In September he led a raid into the east, into areas he missed earlier: Harbottle, Holystone, Redesdale, Corbridge and into the valleys of the North and South Tyne. This raid lasted fifteen days. Fearing Bruce would return the

Northumbrians sent envoys to negotiate a truce until 2 February 1312 ('an exceedingly short time') at a cost of £2000. Bruce also made raids into Lothian where Dunbar was 'heavily taxed' for a truce that lasted until the same date.

These raids were a return to the scale of those led by the Earl of Buchan in 1296 and William Wallace in 1297. The raiders could make 20-30 miles a day, the knights and esquires mounted on chasers, lesser men on ponies and 'gillies' hurrying along on foot. They had no baggage train, carrying meal on their backs and a flat stone under the saddle to bake oats. Otherwise, they lived off the land. The raids lasted for days or weeks. This made their movements extremely difficult to predict and left the northern counties unable to offer any resistance. The larger castles could withstand sieges; most of the smaller castles and peels could hold off a skirmishing party; Carlisle and now Newcastle had walls and castles that protected the citizens. Only the countryside remained unprotected. The raids were well organised and disciplined. Lanercost tells us that on the first raid 'he killed few men besides those who offered resistance', on the second raid 'he caused more men to be killed than on the former occasion' but this may simply have been a result of a better organised county putting up greater resistance.[64]

Slaughter was not the objective of the raids. It seems that only when Bruce himself was absent was any lack of discipline. The raids served a dual purpose—they punished the English and destroyed the north's aggressive capabilities. Troops from the north had always formed core contingents in English invasion armies but from now on they would be denied to the king as they were deployed in the north's defences. The attacks also raised badly needed money for Bruce who could only levy taxes in the areas he controlled north of the Tay. He used these tributes to finance his campaigns against the remaining English garrisons and their Scottish supporters. The acceptance of a truce with the north of England was merely the signal for an attack on English strongholds in Scotland.

In January 1312 Bruce sought a truce from Edward who sent David Strathbogie earl of Atholl and five others a commission to treat with the Scots.[65] At about the same time Bruce began the siege of Dundee, his most ambitious target to date. This was a critical strategic site. Its fall would sever Perth's lifeline: supplies from the sea along the Firth of Tay. In recognition of its importance the town's garrison in 1311 numbered 211, second only to Berwick. Alexander Abernethy received the town's command in 1311 followed by David Brechin in 1312, two of the most stalwart Anglo-Scottish lords.[66] At the beginning of the year Brechin met the king at York, leaving the town in the custody of a Scot, William Montfichet. Montfichet made an agreement with the besiegers to surrender the town in return for the release of prisoners.

When Edward learnt of the agreement on 2 March he angrily ordered Montfichet to break his word and began preparations to relieve the town. Edward had already sent a mandate to the collector of customs at Hartlepool to buy 100 quarters of wheat, malt and beans and peas, and twenty quarters of salt paid out of the town's customs, to be sent directly to Dundee.[67] The order was made on the day David Brechin met the king and explains his journey south, the town's supplies were running low. With a typical lack of urgency it took three weeks before any action was taken. On the 21 March Edward sent letters to the town promising relief; the bishop of St Andrews was commanded to ensure that Edward's messenger got through and may himself have entered the town.[68] The supplies from Hartlepool would not last long in the present crisis so the sheriff of Lincoln received instructions to send triple the original order. Four days later Brechin began raising a force of men at arms and foot to relieve the town. William Jettour, described as an 'amirello', was cruising in a ship off Berwick. He began to organise a fleet of ships, *la Messague, la Nicholas, la Welfare* and two others together with barges to transport the relief force and supplies.[69]

The effort came too late—Montfichet kept word. On 12 April Bruce held a parliament at Inchture, a village lying between Perth and Dundee, where letters patent were issued recording an ordinance that burghs would only negotiate with the Scottish chancellor for military service, tallages and contributions. This was part of the surrender agreement. Around this time the town capitulated.[70] The only business left was to reassign the relief force. Brechin became keeper of Berwick and the troops he collected were to remain for the defence of the town. William Jettour received a commission to arrest all ships with provisions passing beyond Berwick.[71]

Many of the smaller English garrisons in the north had fallen by summer 1312: Banff in 1310, Muckhart in 1311, and after the fall of Dundee, Perth was the last stronghold north of the Forth. South of the Forth the English held strongholds on two lines. Along the Clyde-Forth isthmus stood the great castles at Edinburgh, Stirling and Bothwell. Between these and crucial to their survival were the smaller forts or peels, at Linlithgow and Livingston. In the south of Lothian, along the line of the Tweed, stood Berwick, Roxburgh and Jedburgh on the north side of the river, while to the south were the English castles at Norham and Wark. Scattered between these were numerous smaller castles.[72]

The position in the south-west was just as strong. Bruce's island castle at Loch Doon was still in English hands in 1311 but was under siege. Atholl attempted to relieve the castle but it evidently fell towards the end of the year. This still left the large castles at Lochmaben, Caerlaverock and Dumfries, together with the outposts at Tibbers, Dalswinton and Buittle. It is unclear when the isolated Ayr fell. Bruce held a parliament in the town in 1312, so it may have fallen in 1311. No details of the truce Atholl negotiated survive although a truce of sorts seems to have lasted until the end of the year when Bruce returned to the offensive. Early in 1312 the vill at Norham was burnt; it had either been excluded from the separate truce bought by the northern counties or the truce was ignored as the 'castle had previously done them great injury.'[73] In Summer the truce secured by the north of England elapsed and Bruce returned to burn Hexham and Corbridge. A detachment arrived at Durham on market day and were able to carry off a great deal of booty after slaughtering many in the town and putting much of it to the flame. Durham bought a truce until the following summer for £2,000 that was only accepted on the condition that the Scottish army was given free access through the palatinate. Northumberland paid a similar tribute.

The poorer western counties, Westmoreland, Copeland and Cumberland, could not find enough ready cash so were forced to send hostages. Their failure to pay the tribute led to a warning raid in December followed by an invasion by Edward Bruce. He occupied the bishop of Carlisle's residence, Rose Castle, spending three days raiding the surrounding districts. The bishop saved his manors at Rose and Linstock by offering the release of two Scottish prisoners, the brothers Alexander and Reginald Lindsay. At some point the deal fell through, and the Lindsays were not released until after Bannockburn.[74]

There was now no target in Scotland that was beyond Bruce. On the night of 6 December 1312 the Scots made an attempt on the capital of English occupation, Berwick. A Scottish force approached the walls at night, undetected. A barking dog saved Berwick, alerting the garrison that the Scots were scaling the walls. The ladders were left behind and hung on a pillory the next day to put them to shame. The Lanercost chronicler saw the ladders used in the assault and was much impressed. They were nothing more than a variation on a simple rope ladder with iron hooks that could be lifted over battlements by two men and a pole.[75]

Bruce had none of the traditional weapons to take a large town; at Dundee he could rely on starving the town into submission but he knew that a similar strategy aimed at one of the four square bulwarks of the English occupation, Berwick, Edinburgh, Stirling or Roxburgh, might bring a response even from Edward II given that he would have time to organise an army while the siege was in progress. The last thing Bruce wanted to see was another large English army that might undo the work he had painstakingly achieved. Instead he tried to take these castles by stratagems, surprise attacks or treachery. After the near loss of Berwick the garrisons should have been more alert to the danger.

Having narrowly failed to take Berwick Bruce moved on to Perth, laid siege to on 8 or 10 January 1313. Barbour gives the earl of Atholl, who went over to Bruce sometime in 1312, much of the credit for taking the town. Perth was well defended. It had walls and was surrounded by moats on three sides, the fourth side protected by the river Tay. Its commander since July 1311 was William Oliphant, the man who had led the Scottish defenders at Stirling castle in 1304 and knew a thing or two about siege warfare. He had been released from captivity in 1308 on condition that he served the English. The town put up a stout defence and Bruce saw that it would be difficult to take by open assault.[76] Instead he feigned withdrawal to take the sentries off their guard. After a few days he returned at night, leading his troops through the chill waters of the moat and was one of the first over the walls. A French knight in the Scottish force was horrified that Bruce should put himself at such risk 'to wyn ane wrechit hamlet.'[77] By the time the cry was raised enough Scots had reached the walls to capture the gates and let the main force into the town.

The chroniclers disagree on the fate of the besieged. *Lanercost* says that the English in the town were allowed to go free, the Scots supporters killed. Fordun contradicts this, saying that both Scots and English alike were taken and slain, with 'the rabble spared.' Bower quotes a contemporary poem: 'those who rejected terms while they could, hence have deserved and received destruction.' This seems to agree with Fordun. However the Earl of Strathearn certainly survived the siege, as did Oliphant who received an English safe conduct to go to Scotland in 1313, possibly to pay his ransom. Barbour says that the earl of Strathearn was in the garrison and was taken before Bruce by his son, who sided with the Scots. This is unlikely; as late as 1311 Strathearn and his son Malise were in England, Malise's allowance was being paid by the English in early 1313. It is possible that Strathearn was taken at Perth and died shortly after. It was then that the son came out in support of Bruce.[78]

Bruce took command of the siege of Dumfries. Dungal Macdouall held the castle which will have been an incentive for the king's personal involvement. Macdouall surrendered in February 1313 and despite his history Bruce honoured the surrender terms and allowed him to go free. Caerlaverock and Buittle fell soon after. We next find Macdouall on the Isle of Man where he took command of Rushen castle. The lordship of the Island was the subject of a dispute between Henry Beaumont and Simon Montagu. This left Bruce an opportunity to take the island. A force landed at Douglas on the 18 May. After a five week siege Macdouall lost yet another castle. He was forced even further west, into Ulster.

The peel at Linlithgow formed an important supply point and staging post between the major castles at Stirling and Edinburgh. It was taken sometime in September or October 1313. Following the tradition of popular heroes it was a husbandman, Matthew Binnock, who jammed his haywain in the peel's doorway. Hidden in the hay lay eight Scots who could defend the gate until a force could approach the peel. Once captured the peel was destroyed and all in the garrison slain.[79]

The payments for truces were meant to buy time before the king could come north but he never did. In May 1313 the king accepted an invitation from the king of France to attend the crowning of Philip's son as king of Navarre. The earl of Angus gave a report of Northumberland's plight in 1313. The king merely gave the county a mandate 'to use their utmost endeavours in defending the county.' He told the people of Cumberland that they would have to look after themselves until he returned. Philip's friendship and aid were more important now.[80] Under these circumstances it is easy to understand why Edward I was remembered with such reverence. It would be very difficult to imagine the circumstances in which Edward Longshanks would have left the north undefended for so long or Bruce's raids unpunished.

In 1314 the northern English counties 'neither having nor hoping for any defence or help from the king (seeing that he was engaged in distant parts of England seeming not to give them a thought) offered to the said Bruce no small some of money.'[81] The mere threat of an invasion had been enough to secure a tribute. The north of England lay on the periphery of the kingdom. English wealth was concentrated in the south and the midlands. It was all too easy for the government of England to remain detached from the suffering in the north, an expedient to leave the north to defend itself.

Two events then contrived to bring an English army to Scotland. The first was the arrival at court of Adam Gordon. Much to the astonishment of the Anglo-Scots he had been arrested by the Roxburgh garrison. He was only released on the condition that he appeared before the king to explain himself. Gordon brought with him an appeal for help signed by Patrick Dunbar earl of March. Dunbar and Gordon calculated the county's loss since Edward had left in 1311 at £20,000, with 'matters daily getting worse.' Livestock had not only been plundered from the enemy but also by the garrisons at Berwick and Roxburgh. It is not surprising that the complaints were aimed at these two garrisons, which had few Scottish members, 20 out of 328 at Berwick, only 5 out of 63 at Roxburgh, a far smaller proportion than in other garrisons.[82] Gilbert Middleton's name was conspicuous in the charge against the Berwick garrison: a corrupt and lawless commander.

The Roxburgh garrison had plundered and imprisoned merchants in the town. The Berwick garrison had organised a raid that had taken 4000 sheep and kidnapped thirty citizens. They were accused of killing those who had no money to pay a ransom, throwing their bodies into the Tweed.[83] The king commissioned Angus, the keeper of Berwick, and

John Weston, chamberlain of Scotland, to enquire into the state of Northumberland, Berwick and Roxburgh but it was clear that more strident action was required. Certainly, Gordon's presence galvanised Edward.

Edward also feared that his Scottish supporters might desert en masse. The Lanercost chronicler makes the claim that:

> 'In all these aforesaid campaigns the Scots were so divided among themselves that sometimes the father was on the Scottish side and the son on the English, and vice versa; also one brother might be with the Scots and another with the English; yea, even the same individual be first with one party and then with the other. But all those who were with the English were merely feigning, either because it was the stronger party, or in order to save the lands they possessed in England; for their hearts were always with their own people, although their persons might nor be so.'[84]

This may just be picket fence xenophobia. Some Scots no doubt began to desert which left the remainder under suspicion. The English counties had no option but to make do, to pay the tributes or suffer the consequences of a Scottish invasion. In Scotland, where the lack of protection from the south was probably felt most acutely, there was a choice: Edward's Scottish supporters could fend for themselves or accept Bruce's kingship. Bruce was ready to exploit any remaining doubt amongst Edward's Scottish supporters. In a parliament held in Dundee in October or early November 1313 he proclaimed that those Scots who did not come into his peace within one year would face forfeiture and perpetual disinheritance.[85]

Edward answered this by declaring he would take an army to Scotland in the summer of 1314. By doing so he neutralised Bruce's demand for recognition from Edward's Scottish supporters.[86] Besides, Edward's position at home was now much stronger. He had divided his opponents after Gaveston's death and slowly worn down Lancaster and Warwick's opposition. In October 1313 the king and magnates agreed a shaky truce after the opposition appeared and made a public apology. This was a victory for the king as he was in no way restricted by the ordinances that were declared invalid, although he had not crushed the opposition.

This declaration by Edward added a new urgency to the destruction of English bases. During the feast of Shrove Tuesday (19 February 1314) Douglas 'cunningly' took Roxburgh. His force approached the castle on their hands and knees dressed in black to look like cattle against the night sky—this was not pantomime, medieval cattle were considerably smaller than they are today. Rope ladders were used to scale the walls and a sentry who was roused by the noise of the grappling hooks was silenced by the first man over the wall: 'stekit upwar with ane knyff.' The garrison were celebrating the feast in the great hall, 'dancing, singing and otherways playing,' games that ended when the war cry went up, 'Douglas, Douglas.' The castle commander, the Gascon William de Fiennes, managed to secure the castle's great tower although this fell shortly after. Fiennes was wounded in the face by an arrow while defending the tower and died from his wounds. The castle was razed 'lest the English should ever hereafter be able to lord it over the land through holding the castles.'[87]

Not to be outdone Edinburgh fell soon after to Thomas Randolph. The north face of the castle stands on the steepest and highest side of the castle crag and was believed to be impregnable. A local man, William Francis, told Randolph that he was the son of a former keeper and knew a route up the north face that he had learnt as a boy when he secretly visited a 'wench' in the town. A general assault on the east gate drew the complete garrison. Randolph, Francis and thirty men climbed the crag and gained entry with rope ladders; once in the gates were secured and opened, the English garrison killed, the castle razed. Piers Lubaud, a Gascon knight and sheriff of Edinburgh deserted the English but was later accused of treason by Bruce and hanged.[88]

The English chroniclers say that after the success at Roxburgh and Edinburgh Bruce marched to Stirling and began the siege of the castle. Stirling had ready access to the higher tidal reaches of the Forth so could be supplied easily, while its height made it almost impregnable to storm without lengthy siege operations. Once Bruce had established a blockade around the fortress he left the siege to his brother, Edward. With supplies running low the castle's commander, Philip Moubray, persuaded Edward Bruce to raise the siege if a relieving force did not appear within three leagues of the town by Midsummer Day 1314. Barbour says that the siege of the castle began in lent 1313 and the respite given was a year long. This is unlikely; a year long truce is unheard of, contradicted by English sources and it conflicts with the change of English plans during the Spring. Military writs were issued at Westminster on 23 December for a muster on 10 June at Berwick.

It was only after Philip Moubray came south to press for the castle's relief that these plans were revised: by 26 February 1314 the king had decided to go to Scotland after Easter. Fresh writs were issued on the 24 March, for a summons three weeks later.[89] This type of agreement was common; it brought a welcome relief for both sides from the harsh realities of a long siege. In 1313 those realities were much harsher for the English garrison than for Edward Bruce. What motivated this generous folly is unknown. It was blunder, made in the knowledge that an English army was due to arrive in Scotland in mid-summer. It certainly gained him a severe rebuke from his brother since by the compact Edward Bruce had set the day for a pitched battle, aware that he stood little chance against the full the full array of English heavy cavalry that he could not hope to match.

Chapter 7

BANNOCKBURN

'So many fine noblemen and valiant youths, so many noble horses, so much military equipment, costly garments and gold plate—all lost in one unfortunate day—one fleeting hour.'
Vita Edwardi Secundi

Edward II marched north, confident not just of relieving Stirling but of bringing the Wars of Independence to a close. On 17 June 1314 the host left Berwick and Wark, conscious that no English king had been defeated in Scotland for more than 600 years.[1] Edward believed his problems lay behind him in England. He was 'light of heart' wrote the Monk of Malmesbury, as if on a pilgrimage.[2] His army straddled miles of countryside. From a distance the land, in Barbour's well-turned phrase, glittered as the sun, 'brycht and schynand cler', reflected off their polished armour as embroidered banners, standards and pennons gently blew in the light breeze.

It was a spectacle which stirred Robert Keith and James Douglas who had been sent to reconnoitre. They caught sight of the army as it made its way towards Stirling and returned to the Scottish camp to inform Bruce that he faced 'the stoutest men in Christendom'. Bruce was shrewd enough to suppress the news, telling his men that the English approached in disarray. He well understood that battles could be won and lost in the combatants' minds before a single blow was struck.[3]

For all its apparent strength, the English army had been late to assemble. With the midsummer deadline for Stirling's relief only a week away, the army had to make a gruelling forced march to reach the castle: 'Brief were the halts for sleep, briefer still for food; hence horsemen and infantry were worn out with toil and hunger.' In its wake followed a vast wagon train, 110 wagons drawn by teams of eight oxen, 106 by teams of four horse. Malmesbury believed 'if they had been extended in a single line [they] would have occupied the space of 20 leagues.'[4] (In fact a harnessed wagon measured about 12 metres in length. Given a five metre or so gap between wagons the train, in the unlikely event it found itself in a single column, would have extended over about one and a half miles). Even so the wagon train slowed the army's progress, and many wagons were there to keep knights in the grand fashion of a medieval warrior. Eighty wagons were filled with food, reflecting the decision to cross the country inland, rather than hugging the coast where fresh supplies could reach them from the sea. Yet this was only enough to feed the army for a few days.

The host moved along the Tweed valley and then up Lauderdale, arriving at Edinburgh on 19 June to rendezvous with ships carrying fresh provisions at Leith. It rested two days, waiting for the arrival of the rear of the army and for contingents that had arrived too late for the muster. The army set out again early on the morning of the 22 June, compelled to make a hot, dusty, forced march, covering 20 miles to reach Falkirk — still 14 miles short of Stirling. On the following day they pushed on. A tired host arrived three miles from Stirling a day early. By the terms of the covenant agreed between the governor of Stirling and Edward Bruce, the castle had been relieved.

The following two days have been the subject of intense scrutiny from historians ever since. Speculation has often succeeded in confusing an already complex story. There is only one eyewitness report, from Robert Baston, an English friar captured by the Scots and forced to pen a poetic record which he had promised to write for the English. His account adds little to our knowledge of the battle and still less to poetry.[5]

The fullest accounts are John Barbour's *Bruce*, written in 1375, and Thomas Grey's *Scalacronica,* written in 1355; other useful information can be found in the Lanercost chronicle, written about 1346, and based on an unnamed eyewitness; and the contemporary *Vita Edwardi Secundi*, the closest contemporary source[6], written only twelve years after the battle. Grey wrote the *Scalacronica* while a prisoner in Edinburgh castle between 1355 and 1357; set amongst the works of clerics who never saw a battle it has the rare advantage of being written by a soldier. It is based on a blow-by-blow account given to him by his father who was at the battle, and on no longer extant chronicles of the battle kept in the castle's library. Barbour's sources are unnamed; by the time he wrote *Bruce* most of combatants would have died so that it is to family traditions together with a few veterans themselves that he had to rely on to write his chronicle. He would also have been able to use the chronicles Grey had worked from, chronicles he embellished as his sense of theatre got the better of him.

It is easy to be swept along by Barbour's graphic prose and to lend too much weight to his account when compared to the more pedestrian English chronicles. Although these are not partisan accounts with rival points of view. The English chroniclers could not represent Bannockburn as anything other than a disastrous defeat suffered by a disastrous king. They have an independent consistency which suggests that our knowledge of the essential points of the battle itself, the outline of strategy, the steadfast Scottish onslaught, the gallantry of the English knights, the scale of the disaster, is largely accurate, even though they contain crucial discrepancies in points of detail which inevitably creep into accounts written a generation later.

The first area of dispute involves the number of combatants. The incredible figures given for the strength of the two armies in Barbour's *Bruce*, 100,000 English and 30,000 Scots, were left largely unchallenged until Mackenzie's ground breaking study, *The Battle of Bannockburn*, appeared in 1913 which placed the English army at a more manageable 20,000, with cavalry numbering only 2,000. Since then attempts have been made to scale down the size of the army still further, by one author to 6-7,000 infantry and 450-500 cavalry[7], no larger than the force available to Robert Bruce.

The English army was formed from three distinct groups: at its head was the king with his household, followed by the magnates who brought their own retinues, and lastly the infantry formed from the county levies. The later years of Edward I's reign had seen a decline in the value of foot, which would not be reversed until the reign of Edward III. Edward had hoped to mount a campaign in Easter. Writs had been issued in March 1314 to the northern counties for 6,500 foot soldiers. These were followed onthe 14 April by new writs seeking a further 10,000 men. As spring slipped by and the campaign failed to materialise new writs were prepared for a June muster.

Edward II arrived in the north towards the end of May. On the 27th he wrote from Newminster in Northumberland to recruiting officers to press for greater efforts to raise infantry since he had been informed that 'the Scots are striving to assemble great numbers of foot in strong and marshy places, extremely hard for cavalry to penetrate, between us and our castle of Stirling.' It was an innovative plan: an army dominated by foot soldiers at the expense of cavalry. It showed a grasp of strategy which deserted him at the battle itself. His letter to the recruiting officers indicates he was having difficulty finding troops and was enclosed with fresh writs calling for 21,540 men to muster at Wark on 10 June.

Issuing writs was one thing, raising troops was another. Commissioners of array often had difficulty finding men to fight; the system for choosing troops was open to corruption and once formed infantry forces were dogged by desertion. As a crude measure armies could hope to muster about half of the number of troops ordered, which would give Edward 10,000 to 11,000 infantry at Bannockburn. Sometimes it was far worse: in the Welsh wars one muster had called for 16,000 foot, but only 6,619 reached the front. In 1319 only 25 per cent of the men turned up. Only for truly popular campaigns would the total exceed the 50 per cent mark. And this was not a popular campaign.

Medieval armies were notoriously slow to form, but even if some troops had been made ready by the earlier writs, the short interval between 27 May writ and 10 June muster must raise doubts as to whether even a 50 per cent turn-out was achieved. The writs to South Wales and Lincolnshire would have to travel more than 200 miles, the men arrayed and then marched on foot to the muster. It was not surprising that Edward had to delay the march into Scotland as he waited for contingents to arrive.[8] It therefore seems unlikely that he had any more than 10,000 infantry.

Calculating the numbers of cavalry in the English army is an even thornier problem. The mounted arm was formed from an informal call up of the feudal levy and the king's household. Since no formal feudal muster was ordered, no muster rolls were kept; since no payments were made for cavalry service, no wardrobe accounts were maintained. The *Vita* gives Edward 2,000 horsemen; Barbour, although counting 40,000 cavalry in total, makes a distinction for the 'helit', or covered horse, which he numbers at 3,000. This consistency has some appeal and would have been a fine cavalry force when measured against the numbers mustered for other campaigns: Edward I had 2,400 cavalry at Falkirk, Edward III the same number at Crécy.

Yet Edward had been forced to rely upon the feudal levy. In 1310, the most comparable campaign, feudal writs had been issued to 175 tenants-in-chief. Their liability amounted to 236 knights, for which 51 men-at-arms and 370 *servientes*, light horse, were sent: a mounted force of 421 men. In 1314 writs were only issued to 95 chiefs, which would yield no more than 300 men.[9] Added to their number would be the king's household knights and retainers. One writer suggest these would only number perhaps 200 in all.[10] This is probably too conservative; in the admittedly well-supported Galloway campaign of 1300 the household cavalry numbered 850.

Many of the nobility would have brought far more men-at-arms than their obligation to the feudal levy required. 'The size and splendour of a magnate's retinue signalled his importance in the world; this indeed was very largely its purpose.'[11] But many nobles were missing from the campaign. The army that Edward had hoped would unify his realm and remove once and for all instability in England had gaps, exposing the previous year's reconciliation between Edward and the barons for the hollow sham it was. As early as 23 December 1313 Edward had issued writs of military service to the nobles to meet him at Berwick for the abandoned Easter campaign. They replied:

> 'that it would be better for all to meet in parliament and there unanimously decide what ought to be done in this

matter rather than to proceed so inadvisedly; this moreover would be in accord with the Ordinances. But the king said that the present business was very urgent and he could not wait for parliament. The earls said that they would not fight without parliament, lest it should happen that they infringed the Ordinances. Some counsellors and household officials therefore advised the king to demand their due service from all, and set out boldly to Scotland. It was certain that so many would come to his aid that neither Robert Bruce nor the Scots would resist. What of the earl of Gloucester, the earl of Pembroke, the earl of Hereford, Robert de Clifford, Hugh Despenser and the king's household and the other barons in England? All these would come with their knights: there was no need to worry about the other earls.'[12]

Edward had cancelled a parliament due to meet in April; believing it would bring unnecessary delay to the Easter campaign's preparations, he saw no reason to reinstate it. Hereford, though a member of the opposition in 1312, had proved instrumental in the peace of 1313 which marked him out as a moderate.

The most powerful magnate, Lancaster, reminded Edward that without parliamentary sanction this was a private expedition, and begged leave not to attend personally. From the military muscle of his five earldoms he sent the smallest contingent that his feudal service would allow while he sat in his castle at Pontefract awaiting the outcome. It was 'a transparent excuse.' An earlier parliament, in 1313, had granted a subsidy for this very purpose: sanction for a campaign was inherent in that grant. Lancaster feared a successful Edward would return victorious from Scotland ready to deal with his enemies in England, while defeat would, and did, greatly strengthen Lancaster's own hand.

Warwick followed Lancaster's lead, while Arundel blew with the prevailing wind. Earl Warenne was trying to have his marriage to Joan de Bar, the king's niece, annulled which may have strained his relationship with Edward; he also feared a resurgent Lancaster.[13] The 14-year old Norfolk was just too young to attend. Between them the absent earls may have sent as few as 60 men-at-arms. Edward's plea of necessity made no impression.

If these reluctant lords left the king short of cavalry, Edward might have turned to his domains outside England. Barbour tells us that he had 'a gret mengne' from Ireland, Aquitaine and Bayonne.[14] There is no reliable source to estimate their numbers. From Scotland, Ingram de

Umfraville, and the earl of Angus was there, as was John Comyn, son of the murdered 'Red' Comyn. Patrick Dunbar, whose letter to Edward in the previous November had brought a promise of relief, was not. It is likely that the campaign brought adventurers from throughout the English king's domains, but in no greater numbers than for other campaigns and certainly not enough to make up for those who were missing.

The *Vita Edwardi* credits Gloucester with a retinue of 500 cavalry[15], which is an outrageously inflated figure. It is given by Malmesbury, a chronicler obsessed with his belief that Gloucester's death was the result of the desertion of his own men and he exaggerates Gloucester's contingent to strengthen his case. Historians have long known of the unreliability of such uncorroborated chronicle evidence, yet persist in supporting Malmesbury, using his work to support wild claims for the numbers of English cavalry. Not even Lancaster (with the strength of five earldoms) could match this number in the 1318-1319 campaign.

The single contingent which is recorded (that of Aymer Valence) amounted to 22 knights and 59 men-at-arms, including 18 attached to his retainers, Hastings and Berkeley.[16] Gloucester's retinue is likely to have slightly outnumbered Pembroke's, a ratio can be found in the number of protections each men sought: 86 for Pembroke, 131 for Gloucester.[17] Gloucester lost his life while in command of the van, so it is possible that Malmesbury is confusing his personal retinue with this command.

The command of a second battle went to Clifford, who Grey has with 300 men. If these two figures are correct then we are approaching the likely size of the cavalry. The king's own command would have been the largest of the three English battles. If he had 600-700 men then the total force of the English cavalry would have been 1,400-1,500 men, which, incidentally, is the number mustered for the next comparable campaign in 1319 when parliamentary assent meant the opposition barons did attend.

We are completely in the dark when trying to estimate the size of the Scottish army. Barbour's numbers of 100,000 English, 30,000 Scots have been converted into a ratio of Scottish to English forces: three English to one Scot, but there is no evidence to support this. There is no known method for calculating a country's army from its population[18], and in any case it is unknown how much support Bruce could count upon: many areas and magnates were still hostile towards him. Neither had Bruce resurrected the feudal mechanisms for forming large armies that had existed in Scotland since the times of David I. There would have been little point: the strength of Bruce's army came from the middle lords, not the earls. Few of the important men of the realm were with him, and only five warranted mentioning, his brother Edward, his nephew Thomas Randolph, Walter, the Steward, James Douglas and Robert Keith.[19] Without the top layer of the feudal pyramid the mechanism for calling up a feudal army was redundant—men owned allegiance to their feudal lord, not their country or king.

Bruce had hitherto relied on a small group of guerrilla soldiers, numbered in their hundreds, not thousands, men who he could trust to 'wyn all or de with honour'.[20] Not knowing when Edward would invade Bruce had began assembling his army as early as April or May. Although some no doubt drifted away in the long wait for the midsummer deadline, this early muster offered him an unexpected advantage. Wellington said that his own men frightened him, not by their ability, but by their ability to run out of control. The same was true of medieval infantry, a poorly trained mob whose limited strength came from its weight of numbers. The schiltron was its single answer to heavy cavalry, but it was only as strong as its weakest section.

During the early summer months Bruce was able to train his force, so it would not be a mob that he took into the field. He crafted a schiltron that could move, rather than passively absorb the knights' charge as at Falkirk. Those men-at-arms available to him—too few to fight as a discrete unit—dismounted to join the schiltrons. These veterans gave Bruce's schiltrons a heavily-armed core. It was a tactic used by the English at the battle of the Standard to stiffen the levy and it is ungenerous to suggest that Bruce placed them there so that they could not repeat the desertion of the men-at-arms that took place at Falkirk and Dunbar. There was a limit to the number of men that could form a schiltron before it became too cumbersome to manoeuvre: at most they contained 1,000 to 1,500 men. This suggests Bruce's fighting force was between 3,000 and 4,500 strong.

Those who joined the army late were set aside, perhaps as many as 3,000 'small folk', whose enthusiasm and home made weapons were a poor substitute for good training. They were positioned away from the main force, in a depression north-west of Coxet Hill that would not have been visible to the English. If Bruce lacked the men and equipment of the English he still had a skilled military force, highly committed and better led.

It is known that Bruce only had light horse, 500 or so under the marishal Sir Robert Keith. In contrast to the heavy cavalry favoured by the English, they had been used by Bruce as part of his guerrilla warfare, and although they wore mail they rode light horses able to cross long distances for lightning raids. There was no heavy cavalry in his force since the heavy horse, the *destrier*, was not bred in Scotland. This was a horse reserved for the military elite, the numbers of them in the English army would have been numbered in hundreds, not thousands. They were not protected by armour, a later development which required still heavier horses. Keith's cavalry were of little use against mounted English knights so they stayed out of sight until the English archers showed themselves.

Barbour has the Scots in four divisions: the vanguard under Randolph, the rear under Bruce and a third under Edward Bruce. A fourth battle was under the nominal command of Walter the Steward. These four battles, in a diamond formation, have been largely accepted, yet it relies far too heavily on Barbour and conflicts with the English eye-witnesses. They all specify three Scottish battles: on the second day the *Vita* has 'two divisions advanced like a thick set hedge' (with Bruce behind them); Lanercost has the 'Scots two columns ... abreast so that neither should be in advance of the third'; the *Scalacronica* has them leaving 'the wood in three divisions of infantry.'[21]

Barbour is a persuasive writer. From the start he forms the Scots into four battles, and then sticks rigidly to his story. He has not convinced his most recent editors: 'Barbour's mention of a fourth division, assigned to the 'beardless boy' Walter Stewart and new-made knight Sir James Douglas, is extremely dubious, irreconcilable with English statements and fitting uneasily with the poet's own account of the Sir James's movements.'[22] After seven years at Bruce's side it was only on the eve of Bannockburn that he received his knighthood. By no means was he in the same rank as the earl of Moray or the king's brother. It seems more likely that Sir James Douglas commanded cavalry and dismounted to bolster Randolph's battle which would reveal why the *Scalacronica* places him on the Sunday in charge of the first battle to engage the English, which we know to have been Randolph's. Barbour's editors have explained the Steward's promotion simply as a '1376 ... compliment that would be appreciated by Robert II', his son.

* * *

Barbour has the English in 'batailles ten' for the march north, an array kept for the battle itself. Barbour is playing games with us. Where doubt can be entertained with the fourth Scottish battle the seven surplus English divisions are not credible—they would have been unwieldy, it is at odds with the English sources, breaks standard military convention and leaves men such as the earls of Angus and Pembroke in supporting roles and Hereford and Gloucester sharing a command while presumably lesser men were given their own divisions to command.[23] The English were in three groups, the van under Gloucester and Hereford, the centre under Edward and the right under Clifford. It is the classic medieval military convention: van, centre, right; Gloucester, Edward, Clifford; King Robert, Edward Bruce, Randolph.

The most that can be said of the opposing forces is that the English army was larger, and that its superiority was greatest in cavalry. The debate about the size of the army is in any case irrelevant since the English infantry played so small a part in the fight. The importance lies in the tactics of the battle itself, a contest between trained pikemen and what was considered the pinnacle of military evolution since the battle of Hastings: mounted men-at-arms.

As the English moved towards Stirling Bruce led his army from their mustering point at Torwood, about eight miles from the castle, to the forests at New Park, two miles from the castle. He had chosen his ground well. A muster near Stirling meant that if he chose to give battle he could be sure that the two armies would not miss each other—not uncommon in medieval warfare. It also forced the English deep into enemy land where they would have difficulty finding supplies.[24]

The road to Stirling castle passed through the New Park, an area of heavy woodland planted by Alexander II, where it would be difficult for the English cavalry to deploy, but where Bruce expected that the English would attempt to force a passage. The only open ground for cavalry lay before the edge of the wood, between the Bannock Burn and 'the Entry'. To guard against action here Bruce ordered shallow pits to be dug either side of the road. These 'pottes' which, to borrow Barbour's metaphor, honeycombed the entrance to the wood, were disguised with a light covering which would give under the weight of a horse. Caltrops, small weapons armed with four spikes arranged so one stands upright, were scattered around the entry to cripple horses.

To the east of the wooded plateau the land drops steeply away towards the Forth into a boggy area known as the Carse. The sharp incline would have prevented either arrayed infantry or cavalry from remaining in formation while making a determined attack. An attack either along the road or from the Carse could be beaten off by a determined defence. Denied the road the English would have to cross the Bannock Burn, a tributary of the Forth, to reach Stirling castle.

The Bannock itself would have presented a more formidable obstacle than it does today, although not impassable as much of the burn had a firm bed. The ground between the Bannock and Stirling, now drained, varied: Grey describes it as 'an evil, deep, wet marsh', but there were also areas of firm ground that could take cavalry movements. The Scottish vanguard, under Randolph, was placed nearest Stirling by St Ninian's Kirk, from where he could look out across the Carse and intercept any flanking movement; Bruce himself led the rear schiltron, towards the English, guarding the entrance to the wood at 'the Entry'. On the eve of the battle he had deployed his men for retreat.

The English had arrived late on the afternoon of 23 June. They were met by Sir Philip Moubray who must have brought vital intelligence. The ground was well known to the English, they had held the castle for a decade and Moubray was witness to the general thread of Bruce's movements. He warned Edward that the Scots had blocked the narrow Roman road in the forest which would be difficult to pass and advised him that the conditions of the pact he had made with Edward Bruce a year earlier had been met and a pitched battle could be avoided. It was advice too easily ignored. The English had sought a battle and the Scots avoided it for too long; English contempt for their enemy meant, with some historical justification, that even now they believed the mere sight of the host would be enough to frighten them away.[25]

As the bulk of the English army came together about a mile from the Bannock Burn, Edward ordered a halt so that a plan of action could be devised. In the van the earls of Hereford and Gloucester could see activity across the burn. Whether the order to stop never reached them, or whether they ignored it in the belief the Scots were about to slip away will never be known. The van advanced across the burn along the Roman road. In fact, Gloucester and Hereford been watching Robert Bruce forming his battle into schiltron formation.

* * *

Robert Bruce could be clearly identified by the gold crown that he wore over a heavy leather helmet. The sight of this old enemy so close was too inviting for the hot-headed earl of Hereford's nephew, Sir Henry Bohun[26], who was to the fore leading a Welsh infantry troop. He charged Bruce who took up the challenge. Riding a more nimble horse, 'a litill palfrey grey and joly', Bruce skilfully side-stepped Bohun's lance, in Barbour's words: 'Scher Henry myssit the nobill Kyng'.[27] As the hapless knight, baffled and unbalanced by his miss, rode past Bruce rose in his stirrups and with his full weight swung his axe through Bohun's helmet. The blow was so heavy it broke the axe into two pieces, leaving the head impaled in its victim's skull. In a rash but stirring act of loyalty Bohun's squire leapt to his lord's body to shield it from the oncoming Scots, only to be overwhelmed and slain.

Bruce's men moved forward to drive back the English, who were worsted in the melee that followed and Gloucester was unhorsed. It said much for the discipline of the Scots that they heeded Bruce's call to retire rather than follow up their victory in the chase, although his lords censured him for accepting Bohun's challenge which had placed him and his cause in such peril. Bruce brushed off their rebuke—lamenting the loss of the axe-shaft.

With the Stirling road blocked, Edward determined to carry out a flanking movement. He sent Robert Clifford and Henry Beaumont across the Carse with a 300 mounted men-at-arms[28], intending to reach the castle. Had they succeeded, the strengthened garrison would have been useful for Edward. Located behind the Scottish army, it would also have obstructed an orderly retreat in the event of Scottish defeat, although the force was too small to have prevented Bruce retiring if he wished to avoid battle. Clifford crossed the Bannock and moved parallel to the escarpment, but well away from the trees.

Barbour claims that Clifford had already 'passit by' Randolph's battle before being spotted by Bruce; who then gave Randolph the stinging rebuke that a 'rose of his chaplete was fallyn', sending him scurrying to his own men. Grey offers an alternative version which gives both Randolph and the English more credit. He has Clifford's action taking place at the same time as the van confronted Bruce—in a two-pronged assault that indicates English strategy was better planned than Barbour suggests. The *Scalacronica* has Randolph waiting, presumably with his battle and not by Bruce's side, and not emerging from the woods until Clifford had passed too far along the Carse for English reinforcements to reach him.

It seems unlikely that neither Randolph nor his lieutenants could have missed a cavalry action across the one piece of open ground they had been directed to guard. To move into a position that would threaten Clifford, Randolph must have broken up the schiltron and moved the men down the embankment before reforming close to the cavalry. It was a dangerous and exposed manoeuvre.

Henry Beaumont was heard to call out 'Let them come on, give them some ground' so that he could have space for the cavalry to operate. Thomas Grey questioned the sense of charging the schiltron. As Randolph's men were on foot it would have been easy for Beaumont to continue and reach the castle. Instead Beaumont challenged Grey's courage—an accusation which was ill directed considering Grey's prominent role in the English occupation during the difficult years since Edward I's death. It was also a charge to which hot-headed knights had one resort: Grey recklessly spurred his horse between Beaumont and William Deyncourt and charged into the thick of the schiltron taking Deyncourt in his wake. Grey's horse was killed from beneath him and as the helpless knight floundered the schiltron opened up to take him prisoner. Deyncourt was killed.

It was a small, but desperate engagement. In the heat of the late afternoon the combatants became soaked in sweat. As the knights circled the schiltron, trying to break into its impenetrable wall of spears, a cloud of dust rose up, leaving them veiled in darkness. In frustration the English knights resorted to flinging spears, darts, knives, swords and maces at the infantry until 'inwith thame ane montane was of wapyns.' As the other 'battles' looked on James Douglas pressed Bruce to allow him to relieve Randolph. Bruce refused at first, still believing that the defence of the Roman road was more important. When he finally relented Douglas moved down the escarpment. When the English saw them they gave up their futile task. As they drew off Randolph counter-attacked, pushing his schiltron forward, dividing Clifford's force so that some headed back to the host, others in the direction of Stirling castle. Douglas held off when he saw the English depart, less he should deflect Randolph's glory.

* * *

As the evening drew on the English called a halt to any further attacks on the Scots, deciding to move the bulk of the army across the Bannock Burn. Where and how it took place is unclear, and for many years it was believed that the English remained south of the burn. When Mackay Mackenzie proposed his new site for the battle many critics found the idea of the English crossing the burn one of the most difficult to accept.[29] They argued that it was a poor military decision: a movement of a tired army across a not inconsiderable barrier while exposing its flank. However, the chronicle evidence is not so easily brushed aside: not only do they point to a crossing, but their accounts of the battle can only fit sites on the far side of the burn. Barbour has the English

> 'harboured … that night down in the Carse and as there were pools they broke houses and thatch to make bridges, and some say that folk in the Castle, when night fell, bore doors and shutters with them, so that they had before day bridged them, so that they were passed over every one and had taken the hard field on horse.'[30]

It is unlikely that enough material was found to provide a dry crossing of the burn itself, but peat overlaying clay soil creates a terrain riddled with a maze of narrow, deeply cut streams which could have been filled in places. These streams have been mistaken for generations as pools, a mistranslation of Barbour's 'pols' (streams), so many maps of the battle site are potmarked with ponds![31]

The *Scalacronica* describes how they

> 'debauched upon a plain near the water of the Forth beyond Bannockburn, an evil, deep, wet marsh, where the said English army stayed in harness and remained all night, having sadly lost confidence and being much disaffected by the events of the day.'[32]

The *Lanercost* chronicler sends them across 'a great ditch into which the tide comes from the sea, called the Bannockburn.'[33] The chronicles clearly point to a crossing, but they do not, unfortunately point in a particular direction. Given the size of the army a number of crossing points must have been chosen to avoid creating an exposed bridgehead, and to move the army across in the time it took, probably above the tidal range of the burn. The army then settled down for a restless night. Fearing a night attack—the Scottish army was only a mile or so away— the camp was well guarded, the soldiers keeping themselves awake with drinking and revelry while the crossing itself was not complete until shortly before dawn. Some of the infantry may have remained on the other bank with the baggage train.

Edward's move must be seen in the light of his desire to force a pitched battle. With the English across the burn it would be difficult for the Scots to break camp. Bruce's clash with the English van had shown the English that the road was not passable, and had no room for cavalry action. In any case, why should Edward fall into the trap Bruce had so carefully prepared for him? Clifford and Randolph's engagement had shown that there was firm and dry ground between the Carse and the wood where cavalry could be deployed. This final site was not a battlefield of Edward's choosing, but he, together with the rest of the leadership, did not believe the Scots posed a threat to the whole English army, despite Clifford's defeat. There was no reason for the English to believe this was where the battle would be fought. They assumed they would have time to array their cavalry and archers properly. The thought that the Scottish infantry would approach them never entered their heads, so strong was their conviction that cavalry outranked infantry.

The English were tired, the forced marches in the hot sun over the past week meant that there had been little time to rest or feed men or horses. They had lost confidence after the day's skirmishes. Worse still, Bruce knew it. In 1308 or 1310 Alexander Seton had entered into a solemn bond at Cambuskenneth abbey with Gilbert Hay and Neil Campbell 'that they fought to defend the freedom of the kingdom and Robert lately crowned king, against all mortals, French, English and Scots, to their last breath.' Hay and Campbell became two of Bruce's most constant companions, but Seton had returned to his Lothian estates and remained in Edward II's peace. He now made a critical intervention.[34] The night before the battle, Seton deserted from the English army and revealed to Bruce how disorganized and dispirited parts of it were. Indeed, Seton pledged his head that the Scots would win an easy victory if they fought the next day.

Bruce had been on the point of pulling back to Lennox.[35] He passed up the opportunity to attack the English before they crossed the burn — as Wallace had at Falkirk. He now put the decision to the army, whose leaders unanimously called on him to fight. It is difficult to believe Bruce put the question without being sure of hearing the answer he wanted. A pitched battle risked everything. Defeat would mean the final loss of his cause despite all the ground he had won so expensively in the preceding years.

During the night the earl of Atholl crossed Cambuskenneth and killed Sir William Airth and many others who were in charge of the Scottish supply depot. The motive for his attack will never be known for certain, but it may have been aimed at Edward Bruce who had seduced and then abandoned his sister. Or Atholl simply believed an English victory was imminent. Whatever the reason, Atholl's treachery at such a moment was a powerful reminder—if any were needed—that Robert was still unsure of his friends, and that his enemies were still a force to be reckoned with.

Bannockburn is a typically anonymous battlefield, made more so since the National Trust's interpretative centre is placed on the Borestone, the traditional site for the battle that has long been dismissed by historians. It is at odds with the description of the site in all the chronicle sources, and cannot possibly contain the day's actions.[36] It is the traditional site, but the tradition only dates from the eighteenth century. Medieval men saw no reason to mark the sites of battles and the precise site of the battle is unknown. The general area has been drained for agricultural use and part covered by an industrial estate. A case can be built for three distinct sites: Mackenzie's 'buckle of the Forth', Miller's Dryfield, and Christison's Pelstream/Bannockburn triangle.[37] That the garrison brought material to help cross the 'pols' convinced Mackenzie that the English camped the night in the buckle of the Forth; any other site would have meant carrying these doors and shutters across hostile ground. But if the battle was fought here the English would have had to cross the Pelstream, a considerable obstacle in itself which could only be crossed by the English with their backs turned to Bruce, and which does not figure in the chronicles. Neither does it play a part in the rout. It seems unlikely that the English crossed the Pelstream, but camped and fought somewhere between it and Bannockburn.

The Christison site, adopted by the National Trust, lies between the Pelstream, the Bannockburn and the 50 foot contour. The Reverend Miller proposed a site on the Dryfield, scrub-land above the 50 foot contour. Professor Barrow supports this site, and has demonstrated the the battlefield was named after the location, Bannock, a settlement with its own community on the Carse, rather than the burn. This site is far easier to reconcile with the day's action. Bruce needed to fight on a narrow front. The line between the Pelstream and the Bannockburn is over 1.5 miles long, so his men would have been no more than three men deep: too thinly spread to survive a cavalry charge. Up on the Dryfield, his flanks would have been protected by deep gullies cut into the ridge. This site also accounts for the difficulty the English had deploying their

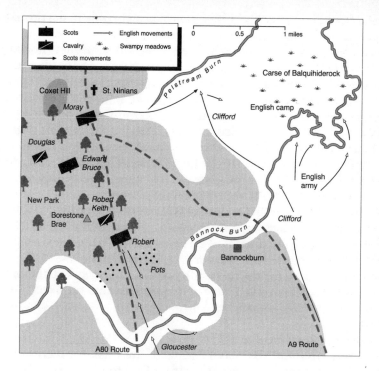

Bannockburn – first moves

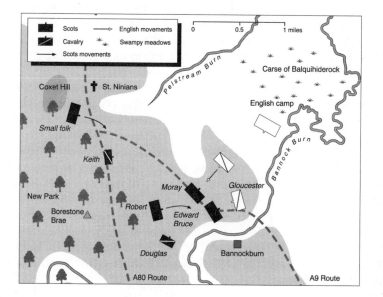

Bannockburn – The Battle

archers: from the Carse, they would have been unable to see the action themselves, only hearing the terrifying roar of battle.

On midsummer's day 1314 the Scots emerged from the cover of the woods as dawn broke. It was about 4 a.m. and Bruce had boldly decided to provoke the English cavalry into battle. As they reached the Carse the Scots formed into schiltrons. The only way infantry could withstand a cavalry charge was to stand its ground and attempt to absorb the force of the impact. The idea that the Scots attacked the English can be dismissed; the schiltron was still a defensive formation. Bruce took the Scottish divisions as close as possible to the English line. Then the Scots stopped, and braced themselves for the first cavalry charge. It was only after the first wave failed that the Scots assumed the offensive.

The English had remained under arms all night, but they were not arrayed. Only Gloucester's battle was prepared, and even he did not have time to put on his surcoat, with its vivid De Clare coat of arms that would have highlighted him as worthy of ransom. The rest of the camp frantically prepared for the fight. Meanwhile, the Scots knelt in prayer. Barbour (whose source must have had remarkable hearing) has Edward II commenting to Sir Ingram de Umfraville:

> 'Those men kneel to ask for mercy.'
> 'You are right,' Umfraville replied, 'they ask for mercy, but not from you. They ask it from God for their sins.'[39]

The 23-year old Earl of Gloucester counselled delay, voicing the concerns of older and wiser veterans who considered that the troops were in desperate need of a rest before battle, and could wait a day. In a fit of pique Edward angrily denounced him as a traitor, a typically absurd accusation.

The *Lanercost* chronicle has the fight beginning with an archery duel, in which the English and Welsh had some success against the few Scottish archers from Ettrick forest. It did not last long as Gloucester's charge interrupted the archers' line of fire and so shielded the Scots. Tempers had flared between Hereford and Gloucester over who should lead the van. The honour would normally have fallen to Hereford, as hereditary constable of England, but Edward had offered Gloucester joint command as a favour. The dispute only ended when Gloucester spurred his mount and headed for Edward Bruce's schiltron.

The result of his suicidal charge was as swift as it was predictable. He called for help from Berkeley, but if help came it came too late. Randolph soon reached the rest of the English cavalry and desperate fighting took place along the front.

'The great horses of the English charged the pikes of the Scots, as it were a dense forest, there arose a great and terrible crash of spears broken and of destriers wounded to death.'[40]

When they failed to ride down the schiltrons with their first charge, the English knights fell into confusion. Their initial impetus was lost, but they had no room to retire, reform and charge again. They were at a standstill. The unprotected horses suffered heavy losses against the schiltron, and as the horses fell the men-at-arms were thrown to the ground. Many were trampled underfoot or suffered the final *coup de grace* from an axe-wielding Scot sallying from the schiltron. Others stood by helplessly since the front rank refused to retire and allow fresh troops to come up. The English infantry were stuck behind the cavalry and could only watch as the knights fell in front of them. Panicked riderless horses fled around them. Some archers attempted to fire over the heads of the cavalry, but many could not find a target and arrows fell harmlessly into the centres of the schiltrons from above. Those who attempted to shoot straight 'hit few Scots in the breast, but struck many more English in the back'.

Edward finally managed to deploy some archers against the Scottish left. The forward march of the schiltrons had left exposed their flanks to the archers. But it was too late, before they could have any influence on the fighting the archers were overrun by Robert Keith's light cavalry. As they escaped back into their own lines many were beaten up by their own side, frustrated by their failure. Why Edward had waited so long to bring the longbowmen into the action is one of the most puzzling aspects of the battle. It is unclear how many archers he had, but earlier writs for the year, later cancelled, summoned 5,000, with more from Wales. It is unlikely that Edward was short of archers at Bannockburn, and astonishing that they did not play a more prominent role. The longbow was the single most effective weapon against the schiltron.

Even then the battle was still undecided. Bruce brought his own schiltron, held in reserve, into the fray. Now all three Scottish divisions were fighting together. Barbour reveals the horror of the intense melee, the war cries of both sides, the groaning of the dead, the ground coloured red with blood, men falling and unable to rise under the weight of their armour and being trampled to death;

'And mony a reale romble rid
Be rought yar apon ayer sid
Quhill throw ye byrnys bryst ye blud
Yat till erd doune stremand zhude.'

['Many a mighty fierce dazing blow
Be rought there upon the other side
Where through the mail coat burst with blood
That went flowing freely to the earth.']^{41}

The English host began moving backward and the cry went up from the Scottish line, 'On them, on them, on them! they fail'. Then the 'little men', the undisciplined rabble, 'yeoman, swains and poveraille'^{42}, could resist the battle no longer and streamed from their position from the Park, screaming 'slay, slay' as they ran. To the English, whose cause already looked lost, it seemed that a fresh Scottish army had reached the field. At the rear the army began to break up.

With defeat imminent, Valence seized Edward's reigns and with Giles d'Argentine led an unwilling king from the field. Argentine and Valence escorted him towards Stirling. It was a prudent decision; had Edward been captured his ransom would have sorely tested English taxation. As it was his path was barely clear, with the royal escort having to fight its way through, the Scots 'laid hold of the housing of the king's charger in order to stop him, he struck out so vigorously behind him with a mace that there was none whom he touched that he did not fall to the ground.'^{43} Edward's horse was killed from beneath him. Sir Roger Northburgh, bearer of the king's shield, was captured, as was the privy seal.

When he was sure of Edward's safety Argentine, noted as the third best knight in Christendom after returning from the Wars of Emperor Henry of Luxembourg^{44}, returned to the battle and lost his life as he vainly charged a schiltron. The king did not gain entry to Stirling, perhaps reminded by Moubray that the loss of the battle would see the castle surrendered to the Scots. Instead, with a force measured by Barbour as 500 mounted men including Hugh Despenser and Henry Beaumont, Edward fled by the Round Table, past the rear of the Scottish army and the road to Linlithgow and finally reached safety in earl Patrick's castle at Dunbar. They were chased all the way by Douglas.

Douglas, with 60 mounted men, was strengthened by the Alexander Abernethy who came late to the battle with 80 cavalry. When Douglas broke the news of the battle Abernethy swore fealty to Bruce and joined the chase. They did not have the force to stop Edward but harassed the English all the way, so much so that they did not have time to 'make water'. From Dunbar Edward took an open boat to Berwick.

As they watched the king's standard leave the field the English army lost heart and the rout began. In medieval battles it was at this instant that the greatest loss of life occurred—a running man on foot stood little chance against a mounted knight. But Robert Bruce did not have many cavalry to follow up the victory. The 'small-folk' could have created more problems for the English, had they not discovered and plundered the wagon train. Many Scots left the field rich from the gold, plate, armour and cloth found in the wagon train. The English scattered in any direction possible, some followed Edward towards Stirling where they sheltered in the shadow of the castle rock. Bruce feared to leave the field in case they regrouped.

Disaster struck as sections of the army tried to cross the Bannock Burn. 'The troops in the English rear fell back upon the ditch Bannock Burn, tumbling one over the other'[45], the 'Forth absorbed many well-equipped with horses and arms, and Bannock mud many whose very names we know not.' The Bannock was so filled with bodies that they formed a bridge, and it was possible to cross without wetting your feet.

The chronicles record the names of 37 men of worth among the English dead, a total never to be repeated in the Anglo-Scottish wars. The Scots lost two knights, William Vipont and Walter Ross. Gloucester's body was found by a Franciscan friar. It was taken to a nearby church where Bruce, Gloucester's brother-in-law, spent the night in vigil. The body was then allowed to be taken back to England. Marmaduke Tweng hid amongst the battle's debris, and only surrendered to Bruce himself as he inspected the battlefield. He was honoured with free passage home.

Another group of fugitives, including the earls of Hereford and Angus, his brother, Ingram de Umfraville, Segrave and Anthony de Lucy, made it as far as the English held Bothwell Castle. But the Scottish warden, Walter Gilbertson knew where his interests lay after Bannockburn. Struck by a convenient fit of patriotism, he took the barons under his protection, and then imprisoned them, holding them captive until they could be handed over to Bruce for ransom. Those left outside were slain. One chronicler had the Earl of Pembroke escaping by foot, unarmed with fugitive Welsh. A large Welsh contingent did make an uncomfortable and harassed journey to Carlisle, though, since Pembroke was instrumental in the king's flight, other chroniclers offer a more convincing escape, in the king's boat from Dunbar.

Chapter 8

ROBERT BRUCE AND THE NORTH OF ENGLAND

'After the aforesaid victory Robert de Brus was commonly called king of Scotland by all men, because he had acquired Scotland by force of arms.'
The Lanercost Chronicle

For a battle that was won so convincingly, it is easy to inflate Bannockburn's real significance. It was unique, the only full-scale battle that the patriots won. John Balliol had died peacefully on his estates in Picardy a year earlier. He had not been a player in Scottish politics for the last decade but the battle and his death seemed to mark the end of the old order, certainly the end of the civil war. Yet for all this the wars dragged on. It is an enduring feature of Anglo-Scottish warfare that battles—however decisive—did not bring victory.

The war had ground into a stalemate. Edward II would not give up Scotland, but neither could he hope to win it. Despite holding the military ascendancy, Scotland was never strong enough to threaten English centres of power, in the midlands and the south, and England was never strong enough to hold a country that had suffered too much to accept its overlordship. By the time a peace treaty was signed, and that only a step in a longer struggle, Edward would be deposed and murdered, Robert an old man close to death.

Edward stayed at Berwick for two weeks after Bannockburn 'for the purpose of repressing the forwardness and malice of the Scots who are preparing to invade the kingdom.' He called Henry of Lancaster, the earl's brother, and 362 barons to Newcastle to protect 'the honour and safety of the kingdom.'[1] It was a response born in desperation and overtaken by events. Two tax collectors sitting at Morpeth when news of the battle reached them from soldiers fleeing south filed a disquieting report:

'suddenly there arrived Stephen Segrave and many others with him and they told them that the lord king was retreating from Stirling with the army and was coming towards England, and on this they were terrified. They fled, and, like others of the county stayed in enclosed towns and castles and forts. And immediately afterwards, before 1 August, there came Edward Bruce and Thomas Randolph leading the Scottish army.'[2]

The Scottish army crossed the border at Norham and reached the Tees. The truces expensively bought by the northern communities were worthless against the victorious Scots. Northumberland was devastated with fire. The Scots spent three days at Newburn before crossing the Tyne into Durham where the people of the bishopric ransomed themselves. At Richmond a detachment went further south, although the town was not entered. The army crossed the Pennines along the Swaledale and Stainmoor where they found herds of cattle. Brough, Appleby and Kirkoswald were burnt, the crops trampled down.[3]

Andrew Harcla and the Carlisle garrison had avoided the debacle at Bannockburn. He intercepted the Scots as they moved north in the pass below Stainmoor, but the loss of 25 horses suggests the English came off worse. However, Harcla was winning a reputation as one of the most tenacious northern captains. In November he regrouped his forces and made a raid to Pennersax in Dumfriesshire where the foray lost eleven horses for the gain of 65 bulls and 35 cows that he sold for £40. Harcla came from a modest background and his rapid promotion was resented by some men of rank. There had been a dispute over his appointment, with the crown putting forward its own nominee, that generated lasting bitterness.[4]

When news of the Scottish raid reached Edward at York he appointed Aymer Valence captain of the troops north of the Trent with sweeping powers to impress the whole of the Yorkshire foot at the expense of the vills.[5] But before he could take any action the raiders were back over the border. This pattern of lightning raid and belated response was now established in the north of England.

The wave of Scottish raids had already broken over the northern counties when Bruce's main army marched over the border in 1314. Before Bannockburn Scottish raids were stoically accepted in northern England since an English army was expected to punish the Scots that summer. After the battle the raids escalated and the purchase of truces became a way of life. The countryside provided easy pickings but the relentless assaults did not allow time for recovery. After 1314 the community wide system of paying tributes collapsed in Northumberland. The county had no money left to pay the tributes and no will to resist.

Communities that did not buy truces had little hope of collecting crops that could be trampled down if wet or burnt if dry. The poor, who had no access to castle refuges, could only flee from the path of the raiders. After a while they could no longer afford to return. Serfs and poorer tenants simply disappeared from the countryside. In 1311 bishop Kellawe postponed a visit to Northumberland because the people had fled.[6] By 1316 the Hexham abbey accounts show 'only half a dozen people on as many manors who preferred to die in their own homes: in one village a man and his wife, in another an old miller and his son.' Durham, further from the border, was able to maintain the payment for truces and escaped the worst damages of the raids. Still, the royal keeper of the bishopric in 1316-17 (when vacant) complained that the county was 'quasi guerrive.' Refugees were roaming the countryside, civil administration and justice was collapsing.

At first the Scots demanded cash, variously described as tributes or ransoms. It was only later that the raids became more savage to destroy civilian morale and foster a demand for peace. The raids were often canvassed well in advance which gave the population adequate time to find safety and organise the collection of tributes. This was a highly successful policy, so much so that the raid in 1313 never took place. Devastation was merely meant to encourage payment. Fire was the easiest and safest method of harrying the countryside, destroying homes and crops. In 1327 Edward III made a determined effort to catch a strong raiding party, and for some time he followed them by the light of burning villages.

Cattle were prized because they could be easily moved, but advanced warning gave local communities time to send livestock into safety on the hills and moors. The monastery at Durham only sent their cattle six miles to Spennymoor. They considered this ample precaution. On one occasion the failure to move livestock led to the loss of 60 horses and 180 cows but this was exceptional; the monastery's accounts normally record the loss of 'an occasional pig or three sheep' in a flock of 500. Lardere lost only 16 head of fatstock in seven years.[7] The most lucrative cattle raids occurred when the raiders penetrated unexpectedly deeply and caught the community unawares.

When ready cash was not available hostages would be taken. At Ripon the burgesses gave hostages and then thought themselves too far south to have to redeem them. The unfortunate hostages remained in Scotland for six years, bar two who escaped, until Edward, who had been badgered by their wives, told the burgesses to pay up. The king had become a 'debt collector' for his enemies.[8] Occasionally the raiders would strike lucky. When a raid in the west reached Furness, the Scots were 'especially delighted with the abundance of iron that they found there, for Scotland is not rich in iron.'[9]

From 1314 the raids became more audacious and began to reach deeper into England. This was not just a sign of Scottish confidence and the inability of the English to organise adequate defences, but reflected diminishing returns in the northern counties that had been so thoroughly plundered. For the remainder of 1314 Berwick became the major concern. The mayor, bailiffs and community wrote to Edward promising that they were taking every precaution for the safety of the town. The walls, ditches and palisades along the circuit were repaired, brattices added to the gates, a barbican added to the great gate; timber, nails, a beam, tanned hides and a 'hangour' were bought for the great engine at a cost of £2 10s; another £15 9s was spent on a portcullis and repairs to St Mary Gate. Between July and December £270 was spent on the fortifications. In November the cities of York, Lincoln, Northampton and London sent cross-bowmen to the town, paid 4d a day at the king's expense. These heavily armed footmen had a slow rate of fire that was more than balanced by greater accuracy.[10]

The town lived in constant fear. When Henry Bentley, the king's coroner, led a foray but delayed his return the community feared that the party had been captured or killed. As tension rose two boys walked through the gate. They had gone to play in the field of St Mary Magdelene, outside the town walls. They lost a rudiment song book and began to cry; when they returned to the field, it could not be found. They were arrested, accused of trafficking, and kept in custody. In October an inquisition acquitted Richard, aged eleven, and Roland, aged nine of trafficking with the Scots.[11]

Carlisle was besieged in 1315 and was under threat thereafter, but no further attempt was made to take the city. In 1317 Newcastle's burgesses sent a request for tax relief citing reasons that must have been common to the northern towns. They had guarded the town at their own expense since the beginning of the war and paid for the enclosure of most of the town with a wall and all of it with a ditch. Owners of land outside the town had seen their property overrun by the enemy, while those inside had no time to trade because they were standing guard over the town. Scottish and Flemish privateers pillaged shipping and artisans had no material on which to work.[12]

A severe famine compounded the impact of the raids.[13] The harvest in 1314 had only been gathered with some difficulty and was poor. In 1315 it began raining in the early summer and continued until autumn. The crops did not mature in time so the harvest utterly failed. The autumn sowing of wheat and rye was no better, the spring sowing of oats and barley severely delayed. Prices rose steeply in 1315 and then went higher still in 1316. A horrific famine ensued, the worst in the medieval age. There was no respite; it extended throughout Europe so grain could not be bought from abroad. The famine touched Scotland, with an English blockade preventing supply ships reaching Scottish ports, but the Scotland was not so reliant on grain, which mitigated the ordeal north of the border.

Government measures to alleviate the famine failed: attempts made to fix prices were abandoned when merchants stopped bringing goods to market and the prohibition on barons eating more that two courses of meat a day was inadequate. High prices made it hard to supply the northern garrisons. In Northumbria, 'dogs and horses and other unclean things were eaten.'[14] The maintenance of supplies to the garrisons became haphazard and infrequent. The cost of maintaining the northern defences, in both wages and food, at a time when the country went into steep economic decline meant that Edward had to tax more heavily just when the people could least afford it.

Edward II had neither the inclination, nor the resources, to alleviate the problems in the north. Yet no-one else could assemble a large enough force to resist the raids. Lancaster's northern lands were spared, suggesting that he had reached some kind of understanding with Bruce. Few other great lords had holdings in the north. The earl of Warwick held Barnard Castle, Valence his estates around Mitford, John of Brittany held the former Balliol barony of Bywell. They could easily compensate for their losses here from their estates in southern England. Many of the north's natural leaders were no longer available: Henry Percy died in 1314, the earl of Warwick a year later. Robert Clifford of Appleby died at Bannockburn where Anthony Lucy, John de Clavering and John de Eure were captured.[15]

Other northern magnates suffered from the loss of their holdings in Scotland, naturally greater amongst the northern lords than those from the south. Cross-border holdings were common to many of the northern magnates: the Umfraville lords of Prudhoe and Redesdale as earls of Angus, the Balliol lords of Barnard Castle as lords of Galloway, the Bruce lords of Cleveland, the Vaux lords of Gilsland who held Dirleton. They were not impoverished by the loss of these lands, but neither were they power they had once been. Roger Umfraville took very little part in the defence of the north, eventually selling many of his lands to the Percys. Other lords had chosen the Scottish side. Some of the lords who had gone over to the Scots in 1296 and had been restored in 1305 returned to Scottish allegiance. 'Others went over in sheer desperation.'[16] Edward I took the liberty of Tynedale, held of the English crown by the king of Scots, into his own hands in 1296. After 1314 many lords in the area returned to Scottish allegiance:

> 'They treated their neighbours the Northumbrians inhumanely, carrying off their goods and taking them away as captives. The women too went riding in warlike manner, stealing the goods which their men did not care about, such as shorn wool and linen and carried them off.'[17]

In 1319 the men of Carlisle complained 'the best and richest of the country about Gilsland and Liddle have gone over to the enemy.'[18] Over the next forty years North Tynedale was regranted six times, often to absentee landlords. Without these lords, law enforcement broke down. There followed the emergence of kinship groups as a unit for defence, which would later gel into Reiver society.[19]

Power devolved to the royal officers, men who owed their position as captains and keepers of castles rather than as landowners. The devastation of lands in the north did not affect them, they had no interest in the peace of the border, rather the reverse: their income was dependent on warfare. When Luke de Wharton was captured in 1317 he mortgaged his lands to Roger de Horsely, keeper of Berwick castle, the only man with ready cash to pay the ransom. Many of these new lords did more harm than good. In August 1314 the people of Berwick complained of the depredations of a gang led by John de Lilbourne, who, in revenge for the execution of some of those who had tried to betray Berwick, had sworn to kill any Berwick man found in Northumberland.[20]

The following year, the people in the ward of Bamburgh castle complained that its constable had refused to let them accept the truce offered by Randolph for £270 unless they paid him as much in addition. He charged them exorbitantly for leaving their goods in the castle, and his porters and servants exacted more money for letting them go in and out. Merchants alleged that the same constable had seized victuals from their ships. Disturbances such as the abduction of Lady Clifford by John Ireys, the custodian of Barnard Castle and well-known local brigand, were inevitable when the central administration in the north was so enfeebled.[21]

* * *

It was rumoured that after his victorious return from Scotland, Edward II planned to have the earl of Lancaster arrested. But the king's defeat at Bannockburn placed Lancaster in an unassailable position. Parliament was called to York to discuss 'certain arduous affairs,' by which the king meant Scotland.[22] The opposition would do nothing until the Ordinances were executed. Lancaster instituted a wholesale removal of the royal officers and replaced them with his own nominees. Warwick was made the king's chief councillor early in 1315 but his death in August robbed Lancaster of the friend with whom he could share or delegate power.

As the parliament sat debating internal affairs, an offer of peace arrived from Robert Bruce. His envoy told the assembly that the king 'and his men persist so strongly to have peace, that all say they desire it earnestly.' There is no extant record of the talks, and some uncertainty whether they ever took place. There seems little doubt that Bruce sought peace, but he did not hold much hope that they would succeed. Only three days before the talks were scheduled to begin Thomas Randolph, who was not covered by the safe-conducts but who must have played the chief Scottish role, was in Durham negotiating an extension on the county's truce. This was either premature or realistic, it not a sign of confidence in the process.[23]

The York parliament made arrangements for an exchange of prisoners. The Earl of Hereford was the Scots' most valuable prize and the king's sister pestered Edward to ensure her husband's release. The price of his ransom was the release of Bruce's queen, his daughter Marjorie, his sister Christian Seton, his nephew Donald earl of Mar and Robert Wishart bishop of Glasgow. The earl of Mar had grown accustomed to Edward's court and company, he set out for Scotland with the others but turned back at Newcastle. Nicholas Segrave was exchanged for five Scottish barons. The other captives were expected to make their own arrangements for ransom.[24] After the battle Edward was forced to issue a declaration that he had 'misplaced' his seal, and that no attention should be paid to writs sealed by it. Bruce returned it to the king with some courtesy.[25]

Robert Bruce held a parliament at Cambuskenneth near the field of Bannockburn in very different circumstances from Edward's at York. All those who had died in the field against the king were now disinherited.[26] This was an enabling statute aimed at Anglo-Scottish die-hards. The king remained conciliatory to his enemies, only demanding loyalty and an oath of allegiance to one sovereign—he would not allow cross-border holdings.

Some now came into his peace. Patrick Dunbar earl of March had watched Edward depart on a boat after Bannockburn and recognized that his support for the English occupation was no longer viable. (And what might have happened if he had followed the example of the constable at Bothwell?) His change of allegiance would have swayed many local barons. Edward's sagacious councillor before the battle, Ingram de Umfraville, followed suit. The young earl of Fife, who had been brought up in the court of the English king, returned to Scotland in 1315 leaving his wife behind.

Some were irreconcilable: David Strathbogie earl of Atholl who had plundered the Scottish camp the night before the battle; Robert Umfraville earl of Angus, an Englishman had interests on both sides of the border and never showed any interest in the patriot cause.

John Comyn earl of Buchan had died without male issue in 1308. His estate was divided between the daughters of his brother Alexander. The first co-heir, Margaret, married John of Ross and received half the Comyn inheritance. The other co-heir, Alice, married the Englishman, Henry Beaumont; her share of the inheritance was escheated to the crown. Edward II awarded the title of Earl of Buchan to Beaumont in 1312. Twenty years on it would be these men, or their sons, dispossessed of their estates and holding empty titles, who would re-ignite the Wars.

As the English prepared to defend the north of England Bruce undertook a course that nobody in England anticipated. In April 1315 he gathered a council in Ayr to settle the succession. For a country that had suffered so much from the need of a male heir the question dogged Bruce. His first marriage to Isabel of Mar had produced only one daughter, Marjorie. His second marriage to Elizabeth de Burgh was still childless, hardly surprising in the circumstances of their forced separation. Their reunion after Bannockburn would bear four children, two girls and two boys. The one surviving male offspring, the future David II, was not born until 1324. Marjorie married the hereditary Steward shortly after the Ayr council. The only offspring from this union was the future Robert II. Marjorie died shortly after. Even these fragile foundations for the survival of the dynasty lay in the future.

The Ayr council published a *tailzie* of the Scottish crown, naming Edward Bruce 'as an energetic man abundantly experienced in deeds of war' as heir over, and with the agreement of, Marjorie.[27] That Bruce swept aside the rights of a daughter that had guided Alexander III's *tailzie* in 1286 was not just a sign of feudal conservatism but of civil defence. The state needed a strong male hand, to guide it after Robert's death. Randolph was named as guardian should both Robert and Edward die leaving a minor to inherit the throne or if no heir existed until the community chose a new king.

* * *

Another issue concerned the Ayr council besides the succession: Edward Bruce's attempt to win the Irish crown.[28] English power in Ireland had long been on the wane. The beginning of the fourteenth century had seen the country go through a crisis from which it had yet to emerge. The government had lost control of much of the country to Gaelic Irish or rebel English lords, a so-called 'middle party' who had not been born in England but were not Irish. As the demands on the government in Dublin increased to combat these rebels so the land they governed and revenues they drew declined. The demands for supplies and troops to fight the war in Scotland had added to the government's problems and made it difficult for the centre to exert control.

The York parliament appointed John Macdougall of Lorn as admiral of the western fleet with twelve ships, paid out of the Dublin exchequer.[29] Before 18 February 1315 his deputy Duncan MacGoffrey recaptured the Isle of Man and its Scottish garrison. This was a rare success and so cheered Edward that he sent instructions to Ireland to raise 10,000 men and 60 ships to invade the west of Scotland in support of the Macdougalls. The Scottish invasion frustrated these plans. Lorn, operating from Ireland and the Isle of Man should have dominated the Irish Sea, yet on 26 May

1315 a Scottish fleet left Ayr carrying Edward Bruce and Thomas Randolph together with 'enterprising and valiant knights'. Landing on the Antrim coast at Larne, their immediate target was Carrickfergus where the town soon fell but the castle, one of the most impregnable in Ireland, held out. It would remain under siege until it finally fell in September 1316. Edward Bruce left men to invest the castle when he went to take Dundalk. His battle-hardened veterans had little trouble overcoming local opposition in Moirie Pass before sacking the town: the prelude to ruthless slaughter where 'the rewys [streets] all bludy war'.[30] It was a policy that became the signature of the invaders, repeated wherever they faced opposition.

From the Lincoln parliament in September Edward II sent John de Hotham to Dublin to investigate the progress of the war. It was only when Hotham sent back an urgent request in February for £500 that the king realised how dangerous the situation was, but he could do nothing to help. It would be another two years before he could send an English force to Ireland. The government in Dublin was not slow to respond to the invasion. By July the justiciar, Edmund Butler, had raised an army that combined with the earl of Ulster's men in county Louth. Ulster persuaded the justiciar that he could deal with the invasion alone. The earl was over-confident but also wanted to protect his estates from the damage the royal army would cause. Butler was happy to disband his own force as the famine had made supplying the army difficult and expensive and a foray into Ulster would stretch his supply lines.

Edward Bruce feigned a withdrawal before the earl and then utterly defeated him at Connor. With this victory Ulster became secure for the invaders and remained a district where they could retire with the protection of a friendly countryside and local support. But Edward Bruce was unable to breakout of the district.

Late in the year Randolph went to Scotland for help and returned in December with more men. It was now that the Scots launched an offensive, through the Midlands and Leinster. Bruce won two swift victories, against Roger Mortimer in Meath and then against the royal army at the battle of Skerries. It was a victory against the odds. The Scots, in the words of an English report, 'by bad luck kept the field' but the fighting had been hard and their ranks decimated and weakened by famine and sickness. His army retreated in disarray back to Ulster.

Randolph travelled to Scotland a second time towards the end of 1316. When he returned in February 1317 it was with king Robert who came to put new vigour into the invasion, if not to rescue his brother. He must have felt that Scotland was safe from an English offensive with a truce in force during the winter months. The Bruce brothers led an expedition towards Dublin and southern Ireland to rouse the Irish into rebellion. The city panicked at their approach. Shops and houses lined the city wall and in places their weight had caused the walls to collapse. These suburbs were burnt to clear a line of fire from the battlements, but the flames spread and destroyed large parts of the city.

The mayor had the earl of Ulster, who became the focus at the governments' failure to stem the invasion, thrown into jail. Despite the chaotic state of the defences the Bruces made no attempt to take the city. Perhaps they had learnt the lesson of Carrickfergus and Carlisle; besides, there was a royal army nearby. Instead they approached Munster and reached as far as Limerick. At the height of the famine the army was unable to live off the land so needed to rely on allies in the countryside. They expected support and fresh supplies from Donough O'Brien but instead found his patrimony in the hands of his rival the unsympathetic Murtough O'Brien. This was the turning point of the campaign. The army returned to Ulster starving. Randolph and king Robert left in May, after four months campaigning.

It is unknown what took place over the following eighteen months. Thomas Dun, the daring commander of the Scottish navy, kept the supply route to Scotland open. John of Lorn died in 1316. He remained in his post to maintain the loyalty of his men in the west of Scotland but he was a shadow of the man that had defeated Bruce. His continued presence as admiral understates the true strength of the Anglo-Irish fleet. The new Irish admiral John of Athy caught Dun in July 1317. He revealed Scottish designs on Anglesey and the Isle of Man before his execution—either island could provide a naval base for operations in the west.[31] Two years earlier Dun had sailed into Holyhead harbour with four Flemish captains and captured an English ship. This may have been testing the defences before an invasion and Edward had the Welsh defences reinforced. It was Man that fell to Randolph sometime in 1317. Instead of strengthening Edward Bruce's hand in Ireland it deprived him of his most important commander.

In 1317 Roger Mortimer was made Edward II's lieutenant in Ireland and landed with a small armed force. Absentee English landlords were ordered to return to defend their lands. Edward Bruce was now trapped in Ulster. He could no longer rely on reinforcements from Scotland; none could be spared as any experienced men were required to defend Berwick. In October 1318 Edward Bruce once more tried to venture out of Ulster. He was defeated and killed with many of his supporters by a royal army led by John Bermingham at Faughart near Dundalk. Bermingham carried Bruce's head to Edward at Winchelsea in a salted box. His reward was the earldom of Louth. The Irish invasion was over. Carrickfergus, the castle that had taken a year to surrender, was now abandoned.

The question that has troubled historians ever since the invasion is whether Robert really envisaged a dual Celtic kingship, or was he just creating mischief? Barbour says that Edward Bruce invaded Ireland because he 'Thoucht that Scotland to litill wes |Till his brothir and him alsua.'[32] His suggestion that Edward Bruce went to conquer Ireland to feed his own ambitions cannot easily be reconciled with the Ayr council only a month earlier that had recognised him as heir to the Scottish throne. It seems unlikely that Robert would have devoted resources just to win a kingdom for his brother, however attractive a pan-Gaelic alliance appeared as a guarantor of Scottish independence. Barbour has made Edward Bruce the scapegoat for the eventual defeat in Ireland to protect his hero, Robert, the author of the policy. He may also have been countering contemporary criticisms of Robert's failure to bring aid to his brother after 1318. Though Barbour's tale may tell part of the story we have to look elsewhere to find the real rationale for Edward Bruce's invasion.

Sometime before the invasion, possibly in 1315, Robert sent an open letter to the Irish appealing to Gaelic national sentiment and calling on a strengthening of 'the special friendship between us and you, so that with God's will *our nation* may be able to recover her ancient liberty.' There was a common ancestry between the Scots of Gaelic descent, mainly in the west, and the Irish. Many of the magnates in Edward Bruce's ranks were from the Gaelic speaking west. The Anglo-Norman Bruce family did not share that ancestry but were not slow to exploit their advantage whether in Ireland or Wales. A second document supports this appeal to common ancestry. In 1318 Domnall Ò Néill the 'king' of Tyrone sent a remonstrance to Pope John XXII claiming the pretentious right to be high king of Scotland, a right he claimed to have presented to Edward Bruce in 1315, despairing that the country would ever by united under a native lord.

Many chiefs and English lords did join him, others rebelled to further their own grudges against neighbours or the Dublin regime, but many were appalled at the devastation the Scottish armies carried in their wake and fought against them. Some were linked to an opposing faction, others felt an antipathy to a Scottish style monarchy that would encroach on their territories: there seemed little point expelling the English only to have Scottish lordship thrust upon them. Ò Néill's remonstrance cannot be read at face value. He was being pressed in his own patrimony in Ulster and sought support from a traditional avenue, the West Highland gallowglasses. For a man with his own pretensions to High Kingship why stop at hiring mercenaries when he could have a king to aid him? As the Bruces were using the Irish against the English so the Irish were using the Scots against their rivals. It was a recipe that would ensure that a united Ireland under Edward Bruce's kingship was out of the question.

The real reasons for Robert's policy in Ireland assume a realistic attitude to the tenuous hope of uniting Irish factions. By invading

Ireland Robert had taken the war to the English. For three years the invasion of Ireland reduced the tempo of raids on the north of England, but these were having little effect on English policy and Bruce did not have the resources to attack further south. He was able to deny Irish resources to Edwardian armies in Scotland and guaranteed that English resources were occupied in Ireland. It was a simple and effective policy. Robert continued to take an interest in Irish politics up to his death in a bid to ensure that a strong English overlordship could not dominate the island. It was not until 1322 that Ireland was again able to send men and supplies to England, and then with such difficulty the request was not made again in Edward II's reign.

* * *

In England the lack of a coherent strategy from Edward II led the northern magnates to take matters into their own hands in the winter of 1314-15. In a bid to protect their lands when the Durham truce secured with Randolph expired (20 January 1315), John de Eure, escheator beyond the Trent, wrote to Edward to tell him that he expected an invasion when the march lords left for the Westminster parliament. He asked Edward to order them to remain and reported arrangements for a meeting of the clergy and nobles at York, convoked by William Greenfield archbishop of York, his dean Robert Pickering, and the bishop of Durham to discuss the defence of the march. The York assembly sat for three days and appointed four northern barons joint captains of the march. They agreed that they would compel the men of the north to assemble with them but sought Edward's aid 'without which his land and people cannot be saved.' Edward was sympathetic to the request and excused twelve northern lords from attendance at Westminster.

The convocation called a non-parliamentary muster, paid for by a levy of 2d in the mark on every vill.[33] It is unknown if this service produced any armed men. The first invasion of 1315 avoided the palatine: Bruce led a raid into North and South Tynedale, through Haltwhistle, Hexham and Corbridge towards Newcastle.[34] Durham may have decided it was prudent to pay for a longer truce until help came from the south.

In April Greenfield, still searching for protection against the raids, summoned a second northern council.[35] They sent representatives to meet Thomas of Lancaster in May. This predominantly northern process was overtaken by events in the south. The king sent the earl of Warwick and Badlesmere to Lancaster with the news that Valence would lead a contracted force from the middle of summer.

Valence left the country early in the year to present petitions relating to Aquitaine to the king of France but he had retained an interest in the north with the purchase of Mitford castle in Northumberland for £600.

His retainer, Maurice de Berkeley, became keeper of Berwick in April. Valence left London for Newcastle by 20 June. On 5 July he was appointed *custos* of the region between Trent and Roxburgh. He was paid 4,000 marks to bring a retinue of 100 men-at-arms, Badlesmere received 3,250 marks for a similar retinue, two lesser captains supplied smaller detachments. When they assembled in York they had 300 men, 60 more than their contracts were worth.[36]

Before Valence could mobilise his forces Robert Bruce took a 'great army', into Durham; the king remained in Chester-le-Street while Douglas plundered Hartlepool, whose citizens fled the town by boat for safety.[37] Bruce had bigger plans. In July a message was taken by Dungal Macdouall from Carlisle saying that 'the whole force of the Scots will enter England at this march this Tuesday 14 July and will make an "assaie" at the city, for which they have prepared ladders and other engines, as he knows by certain spies.'[38]

Since the fall of Lochmaben in 1312 the city had become the English front-line defence. It lay on the path of Scottish raiding parties as they returned home. It was then that they were most at risk: the large garrison had sufficient warning to intercept them as they were slowed down carrying booty. Skirting the city was tiresome for the raiders, but the assault was more than just an attempt to preserve their booty. This was a show of confidence. It would fulfil an ancient Scottish claim to the western counties and so change the nature of the wars, from independence to expansion. The fall of Carlisle would hamper any English invasion and goad Edward into treating for peace or making an effort to retrieve the loss. Much rested on the next ten days. Bruce vowed not to eat meat until the city fell.[39]

When Bruce invested the city on 22 July 1315 the buildings around the castle had already been levelled and the gates blocked up.[40] The heavily garrisoned city had been turned into a fortress. Bruce destroyed the local fisheries and mills and sent raiding parties into Allerdale, Copeland and Westmoreland to gather cattle to feed the army. The city gates were assaulted every day, but the Scots were repulsed by a shower of stones and arrows. On the 27th a siege engine set up by the Holy Trinity church began to cast stones into the city but did little damage and only killed one man. Against this single engine the city could muster seven or eight engines besides springalds.

The Scots constructed a *berefrai*. The town's carpenters competed in a frantic competition to heighten the wall against which the *berefrai* would approach with a wooden palisade. In the event, the summer's torrential rainfall softened the ground so that when the siege engine began to roll into place it came to a sticky halt, bogged down under its great weight. A sow, a mobile shelter to protect miners as they attempted to undermine the town's walls, made no impression.

Faggots thrown in to fill the moat sank without trace into the swollen waters.

Frustrated by the wretched weather Bruce resorted to the stratagem that had won him Roxburgh and Edinburgh. On the 30th a general assault began on all three gates. When the fighting was at its fiercest and the garrison drawn to the assault James Douglas led an onslaught on the Botchergate, to the south where the wall was high and attack thought unlikely. Tall ladders were placed against the walls and a volley of arrows shot thickly to prevent any defender showing his head. For a short time a foothold was gained on the battlements but the defenders regrouped and drove the Scots from the wall, the scaling ladders thrown to the ground.

Bruce ordered a retreat the next day. News had arrived from Ireland— mistaken as it happened—that his brother had been heavily defeated. Valence was heading for Carlisle with the force he had assembled at York. He joined Harcla in pursuit of the Scottish army. The retreat must have been in some confusion, the *Vita* says that many Scots perished, and more were wounded.[41] Valence was back in Newcastle on 24 August. He advanced through Northumberland in early September, devastating the countryside to prevent a threatened Scottish raid. He was forced to retreat at Longridge near Berwick. With his contract about to expire, Henry Beaumont became commander of the march over the winter.[42]

Edward II took the threat to Carlisle seriously. Before he heard of the city's relief (news arrived on 10 August) he had appointed Lancaster (on 8 August) as king's lieutenant, *superior capitaneus* of the northern forces. Had Carlisle fallen the honour of Lancaster would have been the front line defence of the western march. It is likely that Lancaster was preparing to share command with Valence, who would remain commander in the east. After the relief of Carlisle there was longer any urgency, no force went north, but the city's gates remained blocked up for another year, just in case.

* * *

In late August 1315 the king met with John of Brittany, Hereford and Warenne at Lincoln and declared with their advice that he would stay in the north to defend the marches attended by his barons. He expected them to serve at their own cost. The sheriffs had already received instructions to prepare armed levies from south of the Trent and prepare them for service. By October it was clear that the plan was failing. Commissioners appointed to act with the sheriffs to supervise the array of levies could not stop many of the arrayers from abusing their powers, accepting gifts to allow men to stay at home. When the earl of Lancaster wrote to request supplies from 26 religious houses they answered that they had nothing left to give: between them they promised him 14 carts and 22 horses.[43]

The famine, murrain, and the demands for the Scottish wars, had left the country exhausted. Edward wrote to Lancaster to tell him that the barons were not prepared to come north and that he had no money left. Parliament had voted a twentieth from the counties and a fifteenth from the burghs that raised £37,200. The clerical tenth added another £15,900. But Valence's campaign had spent not only these subsidies but much of the general revenues and issues of the realm. Lancaster told the king to stay put as it would cost no more to stay in the north as it would in the south.

* * *

Scottish attention shifted to Berwick, the last English stronghold in Scotland. Berkeley and John Weston (still holding the grand but empty title of chamberlain of Scotland) warned the king of the town's distress. Promised supplies did not arrive; men began to die of starvation; the garrison only stayed for the winter when Berkeley and the mayor gave them food and clothing.[44] The port was blockaded by Scottish vessels and Flemish privateers. In October the master of *La Prest* of Spalding bringing supplies to the town had to throw much of his cargo overboard so that he could outrun the enemy. In May the mayor reported that two vessels trying to enter the harbour were captured with their cargoes. Eventually Newcastle became the supply point, so that ships could unload and goods be taken overland.

Berkeley's hungry men held off an attempt to take the town in January 1316, 'one bright moonlit night.' It was a general assault by land and sea in boats aimed at the section of the defences between the Brighouse and the castle where the wall was incomplete. They were spotted when the moon came from behind clouds. Thus warned, the defenders drove them off. James Douglas made his escape with some difficulty.

On St Valentine's Day 1316 a squadron emerged from Berwick, led by the Gascon Raymond de Caillau. Berkeley had forbidden the foray but his men told him it was better to fight and die than stay and starve to death. They captured cattle and took hostages in the Merse. Adam Gordon, in the process of becoming 'Scottish', spied them leaving the town. He warned Douglas who brought forces to intercept the party's return at a ford on Skaithmuir near Coldstream. The Berwick men disbanded their defensive schiltron when they saw how few men Douglas commanded. The Douglas banner was unfurled and the Berwick men defeated after a stiff fight, which Douglas said was the hardest he had ever known. Most of the men from the garrison were killed, Caillau by Douglas's own hand. Berkeley's report four days later counted 20 men-at-arms and 60 foot lost 'whether alive or dead they know not.'[46] A second party led by Robert Neville, the 'Peacock of the North', was intercepted near Berwick. Neville was also killed.

Berwick's garrison began to desert and many of the burgesses left. 'Whenever a horse dies in the town' wrote Berkeley, 'the men-at-arms carry off the flesh and boil it and eat it, not letting the foot touch it till they have had what they will.'[47] Another month passed and still no relief came from England. Berkeley's pleading turned from desperation to belligerence. Men guarding the walls were dying at their post of hunger. Out of 300 enrolled men-at-arms only 50 could be arrayed mounted and armed, the rest of the horses were dead and their arms pawned for food. He was not prepared to remain beyond his period of office after Easter and warned Edward to 'think of the town, for if he looses it he will lose the north and they their lives.'[48]

* * *

Edward II allowed the local commanders to take a truce from February until Whitsun (30 May) or longer. Henry Beaumont and the earl of Angus went to parley with the Scots in February. A truce of sorts did come into operation. Edward refers to it in the negotiations for the ransom of two Scottish prisoners. It was extended until midsummer when hostilities broke out again.[49] Preparations for war on both sides of the border hampered efforts to obtain a longer truce. In April a meeting planned to discuss peace with Bruce or one of his representatives at Leicester was cancelled. Lancaster, Valence and Badlesmere received a commission to negotiate with the Scots but that in turn was cancelled in favour of three lesser men though there is no evidence that any talks took place.[50]

It is unlikely that any truce covered Berwick. A report arrived from Berwick that Bruce 'with all his force' was at Melrose ready to begin a siege, but Bruce did not arrive at Melrose until between 28 May and 8 June.[51] In May Berkeley reported that Richard Marmaduke had been in the town for three weeks 'and as yet has had no speech with the enemy, but tells him he will do what he can despite treason and envy'.[52] It is a cryptic remark that does not hint at who was being treasonable. Tension was probably mounting between the garrison and the town. The constant stream of letters 'from one day to another' from Berwick in which the king had been warned that his 'enemies are coming to besiege in every manner they can by sea and land' began to concern Edward who forwarded them to Valence, John Sandale and the treasurer, Walter de Norwich, seeking advice on what action should be taken. He also sent copies to Lancaster.

The king told his advisors that 'the keeper and townsmen had done their part', it was now their turn.[53] Parliament granted Edward the army

he wanted. With a temporary heal in relations between the earl of
Lancaster and the king a strenuous effort was made to campaign in
Scotland. A full feudal muster was called together with a demand for the
vills to levy one man to serve for 60 days, at their cost and with arms:
aketons and bacinets and with swords, bows, arrows, slings, lances.
This last measure had a precedent in the 1315 summons but again saw
an extension of the demands on the vill. These were extraordinary
measures justified in the common interest.[54] But as Edward reached the
point where he could make a determined effort in the north, events
conspired to frustrate him. The famine was at its height and a revolt
broke out in Wales.

In June 1316, news arrived at York from Berwick that Bruce was
assembling his army in the Park of Duns for a raid on Yorkshire or an
attempt on the city itself. On the 24th the invasion of England began.
Through Tynedale and the bishopric the raiders crossed into Yorkshire,
reaching as far as Richmond where the local nobles took refuge in the
castle and bought an expensive truce. From Richmond the raiders
travelled west across Swaledale as far as Furness, where they were
'delighted' with the abundance of iron. This was the first time the
wealthier counties of Yorkshire and Lancashire had been touched by the
raids.

The muster of the English army was delayed until 10 August.[55] In June
the levy granted at Lincoln was cancelled. The 2,000 foot who had
already arrived at Newcastle were sent home. On the 16 August the king
reached York.Lancaster arrived three days later. It was here that the two
men quarrelled openly.[56] The relationship between the king and earl had
begun to fray as early as April as Lancaster's attempts at reform and the
enforcement of the Ordinance were being frustrated by Edward's
officials. On the 20th the army was ordered to be at Newcastle on the 6
October for a winter campaign and the earl retired to his castle at
Pontefract.[57]

Bishop Kellawe's death delayed still further plans for the campaign.
Valence, Lancaster, Hereford and Henry Beaumont waited in the
cathedral for the result of the election for a new bishop. Each had his
own candidate. Beaumont was advancing the case of his brother Louis,
the queen's candidate. The monks chose their own man. Lancaster's
candidate came a very poor third. The king was prepared to accept the
decision but the queen was not and persuaded Edward to reopen the
contest. In December the Pope quashed the result and imposed
Beaumont. With this the breech between the king and earl was complete.
The winter array never mustered, further attempts to extend military
service left arrayers facing blunt refusals for service.[58]

While Edward had remained in the north his invasion threat had been
real. In October the abbot of Melrose received a safe-conduct to go to
England to take a message proposing a new truce. Negotiations did not

begin until the end of November, when two English envoys from York arrived at Jedburgh. Initial plans for a truce to last until Christmas were extended to a truce that would last until the summer of 1317.[59] It was only now that Bruce travelled to Ireland with Randolph leaving the Steward and Douglas as guardians of Scotland. He returned in May 1317 when the renewed threat of an English invasion in the summer demanded his presence.

Command of the northern forces over the winter fell to Edmund FitzAlan, earl of Arundel. Arundel led a contract army, with sixteen captains bringing an impressive force of 799 men-at-arms and 750 hobelars.[60] He devised a new defensive policy, stationing troops throughout the northern strongholds whether they were royal castles or not and keeping a mobile reserve of 299 men-at-arms and 470 hobelars. This was a considerable effort; it seemed at last that the English commanders were trying to adapt their numerical strength into a strategy that could combat Scottish mobility and stealth. That they should do it during a truce, when Bruce was out of the country, when there would be no raids, only highlights how he consistently outplayed his enemy.

Arundel's strategy was only meant as a holding operation for a campaign in the following summer but having such a large force idling

Scottish attacks on England 1314-19

away the winter tempted the earl into what seems a private initiative. He attempted an ambitious plan to clear Jedwood Forest as a refuge for Scottish raiding parties. Every soldier was given a felling axe. The army crossed into Scotland over a rarely used northern pass at Carter Bar. Douglas was at his newly built 'fair-manor' at Lintilee with only his personal retinue—50 men-at-arms and a company of archers. Rather than wait for reinforcements he ambushed the English van led by Thomas de Richmond.

The English commander, recognisable by a fur trimmed hat over his helmet, rode straight at Douglas. Richmond fell to the ground as they clashed, Douglas swooped down and stabbed him to death with a dagger. Before the English could regroup Douglas called off his men who disappeared into the forest. Many in the main detachment could not have known a battle had taken place. Arundel withdrew from the forest out of danger. Douglas returned to his manor that had been occupied by an English foraging party under the clerk Ellis who had found a meal laid and stopped to eat it. The only survivors from the savage onslaught that followed were those allowed to escape to warn their colleagues; most were beheaded. One Scot took Ellis's decapitated head and made it kiss his backside.[61]

Bower says that 'when [the English] heard reports of the worth of the Lord Douglas' they no longer thought it safe to invade by land. Instead Arundel led five ships from the Humber with 323 armed sailors to 'raid Dundee and Aberdeen .'[62] Sailing into the Firth of Forth, they landed at Donibristle (Bower) or Inverkeithing (Barbour) and 'began to cause cruel disturbance to the ordinary people along the coast.' The sheriff of Fife turned away with 500 men rather than risk an engagement. As they were in flight they met the bishop of Dunkeld, William Sinclair, who was at Auchertool five miles away when news arrived of the invasion. He had armed himself and was heading in the direction of the English with 60 experienced men. When the two parties met the bishop accused the sheriff of cowardice, threw away his episcopal staff and seized a lance, ordering the sheriff to follow behind him. The bishop's example spurred the Scots who drove the English back into the sea. Many drowned when they tried to escape on a boat that was too small.[63] For the rest of the season Arundel respected the truce and stayed behind his defensive line.

A more serious threat to Bruce's kingship rose in Avignon. The papacy had been vacant for two years until the election of Jacques Duèse as Pope John XXII in 1316. He sought peace amongst the Christian nations so that they could combine in a holy war against the Turks. This took precedence over all things: the question of patriotism and nationality were indulgences that would not move. There could be no crusade whilst Lancaster and Robert Bruce tormented Edward II. John exhorted

Edward to make peace with Bruce 'who at this time governs the realm of Scotland' and renewed the papal excommunication of the Scottish king and those who threatened the peace in England. John sent two papal nuncios to press this papal enterprise.[64] They did not come as mediators but to press the English case and impose a two year truce on both parties.

The cardinals arrived in England in June 1317. In early autumn they travelled north in the party of Henry and Louis Beaumont for the new bishop's consecration and enthronement in Durham. The Beaumonts had been warned that their journey would be dangerous, but Henry boasted that the Scots would not dare to attack him when travelling with two cardinals. However, the threat, when it came, was not from Scotland. The party was attacked by bandits led by Gilbert Middleton about nine miles south of Durham. The Beaumonts were kidnapped and taken to Mitford castle, the cardinals robbed and allowed to go on.

Circumstantial evidence points in all sorts of directions for the culprits. Robert de Sapy, the keeper of the temporalities during the vacancy, entered into an indenture with John de Eure, the constable of Mitford castle to stop Beaumont's consecration before Michaelmas. (He wanted to hold his lucrative office for as long as possible). But Sapy had already lost that office when the temporalities were delivered to the bishop in May.

The most likely conspirator is Thomas of Lancaster, still bridling that his candidate for the bishopric had been overlooked. Certainly the prime movers in the attack were connected with Lancaster, although their association may have come after the attack to afford them the earl's protection.

* * *

One of the attackers seized the royal castle at Knaresborough in October on behalf—he said—of the earl of Lancaster. If Lancaster was culpable he tried to defuse the affair by travelling to Durham to escort the cardinals under his protection. There he met with Middleton in the cathedral and persuaded him to return the cardinal's property. Middleton's indictment says that he had Scots with him while one chronicler says the attackers sought refuge in Scotland; another names Randolph and Douglas at the ambush. Bruce himself was not without a motive for the attack—it was just possible that he was trying to keep the cardinals out of Scotland but did not want to be seen to act openly by denying them safe-conduct. The last and often overlooked possibility, forwarded in the *Scalacronica*, is that the revolt was a reaction to lawlessness and the failure of the government to defend the north. According to this source Middleton's attack was a response to the arrest of Adam Swinburn, Middleton's (distant?) cousin for 'speaking too frankly' to the king on the condition of the north. The event shocked contemporary Europe but remains one of history's 'who done its.' The leading candidate must be Lancaster, possibly in league with the Scots, but the conspirators covered their tracks too well to make a conclusive statement of guilt either now or in 1317.[65] The Beaumont's were released in October. Middleton was captured in Mitford and executed.

The cardinals never reached Scotland. Their envoys only secured access to Robert Bruce when they showed Douglas and Alexander Seton the papal bull requesting the king's co-operation. One of the envoys made an account of the meeting to his superiors that formed the substance of a report to the Pope, a report that Lord Hailes called the 'best original portrait' of Robert Bruce.[66] The king listened to the envoy's messages and then made a 'cogent reply', with a 'cheerful face and amiable countenance.' In the king's own words (as reported by the envoy): 'We cannot say anything in reply to the cardinal's letters which are not addressed to us as king. There are several Robert Bruces who, in company with the other barons, are "governors of the kingdom of Scotland." The envoys explained that the pope's failure to use the royal title was not meant to prejudice either party. Bruce answered that by not using the title they were prejudicing him

> 'since I have possession of the kingdom, and foreign rulers address me as king. Our father the pope and our mother the church of Rome seem to be showing partiality among their own children. If you had brought letters such as these to other kings you might have had a rougher answer.'

Bruce would not make any decision without his council who were dispersed throughout the kingdom and could not be brought together before Michaelmas (29 September). The papal *cursor* (letter carrier) who had arrived with a letter to the Scottish bishops announcing John's election, had been denied entry into Scotland for three months and only entered on the envoys' coattails. When they asked on his behalf if he could travel in Scotland Bruce 'made no answer but with a certain change of expression he silently refused it.'

Before replying to the cardinals Bruce launched an attack on Berwick: he felt that he would need to take the town while he could still withstand papal pressure. An English detachment left York and a ship with 23 soldiers from Whitby went 'for the rescue of the town' The siege failed and was over by late November.[67]

Robert Bruce sent a belated answer to the cardinals, telling them that no discussion was possible unless the pope ceded the use of the royal title. The pope side-stepped Robert's request for equal treatment by cleverly, if not very helpfully, pointing out that he called neither ruler king of Scotland.[68] The cardinals could do no more and so published the papal truce in London. Publication in Scotland presented a problem. In the end they unburdened the thankless task to Adam Newton, a Franciscan monk from Berwick. At some risk to his safety the friar set out from the town in search of the king. He found him in a wood at Old Cambus supervising the construction of siege engines.

With what must have taken some nerve the friar stood before a crowd and proclaimed the truce as royal officers tried to shout him down. He was refused permission to visit the bishops and denied safe conduct back to Berwick. It was an unusual display of malice from a king who normally behaved with Arthurian chivalry to those who could not protect themselves. On his return to Berwick the friar was robbed of the bulls and his clothing. Bruce could then read in private what he was unable to read in public. Newton made a report of the incident to the pope, telling him that Robert had declared he 'would have Berwick' before any peace would be contemplated. The pope told his cardinals to excommunicate the king and place the realm under interdict.

* * *

As the cardinals were making their futile effort to impose a truce on Robert, the English went through the motions of issuing writs for a campaign that was unlikely to go ahead. The *Vita* suggests the plan to campaign was an Edwardian attempt to test Thomas of Lancaster's loyalty[69]. The cardinals arranged a meeting in July between the two men but Lancaster did not attend, claiming ill-health. He announced that he would be at Newcastle in August with his full retinue. By the middle of 1317 the two sides had reached an impasse. The muster was delayed until August by the seizure of Aymer de Valence on his return from France by Jean de Lamouilly, the Burgundian knight who supplied Greek fire at the Stirling siege. Lamouilly had continued in Edwardian service in the north and now held a grudge against Edward II for non-payment of his fees. The king arrived with an army at York in early September. Lancaster had the bridges north of the city dismantled so that the king could go no further nor receive reinforcements.

Lancaster began collecting his forces at Pontefract, but after the Middleton affair he shrank from outright rebellion. When he escorted the cardinals to York they persuaded the two parties to negotiate an agreement. Edward took his army south. When he passed through Pontefract the castle flew Lancaster's flag which so infuriated the king only Valence's intervention stopped him placing the castle under siege.

Edward was confident that papal pressure would secure a truce and sent a high powered embassy to seek peace in March 1318.[70] But he misjudged his opponent: papal interference meant Bruce redoubled his efforts to take Berwick. And after all the hard work of the last few years, this time it fell. Edward had been unable to keep the town supplied, as the profusion of safe conducts issued to burgesses to go and collect food testify. The king told his sheriffs to collect food but little could be found. Some purveyors in Yorkshire sold the corn they collected. He complained that his orders were not carried out and then found it necessary to repeat them.[71]

In 1317 the defence of the town became the responsibility of the burgesses, who offered to keep Berwick for 6,000 marks. The king took hostages (mainly boys) to ensure the burgesses' loyalty but released them when the town fell. The benefits of this arrangement were twofold: the king secured a cut-price defence, while it released the burgesses from the worst excesses of the town garrison. Many of the Scottish burgesses in 1296 had returned to the town over the years so that it had become predominately Scottish. Barbour says that the warden held all the Scottish burgesses with suspicion and ill-treated them.[72]

Disputes between the burgesses, the warden and the castle garrison continued even after these new arrangements.[73] It was one the burghers, Piers Spalding, who offered the betrayal of the town to Robert Keith— the two men may have been related through marriage. Barbour's account of Douglas and Randolph not being told of the attempt on the town to discourage rivalry between them can 'be rejected as a literary device.'[74] It is likely that both men were occupied at the sieges of Wark and Harbottle. The castles surrendered in May because they had not been relieved. This would suggest that they were under siege from the beginning of the year. Bruce probably released Douglas from duty at these sieges to take part in the capture of the town.

Spalding was in charge of the Cow Port, a gate on the eastern wall leading to Magdalen Fields. At midnight on 2 April Douglas and his men climbed the walls. Douglas's men broke their orders, 'so greedy for booty they ran as if they were demented, seizing houses and killing men.' The garrison, scattered around the town, could not muster so fierce street to street fighting followed. Barbour singles out William Keith of Galston, a cousin of the marischal, for his bravery: 'he pressed where he saw the thickest throng so mightily and fought so forcefully that he made a way for his following.'[75] Some of the English reached the castle, some slid over the walls and some were taken prisoner. *Lanercost* says that the English in the town were expelled 'almost naked and despoiled of all property,' but few were killed.[76]

King Robert was not at the assault on the town. He arrived during the siege of the castle but did not stay long. That Bruce does not figure at the assault on the town, the taking of the castle, or the raids into Yorkshire, may be an attempt to deflect papal criticism at him personally. The castle capitulated after eleven weeks when food supplies ran out. The garrison was allowed to depart. Spalding was not among those rewarded by the king, which suggests he was killed during the assault of the town or the siege of the castle.[77]

Bruce felt he was strong enough to hold Berwick. The ditch dug in 1296 was 80 feet wide and 40 feet deep. A stone wall replaced the timber palisade enclosing the town piecemeal. Yet even after years under English occupation and the Scottish siege the defences were inadequate. Barbour says that a man could stand at the bottom and strike another on the walls with a spear, so Bruce had them heightened. He was at Berwick in January and March 1319 supervising the defences and organising an attack on the earl of Lancaster's castle at Dunstanburgh, still under construction and vulnerable. Bruce's son-in-law Walter Stewart took command of the town.

The Flemish pirate John Crabbe supervised the building of mangonels, trebuchets, cranes and springalds, and provided Greek fire for the town's defence.[78] Stewart needed to restock Berwick with new blood. A proclamation in every Scottish town announced the reward of a plot in Berwick for anybody with means to stay in the town.[79] This change in Bruce's policy eventually backfired, although not in his lifetime. The town became a point of pride between the two realms and both spent the next three centuries defending or trying to take it.

* * *

The fall of Wark and Harbottle closely followed that of Berwick. A traitor surrendered Mitford. The great castles at Bamburgh and Alnwick nearly fell, 'the one by means of hostages, the other by collusion.'[80] Moray and Douglas then launched one of the most devastating raids into northern England. In 1317 Archbishop Melton ordered a reassessment of ecclesiastical properties for the 1291 papal crusading tax. Only a year later a second revision, the *Nova Taxatio*, provided relief for those properties that had suffered from this raid. Northumberland, where ecclesiastical income had collapsed, was excluded altogether.[81] These parish revaluations map out a clear trail of destruction. The main party crossed the Tees at Barnard Castle and headed towards Ripon by way of Richmond with a division sent into Wensleydale. At Ripon 1,000 marks was the price of respecting St. Wilfrids.

A second party left the main division to attack Hartlepool and then rode down the vale of York to Northallerton. The two groups converged at Knaresborough. It was here that a Lancastrian supporter captured the town in the aftermath of the Middleton affair. The castle surrendered to royal officers on 29 January but the suspicion remains that Randolph, unaware of the events over the winter, believed that the castle was still held for Lancaster and was coming to its relief. The raiders remained for three days whilst searching local woods to find cattle taken away for safety. Of 140 houses in the town only twenty were left standing. From Knaresborough the raiders crossed the Pennines along Airedale, Ribblesdale and Wharfedale before turning north.

The loss of Berwick drove Edward into a reconciliation with Lancaster at Leake. Lancaster had now lost his position of influence. The vehemence of his alienation from his cousin the king, and the treacherous lengths he would go to humiliate Edward, lost him the support of the other magnates. But his enormous wealth from five earldoms meant he could not be discounted, however unpopular he became amongst his peers. The reconciliation coincided with the first abundant harvest for three years and then the news of Edward Bruce's defeat at Faughart. It seemed that it would be possible to break the 'unhappy circle of shortage of money, extension of military obligation, discontent and military failure.'[82]

* * *

Edward intended to campaign after the York parliament where he received the consent that was missing in 1314. This would be a national effort, with Lancaster's service. At the end of the parliament Edward sent envoys to Scotland to claim the kingdom and offer Bruce peace in return for his safety. It was a sign of Edward's confidence that he was willing to be reconciliatory towards Bruce who replied 'that he did not much care for the king of England's peace.'[83] Edward's plans were too ambitious. The levies went home when parliament overran. The north received new commanders and new defensive measures. Edward relied on his barons to defend the northern counties, who were to be ready with their forces at three days notice to repel any invasion. This meant that he would not have the burden of paying a force waiting for unannounced raids. It is unlikely that the barons could react to a raid before the Scots were on their homeward journey. The spring brought an announcement of a muster at Newcastle.

Edward called for 24,296 foot soldiers. He offered the infantry and sailors the right to as much of the enemy's goods without restitution up to the value of £100. The *Vita* says this encouragement armed many volunteers though the Pay Roll is not so liberal: only 8,080 served. This figure excludes the naval and Lancastrian contingents whose troops did not draw pay (Lancaster was asked to bring 2,000 men, he perhaps brought a quarter of this number with him). Even this inflates the real size of the army, as it is the total number who arrived at Newcastle in late August rather than the number at the siege. On 10 September about 5,500 infantry were being paid although by then most of Harcla's large Cumberland contingent, 354 hobelars and 980 archers had left to intercept Scottish raiders. Besides the infantry and hobelars the English had 1,400 cavalry and a huge fleet of 77 ships.[85]

The decision to besiege Berwick was only taken after the army left Newcastle. This lack of any pre-planned strategy is confirmed by an order to the chancellor to send siege engines and ditchers to the town the day after the siege had begun. The capture of Berwick would serve three purposes: it would return the symbolic town to English hands, protect the army's rear should it venture north, and draw the Scots into a pitched battle since Bruce had sworn an oath to relieve the town. The English arrived 'with trumpets blowing and spent the night in great joy and pleasure and music.'[86]

Siege engines caused great damage inside the town before an assault began with scaling ladders and scaffolds combined with seaward assault from ships moored in the harbour. Barges gingerly towed a ship against the harbour walls. Before the company had time to lower a bridge across to the battlements from the ship's tower the defenders issued from the town and set it on fire, capturing an engineer. As the ship burned in the harbour the assault was abandoned and a general retreat sounded.

This failure was blamed on a lack of siege towers.[87] As the army waited for siege engines to arrive from Bamburgh and Northampton before a second assault, dissension began to grown in the camp. The king began giving awards to his favourites, 'despicable parasites' as the *Flores Historium* calls them. He made Despenser keeper of the castle and Amory the captain of the town—both men were enemies of Lancaster.[88] Rumours spread that he was planning to avenge the death of Gaveston.

At dawn on the sixth day a second, more forceful, assault began. The engineer captured from the English ship operated a mangonel that smashed a sow before it reached the walls. The work was completed by John Crabbe who used a moveable crane to drop burning faggots onto the wrecked engine. A ship held a boat full of men-at-arms hoisted to the top of its mast. The intention seems to have been to lower the boat onto the walls, a plan foiled when it was struck by a stone from an engine.

The town nearly fell to the land assault. The outworks at the Marygate were captured and the tackle to bring the drawbridge down set on fire. Walter Stewart committed his armed reserve to keep the entrance. The fighting continued until nightfall when the English withdrew 'woundit, and wery, and forbeft.' Amongst the defenders 'only a few were slain, but many were very badly wounded, and the rest were desperately weary.'[89]

Bruce would do nothing so foolish as to challenge Edward to a battle which 'mycht weill turn to foly'. Instead he sent Douglas and Randolph in a diversionary raid into England. A spy captured at York told his interrogators of a plan to capture the English queen who was hurriedly packed off to Nottingham for her safety.

Archbishop Melton sought to imitate his predecessor at the battle of the Standard. His hastily gathered force included a large number of clerics in which he pressed all who could travel into service. Against experienced Scottish raiders, it was an unequal contest. Myton lies three miles east of Boroughbridge on the banks of the Swale near the confluence with the Ure. Melton marched—strolled would be a better word, the army was not arrayed—towards the Scottish camp hoping to catch them by surprise. Randolph formed his men into a schiltron. They set three haystacks on fire, the smoke blinding the English who could not make out the Scottish position. From behind the smoke the Scots screamed war cries that frightened so many of the English they turned and ran. The raiders mounted and cut through the fleeing English, and many drowned in the Swale. It was only the coming of night that saved greater loss of life.

So many clerics died that Scottish chroniclers, no doubt quoting contemporary usage, named the battle the 'the Chapter of Myton'.[90] From Myton the Scottish army moved south to Castleford and then west along Airedale and Wharfedale before returning to Scotland via the western march.

* * *

Edward held an emergency council when news of the disaster reached Berwick. The southern magnates wanted to stay, those from the north whose homes were under threat wanted to leave. The king favoured staying but did not have his father's force of personality to determine the issue. The decision to abandon the campaign became inevitable when Lancaster sided with the Northern magnates. The campaign had lasted only ten days. Seven ships from London carrying timber to build a peel when the army moved further into Scotland returned home, their cargoes still loaded.[91] It was not surprising that rumours spread as soon as Lancaster left: that he was in league with the Scots who had not touched his lands, that Bruce had paid him £40,000, and that he had made no effort at the siege. The younger Despenser wrote to the sheriff of Glamorgan that 'before he [the king] had been there eight days news came to him that the Scots had entered his lands of England with the prompting and assistance of the earl of Lancaster. The earl acted in such a way that the king took himself off with all his army, to the great shame and grievous damage to us all.'[92] There would be no further attempts to reconcile the king and his over-mighty earl.

Edward returned to York where he repeated the orders for the defence of the north made before the expedition. On 4 September a Yorkshire county force under Melton was to be ready to go against the Scots with fifteen days provisions at three days notice, the prelates to raise men-at-arms. John Cromwell and the earl of Angus agreed to keep the march of Northumberland with only 200 men-at-arms. On the 13 October a council meeting at York revised the plans: the king would remain in York with 600 men-at-arms including Henry Beaumont, John de St John and the earl of Atholl. They could do nothing to prevent a raid led by Randolph and Douglas which served to remind Edward of his inadequate defences. John of Brittany was ordered to raise a levy to march against the Scots who had, or were about to, enter the march of England but no evidence exists of any action from the earl.[93]

The pressure for a truce was now growing on both kings. Edward had no stomach for northern military life over the winter and the new king of France was pressing him to do homage for his French lands. The capture of Berwick meant Robert Bruce could try and rehabilitate himself with the papacy by allowing a truce, albeit two years late. Negotiations began towards the end of October when twelve Scottish envoys received safe-conducts to Newcastle and English envoys left from London. The ensuing truce, signed on 22 December, would last two years.

It was a humiliating climb-down for Edward. He conceded that the English castle at Harbottle would only be handed over on the condition that it would be dismantled or handed back to Robert at the expiry of the truce if no permanent peace was made. Two years later Edward was compelled to honour the agreement but ordered the castle be destroyed secretly.[94] The magnates were ashamed that the king had been humbled but Edward had no choice, England could not maintain the war effort.

* * *

With the truce in place, Bruce had fences to mend at the curia. Bruce was a deeply religious man and his excommunication and the interdict genuinely troubled him. Although not published in Scotland, their publication on a daily basis in England meant that the bulls were widely known. The Scottish clergy, for so long the backbone of the Wars of Independence, had to choose between their loyalty to Bruce and their devotion to the church. An English chronicler says that 'meny a gode preste and holy man ... were slayn throuz al the reme of Scotland' because they 'wolde singe no masse azeynes [against] the popes commaundement'.[95] By 1319 the failure to recognise the papal truce led to a fresh series of bulls excommunicating Bruce and his lieutenants. The pope called the king with four of his bishops, St Andrews, Dunkeld, Aberdeen and Moray, or their proctors to appear at the curia to give an account of their actions. Certainly, they sent no representation to the pope. Instead three letters were written, from the king (lost), the clergy (lost) and lastly from the barons, to explain in the form of an *apologia* the Scottish resistance to English rule.

A duplicate of the letter from the barons was made and kept at Tyninghame House in East Lothian. It has survived, faded and tattered. It is known as the Declaration of Arbroath. Although the barons' letter runs in the names of eight earls and 31 barons it was the king's initiative. The most likely candidate for its authorship is Bernard Linton, the chancellor. Once the document was completed the barons' seals that run along the base of the faded document like a centipede, were called in and affixed. With the barons scattered throughout the country the king's clerks relied on those seals that could be found locally, there are few from the north or west. An effort was made to include as many names from the former Comyn party to show that this was a national document.

The declaration is a petition to the pope to persuade the English to leave Scotland in peace. It is the appeal of a smaller country threatened by its larger neighbour, a neighbour who anticipates 'a readier return and weaker resistance' than from crusading. Its antecedent is Baldred Bisset's *Processus* from 1301 and the declaration of the clergy in 1309. It begins with a historical account but unlike the *Processus* it is short and avoids the abstract legal arguments that so impressed literate medieval minds. Instead it tapped into a rich vein of nationalism forged through years of bitter warfare.

It says much for Bruce's success in wrapping the nation around him that he could contemplate such a document. Its language is beautifully simple which gives it an impact that has never lost its relevance, the 'most impressive manifesto of nationalism that medieval Europe produced.'[96] The declaration pulses with pride:

> 'for so long as a hundred of us remain alive, we will never in any way be bowed beneath the yoke of English domination; for it is not for glory, riches or honour that we fight, but for freedom alone, that which no man of worth yields up, save with his life.'

The letter was carried to the curia by Adam of Gordon, the Lothian knight who had beseeched Edward's help in 1313, Odard de Maubuisson, a French lord, and Alexander Kinninmouth, a lawyer and cleric. Maubuisson had been admiral of the French fleet. His inclusion not only offered some guarantee of the letter's delivery but was part of the Franco-Scottish rapprochement.[97] The letter sent by the king told Pope John of the new truce and peace negotiations. With this news John wrote to Bruce, 'that illustrious man Robert, who assumes the title and position of king of Scots', and brought a halt to the process against the king and the bishops. He exhorted both sides to make efforts to make a final peace.[98]

Within just five months of this affirmation of Scottish nationhood five of the signatories, William Soules, Roger Moubray, David Brechin, Patrick Graham and Eustace Maxwell had hatched a plot to kill Bruce.

Barbour says that the conspirators wanted to place Soules on the throne, but it is more likely that they intended to warm the seat for a Balliol restoration. The threat of internal dissension seems to have played on Bruce's mind for the last two years. In 1318 a new entail took account of Edward Bruce's death that recognised Robert's grandson, Robert Stewart, as heir. It includes an affirmation of loyalty, echoed in parliament in the same year when rumour-mongers were threatened with imprisonment. Clearly the danger of Balliol sympathy was still present and identified by the king.

On 4 August 1320 a parliament at Scone, 'the Black Parliament', acquitted Maxwell. Soules and his aunt, the Countess of Strathearn, confessed, and were sentenced to life imprisonment. Moubray had died, but his corpse was placed in a litter and bought to the parliament where it was sentenced to be drawn, hung and beheaded. Robert's clemency stopped this sentence from being carried out, but Gilbert Malherbe, John Logie, David Brechin and Richard Brown, died traitors' deaths: a punishment hitherto unknown in Scotland and which shocked contemporaries more than the conspiracy. Ingram de Umfraville was never cited but circumstantial evidence points to him as a chief conspirator. He left Scotland under an English safe-conduct, never to return.

* * *

By the time Pope John replied to Robert Bruce the peace talks held at Bamburgh had failed. They remain of interest only as they are recorded in a series of letters between Edward and his envoys, the bishops of Worcester and Carlisle and Bartholomew Badlesmere.[99] The Scottish delegation was less distinguished, led by William Soules and Alexander Seton. The meeting was delayed twice, firstly to give time for papal and French envoys to arrive, secondly when the leading English envoy, Valence, was detained in France. The papal envoys promised to aid Edward. John of Brittany replaced Valence when it became clear he would not return in time. A note in the exchequer records the 'process of Scotland', that is the documents recording the Great Cause, were handed to John of Brittany who was instructed to refer to them as often as possible.

By chance, the arguments used by the Scottish delegation have been preserved in a fourteenth century manuscript in Córdoba.[100] The English merely repeated the original arguments of 1291, while the Scottish returned to those of 1301. The result was a stalemate. The envoys sent Edward a report blaming Scottish intransigence for the failure:

> 'we have heard many declarations that they desire peace above all things, but in practice they have little to say which suggests it, rather the contrary, and finally, after they had cause great delays, they would agree only to a long truce, for example of twenty-six years.'

Both kings would need to be consulted before such a long truce could be entertained so the meeting broke up—there is no evidence of the negotiations reopening. In their comically unrealistic attempt to reopen the question of English overlordship the English had shown that they were the 'prisoners of their refusal to admit that Scotland was not theirs.'[101] It would take another campaign, and three more devastating raids, before a longer truce could be forced on the belligerent English king.

* * *

1321 started badly for Edward. His choice of favourites was worsening. The younger Despenser was a far more dangerous young man than Gaveston. In Spring the Despensers began to enrich themselves in the Welsh marches through the king's favour. A league of Marcher lords seized the elder Despenser's estates and open warfare began in the west. In mid-summer Thomas of Lancaster called a northern 'parliament' to Sherburn. The number of border captains present show that they had become exasperated with the king and saw that the only hope of rescue from Scottish attacks lay with the earl. They were not the only men relying on him. In December a Lancastrian retainer received a safe-conduct from James Douglas to go to Jedburgh. Earlier evidence of Lancaster's dalliance with the Scots is circumstantial, albeit backed by contemporary rumours. From now on hard evidence of his treason exists as negotiations, cloaked in secrecy, began between the two parties.

The Scots sought from the earl what they could not get from the king. Lancaster sought from the Scots the friends he would need in a final confrontation with Edward. In January 1322 Thomas Randolph extended the safe-conducts until August; in February safe-conducts were given to two of Lancaster's retainers to go north with 40 horsemen; a letter from Douglas to 'king Arthur', Lancaster's inflated pseudonym, sought a meeting.[102] This collusion brought rewards in January, when a Scottish raid at the end of the truce headed for Durham to neutralise the king's supporters in the palatine. Randolph remained at Darlington ready to intervene with Lancaster while Douglas plundered Hartlepool and Cleveland. The Steward secured tribute from Richmond. When northern knights sought help from the earl, Lancaster feigned excuses.[103]

The last letter is the most damning. It is unsigned and undated which allows for the possibility of its forgery, but in it Lancaster and Humphrey Bohun, the earl of Hereford who had led the Marcher lords in their contest with the Despensers, promised that they would not help the king in his war with the Scots. In return the Scots promised to come to the barons' aid.

* * *

In the end it was neither the earl and his northern parliaments, nor the Marcher lords and their private war with the Despensers, but an affront to the queen at Leeds Castle by Bartholomew Badlesmere that stirred King Edward. With uncharacteristic purpose he determined to remove the baronial opposition. Andrew Harcla was now crucial to the northern defences. In March he met Edward in Gloucester where he informed him of the recent raids and pressed him to bring relief. The king told him that his problems in England came first. A truce was made until Michaelmas (29 September).[104] In quick succession Edward destroyed his enemies in Kent, in the Welsh marches, and the north.

Hereford fled with his forces to join Lancaster at Burton-on-Trent. They retreated as the royal army approached from the south. Whether they were headed for Lancaster's bolt hole at Dunstanburgh or the protection of their Scottish allies is not known, but when they reached the river Ure at Boroughbridge they found the bridge and ford blocked by Harcla. He had called out the Cumberland and Westmoreland levies and made a forced night march to block Lancaster's route. Hereford died trying to force a crossing. That night his retainers drifted away, as did some of Lancaster's men. The game was up. Lancaster surrendered, trusting that his royal blood would save him, but after years of provocation the king was not prepared to show mercy . Lancaster was executed and Edward rewarded Harcla with the new earldom of Carlisle.

Riding high on the success of a victory that was not his, Edward looked north. With the baronial opposition crushed, for the first (and only) time of his reign he could campaign in Scotland free from the dissension and quarrelling that had undermined the campaigns in 1310, 1314 and 1319. What was more, the public finances had at long last recovered from the depression caused by the famine. The new campaign would not be financed by a new tax on the laity, although the clergy did give aid. Instead Edward determined to repeat the extension of military service that he had attempted in previous years. Soon after Lancaster's execution a muster was ordered for Newcastle on 13 June, later prorogued until 24 July. Edward called for huge numbers of foot from the counties, paid and armed at local expense. A total of 28,500 were told to muster at Newcastle, another 11,000 at Carlisle. A further 7,000 foot and hobelars with 300 men-at-arms were drawn from Ireland and 10,000 from Wales. Just in case this was not enough in June a further 10,000 foot were ordered along traditional lines, drawing the king's pay.[105]

At the York parliament these plans were modified and the muster postponed. For one of few occasions in the Scottish wars Edward relied on foot from southern counties. Their loyalty was not as suspect as those from the north, but they were poorly trained and their supply from their own localities stretched. The numbers called by Edward were laughably ambitious. Some 1,250 men-at-arms and 20,000 foot served, including 1,500 hobelars; 13,100 served unpaid from the counties, 6,900 from the vills.[106]

The pattern of English attempts to campaign in Scotland by Edward II was now too established to expect anything novel in 1322. As the military build-up gathered pace in the east, Bruce attacked down the west coast. Historical documents form a rich source of evidence for the formation and disposition of English armies. This is in stark contrast to the evidence of Scottish raiding parties, which appear in the records as if from nowhere. On 17 June the Scottish army surfaced, passing Carlisle to burn the bishop's manor at Rose and to plunder Holme Cultram. At Furness the abbot paid ransom to be left alone. Bruce then crossed the sands and burnt Lancaster, the first time the town, without the protection of its lord, suffered. Randolph and Douglas, who had taken another route, now joined with the king. They marched twenty miles further south to burn Preston, before returning, staying five days near Carlisle to trample crops. They reached Scotland on 24 July.[107]

It was not until 12 August 1322 that the English army finally crossed the border. Bruce withdrew before the invasion to Culross, taking whatever provisions could be carried and burning what could not. The English army soon ran out of food. Creighton was reached on the 18th, Musselburgh on the 19th. Henry Beaumont went to Holy Island to see what had become of the supply ships. After good harvests in the previous three years the 1321 harvest was poor and grain for the campaign was imported from Gascony. Edward had known of the dangers presented by Flemish pirates but did little to combat them. Ships from the Cinque Ports and Great Yarmouth received a mandate to go against the Flemings in the south coast where they were preventing supplies getting through but there is no evidence of success.[108] John Bermingham's Irish contingent was told to wait at their embarkation points until the admiral of the western fleet arrived to bring them across safely as the sea was 'infested by the king's enemies with the intention of taking victuals.'[109] Storms prevented some of the ships reaching Leith. Without protection many more refused to put out from their ports. Part of the stores were wasted, allowed to rot in the ships' holds at Newcastle.

The army reached Leith on the 20th. The footmen staying at the expense of the vills were made a payment of ten pence, one third in cash and the rest in flour.[110] This extraordinary payment could not avoid disaster. The contingents brought sixteen days supply of food but this barely lasted until they crossed the border. At Edinburgh the infantry was racked by dysentery and famine. There was little point having money in Leith where no food could be found, the supply of flour soon ran out. After a week without sight of the precious supply fleet the army turned home. The king was at Alcrum Moor in Roxburgh on the 30th, and recrossed the border on 2 September. He dryly wrote to the archbishop of Canterbury that he had returned 'the better to harass our enemies,' that he had found neither man nor beast except a solitary lame bull standing in a corn field. When Warenne saw the poor beast being brought back to camp he said it was the dearest cattle he ever saw. Just to complete a miserable campaign James Douglas ambushed an advance party as it looted the monastery at Melrose.[111]

* * *

With most of the troops starving, Edward disbanded the army the day after he crossed the border. He kept with him John Bermingham, the steward of his household Richard Amory, Ralph Neville as keeper of the March and the younger Despenser. The king's immediate concern was Norham which must have come under threat early in September when he berated the bishop of Durham for not defending the castle with vigour. Durham's constable, Thomas Grey, undertook to find 20 men-at-arms and 50 hobelars for the castle's defence. Attacks had escalated to a full-scale siege by 17 September. The king did not reserve his contempt solely for the bishop. He wrote from Durham to reprimand the constables at Bamburgh, Warkworth, Dunstanburgh and Alnwick for allowing attacks without any challenge from the garrisons 'to the constables' dishonour and shame.'[112] The people of Northumberland began to flee south with their cattle.[113]

The raids in the east were just a prelude to a bold drive in the west. In line with the king, Harcla disbanded his substantial Cumberland force at the end of September. But Bruce then crossed the Solway at Bowness and spent five days devastating the area around Carlisle, preventing Harcla from reforming his division. Bruce sent scouts searching for the English king. Edward was travelling south from Barnard Castle when he heard of the invasion. As a precaution he ordered Harcla and seven other northern magnates to attend him with a levy of Yorkshire foot on 'Blakehoumor', a site identified as Scawton Moor, a summit overlooking Sutton Bank and Roulston Scar on the North Yorkshire moors near Byland.

The king moved to Byland Abbey. On 12 October news reached Edward that the Scottish army had crossed the Pennines. Without his normally huge army, Edward made camp at the safer Rievaulx. Randolph was now only 15 miles to the north-east at Northallerton, only separated from the king by the Hambleton Hills. The king had suddenly found himself in a dangerous position, with Scottish forces preparing to block any retreat south. The next day he sent an urgent message to Valence to make his way to Blakehoumor where he would find John of Brittany and Henry Beaumont.

From the base of Blakehoumor Randolph could see line of unfurled banners on the ridge where Brittany could reconnoitre the Scottish army. The only route over the hill was a small steep pass defended by dismounted men-at-arms. An alternative route around by Helmsley would have given Edward time to abandon the abbey. Douglas's division led the way along the pass. Randolph left his division with four men from his company and placed himself ahead of Douglas to command the advance. Both men pressed the attack on the pass as boulders and arrows hurled past them from the heights.

Ralph Cobham, known as the best knight in England, withdrew when Thomas Ughtred of Scarborough remained to fight, apparently giving up his epithet to Ughtred. Both men were captured. Bruce sent his 'Irschery', the Scottish Gaels from Argyll and the Isles, scrambling up the hillside to outflank Brittany. When they reached the summit they bore down on the English position, a Highland charge that would become familiar to a later generation. Brittany, fighting dismounted, put up a stout defence but was taken together with the nobleman, Henry de Sully, butler of France. Those who could fled.

Edward, 'being ever chicken-hearted and luckless in war ... now took flight.'[114] Brittany's hilltop defence gave him enough time to escape. Just. A payment to an archer for 'following the body of the lord king from the conflict had with the Scots at Rievaulx' is a cool comment on a frantic flight. For a second time the king abandoned his silver plate and treasure to the Scots. Edward moved first to Bridlington. Walter Stewart snapped at Edward's heels so he moved to the safety of York. The Steward followed as far as the city's gates.

The affair was a catastrophe for Edward. The losses may not have been as great as at Bannockburn but his near capture was all the more humiliating for being on English soil. This would be his last action against the Scots. Brittany, a leading light of the English war party, was brought before Bruce. There appears to have been animosity between the two men, possible after Brittany's uncompromising stance at the Bamburgh peace talks.[115] He was not ransomed until 1324.

Yorkshire suffered the predictable consequences of Edward's humiliation. Robert's men raided freely in the East Riding, a district that had escaped the raids until now, as far as Beverley, which paid a ransom to protect the town. The Bridlington monks did not find Edward's presence great comfort, they removed their treasure to Lincoln and some monks sought out Bruce and paid a ransom to protect their estates. Nine horsemen and eighteen horses were billeted on the abbey for the duration of the raid. Unable to reform his detachment Harcla had moved to raise men in Lancashire. He arrived at York to find the king indignant that he had been unable to rescue him so disbanded his force. The Scottish army recrossed the border in early November:

> 'And syne with presoneris and catell
> Riches and mony fayr jowell
> To Scotland tuk thai hame thar way
> Bath blyth and glaid joyfull and gay...
> That thai the king off Ingland
> Discumfyt in his awne countré.'[116]

Scottish attacks on England 1322

Chapter 9

THE SHAMEFUL PEACE

'They have nothing but their naked bodies for his service.'
Petition from men of the English Marches

Edward II was unmoved by his sobering escape from Rievaulx and made no efforts towards a peace settlement. Intermittent fighting continued on the border—in November Archibald Douglas, James's brother, was captured in a skirmish. The king ordered his barons to go to their northern estates with as many men as possible, to be ready to assemble at York if Bruce invaded. English forces were put on alert at least four times from the beginning of 1323 for an invasion that never came.[1]

Northern England despaired of the king's plans. The Archbishop of York issued letters permitting the northern clergy to negotiate private settlements with the Scots. The Bishop of Durham entered direct negotiations. Andrew Harcla was not prepared to see yet another debacle. He had become disillusioned with the king and the conduct of the war. There is a suggestion that he had intentionally not arrived in time for the battle of Byland to see which way events turned. After Byland he disbanded his force and turned north to arrange his own peace with Bruce. This would not be a temporary and expensive truce favoured by ecclesiastics, burghers and constables but a brave and far-sighted initiative to break the deadlock.

Harcla found Bruce at Lochmaben where the two men signed a truce on 3 January.[2] It is likely that this was the culmination of contact over the two months since Byland, or even before. The truce was testament to northern realpolitik. It recognised that 'both kingdoms prospered so long as each kingdom had a king from its own nation, and was maintained separately, with its own laws and customs', and sought to 'let it again be done in the same manner'. The treaty exists in two versions. The first, a Scottish copy (now in Copenhagen) must have been the primary treaty. It proposed the appointment of twelve arbiters, six from each kingdom, who would settle differences over a final peace not between the two kings but between Bruce and Harcla. Neither king would be forced to accept back any who had fought against them.

A second, diluted version of the treaty kept by Harcla was most likely made to pacify English unease. In that copy Harcla negotiated 'on behalf of all those in England who wish to be spared and saved from war by Robert Bruce and all his men'. In the Copenhagen version Bruce promised to respect Harcla's lands in any future invasion. This clause was understandably dropped in case it was seen as self-serving. The most striking difference is the promotion of the arbiters to a council of magnates to consider matters of dispute between the two realms.

On his return to England Harcla began to canvas support for the agreement.[3] But he had made too many enemies in his swift rise to prominence. When the truce became known to the king, Harcla was proclaimed a traitor. A local lord, Anthony de Lucy, entered Carlisle castle with seven men-at-arms. Leaving armed men at the doors he found Harcla in the great hall where he demanded his surrender. Harcla was tried by Geoffrey le Scrope, chief justice of the king's bench, one of the men who would later conclude a peace treaty very similar to that proposed by the earl. Harcla was stripped of his earldom by the ritual removal of the sword given him by the king, then stripped of his knighthood by the removal of his gilded spurs. He was dragged from a horse's tail to the gallows at Harroby, and hanged and quartered. He justified his motives to the end. Harcla's promotion to the earldom made him the pre-eminent northern lord and he was one of the few men capable of defending the border. His death removed the prospects of any proficient northern defence. He may have made the truce in the quixotic hope of the king's approval, but it was too much to ask of this petty, vindictive man. To Edward II, Harcla was 'a private person to whom it in no wise pertained to ordain such things'.

At first, the Lochmaben treaty seems to have been an aberration. Edward's Irish magnates were warned as early as 10 December that he expected them to serve in a summer campaign. A parliament at York gave him a tenth and a sixth. He sought further subsidies from the prelates and Gascony.[4] Yet even before Harcla was executed, official moves had been made towards a longer truce. Henry Sully, the French captive from Byland, became an intermediary. Sully's men had English safe-conducts as early as 28 December.[5] In February Sully himself went to Edward armed with a letter from Bruce requesting peace and returned to Berwick on the 17th with Edward's reply. The two sides were close enough to arrange a parley at Newcastle after Easter.

As the prospects for a peaceful settlement grew in the spring a two month truce was agreed at Knaresborough on 21 March.[6] It was only with the temporary truce that the northern counties could feel safe, and even then invasions were expected when the truces came to an end. Only four days before the truce was due to expire, fears of a Scottish invasion led to orders for an evacuation of the northern counties to deny a

Scottish army sustenance. Any animals were allowed to depasture in the royal forests in Yorkshire.[7] These were valid fears which appear to be founded on reports of Scottish military preparations from English spies on the border. Bruce was toying with the English, applying pressure to secure a peace settlement.

The talks nearly faltered before they began. Robert Bruce sent Sully a furious letter saying that he would not consent to the truce as it did not mention him by name:

> 'You ought to remember well enough, sir, how it was contained in our letters sent to the King of England and also how we charged you verbally, that we desired and desire always to negotiate with the King of England aforesaid in the form of a final peace between him and ourselves, saving always to us and to our heirs our kingdom free and quit ... on this matter we have received letters of yours and transcripts of the king's letters saying that he has granted to the people of Scotland who are at war with him a truce; and this manner of speaking is very strange to us, for, in the other truces which have been made between him and us, we have been named the principal on one hand as he has on the other, though he would not style us king... And do not wonder therefore that we have not agreed to this truce... And we send you a copy of the king's letter, for we think that you cannot have seen it. And if you have seen it, it seems to us that you have treated us too lightly.'

This document is puzzling. The version of the letter kept in the English records refers to 'Sir Robert Bruce and his adherents'. It is possible that this was a simple clerical error, the king being sent a draft. Bruce sent Alexander Seton (the man who had betrayed Edward at Bannockburn), William Montfichet (the man who had surrendered Dundee) and Master Walter Twynham to secure Edward's oath for the security of the truce and safe-conducts for his envoys.[8]

With the removal of the opposition in the civil war, Edward was now dependent on his household staff and the Despensers. He appointed his treasurer, Walter Stapledon, bishop of Exeter, the younger Despenser and his chancellor, Robert Baldcock to make a final peace. They met Randolph and Lamberton in early May. The talks do not seem to have gone well—on the 11th the king wrote to Valence telling him that the truce was extended until 12 June but warning him to be ready to answer an earlier summons if the talks broke down.[9]

No common ground could be found between the two sides. There would be no final settlement. Instead, on 30 May at Bishopthorpe near York, a thirteen year truce, 'at the request of Sire Robert de Brus' was finally agreed.

Edward II probably wanted a short truce, to give himself time to regroup, but had to accept Scottish demands for a longer term or nothing at all. The truce carried the unusual clause guaranteeing its term beyond the life of either monarch. The truce provided clauses to prevent the building of new fortifications on the borders. Wardens would control the border with powers to settle border disputes. Special licences were required to cross the border; no doubt Edward feared English rebels treating with Bruce, and patrols watched for anybody trying to cross the passes without a passport. The treaty protected shipping, giving safe-haven to ships, a provision that was more valuable to Scottish ships having to sail down the length of the English seaboard. It was ratified by Bruce in Berwick a week later. In a small victory the copy of this ratification enrolled in the English records was signed 'Nous Robert roi d'Escose'.[10]

The Bishopthorpe truce must have been a bitter disappointment for King Robert. He knew that England was bigger, stronger and richer than Scotland. The military ascendancy held by Scotland depended on his survival. The Soules conspiracy had revealed latent Balliol sympathies. Worst still, he lost the support of his allies in Flanders. Count Robert de Béthune died in September 1322. His successor, Louis de Nevers, sought talks for a truce with England, which Edward allowed only on the condition that Louis would not aid the Scots. With this, Scotland's tie with the continent, its essential supply of arms and naval support, was severed.[11]

The truce was unpopular with the war parties in both countries. When Edward gave Randolph a safe-conduct, Henry Beaumont was commissioned to lead the guard bringing him to the talks. It was felt prudent to change these orders, with Beaumont becoming a hostage at Tynemouth for the earl's safety. He was joined by other members of the war party to keep them out of harm's way until the negotiations were complete.[12] As a member of the king's secret council, Beaumont was an important player in English politics. At a council meeting when the king asked him for his advice, Beaumont replied in 'a disrespectful manner' that he would not give any. When told to leave he told Edward that 'he would rather be absent than present'.

Beaumont's reaction was mirrored in Scotland. In late April Anthony de Lucy sent a report on the state of the march following a court held to settle matters of dispute on the border. The news from Scotland, he said, 'is that the nobles and commons desire war more than peace'. The *Vita Edwardi* quotes Robert complaining to Edward that he was unable to 'restrain the fury of a raging throng'.[13] Still, the long truce might stifle this opposition. It would give time for negotiations towards a full peace and for recovery in the areas devastated by the wars.

Edward made a solitary concession, promising not to hinder Scottish efforts at the curia to have the papal excommunication and interdict lifted. Towards the end of the year Thomas Randolph travelled to Avignon to argue for recognition of Bruce's title. In the draft of a letter from the younger Despenser to an English official in early October, Bruce is referred to as *le roi Descoce*. A clerk has then struck out the mistake, but if the English king's closest supporter was having difficulty keeping up the pretence it would have been foolish for the pope to continue to deny the validity of Robert's kingship.[14] In January 1324 the pope wrote to Edward to explain his acceptance of Bruce's title. Perhaps Edward thought this went beyond the terms of the Bishopthorpe agreement, perhaps he was just being petty, but he sent his confidant, the new bishop of Winchester, John Stratford, to the papal court to ensure that Pope John gave no further ground. When Randolph returned to the curia in 1325-6 Pope John was no longer responsive to his embassy. The interdict and excommunication stayed in place.

In 1322, Edward's brother-in-law was crowned Charles IV of France. His accession soon led to renewed conflict with England, and the possibility of a Franco-Scottish alliance. Charles gathered around him a new group of advisors, the conciliatory Henry de Sully fell from favour to be replaced by Charles of Valois, the man who had stormed out of Edward's coronation and who had held the French military command during the 1294-8 war in Gascony. Edward's duchy had remained secure since the treaty of Paris in 1303. The short reigns of Louis X, John I and Philip V prevented the French from pursuing an aggressive policy against their English vassal.

When Charles succeeded to the throne he demanded nothing more than his rights contained in the 1259 treaty of Paris — Edward's homage for his French domains. He even gave Edward extra time to fulfil his obligation until the kingdom was secure from the Scots, their Flemish allies and English rebels. Edward would procrastinate in the same way as his father but, however unpopular, homage to the French king was inevitable.

The change in French policy can be dated to October 1322, when Charles authorised the building of a *bastide* at the priory of Saint Sardos in the Agenais, the centre of English territory. The priory, as a dependant of a French Benedictine house, owed nominal loyalty to the French king, but the legality of the new *bastide* was far from clear and immediately questioned by the seneschal of Gascony, Ralph Basset of Drayton. When construction began in the autumn of 1323 the *bastide* was attacked and burnt to the ground. The perpetrators, English officers amongst them, hanged a French official from the stake of the French claim. Edward and his officials disclaimed responsibility but Charles summoned Basset to an inquiry in Paris. War seemed inevitable and in August 1324 Charles of Valois entered the duchy at the head of a French army. The English commander, the Earl of Kent, could do nothing but secure a six-month truce.

Edward was in no position to send troops to the continent. The truce with Scotland was far from clear even though peace negotiations, instigated by Bruce, progressed throughout the second half of 1324. The younger Despenser wrote to Basset that Edward planned to meet Bruce on 18 November. 'If affairs go well between them' Despenser hoped that Bruce would accompany the king to Gascony.[15] The idea that Scottish lords would serve in an English army on the continent illustrates just how divorced Edward's officials had become from reality. They hoped for too much from the peace talks at York, but would not give way on the central issues of Bruce's kingship and Scottish independence which Edward called 'the manifest disinheritance of our royal crown'.[16] It also appears that Bruce raised the price of peace, pressing for a demilitarised zone in the north of England.[17]

Edward's hands were tied. Basset, his hopes of a grand anti-French coalition including the Scots quashed, realised that Edward would need all his men in England, so he would not receive reinforcements.[18] When Pope John suggested that Queen Isabella, Charles's sister, be sent as an English negotiator, the king had little choice but to accept. Rather than cross the channel himself to perform homage he awarded the seisin of the duchy to Prince Edward who could then go to France with his mother.

All the elements that would result in Edward's downfall had now fallen into place. Since his victory in the civil war, his reign, under the destructive influence of the Despensers, became increasingly tyrannical. Isabella, fearing the Despensers, refused to return to England with the prince. Instead she sought out and became the mistress of Roger Mortimer, the marcher rebel who had made a daring escape from the Tower of London and certain execution in 1322. Isabella and Mortimer drew together other survivors who had fled after the civil war in 1322.

The papal nuncio in London reported to the pope that it was believed that if there was a French war 'Bruce will come to Charles IV's aid by every means in his power'. But Bruce did intervene in the war of Saint Sardos in 1324 even though there must have been pressure on him from the war party in Scotland.[19]

Even so, Scotland could not simply view the events across the border and in France as a mere bystander. England was now reconciled with Flanders and at war with France. The opportunity was just too good to miss. English actions since the signing of Bishopthorpe at the curia, and in provocatively recalling Edward Balliol from France, may only have nudged Scotland into what was a natural alliance.

After his rejection at Avignon, Randolph arrived at the French court in October 1325. In April 1326 he secured the treaty of Corbeil. Thus began 'the auld alliance' between Scotland and France. Formally renewed in 1371, 1391, 1428, 1448, 1484 and 1492, it became the cornerstone of Scottish foreign policy until the reformation. In theory the treaty meant that Scotland would no longer be isolated. It promised, once the Bishopthorpe truce expired, that Scotland would enter any conflict between England and France. There was no reciprocal arrangement, French responsibilities remained ambiguous, a promise of help and advice should the Anglo-Scottish conflict flare up again. Support was always implicit, which left England encircled, threatened and dangerous, but was rarely forthcoming: France was to prove a fickle ally.

The French alliance brought Scotland into European politics. It sometimes brought money, weapons and troops, but the balance sheet was appallingly one-sided. French support for Scotland remained at the whim of a wider diplomatic world. When weak, France would abandon her ally, as in 1297 and 1303. When strong, France no longer needed the Scots. The treaty would work to Scottish advantage, providing a stalemate existed across the channel.[20]

The treaty made any permanent peace treaty between England and Scotland void in the event of an outbreak of war between England and France. It locked Scotland into the continental power-struggle and would lead to disastrous defeats such as the battles of Neville's Cross (1346) and Flodden Field (1513). Tension between France and England over English behaviour in Scotland contributed to the breakdown in relations between the two countries prior to the Hundred Years War. But in reality, an Anglo-French conflict had been coming for years. The real benefit to the Scots came with the diversion of English military resources from the north of England to the continent: a by-product of the Hundred Years War.

In the Spring of 1326, with the treaty signed and a threat of invasion from France, tension rose on the Anglo-Scottish border. After a series of small-scale raids on northern English strongholds Edward warned his wardens on the march, Anthony de Lucy and Henry Percy to be more careful granting safe-conducts to Scotsmen crossing the border. He sent munitions to Carlisle and told Louis Beaumont and others to fortify and victual the northern castles. The English were persuaded that Bruce had not sanctioned the raids. War with France reopened in June 1326 and this seems to have led to a renewal of efforts to make a permanent peace in the north. Negotiations continued for the rest of the year but were ultimately fruitless.[21]

The real threat to Edward's regime—although he does not appear to have realised it—came from his own queen. Isabella moved to Hainault, where she promised the count that his daughter Philippa could marry Prince Edward in return for help deposing Edward II. The queen landed in Suffolk in September with 1500 men, including 700 men-at-arms led by John of Hainault.[22] Thomas Brotherton, the king's half-brother and Henry earl of Leicester (brother of Thomas of Lancaster) soon joined her.

The Despensers had alienated too many powerful men. Support for the king crumbled. The Londoners rose in rebellion, forcing the king to leave the capital. Abandoned by the men he trusted to defend the kingdom, he was chased west by the queen's forces. The elder Despenser and Mar tried to hold Bristol but the burgesses' sympathies lay with the queen. Despenser surrendered and was executed, Mar escaped and returned to Scotland. The king and the younger Despenser were taken in Neath Abbey. A 'parliament' in January 1327 demanded Edward's deposition. On 20 January he resigned in favour of his son.

The fourteen-year-old Edward III was crowned on 1 February 1327. In the late hours, as the celebrations ebbed in London, a small raiding party crept over the border and rested scaling ladders against Norham castle's walls. Sixteen men climbed onto the battlements before being repelled by the garrison; nine or ten died, a further five Scots were taken captive.

The timing was deliberate and provocative, a personal insult to the new king. Barbour says that Bruce broke the truce after the failure of efforts to obtain redress for attacks on Scottish and Flemish shipping.[23] In September 1326 an English commission investigated the capture of a Flemish vessel, the *Pelarym*, seized at Whitby. The master, a man called Fosse, nine Scottish merchants, sixteen pilgrims and thirteen women were slaughtered; the cargo worth £2,000 was seized and the ship set adrift.[24] The piracy was certainly not officially sanctioned: the English studiously kept the terms of the truce as the situation on the continent threatened to destabilise the English regime. A case could (and has) been made that the English violated the terms of the truce, but these were actions in the past, they do no explain why Bruce should break the treaty now.

Bruce had decided that the truce no longer served his purpose. This may not have been honourable, but it was pragmatic—and essential in the light of the illness that had befallen the king and would eventually kill him. Bruce no longer had thirteen years to work for a peace. One report, from a hostile source in early 1327, describes him as 'so feeble and drawn that he will not last much longer without the help of God, because he can hardly move anything except his tongue'.[25] The birth of an heir, David, in 1324 meant that the realm would almost certainly be left to a minor. He was desperate to conclude a final peace before his death.

The prospect of peace had faded when Isabella had been joined by Henry Beaumont, Thomas Wake and Henry Percy; all disinherited northern lords. This nucleus of an English war party dominated the Westminster parliament that deposed Edward.[26] The Articles of Deposition accused the king of losing Scotland by bad government: by implication the 'good government' of the new regime in England presented a threat. The situation in England presented two courses of action that might achieve Bruce's aims. He could act to reinstate Edward II, hoping that a grateful king might then conclude peace terms. This was the policy of Edward's close friend, and Bruce's nephew, Donald, Earl of Mar. Bruce had reinstated his earldom when he returned to Scotland, and Mar began to plot the king's release. But in October 1327 his agents in England were captured, and pardoned on condition that they were prepared to fight against the Scots.[27] Two years later the earl was also implicated in the plot that brought about Kent's downfall and execution.

Alternatively, Bruce could negotiate with Isabella and Mortimer, two people who had already shown their willingness to countenance the disinheritance of an English king. Their regime was unstable. Edward II's defeats in Scotland and France, and the humiliating treaty of Corbeil, (which Isabella herself had a hand in drafting) had left the crown in England with little credibility. Mortimer and Isabella had to move quickly if their new regime was to become established.[28] In the early days of Edward III's kingship they were in no position to take any hostile action in the north of England. By March 1328 they had already expended the vast reserves of cash, £60,000 in the king's treasuries together with the estates seized from Arundel and the rapacious Despensers. The regime was nearly bankrupt.[29] Bruce hoped that the assault on Norham would remind them of his military presence.

It was unclear which of these two options held the best hope of success, but they were not mutually exclusive. By pursuing the reinstatement of Edward II, Bruce could so destabilise the new regime that it would be forced to sign a peace treaty.

Mortimer and Isabella tried to avoid a conflict. Henry Percy became warden of the north where, with others, he was ordered to strictly observe the terms of the truce.[30] The abbot of Rievaulx and Ivo of Aldburgh received powers to arrange a meeting where a final peace could be discussed. They concluded arrangements by 20 February. On the Sunday after the feast of Ascension nobles from the English council would go to Bamburgh, nobles from Bruce's council to Berwick. From here they would dispatch delegates to meet at Tweedmouth. In an act of good faith the English unilaterally confirmed the Bishopthorpe truce.[31]

As insurance against the failure of the talks, Bruce began to assemble his forces on the border. The English could only follow his lead. As a precaution, military writs were sent to six earls and 80 barons for a muster at Newcastle on 18 May. If the English military build-up was intended to call Bruce's bluff, it failed. A military solution began to gain its own momentum.

By 20 April the commissioners of array were told to prepare for an expected Scottish invasion and arrangements were made to evacuate the north of England.[32] This was by no means the end of the attempt to reach a final peace. As late as 23 May the English admirals were warned not to take any action that would prejudice the efforts of the envoys, and William de Herle, a noted diplomatist, was kept at Bamburgh for three months.[33] On 10 June the English made a last effort to secure a peace or truce. Twelve English negotiators were enrolled and preparations made to receive Scottish envoys at York.

The English do not seem to have recognised the magnitude of the threat that faced them. The sincerity with which they entered the talks was not matched by a willingness to make concessions. The Scottish envoys left the talks in the middle of the night, pinning an insulting verse on the door of St Peter's church in the Stangate: 'Long beard hertless, painted hoods witless, gaie coatis graceless, maks Englond thriftless.' The Scots refused to meet any more English envoys. Accusations of bad faith, double dealing and treachery could be heard on both sides.[34]

The wardrobe accounts, normally a reliable source for the armies Edward III formed for later campaigns, do not exist for 1327. We can safely say that the English army was far larger than the Scottish, but was shackled by large numbers of foot arrayed against a mounted enemy. After the civil wars the English regime may have feared enlisting professional men-at-arms, whose loyalty was suspect. They turned again to John of Hainault, who had returned to Flanders in March for a tournament on the Scheldt. His mercenaries, 700 men-at-arms, formed the backbone of the army.[35] They included in their number Jean le Bel of Liege who wrote a graphic eye-witness account of the difficult campaign. As a combatant he filled his memoirs with the everyday drudgery faced by the soldiers. His account must be closer to the realities of medieval campaigning than the sanitised story of the poet at Caerlaverock in 1300.

Isabella gave a banquet at York attended by many of these foreign knights. Outside, their retainers, billeted amongst the English foot, began to quarrel with Lincolnshire archers over a game of dice that ended in a riot, only quashed when the Hainault knights armed themselves and turned on the archers. Le Bel estimates 316 Englishmen died, the *Brut* a more sober 80, 'buriede vnder a stone in Seynt Clementis Cherche haw in Fossegate'. The official enquiry blamed the English for the riot ('it was founden by enquest of the citee, that the Englisshe-men biganne the debate.'[36]) The episode did little for international relations, embarrassed the hosts, and was a dire beginning to a campaign that left brooding discontent in the English ranks towards the mercenary forces.

The muster date at Newcastle, 18 May, was over-optimistic. On 24 May the supply fleet from the Cinque Ports was still in harbour. The king himself only reached York on the 23rd, where he stayed for a leisurely five weeks, as the army began to assemble.[37] Mortimer would have been a popular commander, his name drew volunteers to the army based on his reputation after the success of his campaign against Edward Bruce in Ireland. But, suspecting his authority could not sustain a defeat, he decided to stay aloof from the campaign. The army's command fell, divisively, to the earls of Kent and Lancaster and John of Hainault.

Bruce slipped across to Ulster in April. On 12 July the people of Ulster paid for a truce for one year, which included the delivery of wheat and barley to Larne.[38] It is unknown why Robert should leave Scotland at such a dangerous time; the inference must be that the prize was worth travelling for. His father-in-law, the earl of Ulster, died late in 1326. Robert may have seen this as an opportunity to assert his authority in the earldom at the expense of the heir, a minor. By doing so he would deny resources to the English. After the events of his brother's invasion it seems unlikely that he was trying to form a coalition for an invasion of Wales in a new pan-Celtic alliance. Since the administration in Ireland remained loyal to Edward II, Robert may have been trying to forge an alliance to secure the English king's reinstatement now that it was clear he would not gain a permanent peace with Mortimer and Isabella without open warfare.

* * *

Bruce trusted the northern campaign to his lieutenants, Thomas Randolph, James Douglas and, in recognition of his new place in the Scottish hierarchy, Donald, earl of Mar. They would each command their own divisions. Barbour stressed the role of Douglas but Randolph held command.[39] He mentions two other Scottish leaders, Archibald Douglas and James Stewart of Durisdeer, brother of the recently deceased Steward.

On 6 June, Kent and Lancaster took up appointments as joint captains of the English army in the Scottish March, move meant to reinforce the marcher captain, Henry Percy. The two earls moved to Newcastle where they enlisted 40 Tynedale hobelars as scouts to warn of raids.[40]

On 15 June, less than a week after the failure of the talks at York, Scottish raiders advanced across the west march. The English command heard of the raid on the 17th. As he was going to bed on 4 July, Kent's scouts brought news of another raid on Appleby in Westmoreland. He issued instructions that evacuated houses should be set on fire to warn of the Scots' advance. His forces kept watch all night, but the raiders must have slipped back across the border. On 12 July, Anthony Lucy reported an expected invasion in two days.[41] The slow-moving foot soldiers in the English army now began to move north from York. The king and magnates waited for stragglers and then moved out, reaching Durham on 15 July.

The full-scale Scottish invasion of England began in mid-July. It is possible that Mar entered the east march to harry Anthony Lucy at Carlisle, and Randolph crossed into the east march through the Kielder gap. Their movements are then lost.[42] The bulk of the English army had now reached Durham, while Lancaster remained in Newcastle. Le Bel says that the Scots moved so quietly they passed by Newcastle unnoticed. They aimed to outflank and divert the threatened invasion of Scotland but did not want to engage the king. Their presence became known at Durham by the columns of smoke from villages burning in the distance. The host set out in pursuit in three infantry divisions, flanked by men-at-arms on horseback. Slowed by the foot soldiers the army had no hope of catching the raiders and spent the first few days passing through areas already devastated.

On 17 July they arrived at Tudhoe, south of Durham. The Scots, already at Barnard Castle, were running rings around them: 'Fra place to place so sped they past, the Englishmen could not follow fast.'

On 19 July the English reached Bishop Auckland where scouts mistakenly believed the Scots were breaking camp, ready to move north. It was decided to abandon the chase, risk giving the raiders a free run to the undefended York, and attempt to intercept them as they returned home, slowed by booty.[43] At some point the raiders would need to recross the Tyne. The bridges at Corbridge and Newcastle were easily defended. This would mean the raiders crossing one of the fords between Corbridge and the South Tyne.

The English abandoned their baggage train and infantry: heavy wagons were unfit for the moorland crossing, the foot too slow and exhausted by the chase. Few slept in the hours before midnight when the army's trumpeters blew the signal to move out in battle formation. The forced march lasted through the night and all the following day across 'a region called Northumberland, which is a wild poor country full of barren wastes and great hills, and extremely poor, save for the livestock'. That evening the army reached Haydon Bridge, the last contingents arrived after nightfall. They were tired and hungry. Then it rained. It rained for four days, swelling the waters of the ford until it became impassable. They were caught behind their own trap.

Without the baggage train the soldiers only had with them what they could carry, loaves of bread strapped to their saddles that had became soaked from the horse's sweat. Some of the lords had wine but most were forced to drink water from the river. Hunger was only relieved when merchants arrived from Newcastle, charging exorbitant prices for poor bread and thin wine. There were not enough axes to cut wood for fires or shelter so many slept on the open ground, their armour rusting, as they held the bridles of their horses. They could only wait. Days passed but no Scots appeared and nobody had a clue where they were. In desperation Edward announced a prize of a knighthood and estates worth £100 a year to whoever could find them.[44] Fifteen esquires sheepishly crossed the ford to set out in search of the Scots while the army headed up stream for a safer crossing. They reached Haltwhistle on 28 July.

It was one of the esquires, Thomas Rokeby, who ran across the Scots, literally. He had the bright idea of looking where they had last been seen, but not the sense to keep a low profile and was captured. As the English became drenched on the banks of the Tyne the Scots, only nine miles distant, were equally at a loss to where the English had gone. They had lain undetected in the valley of River Gaunless for ten days. Archibald Douglas overran the countryside for supplies. At one point his men fell on a detachment of infantry making their way from Darlington to the main body of the English army.[45] Both sides cheered Rokeby's success—he was released so he could report his find to Edward. With this news the English army marched south, camping at Blanchland, and finally reached the Scottish position on the next day, 30 July.

As the English approached, the Scots grouped into battle formation. There was little point: the river Wear, in full spate from the week's rainfall, divided the two armies. The Scots were lodged in defensive positions about half a mile from the river bank, out of bowshot of the English archers. The English cavalry dismounted, the men-at-arms took off their spurs and formed three divisions. The divisions marched forward at a slow pace towards the enemy hoping that it would draw them on, until they reached an embarrassing halt at the banks of the river. The bemused Scots did not budge an inch.

A company of archers, supported by men-at-arms, crossed the Wear with the intention of drawing the Scots from the outcrop they defended. Douglas lured them forward with a feigned retreat, into an ambush, but an English squire recognised Douglas, and brought the archers back before the ambush could be sprung. William Erskine went too far forward in the chase, into the main body of the English and was captured,then released a few days later in an exchange of prisoners. When the archers failed, the English sent heralds to offer battle on even terms (though not even numbers) on level ground. They replied that 'the king and his council could see that they were in his kingdom and had burned and ravaged it; if he dislikes that let him come and amend it, for they would stay there as long as it pleased them.'[46]

The hours grew into days in the hope that the Scots would be starved from their position, interrupted by daily skirmishing and night-time revelry. Horns and cries made such a noise it seemed 'like the biggest devils in Hell were there to destroy us'. 'We were not too comfortable,' says le Bel, 'for we didn't know where to camp, nor with what to cover, nor where to go to forage apart from the heath. And you can guess that we greatly missed our tents, our carts and our tools which we had bought to make things easier, but which we had left in a wood without a guard, where we could not get them back because we had forgotten where it was.'

After three or four days the Scots built up their fires and broke camp, moving two leagues to Stanhope Park under the cover of darkness—to an even better defensive position. The medieval park, a hunting lodge belonging to the bishops of Durham, lies on the north bank of the Tees. On the first night at this new camp Douglas led a hit-and-run raid into the heart of the English camp. He crossed the Wear upstream and attacked the unguarded English rear. A hand-to-hand combat ensued as the war cry 'Douglas, Douglas' rang through the camp. Douglas nearly reached the king's tent and was able to cut two or three guy ropes before being pushed back by an improvised defence in which the king's chaplain was killed.

The wait continued, now with 200 men-at-arms guarding the camp's three unprotected sides. The Hainaulters had to contribute both to the pickets and to the protection of their own ranks from the English archers, for fear that they would take out their frustrations on the nearest foreigners. On 6 August a young Scottish knight was taken and could only tell his captors that his lords had agreed that in the morning every man should be armed and ready to follow Douglas's banner. The English believed that an attack on the camp was imminent. That night the army split into three divisions, with each division charged with defending one side of the camp. They lit large fires so that they could see each other. No attack came. Next morning two Scottish trumpeters were bought to the English camp. They were the only Scots left. In the night the Scots had again built up their campfires and left the trumpeters to make a noise from the camp. They outflanked the English and were now heading home, crossing a treacherous bog on foot, the ground covered with hurdles made during the stand-off in the Park.[47]

Concerned that his raiding party had been gone so long, Bruce sent a hastily gathered relief force under Patrick Dunbar and John Stewart.[48] They nearly threw caution to the wind and turned around to face the English again but lack of supplies counselled a return north.[49] Le Bel and some colleagues crossed the river and climbed along the awkward and steep slope of the mountain, and went into the Scots camp.

'We found more 500 good, fat beasts, already dead, which the Scots had killed because they could not take

them with them, and did not want to leave them alive for
the English. We found more than 400 undressed-leather
pots, hanging over the fire and full of meat to be roasted...
We found five poor prisoners whom the Scots had left in
this wood, all naked, tied to trees in spite, two of them
with broken ribs.'

When he returned to the camp the army was preparing to march home.
When told, Edward burst into tears. The failure of his first campaign left
a deep impression on the king.

Barbour notes two military developments in this campaign. Firstly,
the crests worn on the English helmets, a new livery meant as a
'landmark' for magnates. The second he called the 'Crakys of war': the
first use of artillery in England. It may have been a side show in
Weardale, more notable for its bark than its bite.

The king reached Durham first, followed by the army, who for the
first time since leaving the town had proper shelter. The baggage train
had also found its way back to the town. The campaign had been a
fiasco, a disaster in which the English had been outwitted and
outfought. The plodding, rain-sodden soldiers trekked across the
inhospitable Northumbrian moorland in vain. Randolph had shown
that the Scots could do as they pleased in the north of England,
regardless of the presence of an English army that was twice its size.
Accusations of treachery naturally began to be bandied about to
preserve the young king's reputation.[50] Fresh writs, cheekily claiming
the Scots had fled rather than face the English in battle, were issued from
Stanhope, summoning a parliament at Lincoln to consider how to
combat the Scots.[51]

The Hainault mercenaries charged the enormous sum of £41,304 for
the campaign. Much of this sum was due to 'gross profiteering':
£21,482 paid in compensation for horses left behind in England. When
they came to be resold they fetched just £920.[52] The Hainaulters had not
yet been paid for their service to Isabella the previous year, and the
exchequer had no money left to pay them. This led to the undignified
pawning of the crown jewels to raise money to make the first instalment
as the Hainaulters passed through London on their journey home.[53]
They rode fully armed to Dover to embark for the continent.

Henry Percy was left to defend the border as best he could. Any new
initiative would have to wait for the Lincoln parliament. It was here that
a secure but temporary base for royal finances was found by raising a
tenth from the clergy. William Melton, the Archbishop of York, wrote
to the Bishop of Durham that the subsidy was granted to prevent
outrages by the Scots[54], but the Lincoln parliament did not devise a new
means to achieve this policy. The regime waited on events in the north.

Bruce's return to Scotland from Ireland reinvigorated his lieutenant's campaign. The king 'assemblyt all his mycht, and left nane that wes worth to fycht'.[55] Three divisions invaded Northumberland. One division invested Norham, a second under Randolph and Douglas invested Alnwick, as Bruce led the third on a raid across Northumberland. With little hope of succour from the southern government the northern counties, Durham, Carlisle, Westmoreland, Cleveland and Richmond bought truces with Bruce that protected them until the following May.[56] Northumberland was excluded.

Bruce was now so confident of his military superiority that he could keep an army in the field, immune to the threat from the English regime. It appeared that he was trying to absorb Northumberland into Scotland by seizing the great border castles that would safeguard an occupation. He began to give lands in Northumberland to his men; the grant of one, of Belford to Nicholas Scrymgeour the hereditary standard bearer, survives.[57] Bruce had awarded northern English lands to his supporters before, in Tynedale after Bannockburn, but not outside the lands owned by the kings of Scotland until 1296. Never had the prospect that they might be able to enjoy them been so real.

The military engineer John Crabbe supervised the siege engines at Norham before Robert himself arrived at the castle. Facing him was the governor Robert Manners. A Scottish banneret, William Mowat was killed for 'want of skill'. Manners made a sortie that defeated the Scottish watch who could not be rescued as the river was in flood.[58] Randolph and Douglas remained at Alnwick for two weeks. As the stronghold of the march captain, Henry Percy, Alnwick had a large garrison. The siege here may have served to keep Percy occupied while the raiding parties pillaged the county. After two weeks of skirmishing with the castle garrison they moved on to Warkworth, then joined Bruce at Norham. Percy immediately led a counter raid into Teviotdale. Douglas cut off his retreat to Alnwick, forcing him to make a night march to the safety of Newcastle.

The southern government had long been immune to the suffering of the north of England. But with Bruce apparently set on dismembering the realm, he had to be faced. Isabella and Mortimer could renew the war or treat for peace: a temporary truce was no longer an option. In September the regime attempted to gather a new arm. Archbishop Melton sent a letter to local lords as late as 14 October calling them to muster with him at York.[59] Even before then it was clear that there was no appetite for another campaign. Mortimer's fortunes were waning, the experience of the Weardale campaign had shown him the folly of resisting a Scottish invasion even if he could muster the full might of the realm. His 'best chance of maintaining his power was to make peace at any price'.[60]

At the beginning of October William Denum, an experienced common lawyer, was sent to Bruce at Norham. This was the first step towards offering a final peace settlement. On 9 October he and Henry Percy received powers to negotiate a final peace. Nine days later Bruce dictated six terms that he insisted would form the basis of any settlement: chiefly Scotland would be 'free, quit, and entire, without any kind of feudal subjection, for himself and his heirs forever'. The peace would be guaranteed by a marriage alliance between his son and Joan of the Tower, Edward's sister; it would include a ban on cross-border holdings; a military alliance of mutual support saving the treaty of Corbeil; and a Scottish payment to the English of £20,000. For their part the English would have to promise support at the curia for the removal of papal censures.[61]

On 30 October 1327 the English regime replied. Not surprisingly they were willing to accept the ex gratia payment, but wanted the question of the restoration of forfeited lands and the mutual aid treaty to be discussed further. The marriage was especially important for the English, as it would prevent a match being found for David from a French royal household. If these points could be agreed, then recognition of the key point, the legitimacy of Scottish independence, would be granted. This was enough to move the talks forward. A truce was arranged to last until 13 March 1328.

There are no records of the negotiations that took place between November and December at Newcastle where the fine detail of the treaty was discussed. On 22 January, 100 Scottish envoys entered York to attend Edward's parliament. It was here, on 1 March, that Edward declared

> 'we, and certain of our predecessors as kings of England, have tried to assert rights of rule, dominion, or superiority over the realm of Scotland, and in consequence a grievous burden of wars has long afflicted the realms of England and Scotland; therefore, considering the killings, slaughters, crimes, destruction of churches and ills innumerable which so often befell the inhabitants of each realm, by reason of these wars, and the advantages which would accrue to each kingdom, to their mutual gain, if they were joined by the stability of perpetual peace ... we wish, and grant by the present letter, on behalf of ourselves, our heirs, and all our successors, with common counsel, assent and consent, of the prelates, magnates, earls, barons, and communities of our realm assembled in our parliament, that the realm of Scotland, defined by its true marches as they existed and

were maintained in the time of Alexander, of worthy memory, the late king of Scotland, shall remain for ever ... divided in all things from the realm of England, entire, free, and quit, and without any subjection, servitude, claim, or demand. Any right in the realm of Scotland which we our ancestors have sought in past times, in any manner, we renounce and surrender, by the present letter, to the King of Scotland and his heirs and successors.'[62]

This quit-claim was not the final peace, the letter would not be handed over until the treaty was made; although as an unambiguous admission by an English king in his own parliament of Scottish independence, it was essential to it.

A powerful English delegation was now appointed with full powers to sue for peace. They arrived in Edinburgh on 10 March. Agreement was reached concerning outstanding matters—the dowry the Scottish king would grant Joan (lands worth £2,000 a year), the return of documents 'touching the freedom of Scotland' and marcher laws—after only seven days. Bruce was confined to bed with what seems to be a periodic bout of illness. It was in his bedchamber in the palace of Holyrood that the final meeting took place.[63] The agreement finally brought the wars to a close. Peace was proclaimed in England on 17 April. On 4 May the treaty was ratified in an English parliament at Northampton.

* * *

Much of the Edinburgh-Northampton treaty was determined by Bruce in 1327. But no common ground could be found over the question of the so-called disinherited. The final treaty made no mention of them, merely recording the rights of the church: ecclesiastical lands were restored in the summer of 1329.[64] Bruce's antipathy towards the Anglo-Scots, and his insistence in October that cross-border holdings should not be allowed, was confronted by English negotiators with a vested interest in restoring disinherited lands. It explains why the negotiations were not complete until March. By then Bruce had softened his attitude, agreeing to set aside the question for fear of bringing the whole process to a halt. The treaty's great weakness was its failure to deal with the question of the inheritances of some very powerful figures. In the end they would settle the dispute themselves—by going to war.

When Isabella went to the marriage of David Bruce and Joan in June 1328 she carried letters sanctioning the reopening of the inheritances issue. She had some success. Henry Percy received a charter from Robert Bruce confirming his lands in Scotland. There is evidence that a similar process began for Thomas Wake for Liddesdale and Henry Beaumont for Buchan and William Zouche for lands in Galloway, but in the end they were rebuffed. On the other side of the border James Douglas was restored to his father's lands in England.[65]

The English promised to return all documents touching the subjection of Scotland. This part of the agreement was not honoured. The return of the stone of Scone was not mentioned in any of the surviving documents, though English chroniclers believed it was part of the agreement. The stone's return may have been unilaterally decided by the king's council to moderate Bruce's attitude to the disinherited. A royal writ addressed to the abbot of Westminster requested the release of the coronation stone to Isabella prior to David and Joan's wedding. The abbot, backed by an angry London mob, refused, saying it no longer belonged to the crown. The stone stayed put.[66] Similar confusion surrounds the other relic that Edward stole in 1296, the Black Rood. It may or may not have been returned now. Tradition had it being recaptured at the battle of Neville's Cross in October 1346, but a treasury memorandum records it being taken from the Tower of London in January 1346 to be kept by the king's side on the Crécy campaign. An earlier list of relics, among them St Margaret's bones, lists 'a silver gilt cross, with a part in the middle of black wood'. It arrived at Durham Cathedral after 1346 only to be lost much later, during the reformation.[67]

* * *

Bruce held a parliament in February 1328 where he was granted a tenth for three years to meet the payment of the £20,000 promised in the treaty, spread over three instalments. The price had fallen since Harcla's aborted treaty, when Bruce offered 40,000 marks. There has been much debate over this payment for an agreement that had already been won in the field. The Scottish records merely record it with the vague comment that it was *contribucio pro pac,* a contribution for peace. Otherwise the official records are largely silent. There are three possible explanations for this remarkably generous payment, the first is that it was intended as compensation for the blackmail that had been extorted from the northern shires; the second that Bruce saw the weakness of the regime with which he reached an agreement and needed to shore it up; the third, and most plausible, that it was an implicit recognition of the loss of English sovereignty. It was an age when it was considered reasonable that any material loss of rights should not be surrendered without compensation.[68] If it was meant to placate English misgivings it failed, since Isabella appropriated the sum for herself. It fuelled the belief amongst the chroniclers that the peace had been bought to benefit Isabella at the cost of national dignity.

David Bruce and Joan went through a betrothal ceremony at Berwick on 16 July 1328. The Scots spent £1,500 on food and luxuries for the celebrations—so many guests attended that a wall in the churchyard collapsed. What should have brought the two kings face-to-face, and their kingdoms closer was soured by Edward's refusal to attend. Bruce saved face by staying away. To add to the undoubtedly intended insult Edward refused to give his sister a dowry.

Edward III was not in a position to prevent the peace. Isabella and Mortimer had earmarked the Scottish contribution for their own use, and had already exhausted the treasury's reserves during the Weardale campaign. Historians see the treaty as one 'concluded by two kings of two independent nations'.[69] This is true in part: Bruce's *de facto* kingship now received legal recognition, and both nations had independent status. But the treaty was not negotiated between two kings. It was a treaty between Bruce and the representatives of King Edward, a puppet in the hands of Isabella and Mortimer. The illegitimacy of the queen mother's rule would give Edward an excuse to back out of the peace.

The English chroniclers are united in their disapproval. The treaty became known as *turpis pax* (the shameful peace) a common view shared by Edward: it 'was not in accordance with the king's will but because of his minority the queen and Mortimer arranged the whole thing'; it was 'in the name of the king but not by his inclination' and the king was through 'false conseile ... falsely disherited'.[70] He certainly seems to have been excluded from the negotiations for the peace.

A smaller country had defeated a much larger neighbour. In 1300 England's population reached four million; Scotland's population was about a quarter of this. England's size and wealth certainly brought many advantages, but not in a ratio of four to one. For many Englishmen the war in Scotland was remote; a Cornish peasant (for example) had little motivation to become involved in the war and his services were never called upon, even though his taxes were. This was in stark contrast to his equivalent in Scotland, subject to devastating raids aimed at crippling the rural economy. This was primarily a contest between the English barony combined with the population of the north of England, counties north of the Trent, and Scotland.

This was compounded by fighting on two fronts when the resources of southern England were commandeered for the war in France (population, fifteen million). England's war on the continent made it easy for Scotland to find allies abroad: France between 1296 and 1303, and then Flanders between 1307 and 1320. The French never sent much aid, but the Flemish supply of weapons and armour bolstered the Scottish war effort. The capture of Aberdeen in 1307, far enough north to be safe from anything but the longest forays, reopened the sea lanes to Flanders, Germany and Scandinavia.

English strength lay in campaigning, forming great armies that could dominate large territories, but they were short term. English military institutions and traditions were designed for short campaigns, ideal for defence or fighting a campaign with limited objectives. Over a longer period they were chronically disabling. The mechanisms for raising money and forming armies were unsuited to a war that was best waged by small mobile forces, kept in the field for prolonged periods. Without an enemy army to engage, campaigns could only win towns and castles. Scottish armies were smaller, they had neither the heavy cavalry nor archers to match that most potent English combination, the peasant archer and mounted noble.

The impact of England's wealth and resources was further reduced by fighting over long distances in hostile territory. The Highlands were inaccessible to English armies, giving Scottish leaders a safe haven to retreat to when the English approached. Long lines of communication over poor roads made supplying castles and armies haphazard and vulnerable. The Highlands, Galloway and the central forests were ideal for guerrilla warfare.

* * *

Edward I had played on Scottish disunity. He had been able to appeal to nobles who held lands in Scotland, but whose wealth came from England. He might have overcome these difficulties but they were beyond Edward II. The trouble in his court coincided with repeated famines that had left the country unable to afford the tax bill his strategy demanded. The energy of the state was put into the gruelling, unpopular and expensive mechanisms of forming campaigning armies—in 1308, 1309, 1316, 1317 and 1318—only for the campaigns to be cancelled. Discontent was compounded by the cost of keeping large numbers of men in arms in the north, feeding them and paying their wages. After Bannockburn, it became increasingly difficult to rally the realm behind the war effort. Edward II had no successes in Scotland with which he could offset these great costs.

Just at the point when the English were forced to sign a peace, the elements that had contributed to their defeat began to turn in their favour. New men replaced the discredited figures who had reigned in the country since the death of Edward I. Edward II was murdered in September 1327. It was a pitiful end to a pitiful reign. He lacked all the characteristics of successful medieval kingship: common sense, dignity, energy, authority, intent. Scotland was fortunate to face England at a time when the king and his over-mighty cousin, Thomas Lancaster became bitter enemies. Their feud, which paralysed the court, combined with renewed famine that denied resources to garrisons and made supplying armies impossible.

The Scottish military ascendancy reached its zenith at Weardale. The English army that trudged across the northern moors was slow, difficult to supply and failed to engage the enemy. But the English commanders were aware of the limitations of the English foot soldier, who was no match for lightly armed Scottish cavalry. They tried to recruit several thousand hobelars for the campaign. A general proclamation for aid had called for soldiers to bring 'swift, strong, and hardy rounseys to ride and to pursue' the Scots but did not achieve the numbers wanted.[71] The Weardale summons assembled the last English feudal army: later calls for feudal armies were for political effect not military effort. Even then, feudal service only supplied part of the army. Thereafter, the feudal levy, restricted to 40 days' service and the use of large numbers of foot, was abandoned. This was combined with new measures to finance and levy armies.[72]

At the battle of Boroughbridge, Andrew Harcla, a man who learnt his craft in the Scottish wars, had demonstrated the defensive power of dismounted men-at-arms combined with archers.[73] Boroughbridge as the motor of changing military strategy is an appealing theory, but its case may be overstated. Dismounting to defend a bridge and ford was almost inevitable. There had been no actual battle at Weardale, but the array of the English army shows the development of this new technique, with archers in three units, protected by men-at-arms on the flanks. Later these positions would be reversed as the archers took up a position on the flanks. The hobelar would be attended by the horse-archer, making the English forces highly mobile and giving them the means to catch their enemy and compel them to engage.[74]

There would be no more vain cavalry charges at the serried ranks of Scottish spearmen; instead the knights and men-at-arms dismounted to await attack. They were closely integrated with the longbowmen whose withering fire ravaged the schiltrons, destroying their cohesion and impetus before they could get to grips with the English. Hereafter, this devastating combination of armoured knight and massed firepower would send a shiver down the spine of European armies and would usually achieve victory for the English on the battlefield. The system triumphed at the battles of Dupplin (1332), Halidon Hill (1333), Neville's Cross and Crécy (1346) and Poitiers (1356), even when vastly outnumbered.

Just how much the Scottish victory depended on Robert Bruce would soon be tested. Pope John XXII released Bruce from the sentence of excommunication in October 1328. Alexander of Kinninmouth, later to become bishop of Aberdeen, appealed to the pope to sanction the anointment and coronation of Scottish kings. The pope gave his authority in a bull of 13 June 1329. This final confirmation of the independence of the Scottish crown and its equality with the other princes of Europe came too late for Bruce. The illness that tormented his last years took the king, aged 54, six days later at Cardross, in the manor he had built on the banks of the Leven.

His body lies in Dunfermline Abbey, resting place of Alexander III. Normally reliable and near contemporary English sources say that he died of leprosy, described by Jean le Bel in the common euphemism as '*la grosse maladie*'. His recovery after the Irish expedition in 1327 to lead the *chevauchée* into Northumberland suggests that it was a form of paralytic leprosy. This has been hotly debated. The Scottish chroniclers do not mention the disease. Barbour says his illness stemmed from *enfundeying* (numbing) of his body from lying in cold ground 20 years earlier. This attitude derives in part from the disease's social stigma: the belief that it was divine punishment for sexual depravity. Modern medical experts have not been able to resolve contemporary evidence.[75]

Robert Bruce died as one of the great medieval kings. Unlike many of his European contemporaries, posterity has not tempered this judgement. His character is not beyond reproach. To criticise him for repeatedly turning his back on Scotland before 1306 is to judge him with later values. His contemporaries, and not just his enemies, voiced trenchant criticism over the murder of Comyn in the Greyfriar's church, the execution of Scottish burghers at Dumfries, and the fate of the opposition at the Black parliament. This is not the time to dwell on such points, merely to recognise that the man is far more complex than his legend. He achieved what was thought impossible in 1306. The story of the spider in a cave is fiction, and yet it so sums up Bruce's determination. His methods of warfare, making his forces difficult to engage in a swift-moving, mounted, guerrilla campaign were not new, but the destruction of castles and the devastation of the northern English countryside to wear down the English were revolutionary: the twin keys to his eventual military victory. This latter policy would be adopted by the English in France to chilling effect.

Bruce's success was not confined to military strategy, and he is one of history's great generals. As a politician he changed the very nature of Scottish kingship. When he usurped the crown in 1306, his was the minority party after a struggle in which many Anglo-Scottish lords (whether from self-preservation or self-interest) had fought for the English or sat on the fence. The Declaration of Arbroath set out the new political ideology:

> 'We are bound to him for the maintaining of our freedom
> both by his right and merits, as to him by whom salvation
> has been wrought unto our people, and by him, come

what may, we mean to stand. Yet if he should give up what
he has begun, seeking to make us or our kingdom subject
to the King of England or to the English, we would strive
at once to drive him out as our enemy and a subverter of
his own right and ours, and we would make some other
man who was able to defend us our king.'

Scotland was no longer the personal fiefdom of a king. The king was
now an agent of the community. The community, or nation, transcended
baronial self-interest.[76] It is an important step in the creation of a unified
nation state.

Bruce's final wish was to crusade. He asked that his heart be removed
and carried by James Douglas to 'be born in battle against Saracens'. In
September 1329 Edward III issued Douglas with letters of protection
and commendation to Alfonso XI of Castile. He sailed in early 1330,
making Flanders before travelling to La Coruña in Spain to fight the
Moorish king of Granada. It was probably at the taking of the fortress
of Teba de Ardules in August 1330 that Douglas lost his life.[77] Fordun
says that he went too far ahead of the main force and was ambushed.[78]
The king's heart, in a silver casket around Douglas's neck, was returned
to Scotland and probably buried in Melrose Abbey. Douglas's bones
were brought back to Scotland by William Keith and interred in St
Bride's Kirk in Douglas. Thomas Randolph assumed the office of
guardian in the name of David II.

It had been 32 years since Edward I had gathered the English host at
Wark before storming Berwick. Thirty-two years of savage warfare that
had left the nations in much the same position as they had been in the
thirteenth century, except that the question of English overlordship
appeared to have been finally settled. The English were exhausted by
years of fighting for a cause that had been lost at Bannockburn, and its
continued pursuit could only bring more suffering for both countries.
Peace was both desirable and, in 1328, attainable.

The treaty of Edinburgh-Northampton should have governed Anglo-
Scottish relations for the rest of the Middle Ages. It did not. New men
were beginning to take power who knew nothing but war between
England and Scotland. In 1330 Edward III deposed Mortimer in a
palace coup at Nottingham. A warrior king in the mould of his
grandfather, he was not yet 18 years old. Edward burned to avenge the
humiliation heaped on his father and English arms at Bannockburn and
felt deeply the fiasco at Weardale. The 'perpetual peace' would only last
four years.

Chapter 10

FOR NEW MOTIVE, NEW WAR

'This English nation, which is capable of quite angelic things ...
they jab with a scorpion's sting.'
Walter Bower

Thirty years of war had created a militant body of influential nobles on both sides of the border: men who had lost lands and titles and become known as 'the disinherited'. Their loss was the result of a political decision, made by Robert Bruce. He attempted to resolve the dispute over divided loyalties by severing cross-border holdings. Bruce had not been vindictive in his confiscation of land—the name Balliol or Comyn did not bar an inheritance—forfeitures only took place when landowners had no intention of becoming Scottish subjects at the expense of their English lands.[1]

There was no attempt to silence their claims by buying them out or redistributing estates. The continuity between the second and third wars of independence should not be underestimated, but this was no longer a war concerned with high ideals, of the feudal rights of kings, of nationhood and the nature of Anglo-Scottish dependence. This war was begun by private men for personal gain.

The list of those who had lost property was a formidable cross-section of baronial society. Although dominated by men from the borders, it was a closely knit international cause focused around three titular earls: Buchan, Atholl and Angus. When Buchan died childless in 1308 his inheritance was divided between his two nieces. Margaret married the loyal younger brother of the earl of Ross and received her half of the inheritance; her sister Alice married the militant Frenchman Henry Beaumont. Edward II bestowed the title earl of Buchan on Beaumont when Alice came of age in 1312. It was a reward for years of service in the wars dating from 1302 where he won a reputation as a professional soldier. He was a member of Edward II's inner circle until his expulsion after the Bishopthorpe truce—with which he was never reconciled. Beaumont was 'an arrogant man with a weighty disposition', the most experienced of the group and the driving force behind the scheme.[2]

David Strathbogie was eighteen when he became Earl of Atholl in 1327. He was a ruthless and dangerous young man who worked consistently to further the only cause he believed in: his own. His father was a firm supporter of the English in Scotland until 1312 when he swore allegiance to Bruce, who restored his earldom. Since Bannockburn the family's fortunes were firmly coupled to English success in Scotland. Besides the earldom, Atholl inherited a half share of John Comyn of Badenoch's lands from his mother, Joan Comyn. He married Katherine, Henry Beaumont's daughter.

The earldom of Angus had been in the hands of the English Umfraville family since 1243, but the family, lords of Redesdale, never showed much interest in their Scottish title. Gilbert de Umfraville was Beaumont's great-nephew, also of Comyn descent. He lost the earldom when Robert Bruce granted it to the Berwickshire lord, John Stewart of Bunkle. His Northumbrian lands, close to the border, had also suffered more than most from the border raids.

These men could do nothing while the architects of the peace survived. Even on his death-bed Robert Bruce's personality towered over Anglo-Scottish relations. His death still left the other signatories to the peace. The formidable Earl of Lancaster, with the backing of the leading disinherited lords, attempted to topple the Mortimer regime six months after the Edinburgh-Northampton settlement. Their rebellion petered out and was leniently dealt with by the imposition of heavy fines. Four nobles were excluded from settlement and fled abroad, including Beaumont and another of the leading disinherited lords, Lancaster's son-in-law, Thomas Wake.

Mortimer's regime became increasingly tyrannical as his hold on power was threatened. Lancaster prudently kept a low profile but Edward III's uncle, Kent, was not so careful. He and his supporters, including Donald of Mar, believed that Edward II was still alive and plotted his restoration. In March 1330 he was arrested, confessed rebellion in the belief his rank would save him, but was executed. He had to wait until a drunken criminal volunteered to swing the axe, nobody else dared do it.[3] Kent's execution served notice to Edward III that Mortimer was capable of any atrocity to keep power and that as the young prince grew older he knew he would represent a threat to the regime. Edward struck first: in a daring palace coup he and a hand-picked group of close associates entered Nottingham castle with the aid of the constable. Mortimer was found, arrested and executed. Isabella was allowed to retire to a convent.

Edward III did not have the towering physical stature of either his father or grandfather, but he was, before all things, a soldier. One of

England's finest military leaders, he combined energy and purpose with an ability to inspire men with faith in his cause. It would result in stunning victories against desperate odds. His chief fault was an inability to define achievable goals; he had no concept of the 'relation between ends and means', a 'want of definite policy and clear ideals'. His over-confidence, limited sense of proportion and unlimited energy led him to believe nothing was beyond his reach.[4]

His reign became closely entwined with a new chivalric ideal, a social code enveloping the personal ideals of knighthood, of bravery and courtesy. The image should not be confused with the reality of Edwardian warfare: most of his campaigns in France and Scotland were episodes of slaughter and destruction that fell far short of any ideal. Chivalry and nationalism were there to be aggressively manipulated to his advantage.

His reign faced crisis, particularly in 1340-1, before military success offset years of heavy taxation and poor administration. But it was a reign of political stability unmatched in medieval England. He never had to face the rebellions, real or threatened, that dogged all his predecessors and would menace most of his descendants. He learnt to compromise with his critics, and kept the support of his close family members and the chief magnates through the judicious use of patronage. By consulting them and including them in his plans, he never alienated the barony. His European contemporaries viewed him as the consummate king.

Although free from Mortimer's supervision, and with Robert Bruce dead, Edward's hands were still tied with velvet twine. He would do nothing until the outstanding payment of the Scottish war restitution was paid. The last instalment fell due in 1331, and was only made with some difficulty.[5] Until then, Edward explored the possibility of silencing the disinherited lords by pursuing the claims of two leading members, Beaumont and Wake. Edward owed a debt of gratitude for their consistent opposition to Isabella and Mortimer, and he pressed the Scots to make good their promise to allow restoration of their inheritances. There was a belief in Edward's court that the Edinburgh-Northampton process had agreed their restoration and a degree of irritation when repeated attempts to gain satisfaction in Scotland were ignored.[6] This attempted settlement was concurrent with the bishop of Durham's protracted dispute with the guardian for the restoration of Upsettlington, which, when finally settled was followed by an unprecedented claim for his homage to David II.[7]

Edward did nothing to promote the cause of the many disinherited who had not been included in the 1329 settlement: Atholl, the Talbots who shared the other half of Comyn of Badenoch's inheritance, the Comyns or the Moubrays. Some received desultory royal pensions, but most were ignored.

The breakdown of Edward III's policy to restore Beaumont and Wake to their Scottish lands threw both men into the camp of those disinherited who had not received the diplomatic support of the king in 1330. They did not need to look far for a figurehead. One man had suffered a greater disinheritance than all the others: Edward Balliol, son of King John. No settlement could have met his claim. In the summer of 1331 Beaumont travelled to France on the king's business and made a second trip in the winter: it was during these foreign journeys that he made contact with Balliol.[8]

Once heir to the kingdom of Scotland and betrothed to a niece of the king of France, Edward Balliol had remained in England as a hostage when his father was released into papal custody in 1299. Embarrassingly shifted from one custodian to another, first the bishop of Coventry and Lichfield, then the Earl Warenne who petitioned the king to remove him from his care in 1309, Balliol was shuffled into the English royal household to be brought up with Edward II's half-brothers. When his father died he retired to his family's Picardy estates where he remained a largely forgotten figure.[9] However, he was never reconciled to the loss of the throne, and his ambition to restore his fortunes was fuelled by his father's heavy debts. During Edward II's reign he had merely sought restoration of his English lands, which had been made over to Warwick in 1307.

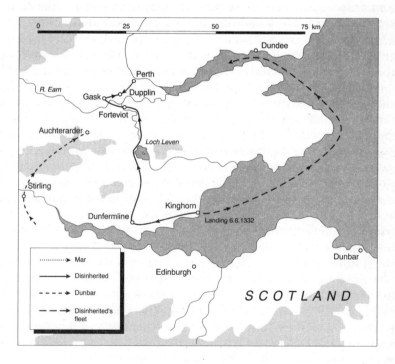

Invasion of the disinherited 1332

Historians have treated Edward Balliol with even more contempt than they reserve for his father. Had John Balliol kept his crown, Robert Bruce might have been remembered as a historical footnote: an embittered earl sulking on his ancestral lands, nursing an ancient claim to the throne. As it was, Bruce won the victory and it was Balliol's son who was so condemned. 'Young and warlike, poor and ambitious, with few lands and great pretensions' he was a dangerous foe.[10] His case was simple: his kingdom had been seized unlawfully through conquest, and he took the only honourable course available to a medieval noble in such circumstances. He took up arms.

In the autumn of 1331 Beaumont brought Balliol back to England. The disinherited lords gathered in Yorkshire and began making plans for a campaign in Scotland. Beaumont leased his lands to raise funds for the campaign—the archbishop of York advanced more money. Edward III turned a blind eye. Outwardly he did nothing to help them, but he did nothing to stop them either. The terms later used by Balliol for Edward's sanction are 'sufferance' and 'toleration'. Edward would not allow an overland invasion, but he did not prevent a fleet fitting out on the Humber, ready for a seaborne assault. Edward kept up the pretence of maintaining the Edinburgh-Northampton peace: at the end of March, he sent orders to his northern officers to arrest any persons planning to infringe the peace, but since nothing was done, secret verbal instructions to do no such thing must have accompanied the orders.[11]

Edward had nothing to lose by any invasion—providing he kept up the pretence that he knew nothing of the plans. This was still only a band of die-hard adventurers. Their failure, which seemed more than likely, could see their English estates forfeited to the crown as an outward sign of royal disapproval.[12] The main danger lay in the type of retaliatory raid favoured by Robert Bruce, but this was unlikely: against whom could the Scots retaliate? And any raid carried the danger of bringing Edward III into the conflict; not a policy to commend itself to the Scottish leadership. On the off-chance that the Scots would risk a raid, Edward calmed northern nerves by appointing his most experienced northern captain, Henry Percy, as warden with the power to summon the northern host. When the threat became manifest in October, the king sent writs to array 2000 troops from the northern counties for the defence of the March.[13]

The leaders in Scotland responded to the well-flagged threat presented by the disinherited with a dangerous lack of concern. They 'marvelled how so few men dared to attack so fearlessly the kingdom of Scotland'.[14] Their only concession was to bring forward the coronation of David II. On 23 November 1331 Thomas Randolph knighted the seven-year old David. The following day he was anointed and crowned king of Scots.

Edward gave the Scots one last chance to make amends to the disinherited in April 1332. Beaumont, who was openly leading the war movement, was dropped from the request, leaving just Wake, who did not sail with the disinherited because of problems on his estates in Lincolnshire. The petition reached Randolph, who replied that Edward should allow the disinherited to gather and 'let the ball roll'.[15]

Randolph was in Musselburgh preparing Scotland's defences when he died suddenly, on 20 July. The disinherited were accused of sending a friar to poison the earl but it is more likely that he died of natural causes.[16] There was no one to step into his place to protect the infant king's throne. The magnates met at Perth on 2 August 1332, only four days before the disinherited landed. After much dispute, they elected Mar as the new guardian, despite misgivings over his long, self-imposed exile in Edward II's court. There was no other candidate—he was the only surviving commander of the Weardale campaign, and as nephew of Robert I, he was the most senior noble in Scotland. Mar's ties with England were suspicious enough: even more intriguing was the ambiguous evidence that he maintained contacts with the disinherited and was willing to support them. Concern over Mar's loyalty soon proved to be misplaced, unlike well-founded concerns over his military and political ability.

Randolph's sudden death was just the piece of good-fortune the disinherited had been waiting for. Their 88-ship armada set sail from the ports of Ravenser, Barton and Hull on 31 July. Their numbers can only be roughly estimated. It was certainly a small force, somewhere in the region of 1500 men, including 500 men-at-arms.[17]

News of Balliol's fleet reached Scotland soon after Mar's election. Unsure where they would land, he divided his army. Patrick Dunbar held Scotland south of the Forth, Mar himself took command in the north. The disinherited landed at Kinghorn in Fife on 6 August. Beaumont landed first, under the covering fire of archers. The Scottish force sent to repel the landing was commanded by Fife, with Alexander Seton and Robert Bruce, a bastard son of the king. Balliol drove them off with losses, remaining at Kinghorn for two days. His fleet left under orders to move into the Tay estuary. On the third day the invaders moved 14 miles inland to Dunfermline Abbey where they found supplies and arms stored to repel the invasion. On 10 August they pushed north, towards Loch Earn and Perth.

They sighted the Scottish army on the far banks of the Earn, encamped on Dupplin Moor overlooking the river, holding the only bridge. The disinherited pitched their tents on the south bank, at Forteviot. Even though the Scots heavily outnumbered the disinherited, they were unwilling to force a crossing so late in the day. Instead they spent the night, confident in their superior numbers and awesome military reputation.

'Cheerfully drinking wine, they expressed their contempt
for the small numbers of the opposition side, singing
songs and saying that ... they would make ropes for
themselves from the Englishmen's tails to tie them up on
the following day.'[18]

Balliol had to confront Mar's army before Patrick Dunbar's force
arrived. The earl's forces had hurried north, crossing the Forth at
Stirling to reach Auchterarder, only eight miles away.

Mar met the leaders of the disinherited, and soon dispelled any hopes
that he might aid them. The die had already been cast. They declared
they were the 'sons of magnates of this land. We are come hither with the
lord Edward of Balliol, the rightful heir of the realm, to demand the
lands which belong to us by hereditary right.'[19]

Fearing they would be caught in a pincer between two superior forces,
the disinherited risked a night assault on the Scottish camp. A local,
traditionally thought to be Andrew Murray of Tullibardine, showed
them a crossing at an unguarded ford over the Earn. They skirted the
main Scottish position before falling on the infantry encamped at Gask.
The footmen were slaughtered, 'like cattle in the meat markets'. The
main body of men-at-arms were still at their posts guarding the bridge.

Balliol's army regrouped early on the 11th. In the morning light, they
discovered that the bulk of the Scottish army remained intact, formed
up in two divisions. Mar had in his following Fife, the young Thomas
Randolph of Moray, Murdoch of Menteith, John Campbell, a Scottish
earl of Atholl and Alexander Bruce of Carrick. A vast superiority in
numbers led Scottish leaders to engage the enemy in the first full-scale
battle since Bannockburn. But Mar was no Robert Bruce, and Balliol no
Edward II.

Both armies fought on foot. The disinherited formed up behind fixed
pikes, with archers positioned on either flank. The horses were sent to
the rear where German mercenaries remained mounted, ready for
pursuit or flight. The disinherited had chosen their ground well, a
bottleneck at the end of a valley. As the Scots advanced along the narrow
glen, the English archers fired into their faces. The flanks of the Scottish
division crowded into the centre, so that by the time they reached the
English line they were in some disorder. The first division, of about 800,
drove the English line back twenty or thirty feet until Ralph Stafford
cried out 'Ye English! turn your shoulders instead of your breasts to the
pikes'. The line began to hold.

Mar's intention was to crush the disinherited by sheer weight of
numbers. But his own division advanced, precipitately, into the back of
the other Scottish division which was fighting the English. A horrific
crush ensued. Men were trampled underfoot and killed, without ever

reaching the enemy. The disinherited gained the upper hand against a confused and struggling crowd.

Fife gave the order to retreat. The disinherited men-at-arms mounted and rode in pursuit, killing anyone not worth a ransom. Some 3000 Scots were counted dead, including 360 men-at-arms. The English chroniclers marvelled at the pile of dead where the disaster had struck, 'greater in height from the earth toward the sky than one whole spear length'.[20] Donald of Mar died in the crush of bodies, together with the earls of Moray and Mentieth. Another casualty was Robert Bruce, whose accusations of treachery may have stung Mar to attack so recklessly.

The disinherited moved to Perth, which they fortified with wooden palisades and a ditch. Despite Balliol's overwhelming victory at Dupplin Moor there were still real threats to the new regime. Patrick Dunbar, with an army equal in number to the one the disinherited faced at Dupplin, learnt of the defeat from a mortally wounded man-at-arms 'holding in his own hands his intestines and internal organs which were hanging down from the saddle'.[21] He led his force to Perth where a half-hearted siege began.

On 24 August the English fleet on the Tay was attacked by a squadron led by John Crabb with ten Flemish vessels manned with Scottish troops. Beaumont's ship was isolated, captured and its crew killed. But the wind changed direction, allowing the disinherited's fleet to join in the action and beat off the attack.[22]

As news of the victory spread, Eustace Maxwell of Caerlaverock[23] and Duncan Macdouall of Wigtownshire rallied to Balliol's standard. Even after 30 years, the name Balliol still stood for something in Galloway, and the encroaching influence of the Scottish crown under Robert I was deeply resented in the region. Maxwell led a force out of Galloway and raided the besieger's lands. The siege was raised to let John Randolph, Andrew Murray and Archibald Douglas retaliate by leading a ferocious foray into Galloway. For the moment Dupplin was decisive.

Balliol now mimicked Robert Bruce's pilgrimage to Scone. On 24 September Edward was created king. Fife, captured at Dupplin, was one of the first Scottish magnates to enter into Balliol's peace in return for his freedom. He performed the secular ceremony claimed by right of his earldom's seniority. Bishop Sinclair of Dunkeld, promising the support of all the Scottish bishops bar James Ben of St Andrews, performed the religious ceremony. Ben could not face the trauma of the defeat at Dupplin and gave up his see. When Balliol's supporters sat down for the coronation feast they remained in full armour for their own safety, only removing their helmets to eat.

Andrew Murray, the posthumous son of the victor of Stirling Bridge, was named as guardian, presumably since Donald of Mar's death at

Dupplin. He was a man with considerable ability and sense of purpose but would not have much time to reveal his qualities in this, his first term as guardian.

Fife commanded the garrison installed by Balliol at Perth. The rest of the magnates set off to visit the estates they had now recovered. Balliol himself left to relieve Galloway, moving through Kyle and Cunningham before turning east to Roxburgh. The fragility of the occupation regime was soon exposed. On 7 October James and Simon Fraser, Robert Keith, and John Lindsay recaptured Perth. Fife was captured and imprisoned in Kildrummy castle. Andrew Murray of Tullibardine, the man the Scots believed led the disinherited across the Earn, was amongst the captives. He was executed for his treachery. Lindsay took command at Perth after the town's defences were demolished so they could not provide protection for the disinherited.

Balliol was at Roxburgh when Perth fell. He left his army and took up residence at Kelso. Murray now saw his chance. He 'continually dogged the king', and then ordered the destruction of the bridge over the Tweed that divided Balliol from his army. A frantic effort was made to repair the bridge, and some of Balliol's men plunged into the waters and then pursued the Scots for eight miles. Andrew Murray was surrounded and captured making a bold attempt to extricate one of his followers. Scotland had lost another guardian. He was sent to Edward III, and ransomed two years later. The king paid Walter de Manny 1,000 marks for another captive from the same raid, the 'cruel and determined pirate', John Crabb. He became 'a most bitter persecutor of his people' when the Scots refused to pay his ransom.[24]

Balliol recognised the debt he owed the English king in winning the kingdom, and that he would need his help to hold it. In November he issued two open letters from Roxburgh announcing the new relationship with England. Scotland would be held by Balliol of the English king by homage and fealty, as, so the letters went on, it always had been. He revealed that homage had already been rendered, presumably in private prior to disembarking from Hull in 1332. No mention was made of the services that this subjugation would entail, except that Balliol volunteered to perform military service overseas for at least six months with 200 men-at-arms. In recognition of this subjection Balliol promised 2000 librates (a unit of land worth £1 a year) in southern Scotland that would be divided from the crown of Scotland forever. The land would simply become part of England. As a final usurpation of the Bruce cause, Balliol suggested that if the marriage of David and Joan did not take place, he should marry her as an appurtenance of the Scottish crown.[25]

Edward III had keenly watched events across the border. A parliament gathered at Westminster in September 1332 to consider affairs in

Ireland. It was here that reports began to trickle in of the victory at Dupplin. Success had been so unlikely that Edward had made no plans for the eventuality, he even kept up friendly communications with the national government.[26] The members told him to go north at once and voted him a subsidy. He moved the offices of the English government to York, where he arrived in the third week of September.

Balliol sent Henry Beaumont and David Strathbogie to a parliament at York in early December where they must have been expected to present Edward with the letters patent Balliol issued in Roxburgh. Instead they had equal place with envoys from David II, and had to listen to Geoffrey Scrope present Edward's case to the parliament. He began with the dubious legal argument that the 1328 treaty was forced upon him by others, and so could be disregarded. Scrope then made the astonishing statement that the causes of the English and Balliol were not one and the same. His parliament was told to advise the king which of two options he should pursue: the support of one or other of the claimants to the Scottish crown or the establishment of direct overlordship of Scotland. But the parliament was weary of war in Scotland and refused to play Edward's game. After a long debate he was told that there were too few magnates present, that he should adjourn the session until after Christmas.[27] It was during this adjournment that Balliol's regime in Scotland disintegrated.

The dramatic turnaround was achieved through a sudden strike led by Archibald Douglas. 'The Tyneman' or 'loser', he was a younger brother of the good Sir James Douglas, who became guardian after the capture of Andrew Murray. He made a truce with Balliol to protect his lands in the south, and Balliol dropped his guard. With John Randolph, earl of Moray since the death of his brother at Dupplin, Robert the Steward, and Simon Fraser, Douglas led 1,000 men from Moffat to Annan where Balliol planned to spend Christmas.

On the dawn of 16 December they found Balliol and his entourage still in bed, 'naked and unarmed and utterly unprepared for their coming'. They killed a hundred of Balliol's supporters, including John Moubray, Walter Comyn and Henry Balliol, Edward's only brother, who died defending himself with a staff. Alexander Bruce, earl of Carrick, the illegitimate son of Edward Bruce, was with Balliol. He was only saved when recognised and taken prisoner by Randolph. Balliol broke out 'through a walle by an Hole in his chambre' before making his escape to England on an unbridled horse, 'with one leg in a boot and the other one bare'. Many of Balliol's supporters now deserted him. He spent Christmas at Carlisle and then left for Westmoreland where he stayed with Robert Clifford and then with Lady de Gynes at Moorholm.[28]

Balliol's humiliating expulsion had shown what should have been clear to Edward's advisors. Scotland would not accept a Balliol restoration so dependent on English intervention, a severing of the realm, and the imposition of anglophile lords. Edward's adjourned parliament was not deluded at the size of the task the king had set himself. When it resumed, debate ran from 21 January through to the 26th, an unusually long time for a medieval parliament. The chancellor, Stratford, had to admit that no conclusion could be reached. Edward promised to refer the question to the king of France and the pope. Needless to say, he did no such thing.

Parliament held the purse strings, but it did not determine foreign policy. That rested with the king and his council. Parliament was sent home. Its last action was to appoint a six strong council to help Edward frame Scottish policy: Edward made sure that he recruited like-minded men. The policy was now conveniently reframed in terms of Anglo-French relations. England could never settle its disputes with France while the Franco-Scottish accord stood. There was now an opportunity to break that accord. In reality Edward coveted military glory, his council craved to 'repair their dented prestige'. They gave him the blunt answer he had wanted from his parliament: 'for new motive, new war'.[29]

The chronicler Geoffrey Baker says that in 1333 Edward put away childish things.[30] Conquering Scotland would take the sort of effort made by his grandfather. The chancery had already moved to York; it was joined by the exchequer and the court of common pleas as Edward moved his capital to York, which became the centre of English administration for the next five years. Writs to raise troops were sent on 30 January 1333. Earlier writs to raise Welsh troops, Marcher lords and some counties had already resulted in an array of troops who were told to stand ready, but not to head north. This was not a logistical problem, but a financial one. Without parliamentary aid Edward's exchequer was under pressure to find money from whatever source it could. Between February and April they called in all money owed to the king who stopped payments from the exchequer to his creditors. Edward came increasingly to rely on his bankers to fill the gap between the crown's income and the expense of campaigning.

In March 1333 Balliol moved into Scotland from Carlisle with a combined Anglo-Scottish force and crossed the country towards Berwick-upon-Tweed, destroying the small tower at Oxnam that lay in his path. The title 'the disinherited' was no longer appropriate: unlike the army that invaded in 1332, Balliol's supporters now included prominent English lords and some Scottish supporters.

Berwick had been made ready for the siege, its walls repaired, the keepership of the castle trusted to Patrick Dunbar, that of the town to Alexander Seton. Balliol set up camp outside the town in the first week of March, in a position defended by a ditch. A second ditch was dug to seal the town. The town's water supply, through fresh water conduits, was found and cut while digging the defences. Berwick's hinterland had not been subject to a scorched-earth policy that might have deprived Balliol's men of supplies. David Strathbogie raided the neighbouring countryside and supplied the army with cattle. Haddington, oblivious to the war around it, even held its market. The town was sacked and the traders slaughtered.[31]

Archibald Douglas organised two raids into England. The first into Northumberland, the second on the west coast into Cumberland and Gilsland on 22 March. The English retaliated with a raid led by Anthony de Lucy that reached twelve miles into Dumfriesshire. As the English headed home, slowed down by booty, Humphrey Boys and Humphrey Jardine led the Scottish garrison from Lochmaben against them near the village of Dornock. The English beat off the attack, both Scottish knights were slain and William Douglas captured. This Douglas, the son of James Douglas of Lothian, became instrumental in the recovery of the ceded counties when he was released from captivity two years later. He earned the epithets 'the Knight of Liddesdale' and 'the Flower of Chivalry'.

Edward had forecast the raids as early as February, and on 1 March, when he called up troops for the defence of the Marches, said they were unavoidable. These raids, no more than banditry, played into Edward's hands as useful propaganda to encourage English participation in the wars, and as justification of English aggression. The Scots had entered England with banners unfurled and the English could now fight a legitimate war. Although he had connived at Balliol's invasion that had prompted the raids, Edward III kept up a fine show of indignation for the benefit of the pope and the King of France.[32] He maintained the barefaced lie that the invasion was a private initiative of his subjects, who were laying claim to their inheritance. On 20 March he ordered supplies to be sent north to help his lieges defend the border. The following day he called a muster of his military tenants.[33]

Edward moved north in early April, he was at Durham on the 8th, before spending a month in Northumberland preparing his campaign. He did not reach Tweedmouth until 9 May when an assault was made on the town to honour his arrival.

The town's defences were too strong to be taken by assault, even with John Crabb, a man who knew the defences better than anyone, fighting for the English. The garrison would be ground into submission. Three ships, the *Gracedieu, Jonete* and *Nicholas,* brought an engine from York castle and two others, built by Richard the Goldsmith at Cowick in Yorkshire, that had required the felling of 40 oaks, beside 691 stone missiles carved by 37 stonemasons.[34] They

'made meny assautes with gonnes and with othere
engynes to the toune, wherwith thai destroiede meny a
fair hous; and cherches also were beten adoune vnto the
erthe, with gret stones, and spitouse comyng out of
gonnes and of othere gynnes.'[35]

The power of medieval artillery should not be underestimated. Large
areas of the town were flattened. The following year the Maison Dieu
sent a petition for help repairing their church and houses that had been
cast down by the engines during the siege. The Master had pawned the
chalices and vestments but the work was unfinished, and without the
king's help they could not 'endure the winter without being utterly
perished'.[36]

On 27 June Edward III and Balliol delivered a joint assault. Ships from
the English fleet were bought up to the walls at high tide. It may have
been now that William Seton, the son of the keeper, was killed, drowned
underneath the ships. Faggots soaked in tar, meant to set light to the
ships, started a major fire in the town itself. As the fire raged the Scots
sought a truce until the following day to give them time to extinguish the
flames when they promised to surrender. Failure to do so infuriated the
king who renewed the assault. Tweedmouth was now close to
exhaustion after months of bombardment; they agreed a new, verbal,
truce, promising surrender after 15 days if the town was not relieved. On
this occasion the king took twelve hostages, including Thomas Seton, a
second son of the keeper, to make sure they kept their word.

During the long blockade in the spring and summer, Archibald
Douglas had been mobilising a host to invade England. He hoped to raise
an army that would equal Edward's.[37] Edward expected an attack in
force by mid-summer; so many of his troops had deserted he ordered the
chancellor to find as many new recruits as possible.[38] Douglas wasted
valuable time building up his army, and when he was finally ready to
move out it was too late to wreak the sort of havoc on the north of
England that might have drawn Edward from the siege. On 11 July, the
last day of the truce, the Scottish host crossed the Tweed at Yair ford and
moved along the river on the English bank to Tweedmouth, which they
spent the day burning, unhindered by the English on the far bank. At low
tide Douglas began to send reinforcements and supplies across the ruined
Tweed bridge before William Montagu could bring English forces
around to contest the crossing.

William Keith, who had led the force across the river, replaced
Alexander Seton as warden. The next morning Douglas drew up his
battalions at Sunnyside, a hill south of the Tweed, banners flying, where
the English could see the size of the force he had gathered. Just in case
any doubt at his purpose existed, he sent messengers to Edward telling

him that they planned to head south into England. Douglas moved off to lay siege to Bamburgh where Edward's queen had been sent for safety. The castle was one of the most impregnable border strongholds; it could easily hold off a poorly equipped army for months. Douglas was free to do his worst in Northumberland. Edward stayed put.

The defenders now demanded the release of the hostages as a relief of sorts had reached the town. Edward, splitting hairs, pointed out that the town had been relieved from England, the truce had specified it be relieved from Scotland. He made his own demand, the submission of the town. When they refused, Edward hanged Thomas Seton on a gallows before the walls.[39]

Edward now ordered that two hostages a day would be hanged until the town surrendered or he ran out of hostages. Under this threat the two sides gathered again to make a new agreement. This time, to avoid confusion, the agreement was set in writing in two indentures, one with Patrick Dunbar, the other with William Keith. The terms of the indentures attempted to deal with all eventualities. A truce would exist until sunrise on 20 July 1333. The town would be considered relieved under one of three conditions: if the Scots crossed the Tweed at Berwick and relieved the town; if they won a pitched battle on Scottish soil, or if 200 men-at-arms could force their way through English lines with the loss of only 30 men from land not sea. Unless one of these conditions was met the town promised to surrender. Those who wished to become English would be allowed to remain, others could leave peacefully. The readiness of the besieged to offer battle, albeit on somebody else's behalf, was in the knowledge that the Scottish army was larger than the English.

William Keith set out under a safe-conduct to inform Douglas of the agreement. He found him near Morpeth. Douglas's hand was forced; any hope that his raiding in Northumberland would draw off Edward and avoid a pitched battle were dashed. Keith threatened that if Douglas did not come to fight he would surrender the town at once. Douglas had no choice and began to move the host towards Berwick.

The English occupied a well-chosen defensive position on Halidon Hill, where one man 'mycht dyscumfyte thre', two miles north of Berwick. The hill rises to 500 feet and dominates the northern approach to the town. The king left 500 men to his rear to guard against a sortie from the Berwick garrison, allowed under the terms of the compact. Edward arrayed his men in a similar formation to the one that had won the battle of Dupplin, although because the army was larger it formed into three divisions. The earl Marshall, the king's uncle Thomas Brotherton, commanded the first division nearest the sea, with the king's brother, John of Eltham, Henry Beaumont and Edward Bohun representing his brother, the constable. Edward himself held the centre; Balliol, the landward division.[40] Each division was flanked by wings of archers. It is unknown exactly how they were arrayed, but probably at an angle to the division to form cross-fire, forming hollow wedges to link the brigades.[41]

It was the English archers that were the key to the formation, the men-at-arms served only to protect them from any troops reaching the line. The heaviest of English longbows had a range of 400 yards, at 200 they became accurate, and at 100 yards an arrow could pierce armour. They had a rate of fire of up to ten flights a minute—men said that arrows would fall like snow. The fearsome noise of the flights scared both men and horses alike.

Douglas crossed the Tweed on the night of 18 July and camped in Duns park, thirteen miles west of Halidon. On the morning of the 19th the army marched to the high ground on 'Witches' Knowe', or 'Bothul'. They were spotted by midday. A Goliath-sized Scotsman called Turnbull challenged all comers to a single combat before the battle started, and he was slain, together with his mastiff, by Robert Benhol, one of Edward's household knights.

The majority of the Scottish soldiers were footmen armed with pikes, so the men-at-arms dismounted to keep pace. Formed up in three divisions, the Scots charged down the slope, losing momentum when

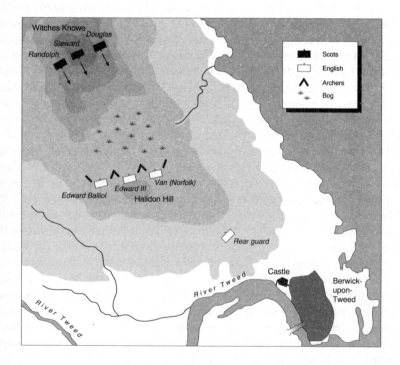

The Battle of Halidon Hill 1333

they reached the foot of Halidon Hill, where they had to negotiate a bog. (The land has now been drained, but there is still a farm called Bogend.) Then, as they started to climb the hill, the skies darkened. A hail of arrows struck their ranks.

The first Scottish division, led by John Randolph, made for Balliol's division on the left but 'were so grievously wounded in the face and blinded by the host of English archery ... that they were helpless, and quickly began to turn away their faces from the arrow flights and fall'. Those who did get through were cut to pieces by the men-at-arms. The second division, under the Steward, and third division, under Archibald Douglas, fared no better.

Douglas had with him the 200 men-at-arms picked to relieve the town, and they impressed the English with their fierce resistance. The three divisions crowded together under the rain of arrows until they formed one untidy mass. Then the rear took to flight. The camp followers were first to leave, with the horses. Ross refused to run, fighting a last desperate rearguard action until he fell with all around him. Then the English mounted to begin a deadly pursuit, 'felling the wretches as they fled in all directions with iron-shod maces'.[42] The fleeing remnants from the army were followed for miles, very few were given quarter. The butchery only came to an end when darkness fell.

The battle of Halidon Hill involved a terrible slaughter of the Scottish nobility. Five earls died: Hugh of Ross, Malcolm of Lennox, Alexander Bruce of Carrick, Kenneth Sutherland, and John Campbell of Atholl. Alexander Douglas fell at a spot now known as Douglas Dyke. Three Fraser brothers fell: Andrew, Simon and James. Fordun, the compiler of the list, then breaks off, declaring it 'would be more sad than profitable to repeat [the names] one by one'.[43] On the following morning Edward ordered the captured Scots put to death. So much for chivalry.

Berwick opened its gates. It was now ceded to Edward, on account for the 2,000 librates he had been promised. He organised the town along the lines of an English sherriffdom before returning to England. Henry Percy was appointed to the custody of both the town and castle. From 27 July until 20 November 1333 Berwick was considered so secure that only eight sentries and two check-watches were posted on the walls.[44]

Edward, still a young man learning the craft of kingship, read too much into the victory at Halidon. He was swept along by the widespread belief that the battle concluded the war. 'And so men freely declared that the Scotch wars had been brought to their close,' said Murimath, 'that nothing remained of the Scotch nation which was willing or able to defend or govern itself.' Edward did not follow his grandfather's example after the battle of Dunbar with a victorious military procession through Scotland, and in this he made a glaring error. He began the journey south only ten days after the battle to attend tournaments. The refusal of Edward's parliament to back his military project reflected unease throughout England at the prospect of re-igniting the wars, and the jubilation after the victory was the more spontaneous because of it. There was a new sense of confidence that would be converted into militancy when the Scottish recovery began.

After the battle, the Bruce cause could count the strongholds it held on the fingers of one hand: the strongest at Dumbarton, under its keeper Malcolm Fleming became a nest of patriot dissent; Kildrummy kept by Christian Bruce, the sister of Robert Bruce and since 1326 the wife of Andrew Murray; Urquhart held by Robert Lauder; Loch Leven by Alan Vipont; and Loch Doon by a servant. David II found refuge at Dumbarton where he was taken in great secrecy. He was joined by his nephew, Robert the Steward, heir to the throne after David. The Steward had been in hiding in Rothesay Castle from where he escaped in a rowing boat with two servants, a chamber boy and the family charters. Malcolm Fleming and Alan Vipont received safe-conducts to go to England in November 1333. This can only have been to negotiate surrender. Although there is no evidence of them taking up the safe-conducts, Scotland's independence hung by a thin thread.

Balliol did nothing to extinguish these last scattered remnants of the Bruce cause: once Edward retired south he did not have the manpower to campaign in the north.[45] Instead, Balliol traversed the lowlands granting lands to his supporters. In October he held a parliament in Perth at which he foolishly revoked all the deeds made in Robert I's name. He planned to expunge Robert from the record in much the way Robert had done to his father, and ordered that all lands granted by Robert had to be returned to their original heirs.

Henry Beaumont received the Randolph earldom of Moray, Richard Talbot became Lord of Mar, David Strathbogie received the Stewardship, Percy claimed Annandale and John de Warenne, Balliol's cousin, was granted the earldom of Strathearn. Earl Malise had been one of few who escaped Halidon, after which he surrendered the earldom to Balliol, for which he was tried for treason in June 1344. Patrick Dunbar 'became English'. He refortified Dunbar Castle, dismantled during the second Wars of Independence, and granted the lands of his own tenants who would not submit to Edward.[46]

Balliol now had to acknowledge his debt to Edward III. It had been nearly a year since he had issued the letters patent at Roxburgh, a sign that he was dragging his feet. No doubt Edward got wind of this reluctance and sent Henry Percy, Ralph Neville and Henry Beaumont to the Perth parliament as his representatives to press Balliol to give effect to the treaty.[47]

Four months later, English ambassadors William Montagu, Ralph Neville, Geoffrey le Scrope, Edward Bohun and Henry Percy pressed for the implementation of the Roxburgh convention at a parliament in Holyrood outside Edinburgh. Half the Scottish episcopates presented themselves, but pitifully few magnates. With so many dead at Dupplin and Halidon or forfeited at Scone there were few available. With the agreement of what passed for a representative assembly in Balliol's Scotland, Edward's demands were sanctioned. The king no longer trusted his client. He began to cultivate his own party in Scotland: Beaumont, Strathbogie, Montagu and Patrick Dunbar would ensure that his voice was heard north of the border.

At the York parliament in February 1334 Edward ratified the terms of the agreement his ambassadors reached in Edinburgh. Edward was willing to sweeten the pill of English overlordship. He released and quitclaimed to Balliol and his heirs the rights to demesne lordship of Scotland; neither would they be obliged to attend English parliaments or have Scottish appeals heard in English courts.[48]

The two Edwards met in June 1334 at the consecration of Richard de Bury as bishop of Durham. On the 12th, in the Treaty of Newcastle, Balliol, in his own name, ceded the counties and towns of Berwick-upon-Tweed, Roxburgh, Edinburgh with Haddington and Linlithgow, Peebles, Dumfries and the forest of Selkirk, Jedburgh and Selkirk. He recognised Edward as his overlord as payment for 'great assistance' the king had given him. Edward had already annexed the Isle of Man in 1333. A week later, at the Blackfriary in Newcastle, Balliol did homage for what was left of his kingdom.[49]

By leaving Balliol self-reliant, far from English interference, in a truncated regality, Edward believed the Scots might be reconciled to his kingship. Balliol was now caught between the mistrust of Edward and the hatred of the patriots. He was no fool and understood that he faced the same dilemma as his father; compliance with the English regime would shore up his kingship but alienate his subjects. He was no weakling, but he had no firm ground on which to make a stand. By cherry-picking the wealthiest parts of Scotland, Edward denied Balliol the resources that he required to maintain his kingship or the respect of his people.

It was not until the spring of 1334 that a new offensive was taken against the remaining patriots. But Balliol's chance had slipped, events in Europe overtook him.

Edward had already shown concern at how his behaviour in Scotland would be regarded in France. The southern counties of England were placed on alert in case of French intervention. Three days before the battle of Halidon, the men of the Cinque ports were warned not to start trouble 'so that the said Ports may not be the cause of war between the king of France and us'.[50] Unknown to the English, Philip fitted out ten ships packed with arms and food for Berwick. They set sail from Dieppe but were blown off course and never arrived.

Since 1329 Philip VI had pressed for a new crusade and hoped to take Edward with him. In July 1332 he formally took the Cross and his energies became absorbed by the crusade for the next four years. English policy in France consisted of holding out the possibility of Edward's participation in a French-organised campaign in return for a settlement of disputes in Aquitaine. Edward's new interest in Scotland complicated the relationship. Edward was careful to manage the news reaching France. Philip wrote two polite letters to Edward in early 1333 asking for news of the events in Scotland. Embassies and the chancellery were told to discuss any matter with France but were on no account to discuss Scotland.[51] When French agents arrived in England, they were told that there were no escorts available to take them to Edward at the siege of Berwick. When they finally reached the town in July they were not allowed to leave until the siege was over. This embassy was hopelessly out of date, they had been appointed to press for Edward's participation in the crusade and had no remit to deal of Scottish affairs.

When Scottish refugees began to arrive at the French court after Halidon, in particular John Randolph, they badgered Philip to fulfil his obligations under the Corbeil treaty. Clearly, David's safety could not be guaranteed in Scotland, so Philip offered the king safe-haven in France. It was the least he could offer, but it bound him to the patriot cause. He gave Randolph 1,000 marks to fit out two ships to bring David II to safety. Randolph arrived at Dumbarton in the spring of 1334, soon after Malcolm Fleming took the king to shelter in France. David and his queen were made comfortable in the magnificent Château Gaillard on the Seine: once the stronghold of Richard I. His little court was maintained by generous grants from Philip together with money and salmon from Scotland. He would not return to Scotland until he was seventeen, in 1341.

David landed in Normandy just as an English embassy was completing negotiations over an end to the Agenais dispute. An agreement seemed to have been reached, town criers began to proclaim the settlement. Then Philip recalled the English delegates from their lodgings and dropped a bombshell. They understood, he told them, that any agreement was conditional on including the Scots. It was the first time Scotland had been mentioned—David's presence on French soil had shamed Philip into making this concession to his ally. The delegates were stunned by this new condition, they had no instructions or powers to negotiate Scottish affairs and knew less of the events in Scotland than the members of David's court. They left France humiliated and defeated, with a last passing remark from Philip that 'there would never be friendship between England and France until the same man is king of both'. When Stratford arrived back in England he had to tell Edward that Philip was committed to the Bruce cause. The king now considered Philip his enemy.[52]

Randolph's arrival at Dumbarton revived the patriot cause. There are no records of Scottish leadership between the battle of Halidon and April 1334, when Robert Steward issued a charter. In May two charters were issued in the joint names of the Steward and Randolph.[53] The eighteen-year-old Steward and the still younger Randolph (Thomas Gray describes him as *'un enfant parcru'*), set themselves up as joint guardians in an alternative rebel government. This joint guardianship may have come at the instigation of David's advisors. It was resented by the Steward, who might have hoped for sole guardianship by right of his royal blood. There was certainly tension between the two men from an early stage. The guardians now led the resistance, beginning with the recovery of the Steward's lands in the south-west. The source followed by the Scottish chroniclers Wyntoun and Bower gives the Steward the central role in the recovery of the south-west. Writing in the first half of the fifteenth century, they have an understandable Stewart bias. There is an element of distortion and propaganda in their accounts where the action incorrectly predates Randolph's return.[54]

David Strathbogie had been awarded the Steward's lands, and the Stewardship, in 1333. He took possession of the patrimony with necessary force and accepted the fealty and homage of the freeholders. The Steward resented the loss of his estates, and led a force of 400 men on Campbell galleys down Loch Fyne. He captured Dunoon where he installed a garrison. This sparked rebellions throughout the Steward's former tenantry. The Brandons of Bute overwhelmed the sheriff and took Rothesay: largely unarmed they used rocks from the hillside as missiles (in the 'battle of the casting stones'). They took the head of the sheriff to the Steward as a present. Bands of rebels began to roam Annandale and Kyle.

The grant of Dumfriesshire to Edward III as part of the 1334 settlement alienated some of Balliol's key supporters in the west. Duncan Macdouall brought Wigtownshire back to David's allegiance. The Lanercost chronicler tries to give Macdouall's treacherous behaviour a veneer of integrity by remarking that he was enticed to defect by his new wife. A concurrent raid by Randolph, Robert the Steward, Lawrence Abernethy and William Douglas may have been more persuasive. The men east of the Cree (Kirkcudbright) who remained loyal to Balliol, and those from the west (Wigtownshire) 'mutually destroyed each other'.[55]

Balliol sought help from Edward. The king did not misjudge the threat, appointing Henry Percy and Ralph Neville wardens of the Marches with power to raise local levies. Edward expected Balliol to hold his own until help arrived, but at a parliament in Perth in August 1334 he contrived to lose the support of his two key lieutenants: David Strathbogie and Henry Beaumont. The dispute arose out of the inheritance of John Moubray, who died defending Balliol's escape from Annan in December 1332. His brother, Alexander, claimed his estates as senior male heir. This was contested by Moubray's three daughters, supported by Beaumont, Strathbogie and Richard Talbot. Balliol's foolish support for Alexander Moubray isolated the king: the parliament broke up with each man heading off in a different direction. Balliol towards Berwick, Beaumont to Dundarg in Buchan, Strathbogie to Lochindorb and Richard Talbot home to England.

The dispute gave the patriots the opportunity to pick off the disinherited lords one by one. Moubray and his brother, the sheriff of Roxburgh, realising that Balliol did not have the muscle to force his claim, threw in their lot with Andrew Murray. Recently ransomed, Murray had lost no time in resuming his career as a guerrilla leader. Together, they besieged Beaumont at his remote castle at Dundarg. Beaumont surrendered the castle on 23 December in return for safe-conduct, and a promise to work towards a restoration of the peace. He took a boat from Dundee and headed for England to raise his ransom.[56]

Randolph went after Strathbogie, and after a 'dogged' pursuit into Lochabar, Strathbogie submitted and took an oath of fealty to David II. Randolph left Strathbogie as commander in the north of Scotland on behalf of David II, a task he completed 'with no lack of zeal as long as he remained on the king's side'.[57] On his way back to England with six knights, including John Stirling, Richard Talbot was captured in Lothian by William Keith and Godfrey Ross. The knights took refuge in a kirk near Linlithgow, but were captured. Those not worth a ransom were executed.

Edward now acted to restore his position. First he ensured that there was no conflict between his senior lieutenants. In August 1333 Balliol assigned Henry Percy to reduce Lochmaben and was promised the forfeitures of Annandale as a reward. In the event the castle surrendered to David Strathbogie and Edward Bohun under the same conditions offered at Berwick. So there were few forfeited estates to be granted, leaving Bohun and Percy on frosty terms. When Balliol awarded the lordships of Lochmaben and Annandale to Percy they were contested by Edward Bohun. Seeing discord between his lieutenants Edward III rejected Balliol's grants and ordered the castle to be handed over to Henry Beaumont and Ralph Neville 'to preserve the peace', until the title could be settled in an English parliament.

Edward used the largesse available to the king to settle the dispute and ensure that both great families, Bohun and Percy, had an interest in serving the king in Scotland. Henry Percy surrendered his claim to the lordship of Annandale to Edward in return for the castle and constabulary of Jedburgh, 500 marks a year from Berwick's customs and custody of Berwick castle for which he was to be paid £200 a year in wartime, £100 in peace. Edward then conferred Annandale and Lochmaben on Edward Bohun in return for a *reddendo* of a goshawk at Michaelmas. Bohun died in 1335 trying to rescue a valet from drowning in the Annan.[58]

The English position in Scotland was grave. Of the disinherited, Talbot was in captivity, Strathbogie had gone over to Bruce, Beaumont was under siege at Dundarg, soon to yield, and Balliol had been forced to seek safety in Berwick. Only Patrick of Dunbar remained and he would soon revert to his former allegiance.[59] There were no English forces of any number in Scotland. Even in Berwick the burgesses had to divide themselves into watches to man the walls and hired 24 sentinels. The garrison amounted to 18 *armati*, and 140 hobelars or sentries. Outside Berwick the warden of the marches, Ralph Neville, retained 60 men-at-arms and 60 mounted archers. Henry Percy joined him on 13 October with a further 120 men-at-arms and 100 mounted archers.[60]

For the next three years Edward's finances were stretched as the war moved into a new phase, from a 'short term levy of the military tenants and the shire infantry' to the need to maintain 'professional warriors, permanent garrisons and mobile columns to conquer Scotland'. Although some money was raised through the exchequer at York, Edward's agent in the field was the wardrobe. In the year of Halidon the wardrobe's expenses had reached £23,090 2s 3d, double the previous year's expenses (£11,160 3s 9½). For the next three years the average expenditure exceeded £40,000.[61] Such expenditure was beyond the king's resources. Fortunately the news of Balliol's expulsion reached Edward in parliament. The victory at Halidon, combined with the news of the treatment of Balliol's English followers, opened parliament's purse and Edward was awarded a new subsidy of a fifteenth from the counties and a tenth from the burghs, followed shortly afterwards by a tenth from the ecclesiastical provinces.

A valuable record of the army is contained in the books of Richard Ferriby, the keeper of the Wardrobe. Edward formed a contract army, made up from the royal household, magnates, shire levies and Welsh troops. The king's household formed the core of the armym which, when included with the retinues of six earls, amounted to 1240 men-at-arms, 40 foot archers and 1200 mounted archers. The counties north of the Trent sent 70 men-at-arms, 460 hobelars and horse archers and 1750 foot archers; the Welsh sent a contingent of 60 troopers, 50 hobelars and 900 foot. Added to these are various small groups, 24 miners from the Forest of Dean, 99 mounted archers from Chester who formed Edward's personal bodyguard, 100 'armed men' from the city of York, Richard Goushill and his company of 54 masons, and Alan Kirk, keeper of the king's tents. Felons promised a pardon for taking part in the campaign formed two 100 strong companies. In all 6,200 men

served, though the army was never at its full strength during a harsh
winter. When he left Newcastle on 14 November he had 4,000 troops
with him, and many of the shire levies had still to arrive.[62]

This is the first evidence of the use of mounted archers in England.
Their horses were purely for mobility: they fought on foot, unlike the
hobelar who did not carry a bow and fought mounted. The significance
of the mounted archer would not be realised until the early campaigns
of the Hundred Years' War, since the bulk of Edward's archers remained
on foot. The men-at-arms were hired under contract and paid the flat
rate of £100 for every group of twenty, regardless of rank. Archers were
paid 6d a day in England, 4d in Scotland: reflecting the possibility of
supplementing wages by living off the land.

Edward left London in the first week of October. He reached
Roxburgh, which he made his base for the campaign. It was here that he
held a Christmas parliament. Little is known of the short campaign: for
the most part Edward stayed at his Roxburgh base where he repaired the
castle. Edward sent writ after writ demanding more troops but had little
success. The shire levies and men-at-arms somehow resisted the
attractions of a harsh winter trooping over the Scottish moors.

* * *

Edward wanted to do much more after the collapse of Balliol's regime in
the summer of 1334. On 28 December he moved out of Roxburgh on a
military promenade through Ettrick Forest. Balliol, Warwick and
Oxford combined their retinues with the March levies under Anthony
de Lucy, to protect the north west from the threat of raids. They were
diverted to Peebles when news arrived that Randolph was in the area,
but he had gone before Balliol arrived. The two columns spent their time
laying waste to the countryside through which they passed, indifferent
to the loyalties of the local population. Edward and Balliol agreed that
all those who took part in the campaign could keep whatever they could
seize which led to 'indiscriminate looting', alienating any residual
support Balliol might have had. In October, Isabella of Mar petitioned
the king for a pension as her lands in Scotland were wasted by both the
patriots and the king's army. Edward allowed her two marks weekly,
later increased to 50s. The following February, Eustace Maxwell was
granted £40 for his losses. Few others qualified for the king's help.[63]

Edward had hoped to maintain the campaign through spring but
relied too much on the arrival of fresh troops. By the end of January it
was clear that the campaign was faltering. On the 30th he redirected
supplies from Berwick to Newcastle and York, but with no money left
to pay them, his troops began to leave as their quarter-year contracts
came to an end. Edward left for the south on 2 February, leaving John of

Eltham, Percy and Neville to defend the Marches. They left royal service in the middle of March, leaving the defence of the border in the hands of household knights.

When Edward arrived at Newcastle on 18 February he was confronted by a French ambassador demanding to know why he was supporting Edward Balliol against the rightful king of Scotland, David II, the husband of his sister. Edward refused to answer, telling the ambassador that a considered reply would be sent later. He allowed the embassy to send members to Perth to meet the patriot leaders. At a conference in York the Scots met the French envoys who persuaded them to observe a truce to last from Easter to mid-summer 1335 to give time for French and papal negotiators to pursue a peace treaty. With no army in the north, no money, and no possibility of an offensive until the summer, the truce served Edward's purpose.

Envoys from France, Scotland and the curia, sent by the new pope, Benedict XII, worked in vain. Within weeks Edward had started to organise a new campaign. The only concession Edward made to the truce was to delay the muster until 23 June to coincide with its expiry. At the beginning of March, John Crabb and James Kingston equipped a squadron of ten ships from the eastern ports, pressing 1000 men to complete a naval blockade. The western admiral, Roger Hegham, had twelve ships stationed along the western approaches.

The Scottish government had still barely recovered from the loss of so many nobles at Halidon Hill, and Balliol's brief rule. The joint guardians had already fallen out with each other when a parliament met in April 1335. The dispute began when Randolph and Strathbogie contested the lands of John Comyn of Badenoch. The Steward, with an unfortunate lack of judgement spurred by jealousy of his colleague, lent support to Strathbogie, while Patrick Dunbar, Andrew Murray, Alexander Moubray and William Douglas supported Randolph. This was not a split over policy but one centred on personal recriminations. Old grudges resurfaced: Andrew Murray, recently ransomed from English captivity, blamed Strathbogie for blocking his release. Each guardian tried to seize what royal revenue the administration could gather from a country in a state of near anarchy. Even without such disharmony the scorched-earth policy ordered by the magnates was the only one which had resulted in any sort of success. They told the lowlanders to go into hiding in the hills with their livestock, while ecclesiastical communities sought protection from Edward III.[64]

The army that gathered in Newcastle was the biggest that Edward III would take to Scotland. Over 15,000 soldiers received pay from the wardrobe during the campaign, the army reaching a peak strength of 13,000. Edward crossed from Newcastle to Carlisle with the earls of Warwick, Cornwall, Lancaster, Hereford and Buchan. The army included a contingent led by Count Juliers, married to the sister of the queen of England, who came with a 'splendid following'. Balliol led a force in the east, with Surrey, Arundel, Oxford, Angus, Henry Percy, Ralph Neville, Thomas Berkeley and William Latimer.

Armies on both sides of the conflict had begun to indulge in excesses rarely seen in the war between Edward I and Robert Bruce. The two columns

> 'freely marched through all the land on this side of the Forth and beyond it, burning, laying waste, and carrying off spoil and booty. Some of them, especially the Welsh, spared neither the clergy nor their monasteries, plundering regulars and seculars impartially. Also the seamen of Newcastle burnt a great part of the town of Dundee, with the dormitory and schools of the Minorite Friars, carrying away their great bell; and they burnt one friar who formerly had been a knight, a man of wholly pure and holy life. The bell they exposed for sale at Newcastle, where it was bought by the Preaching Friars of Newcastle for ten marks, although one party had no right to sell it and the other none to buy.'[65]

The two armies converged and met at Glasgow before pressing on to Perth. They reached Airth on 31 July where the Forth is navigable and the army could be resupplied and ferried across the river. After raiding the ports on the eastern seaboard, the English fleet entered the Forth on 5 July, where the admiral's flagship was wrecked on rocks. Reaching Perth on 7 August, Edward stayed in the town as his army plundered the countryside.[66]

Though unopposed, Edward and Balliol did not have control of Scotland. The Scottish leadership wisely refused to engage Edward. Randolph led guerrilla activity aimed at exhausting the English, with small raids on the March and attempts to cut off supply routes. At Tarbert castle he secured a truce with John, Lord of the Isles, a Balliol supporter, so he could freely move south of the Forth.[67] He intercepted a force led by Guy, the Belgian count of Namur, who had come to England with seven or eight knights and 100 men-at-arms, reached Berwick with the help of English guides, and then travelled into Scotland to Edinburgh. Randolph and Patrick Dunbar ambushed count Guy on the Burgh Muir near Edinburgh. When William Douglas arrived with men from the Pentland Hills, Namur fled for safety into Edinburgh, fighting a street-to-street battle along Friar's Wynd (now Blackfriars street) and then St Mary's Wynd (St Mary's Street). Edinburgh castle had been dismantled on Robert Bruce's orders, but the Namur men defended the castle rock, killing their exhausted horses to fill breeches in the wall's circuit. Without sleep, hungry, cold, thirsty and weary the count surrendered the following morning. For fear of alienating continental support, Patrick Dunbar and William Douglas took Namur back to England and set him free. *Lanercost* was unimpressed with his reckless foray into border warfare, 'a mighty piece of presumption that he should have dared to enter Scotland in time of war with so slender a force'.[68]

Namur took a ship with the queen from Berwick to Perth, but kept his oath not to take up arms against Scots and soon returned home. At some point before or after escorting Namur, the Scots encountered an English raiding party, a sortie from the Roxburgh garrison. The skirmish was 'vigorously' resisted by Randolph who lost his freedom to 'men of low birth'. William Douglas escaped 'into thin air', but his brother James was killed.

Randolph's capture was a devastating blow to the patriots, leaving command to the ineffectual Steward. Persistent English attacks began to eat into Scottish resolve. Emissaries from Strathbogie arrived in Perth on 7 August, and by the 18th they had reached a surrender agreement. Strathbogie's emissaries had power to negotiate on behalf of his ally, Robert the Steward: though no firm evidence exists, the Steward, after ferocious raids on his lands, probably submitted to Edward now. Strathbogie's betrayal led to deep recriminations amongst the nationalists. Balliol attempted to sow further division by offering an opportunity to come into his peace on 26 November. The treaty followed the normal formula: all offences until 18 August would be pardoned, the franchise of the church would be guaranteed, the customs and laws of Alexander III's time would be respected and only Scots would be awarded Scottish offices—a formula that had failed in the past. Fife, who had surrendered Cupar castle without a fight on 7 August and Mentieth, together with the Moubrays, came over. John of the Isle's earlier submission was rewarded with the grant of large areas of the west of Scotland. Attempts to persuade Randolph, in captivity, to do the same were in vain.[69]

Edward III remained in Perth for a month, without an enemy to fight, placing his hope in a political settlement. Edward Balliol, Gilbert de Umfraville and Henry Beaumont left Perth with a small army, perhaps 800 men, enlisting English support from Warwick, Henry of Lancaster and Ralph Neville. It was an attempt to join forces with an Irish contingent and put pressure on the patriot stronghold around Dumbarton.

The task of taking the castle was given to an Irish force led by the justiciar, John Darcy. The initial intention was to meet up with Edward in the Clyde before the king moved off to Perth, but he had already been and gone before the 50-strong Irish fleet left port between 23 and 28 August. They swung round to attack Robert the Steward's lands of Bute and Arran and laid siege to Rothesay castle, which protects the approach to Dumbarton. After three weeks, Ormonde and most of the troops went home. The earl of Desmond, who remained with 30 men-at-arms, left with the justiciar on 15 October. There is no evidence that the castle surrendered.[70]

Edward's army began to disband towards the end of August. On his journey south he sent Thomas Rosslyn to rebuild Edinburgh castle, the work being paid for from special fines levied on the surrounding counties. He was at Berwick on 30 September, when his household troops ceased to draw wages. The campaign had succeeded in pushing the English defences north, to incorporate the ceded counties. The counties were organised as English sheriffdoms, Berwick, Edinburgh, Dumfries and Roxburgh. The sheriffs began to collect taxes but most of the revenue came from forfeitures—where the campaign's destruction had left anything to collect.

* * *

By October the patriot cause had reached its nadir. The resistance to Balliol was now patchy. Bower can only name three Scottish magnates who refused to come into Edward's allegiance: Patrick Dunbar, who held a base at Dunbar castle where he could launch raids into Lothian; William Douglas of Liddesdale, who attacked the south-western supporters of Balliol and the Lothian garrisons; and Andrew Murray, made guardian after Randolph's capture and the Steward's surrender. Their attacks had little effect.[71]

On 17 October William Montagu, Edward's lieutenant in Scotland, granted Murray a three-week truce. Negotiations began in Bathgate near Edinburgh in the first week in November under a truce initially set to last until the 12th, and then extended until Christmas. Edward III remained in the north of England, at Doddington and then Alnwick, during the talks. Ostensibly, this was the prelude to a final peace.

Then disturbing news arrived at the Scottish delegation. Edward Balliol had made David Strathbogie guardian or lieutenant of Scotland north of the Forth. Strathbogie was not making himself very popular: 'For some he disinherited, some he imprisoned in dungeons, some he even banished and murdered; and in the end he ordered the destruction of all freeholders of the land without fail.'[72]

Despite the truce, he besieged Kildrummy castle, where Andrew Murray's wife, Christian Bruce, was making a 'stowt and manly resistance'. Andrew Murray met with William Montagu and gained permission to break off negotiations to take a relieving force to Kildrummy. Montagu realised that this was the action that Edward had sought in vain for the last few months, the Scots that it was a matter of honour and a last chance for their cause.

Dunbar and William Douglas moved in on Strathbogie with 800 hand-picked men from Lothian and the Borders. They were joined by 300 local men led by John Craig, possibly the captain of the Kildrummy garrison. Murray forded the Dee and entered the forest of Culblean. The English had warned Strathbogie who abandoned the siege and took up a defensive position. Wyntoun suggests he had 3000 men, but adds the qualification 'men said'. On the night of 29 November Murray took his division on a circuitous route to try and surprise Strathbogie with an attack on his flank. Douglas marched towards Strathbogie, showed himself, then feigned withdrawal. Believing the Scots had lost heart, Strathbogie ordered a charge. His men lost cohesion as they negotiated rough ground and impetus as they crossed a burn. Douglas ordered his men to level their spears and charged into Strathbogie's force. Andrew Murray now arrived with the second Scottish column and launched an attack on Strathbogie's flank. As Murray joined the combat, many of Strathbogie's men fled into the woods. Strathbogie refused to yield and died fighting.[73] Murray took his force south and laid siege to Cupar Castle and Lochindorb, where Strathbogie's widow, Katherine Beaumont, had fled.

Henry Beaumont vowed that all who had been at Culblean 'should be tortured without mercy and various punishments and killed'; Bower adds that 'there was also much innocent blood cruelly shed among those men'.[74]

For the remainder of the winter, Balliol was forced to remain in England 'because he did not yet possess in Scotland any castle or town wherein he could dwell in safety'. He stayed on Holy Island, running up bills he could not afford to pay. Edward III ordered the sheriff of Northumberland to seize his goods to the value of £45 but was eventually forced to pay off his debts and began to subsidise him.

As the invasion of 1335 progressed, Philip VI became increasingly hostile. It is likely that when Randolph returned to Scotland in 1334 the ships that would carry David to France were filled with supplies. Confirmation of French assistance came when a ship was seen unloading wine and armour at Dumbarton. Edward sent clerks to Liverpool and Dartmouth to prepare warships to intercept the French ship on its return journey[75]. An English ship, the *Litle Lechevard,* was captured by Scottish and Norman pirates as she entered the Seine. The master and some of the crew were killed, the cargo looted and the ship scuttled. Despite Edward's complaints that the French were supposed to be neutral, Philip did nothing to redress events.[76]

In July 1335 Philip stepped up the pressure, announcing that he was planning to send a royal army to aid the Scots. Philip wrote to Edward

that the Scots had sought his help, and that as a matter of honour he had
to oblige. At the same time he held out the olive branch: arbitration by
himself and the pope. Edward received the letter at Perth in August. He
replied immediately, rejecting arbitration on the grounds that he had
established peace in Scotland.

Edward heard reports from spies in Norman ports that ships were
being requisitioned for attacks on the south coast of England, a threat
which forced Edward to mobilise shipping in the south. Ships over 40
tons were to be held ready to head-off the invasion fleet, warning
beacons were built along the hills and the coastal forts were made ready.
Reports of a massive fleet began to reach England, but by the time it
arrived, the massive force had dwindled to nine ships. Two disembarked
for a raid, but the English got between them and their boats, and
captured those left aboard. The remaining boats took to flight.

Edward was not alone in realising the threat French aid to Scotland
would pose to the peace of Western Europe. The new pope, Benedict
XII, told Philip that he had not thought through the decision to send
troops to Scotland. He lectured him on the threat of instability that such
a move would create in France, the cost, the cancellation of the crusade
and the probability that Edward would succeed regardless of French
intervention. Besides, Philip's support for one of the protagonists was a
barrier to his attempts to force a reconciliation between Edward III and
David II. Instead the pope appointed two mediators, led by Hugh
d'Aimery who had been employed to try and reconcile Edward II and
Charles VI between 1324 and 1326, to act on his behalf in England.[77]

Bishop d'Aimery did not arrive in Newcastle until 1 November 1335.
The French emissaries were now bystanders, sent to observe. Over the
next two months the talks progressed under the constant threat of
renewed hostilities: Edward would only allow short truces, sometimes
for only a few days. In late November a Scottish delegation, Murray,
Douglas, Robert Lowther and William Keith, came to England where
the talks resumed. By 26 January an outline settlement had been
reached. With his army gathered, Edward accepted a truce that would
let a parliament, set to meet in London in March, study the agreement.
The Scots in turn lifted the sieges at Lochindorb and Cupar, the only
military operations in the country, and sent a party to Château Gaillard
to get David's support.[78]

The settlement was based on Edward Balliol's recognition as king of
Scots, with David II becoming his heir. Edward Balliol's abortive
marriage betrothal to Jeanne Valois in 1295 had been his only recorded
attempt to prolong the Balliol dynasty. He was now middle-aged. His
only brother died childless at Annan. To Edward it seemed the perfect
solution; he was so confident of the settlement that he ordered a survey
of lands that would form the basis of compensation of David Bruce and

his sister, Joan. But when parliament met, the Scottish ambassadors failed to appear, sending instead the news that David II had refused to accept the agreement. English public opinion correctly blamed Philip VI for blocking an agreement that was too much in Edward's interests.

Worse for Edward, Benedict XII came to the conclusion that the French king was not the man to lead the crusade. Recruitment had been poor. Benedict feared the consequences for Christendom of failure in the east. Philip was devastated, his pride dented. Edward could no longer trade his participation in the crusade with French compliance over Scotland and the Agenais. Philip now returned to his plan to restore David II. He directed the Mediterranean fleet, which had been assembled for the crusade, from Marseilles to the Norman Ports. A seaborn expedition was planned on a scale not seen since the high days of the crusade.

Edward III kept a cool head. He appointed Henry of Lancaster to command the army in the north. With Balliol and a small English army of 500 men-at-arms and 600 hobelars or mounted archers he entered Scotland. They met little resistance as they made their way towards Perth. They found the fortifications they had constructed reduced to ashes, so built new works including a mud wall surrounded by a ditch, and made the town their base. Thomas Rosslyn commanded a naval expedition with ships from King's Lynn. Rosslyn was mortally wounded in the resistance to his landing at Dunottar but his men secured the castle and began to rebuild the fortifications.

John Stirling, governor of Edinburgh Castle, relieved Cupar Castle in Fife with an audacious sortie. With a token force of only 40 men-at-arms and 80 archers he secretly crossed the Forth. Burning surrounding villages to make his force appear greater he attacked the nationalist force, while the castle garrison made a simultaneous sortie. Fearing the complete English army, the nationalists took 'instant flight, abandoning their siege engines, arms, stores and all that they had'. After a pursuit to kill or drive away the rebels Stirling returned to Edinburgh.[79]

In June Edward's spies in France brought dramatic news. Philip had met the Scots at Lyon where plans for a French invasion were completed. Walter Tynham and Alexander Seton, two members of David's court, were to travel to Scotland to assume command of the Scottish forces in preparation for a French invasion fleet that was to land on the east coast of Scotland. A combined Franco-Scottish army would invade northern England. This would be combined with naval attacks on the Solent ports.

Edward gambled that the French threat was idle—and he was right. For all Philip's plans the French were not willing to commit major forces to help the Scots. Philip felt unable to levy taxation for a policy that had no direct French interest. He turned to the church for a levy, only to be rebuffed by Benedict for his recklessness. The proposed captain of the armada, the count of Eu, resigned when he realised the implications for his estates in England and Ireland.[80]

Edward III left London on 11 June with 400 men, mostly household troops and the retinue of William Montagu. He moved swiftly all the way to Perth where his sudden arrival was greeted with great surprise. On 12 July, with the addition of Henry of Lancaster's men, he pushed north from Perth.[81]

This dashing raid had as its immediate and gallant purpose the rescue of Katherine Beaumont, widow of David Strathbogie, besieged in the island castle of Lochindorb by Andrew Murray. On 15 July Edward rode 20 miles from Kincardine-on-Spey to take Murray by surprise. Murray was holding mass in the wood of Stronkalter. The English were so close that scouts from both armies came into contact. The traditional story has Murray's lieutenants too frightened to interrupt mass until he had finished. He then told them 'Na hast' as he cut a strip of roe-deer skin to repair his thigh armour, and then led his men away. The story from a contemporary English source, a man on the expedition, tells of the English reaching within two miles of Lochindorb when they came across the Scottish scouts who gave the alarm. The Scottish army then withdrew into Ross.

The king now revealed the real purpose of his race north, and it had nothing to do with chivalrous rescue. He would prevent Moray becoming the springboard for a French invasion. The English held the east coast as far as Dunnottar, 18 miles south of Aberdeen. This was the farthest point south that a French army could disembark in safety. The French would have to supply the army locally rather than risk supply ships passing along the English eastern seaboard. Edward would make sure that they would find nothing standing. He reached Forres and Kinloss on 17 July, razing both to the ground. At Elgin on the 18th he spared only the cathedral. Aberdeen was reached on the 22nd, and in revenge for some English sailors killed in the town, Edward made a personal inspection to make sure no houses remained standing. Crops were trampled down, and on the first day alone 1,000 head of cattle were rounded up and slaughtered. Edward refortified the three neighbouring coastal castles at Dunnottar, Kinneff and Lauriston. He was back in Perth in late July.

John of Eltham arrived in Perth with the Yorkshire levies, reinforced by the men of Northumberland. He had joined Anthony de Lucy with the men of Cumberland and Westmoreland and marched into Carrick and the west of Scotland, continuing the policy of destruction. William Douglas 'hovered craftily on the skirts of the English army, inflicting upon it all the injury he could' without risking a battle.[82] A large part of the army returned home with its plunder when Eltham and his column moved on to Perth to meet up with the king.

At Perth Edward ordered that the town be enclosed with walls and moats: six local monasteries paid for the three main gates. Behind the protection of stout walls, Edward Balliol now stayed in his nominal capital, but a Yorkshire knight, Thomas Ughtred, was installed under Edward's authority as keeper. Henry Beaumont rebuilt the castles at Leuchers and St Andrew; Stirling was rebuilt by William Montagu; Edinburgh (of which only the chapel stood) by John Stirling, and Roxburgh by William Felton.[83]

John of Eltham carried with him news of a Great Council meeting in Northampton in June that he had presided over in the king's absence. The council sought advice from the nobility, and concluded by sending an embassy to France. It was to gauge Philip's hostility, offer an unknown compromise, and—for the first time—to negotiate directly with David II. The ambassadors, the bishops of Durham and Winchester, travelled to France when safe conducts became available. They held bad-tempered meetings with Philip and his council where the questions of the crusade, the restitution of the Agenais, the support for Scotland and the offer to David II were raised. On 20 August Philip announced that their compromise was unacceptable. He planned to assist the Scots in every way he could. War between England and France was now inevitable.

The bishops, startled by Philip's candour, sent a clerk with the news post haste. William Tickhall reached Dover on 23 August, and was at Northampton late on the 24th—a remarkable ride. Here he found Stratford and other senior councillors who immediately summoned a parliament for 23 September, the earliest possible date. Tickhall was told to take the news to Edward in Scotland, but when he arrived at Berwick, he learnt that Lothian had been devastated by William Douglas. Tickhall's bodyguard refused to take him beyond Fife, and there were no ships that could carry him along the coast. The king finally received the message in the second week of September and immediately headed south to take part in the council meeting.

Raids had already begun on the south coast. The parliament organised a huge defensive army. The war in Scotland had already cost Edward dearly; he was paying both for his own army and the one organised for Balliol. Parliament now granted the second fifteenth and a tenth of the year. He borrowed another £100,000 from Italian bankers, a sum of money far in advance of expenditure seen in the wars in Scotland. He raided the chests from cathedrals around the country where the crusading tenth was being stored.[84]

The king now returned to Scotland where he spent the next six weeks. On 18 October he moved to Bothwell castle where the people submitted to his peace. The castle was rebuilt and a garrison put in place. Edward left Scotland in the middle of December.

Throughout his attempts to overwhelm Scotland, Edward had tried to ensure that the alliance between France and Scotland remained a paper one. His patience had been tested with the gradual increase in French interference. Anger at French involvement in Scotland stoked the embers of Anglo-French hostility. English aggression in Scotland certainly contributed to the breakdown in relations between England and France, but this was not the true cause of the Hundred Years' War. The origins of this famous conflict went back many years and were concerned with the feudal relationship of the kings of France and the Plantagenet dukes of Aquitaine, a relationship now tested by the long-running dispute over the Agenais. The centralising policies of the French kings as they attempted to bring fiefs back into the kingdom of France were resented throughout the French regions that owed nominal dependence to France—Aquitaine, Normandy, Flanders, Burgundy and Brittany—but which had developed as autonomous states.

English relations with France had become complicated in 1328 with the death of the last Capetian king, Charles IV—Edward III's uncle. The French magnates elected Philip, count of Valois, ignoring the rights of Charles' nearest male kin, Edward III. Philip was the French candidate, older and more experienced, his degree of kinship close enough (a grandson of Philip III) not to cause concern. Edward's claim was declared invalid as it had passed through a woman.

The peace negotiations between France and England reached deadlock over English claims to the Agenais, which had been ceded to France in the treaty of Saint Sardos. The presence of Robert of Artois in Edward's court from 1336, sheltering from Philip, poisoned Anglo-French relations still further. In April 1337 Edward sent embassies to the continent to begin recruiting allies in the Low Countries. In May, Philip occupied and confiscated Gascony. Hostilities would not begin until the following year, but Edward abandoned the invasion of Scotland in 1337 when he was called south to prepare for a threatened French invasion, and from then on he was preoccupied with the war on the continent. This was the turning point in the war with Scotland.

Bower attributes the change in fortunes to events in France, 'which was cruel and fearful enough, but yet a fortunate thing for Scotland, for if the aforesaid king had continued his war in Scotland, he would (as far as human judgement is concerned) have occupied it wholly and without difficulty'. This is not easily acceptable to many historians, and yet Bower's theory, formulated far closer to the events, should not be dismissed so lightly. In the 1330s Scotland's independence was only narrowly preserved. The disastrous battles of Dupplin and Halidon witnessed a devastation amongst the ruling class unparalleled in medieval warfare. The turnover of guardians was incredible. Moray died in 1332; Mar was killed at Dupplin in August 1332; Andrew

Murray was captured in October 1332; Archibald Douglas was killed at Halidon; John Randolph was captured in 1335; Robert the Steward changed sides in September 1335; Andrew Murray died in 1338. It was a recipe for unstable and anarchic government as the magnates quarrelled and old scores were settled.

Just as during the wars conducted in the reign of Edward I, the majority of Scots merely wanted to survive. They were subsistence farmers. Feeding their families was of far more concern than political issues. They tolerated English garrisons; some helped the patriots, but most left the fighting to a few determined guerrillas. Scotland owes a debt to men such as Alexander Ramsey, James Douglas of Liddesdale and above all Andrew Murray, whose consistent opposition and victory at Culblean gave a massive boost to patriot morale that is rarely acknowledged.[85]

Andrew Murray avoided contact with the English host after Stronkalter. From 1336 until his death two years later he moved from guerrilla war to the expulsion of the English and their Scottish allies. Away from the main centres of English occupation, the Scots began to gain the upper hand. The war now became fragmented and isolated. Contemporaries had a word for this type of warfare, *guerre guerroyante,* 'made up of losses and recaptures, surprises, incursions, ambushes and sallies'.[86] Murray would win back southern Scotland 'part by strength, part by treason, part by famyne'.[87] He made territories uninhabitable for English armies, garrisons or Scots. The war of devastation that Bruce inflicted on the north of England was now copied in Scotland. Great swaths of the country were made desolate. Wherever the field of operations was most intense, as the patriots dislodged the English from one region to the next, ruin followed. It created such a severe famine that many Scots left to live in England, others 'ate pods in the manner of pigs for want of food, and swelling up all over after a short time, they ended their lives wretchedly'. In 1339 the whole of the surrounding area of Perth

> 'was to such a degree laid waste that there was almost no inhabited house left, but wild beasts and deer coming down from the mountains were often hunted around the town. So great then was the dearth and lack of provisions that the common folk were starving everywhere; and eating grass like sheep; they were found dead in pits. Nearby there lurked in a ruined building a certain peasant called Christy Cleke with his fierce woman; they lay in wait for women, children and young people, and after strangling them like a wolf, lived on their flesh.'[88]

Many of the conditions that had denied Edward I victory still pertained: Scotland's geography, aid from the continent, the inability to finance a standing army or find an answer to guerrilla warfare. There was now an added factor. This was no longer a civil war. Ordinary people regarded the disinherited as Englishmen rather than as inheritors of the Comyn party. The indiscriminate devastation, and the appropriation of freeholders, was acknowledged by the Balliol party as the root cause of their unpopularity. They could not obtain the collaboration that had been such an important part of Edward I's wars.

It had taken a massive English military intervention to shore up Balliol's regime, and then only in southern Scotland. Balliol's authority evaporated as soon as the English army marched home for winter. All medieval kings were peripatetic, but none more so than Edward Balliol who only toured his realm on the tails of an English army. His cause was lost. In 1339 Edward even began to pay for his personal bodyguard of 40 men-at-arms.[89]

Edward III's enthusiasm waned. He would take virtually no part in future operations in Scotland. The great armies that three generations of English kings had used to try and subdue southern Scotland were a thing of the past. In September 1338 the exchequer moved south from York to Westminster.[90] The Scottish wars were now secondary to the war in France, which required the marshalling of the realm's resources on an unprecedented scale. Edward would no longer bolster Balliol's kingship. Raids against Balliol's enemies served only to keep the patriots occupied so they could not assault Edward's strongholds. Edward determined to keep the southern counties of Scotland by garrisoning the fortresses, although he did not have the resources to sustain such control.

The weakness in this new strategy was the possibility of a Scottish onslaught on the north of England on the scale accomplished between 1312 and 1327. The king instituted provincial assemblies which became the recruiting agents for northern forces. The northern defences were now far more flexible. The March counties, Northumberland, Cumberland and Westmoreland, supplied troops on a continual basis, in what was rapidly becoming a standing army. Small-scale raids could be dealt with by the March counties, the now mobile forces of hobelars and mounted archers. When tension rose, they were supplemented by men from further south, particularly from the endless recruiting grounds of Yorkshire. Edward meant to finance the Scottish wars from the eight counties north of the Trent. The wealthier south financed the more expensive war in France.

The northern levies were led by indentured border captains, the Percys and Nevilles, families who were given real power and independence to develop the defences in the north of England. The

Percys' territorial advance in Northumberland came by serving Edward III at the expense of the disinherited.[91] The northern lords used their enhanced status to become central to the government of the country, with the power to make or break kings.[92]

When Edward retired to England in October 1336, Murray collected an army to besiege the Kincardine castles at Dunnottar, Kinneff and Lauriston. Without the king's presence Edward's captains were powerless to come to the aid of these poorly supplied, poorly manned outposts. All three castles were taken and levelled. Murray conducted a guerrilla war throughout the winter in Angus, leaving the locality devastated. In February he took and levelled Kinclevin, the fortress north of Perth. Thomas Ughtred returned to the command in Perth where he received reinforcements and supplies in preparation for an attack.[93] He managed to hold his own; an order in February for Neville and Percy to raise the northern militia to go to the town's rescue was rescinded in March. Balliol did not stay in the town.

Murray was joined by Fife, Dunbar and Douglas to reassert patriot authority in Fife. They levelled the forts at Falkland and Leuchars, 'plundered the land everywhere around, took the inhabitants prisoners, and put them up for ransom'. St Andrews was besieged for three weeks with the siege engine *Bourstar* or 'buster'. The castle surrendered on the last day of February. *Bourstar* was then transported to Bothwell. Without its warden, Robert de Ufford, the newly created Earl of Suffolk, the garrison surrendered while they still could in return for safe-conduct. The castle was 'scattered from the foundations'. Only William Bullock at Cupar was able to resist *Bourstar's* persuasion.[94]

Edward now needed two armies. He sent one under William Montagu to Gascony, another under Warwick to Scotland with the northern host. Warwick's force never amounted to more than 3,500 men.[95] This attempt to put two armies in the field in two countries requiring the division of the household was foolishly optimistic.

In late May 1337 Murray began to besiege Stirling Castle. Edward rushed to the border by forced marches in the forlorn hope that the Scots would offer battle. They would do nothing of the sort and lifted the siege after making a final bid to take the castle by assault. Edward reinforced the castle, then abandoned the invasion to return south with the wounded to prepare English defences against the threat of invasion from France.

The summer progressed with small-scale raid and counter raid. In September the bishop of Carlisle, Wake, and Clifford drew a levy from the west to raid Galloway. They combined forces with Warwick and marched through Teviotdale, Moffatdale and Nithsdale. Anthony de Lucy led a detachment into Galloway. Poor weather and flooded rivers prevented their progress north. When they returned to England and disbanded, Murray led a retaliatory raid through Coquetdale and Redesdale where Umfraville led a 'bold' resistance. But the raid was fruitless; most livestock had already been driven off for safety. A second raid in October skirted Carlisle. The bishop's palace at Rose Castle was destroyed for his part in the raid earlier in the year. The arrival of Percy and Neville pushed the raiders back over the border after only three days. A brother of William Douglas was captured but nothing could be done to save the booty, which had been sent off in advance.

Towards the end of the year, Murray turned to the siege of Edinburgh castle. The bishop of Carlisle called up the host for Cumberland and Westmoreland. He met up with forces from the east led by Lucy and Balliol with the Berwick garrison. Murray broke off the siege and met the relief column at Crichton, where an inconclusive engagement saw many slain on both sides.[96]

Warwick's term as captain of the March ended in November. William Montagu and Arundel, accompanied by Hugh Audley, were appointed in October to lead a new army. Montagu and Audley had been created earls of Salisbury and Gloucester respectively in a rash of promotions in March 1337. The king wanted a broader base of military leaders to fight on two fronts.

Dunbar castle was 'irksome and oppressive to the whole district of Lothian'. It was here that the English decided to concentrate their attack, as the castle's capture would ease the pressure on Lothian. The siege began on 13 January and lasted for 22 weeks. At any one time 50 miners and 50 carpenters were employed. Siege engines were brought from Berwick and the tower of London, and two Genoese galleys armed with crossbowmen blockaded the castle from the sea. The formidable countess of Dunbar, 'Black Agnes,' (apparently a description of her complexion) the sister of Randolph led the castle's defences. The countess was active in the defence of the castle. She apparently showed 'manly feelings', 'ridiculed the invaders wittily with gestures and words', and wiped the walls hit by the English engines with a napkin.[97]

William Montagu was forced to leave with a detachment to rescue Edinburgh. John Stirling had ventured out of the castle with two or three knights and 20 men-at-arms, but had been captured by William Douglas. Douglas brought his prisoners before Edinburgh's walls, threatening to draw Stirling between the tails of two horses and then to behead him if the castle did not surrender. The garrison, though offered safe-conduct, asserted that it was Edward's castle, not Stirling's, and that they would stay put. It was an idle threat: Stirling was sent to Dumbarton. Montagu raised the siege, installed a new warden and returned to Dunbar. The English attempted the same trick at Dunbar, when they brought John Randolph from captivity in Nottingham. 'Black Agnes' replied 'if ye do that, then I shall be heir to the earldom of

Moray', in the face of which the English were forced to take him back.[98]

Edward was now in the final stages of preparations for taking his army to the low countries. Many of those in the English army at Dunbar hungered to go with him. The Scots sought a truce which the English were only too willing to accept as it enabled them to extricate themselves from a siege that had left them weary but could not be abandoned without loss of face. Montagu then left to fight with Edward on the continent. Amongst those who went with him was Henry Beaumont, who saw the chance of greater rewards elsewhere. He died in the Low Countries in 1340.

Andrew Murray, the guardian, died in the spring of 1338. Architect of the Scottish recovery, it had been Murray who cleared the disinherited and their English allies from north of the Forth in all but Cupar and Perth. Fordun identifies his abilities as a great commander, but his eulogy is tinged with sorrow for the regions he passed through 'reduced to such desolation and distress, that more perished afterwards through starvation and want, than the sword devoured in time of war'.[99] Robert the Steward now became guardian for his second term in office. He had shown little flair for fighting or government, going largely unnoticed since his short flirtation with the English in 1335. A man 'young in years [22] but old in deeds'. Murray had already completed the hard work— the English were in retreat. With a truce in place until Michaelmas 1339 the Steward had plenty of time to plan operations.

North of the Forth the English still held Cupar in Fife and Perth, in the south Edinburgh, Stirling, Berwick, Roxburgh, Jedburgh and Lochmaben. When the truce came to an end the castles still in English or disinherited control could be reduced.

Perth was the first target. The siege here may have been the initiative of David II. Douglas visited the king in France and returned with French mercenaries. A hired pirate, Hugh Hampyle blockaded the Tay with five heavily armed barges. The Steward, with Patrick Dunbar, Ross and Maurice Moray, later earl of Strathearn, began the siege in June 1339. Balliol was ordered to England for his own safety. He was part of a 1200-strong relief force of Cumberland and Westmoreland hobelars, but the town fell before any action could be taken.[100] *Lanercost* says that the siege lasted five weeks 'without much fighting'. Bower, perhaps milking the literary tension, contradicts this, asserting that assaults were made on the town nearly every day for 22 weeks.

The town's governor, Thomas Ughtred surrendered on 17 August after Ross's miners drained the surrounding moat: the defenders embarked on ships to England 'amid much jeering'. It was Douglas who took Cupar, which was commanded by Edward Balliol's chamberlain and lieutenant, William Bullock. Bullock handed over the castle in return for a grant of lands. He became David's chamberlain instead, but

fell from grace when suspected of treason and was later imprisoned by
David Barclay.

A siege at Stirling was lifted in October when Balliol arrived with a
border force.[101] Under the steward's guardianship there was now a
downturn in military activity. This may partly be explained by a serious
injury, a bolt from a crossbow in his thigh, that Douglas sustained at
Perth.

Edward and Philip made a truce in September 1340 at Esplechin. The
Scots had the right to accede to the peace, and it is unclear whether they
decided to exercise that right (and the capture of castles was in breach
of the peace), or whether they decided to fight on. Unlike the truce made
in 1343 at Malestroit, it is likely that the war in Scotland was governed
by short-term truces of local origin, which were open to abuse and
misinterpretation. The leaders in Scotland sent a message to Edward
asking if one such truce was to stand or not.[102]

In late 1340, after five years in captivity, John Randolph gained his
freedom from Edward III in return for the release of William Montagu,
captured in France, by Philip VI. The first months of his release were
spent in France on matters of his ransom, but when he returned to
Scotland in the summer of 1341 he launched a new Scottish offensive'.[103]
When he returned to Scotland he found his castle at Lochmaben
occupied by William Bohun and launched a raid on Annandale.
Randolph received the custody of the West March from Robert Steward
to expel the English, William Douglas the Middle March and Alexander
Ramsey the East.[104]

Edinburgh fell on 16 April 1341. The captain, expecting supplies
from a ship moored at Inchkeith, opened the castle gates to William
Bullock, disguised as a merchant, with twelve armed men. They cut the
gatekeeper's throat, jammed opened the portcullis with a stake and blew
a trumpet as a signal for William Douglas to appear from his hiding
place. Despite a vigorous fight from the garrison, the castle was taken.
Douglas went from here to recover Teviotdale.[105]

* * *

David II had accompanied the king of France to resist Edward's invasion
of Flanders, but had not taken part in any action when Philip retired
with his army. In 1341 he was 17 years old, an age by which he might be
expected to take on the reigns of government. The recapture of
Edinburgh signalled that his realm was ready for his return. Relations
between Randolph and the Steward had not been improved in the years
of Randolph's captivity. Now he was free, the political situation
demanded an end to the Steward's regency. The king crossed the north
sea secretly with his queen and landed at Inverbervie on 2 June 1341.

Within weeks of his return, he led raids into northern England, emulating his father's actions. In the first he travelled incognito, under Randolph's banner. The raid reached Heddon Laws, west of Newcastle, on 26 August 1341.[106] It brought Edward north. He spent Christmas at Melrose, 'exposed to much danger by cunning assaults of the Scots'.[107] William Douglas captured his provisions and used them to supply Hermitage Castle. Henry of Grosmont, earl of Derby was now Edward's lieutenant in the north.

* * *

A series of truces, the first for six months, beginning in December 1341 kept military activity to a minimum. Edward departed from Melrose 'half in a melancholy with them that movid him to that jornay'.[108] To while away the time, Grosmont organised a series of tournaments. The first, with William Douglas at Roxburgh had to be abandoned when Douglas injured his hand from a broken lance in the first tilt. Grosmont challenged Alexander Ramsey, reputedly one of the best knights in Scotland, to a second tournament in January 1342. Two English and two Scottish knights died during the three-day tournament.

When Grosmont disbanded his force in early February David II led a raid under his own banner. A third raid reached the Tyne in the summer of 1342.

Balliol's position collapsed throughout Scotland, with the exception of the south-west. After the defection of Duncan Macdouall in 1334, Eustace Maxwell, lord of Caerlaverock castle, became Balliol's key supporter in Galloway. Balliol went to some lengths to safeguard his loyalty, making him Sheriff of Dumfries in 1335, but he went over to the Scots, shortly after Edward III had resupplied him with money, flour and wine. Now both Macdouall and Maxwell returned to Balliol's allegiance, together with a local chieftain, Michael M'Ghie. What motivated these men, when Balliol's fortunes had sunk so low, is unknown. Balliol was able to return to Galloway and built a fortification on the island of Heston, captained by Macdouall. It was the Indian summer of Balliol's kingship.

In 1341 David made his long-time companion, Malcolm Fleming, earl of Wigtown; one of a number of promotions of his supporters in the south-west to displace the region's natural leaders. William Douglas was granted the lands of the Moubray family; a Fergus Macdouall received the Moubray barony of Brogue. His relationship with Duncan Macdouall is unknown, but the award seems to have been an attempt to divide the loyalties of the family.[109]

In the spring of 1342 the last English-held strongholds outside Berwick, Jedburgh and Lochmaben fell. In April 1342 Stirling capitulated with little more than a whimper from England. The constable, Thomas Rokeby, surrendered following a six-month siege.

On the dawn of 30 March, Alexander Ramsey and his men scaled Roxburgh castle's walls with ladders, surprised the guards, who were slaughtered, and took the castle. David granted Ramsey the custody of the castle, which clashed with William Douglas's interests on the border. The two men met in Hawick church, Douglas abducted Ramsey, and took him in chains to his castle at Hermitage where he was starved to death over seventeen days. David attempted to have Douglas arrested. The crime was only remitted on the intercession of Douglas's ally, the steward. The episode was only closed in 1353, when Douglas was murdered by his godson, William Douglas, later first Earl Douglas. William Bullock, David's chamberlain, was accused of treason and led away by David Barclay to a castle on Lochindorb, where he suffered a similar fate. These Scottish feuds help explain the peace on the border from 1343-4.[110]

Suffering reverses in France, Edward III accepted a three-year truce with Philip VI organised by the papacy at Malestroit in January 1343. It would last until September 1346. In Scotland the truce was ill-observed, interspersed with raid and counter raid.

John of the Isles and Ranald MacRuaridh made concords with David II in 1343, settling the Western Highlands. John of the Isles was described as an ally of Edward III in the treaty of Berwick in 1357, but he seems to have been on good terms with both sides.[111] In 1345 Duncan Macdouall reverted once again. He brought with him Balliol's stronghold on Heston. He had been under pressure despite supplies from England, and could probably have held the castle, but he could not stomach the slow loss of his ancestral lands.

Macdouall's desertion brought a swift response from the English. William de Dyfford and Thomas de Lucy took Heston from the sea, capturing Macdouall with his family. He remained in the tower for two years before being released to support Balliol; his family remained to guarantee his loyalty. Balliol himself remained in Galloway for most of 1346 on another isolated stronghold of Burned Isle on Loch Ken. He could do little but watch the raids on the lordship from John Kennedy and Alan Stewart, operating from Carrick.[112]

* * *

War was renewed on both fronts in 1346. Edward III landed in Normandy with an army of 15,000 men. He sacked Caen and marched along the Seine towards Paris. On 26 August the French finally gave battle at Crécy, and Edward won one of the most decisive victories of the medieval period. Edward then turned north to begin the siege of Calais.

Once Edward III's intentions became known in France, Philip wrote to David twice, in June and July 1346, pressing him to create a diversion in the north. David did not need persuading—he longed to fight the English. His confidence was bolstered by the knowledge that Edward III had left England with the bulk of the country's fighting men. He believed only 'priests, friars and clerks, craftsmen and tradesmen' lay between him and London; the country was 'weakened in fighting-strength, devoid of men and destitute of all help'.[113] This impression was reinforced when he led an unopposed raid in July under the Randolph's banner through Cumberland, Derwent and over Aldstone Moor.[114]

On 6 October David gathered an army from all parts of the kingdom, a rare example of a national effort, for a *wapinschaw* at Perth. The English estimated he had 12,000 men, many armed with weapons supplied from France. Ross abandoned the king when he became implicated in the murder of a rival, Ranald MacRuaridh. But the king refused to be derailed by the dispute, 'impelled by pride and led by the devil'; he invaded England.

The army made its way to Thomas Wake's border peel of Castleton in Liddesdale on the confluence of the Esk and Liddel. William Douglas arrived in the morning, David in the evening. They wasted three days laying siege to this pitifully small target. A general assault began when the ditches were filled with beams and house timbers, earth, stones and fascines. Protected by the shields of the men-at-arms, a detachment broke through the bottom of the walls and entered the fort. The governor, Walter Selby, a supporter of Robert Bruce in 1318, pleaded to die in single combat; but David would have none of it—Selby was beheaded, and his son taken prisoner.[115]

An English source points to an earlier siege by Douglas and Randolph that had to be abandoned when the two men quarrelled. It may be that the king now intervened, on Douglas's behalf as lord of Liddesdale, to take the castle. Once it fell, Douglas attempted to persuade the king that his commitment to the French had been fulfilled, and it was time to turn his army around. David's commanders, jealous of their colleague, counselled that Douglas had been enriched by English spoil and was acting in his own self-interest by denying the other Scots access to English booty.

Carlisle was ripe for picking. The castle buildings had decayed. A report in 1345 found a garrison of eight men-at-arms and seven hobelars with few weapons. On 25 September the town only had food for three weeks.[116] But instead of concentrating his attack here, David accepted a heavy indemnity and moved on: Durham and Yorkshire promised still richer pickings.

It was already clear that David had no strategic objective. From Liddesdale the army moved to sack the priory at Lanercost and then moved along the Tyne valley. Hexham priory was despoiled, but the king ordered that Hexham, Corbridge, Darlington and Durham should not be burnt so that they could provide food and shelter for the army as winter approached. A section of the army may have moved as far along the Tyne as Ryton but this was not along the line of march. After three days at Hexham, the army crossed the Tyne and moved south to Ebchester before reaching Bearpark, near Durham, on 16 October. They were now short of rations, so raiding parties were sent into the surrounding countryside as the king waited for the priors to bring £1,000 protection money, payable two days later.

As the Scottish army loitered in the north, the local English commanders, the two march captains Neville and Percy with William Zouche, Archbishop of York, were assembling a scratch force that mustered at Richmond. Besides the local levies from the border counties and Durham, expected to serve in defence of the north without pay, forces were raised in Lancashire and Yorkshire. They had perhaps 3-4,000 men. The archbishop decided not to wait for the Yorkshire contingent, another 3,000 who were expected to catch up.[117]

On 14 October the army moved north along the 'straight road' (A66) behind St Cuthbert's corporeal cloth, carried into battle by the *Haliwerfolk*. They reached Barnard Castle the next day and took up a defensive position on a hill behind the castle. The army was now in the three-division battle formation in which it would meet the Scots. Henry Percy commanded the van, with Gilbert de Umfraville and Ralph Neville. John de Moubray, Thomas Rokeby and John Copeland led the second division. Behind them lay the archbishop's division. On the 16th they moved to Bishop Auckland, only nine miles south of the Scots.

During the night the English forces moved north to Merrington, Ferryhill and then Sunderland Bridge. The Scots had no idea of the force sent against them until they made contact by accident on the morning of 17 October. Douglas led a 500-strong raiding party south towards Merrington. As he returned, a thick fog developed. At Sunderland Bridge the Scots could hear the 'trampling of horses and shock of armoured men' but could not see the English. Panic set into the ranks. In the dense fog Douglas had stumbled into the columns led by Rokeby and the Archbishop. Douglas fled with heavy losses.

Douglas returned to the camp and warned the king of the approach of an English army. David was unruffled: 'There are no men in England but wretched monks, lewd priests, swineherd, cobblers and skinners. They dare not face me: I am safe enough.' The king ordered the fringes on his standard to be made larger and his breakfast to be made ready, declaring that he would return to eat when he had slain the English. He made no effort to move to more favourable ground.

The armies arrayed for battle over a wide area a little north of Neville's Cross. They faced each other with similar formations, the Scots having adopted English tactics with archers on the wings of each battle.

Randolph and Douglas led the first division on the west, opposite

Percy and Neville. The king's division in the centre faced Rokeby; on the east Patrick Dunbar and Robert the Steward faced the archbishop. The armies remained in position from about nine or ten in the morning, but the action did not begin until the afternoon. The battles of Dupplin and Halidon had both been won by the defence, and it seems both armies were waiting for the other to attack.

Irritated by the delay, the English archers moved forward. The Scottish short bow proved no match for the English long bow. John Graham was refused a troop of lancers to break up the archers and, in a fit of anger, went forward alone until his horse was killed by an arrow. The earl had to run back to his own lines.

Under a hail of arrows, the Scottish divisions were goaded to attack, heads down to protect themselves from the English archers. Randolph's first division lost their formation when they had to climb over the dikes that bisected the field. Their numbers were so depleted by the time they reached the English lines that they were quickly dispatched by the men-at-arms.

As they watched the first division being mauled by the archers, Robert the Steward and March decided that discretion was the better part of valour and fled with their men, 'without a single wound'. The king's division faced the English alone.

King David displayed great personal valour before surrendering to John Copeland, a Northumbrian esquire, but not before he had knocked out two of the captor's front teeth. The king was seriously wounded from two arrows. The first was extracted by two barber-surgeons brought from York, at Bamburgh where he was sent to recover after the battle. He still had a piece of metal in his head, which gave him headaches during a full moon, when the chronicler Froissart visited the Scottish court in 1365.

The battle of Neville's Cross was another disaster for the Scots. Randolph, Strathearn, the constable, the chancellor and Robert Keith the marischal were killed. Another four earls were captured: Duncan of Fife, John Graham of Menteith, William of Sutherland and Malcolm of Wigtown, together with William Douglas. The Yorkshire contingent, making its way north, never reached the battle site and was paid off on 16 October, the Lancashire men on the 17th. They had only received four days' pay—the total campaign only cost the king £307, which was more than offset by the value of the ransoms.

Chapter 11

DAVID II'S CAPTIVITY,

The capture of David II presented Edward III with a dilemma. He was worth far more as King of Scotland if he was recognised as such by the English, but Edward still nominally supported his ally, Edward Balliol. For a time, England recognised two kings of Scotland, before Balliol was pushed to one side. With David in captivity and Randolph killed at Neville's Cross, the Scots had little choice other than to appoint the Steward as guardian; but the experience of his two terms of office had taught him nothing of leadership. His rule was noted for the territorial advance of his family and the collapse of central authority. Thomas Gray, author of the *Scalacronica*, wrote while in captivity in Edinburgh castle of the envy amongst the lords and their destructive competition to outdo their rivals 'for every one rulid yn his owne cuntery'.[1] The Steward was the man with most to lose from David's release, so his foreign policy consisted of frustrating increasingly desperate attempts by the king to gain his freedom.

Buoyed by his successes at Neville's Cross and Crécy, Edward's primary aim during 1347 was to convert the victories into territorial gains. He left England with an army of 32,000 men, the largest mustered during the Hundred Years' War, to renew the siege of Calais. That he felt able to take so many of the kingdom's fighting men was due to the security of his northern border.

Henry Percy and Ralph Neville, contracted to bring 180 men-at-arms and 180 mounted archers between them, were hired to serve under Edward Balliol for a year.[2]

It was not until May 1347 that Balliol was given a last opportunity to recover his realm but, with only 3,360 troops, hardly the means to achieve it. He led a force from Carlisle and recovered much of the English districts lost in the previous ten years: the sheriffdoms of Berwick, Roxburgh, Peebles, Dumfries and the forests of Jedburgh, Selkirk and Ettrick. The Scots had refortified the castles at Edinburgh and Stirling. With such a small force and no siege train, Balliol balked at crossing the Forth, so let the Scots buy a truce for the considerable sum of £9,000 until 9 September.[3]

This half-hearted invasion was Balliol's last attempt to secure Scotland. Balliol's failure to take any of the strategic strongholds except those along the border meant he was unable to hold the countryside. Over the next ten years the 'lordes of Scotland, by a litle and a litle, won al that they had lost at the bataille of Duresme'.[4]

The army returned to England after repairing Heston, where Balliol remained. For a short time, as Scottish forces recovered from Neville's Cross, Balliol's possession of Galloway was very real. During the long truce he used his time to restore his position. He moved from the isolated Heston to his family fortress at Buittle, which was strengthened. As late as September 1347 Balliol was resident in John Maxwell's castle when Maxwell surrendered to Northampton.[5] But it was temporary. It was the last foothold of the Balliol party in Scotland.

Edward succeeded in taking Calais, then made a new truce with Philip that included the Scots. Edward's campaigns had overstretched his means to pay for them. His subjects, many made rich by the Crécy campaign, wanted time to repose, and his allies in Europe abandoned him.

Catastrophe loomed over Europe. While Edward completed the siege of Calais, the Black Death appeared in Constantinople and spread to southern France. In August 1348 the plague reached England. Estimates of fatalities over the next two years vary; recent research points to mortality as high as 50 per cent. The plague barely touched the nobility, but it deprived them of manpower and income: rents fell, land was left uncultivated, and the cost of labour rose sharply. Under such conditions there was no serious warfare and would be none for nearly ten years. Europe was too exhausted to fight.

Scotland escaped the plague until its remorseless progress reached the borders in 1350. At first this respite was thought to be divine intervention; the plague was seen as the 'foul death of England'. The Scots 'are greatly cheered by the pestilence', wrote the Berwick burgesses seeking help from the king when reports of preparations to mount a siege reached the town. The Scots gathered an army in Ettrick forest to exploit the weakened border when the plague struck for the first time, amongst the ranks of the soldiers.[6]

Edward III had learned from painful experience that the real value of captives came from their captivity, not their ransoms. When news was brought to him at Calais of the victory at Neville's Cross, he sent instructions that all the prisoners were to be sent into the king's custody to the Tower of London. David was taken to London in February, where he was paraded through the streets on a black charger. The Tower would be his home for the next eleven years.

David's captor, John Copeland, was rewarded with a pension of £500 per year, promotion to the rank of banneret and a royal pardon for all homicides and felonies he had committed during his life. Others fared less well. Some of the captors came to private agreements with their captives, colluding in their 'escapes' rather than surrendering them to the king. Malcolm Fleming was allowed to stay at Bothal castle where he recovered from the injuries he sustained during the battle. He escaped without paying ransom.[7]

Menteith and Fife were both tried for treason on the king's record, without possibility of offering a defence. Edward's vindictiveness to these two earls sprang from their personal debt to the king. Menteith, who had been sworn to Edward's privy council, was hanged, drawn and quartered in London in 1347. Fife was spared by reason of his kinship to Edward (he was a great-grandson of Edward I). The king might also have figured he would be worth a better ransom.[8]

In 1347 David summoned his confessor and his doctor to London. This was the only contact with Scotland; there was no attempt by David's nephew to redeem the king or even to seek terms for his release. The initiative fell to David. A fellow captive, William Ramsey, travelled to Scotland and returned in January 1348 seeking safe-conducts for an embassy. This four-man party arrived in London in April 1347 but made no headway while Edward was still basking in the glow of victory at Crécy and Neville's Cross. Edward saw the possibility of reviving his claim to overlordship. A second, smaller, embassy in October had the same result but managed to secure an extension of the truce.

In 1350 David appealed for help from Pope Clement VI.[9] The appeal, taken by two Scottish knights, was recorded by a notary at the curia. It is divided into two parts. The first exposes David's plight—he complained that he had been in captivity for four years, he had been despoiled of his goods (a literary invention) and had no means to pay his ransom. The second highlights the excessive demands Edward was making for his release: homage; military service against the French; attendance at English parliaments; restoration of the disinherited; recognition of Edward III, or one his sons, as David's heir if he died childless; and custody of Scottish castles as surety. It seems likely that these were the terms set before the embassies two years earlier. They are confirmed by a memorandum dated November-December 1350 'of things to show Sir Ralph'. Its details were too secret to write down, but the use of the subject's initials leave little room for doubt about the contents. It concerns an agreement 'reasonable to one party and the other' that '[EB] will not agree to'.

The memorandum's most likely recipient, 'Sir Ralph' is Ralph Neville, who was charged with persuading Balliol to waive his objections. Neville was instructed to inform Balliol of the 'new offers of DB [David Bruce] and WD [William Douglas of Liddesdale]'. Balliol's objections carry, somewhat surprisingly, enough weight for the king to send assurances of 'the truce for EB's lifetime if he will not agree'. The king adds the caveat that 'all these things depend upon whether DB can carry out what he has promised'. The memorandum takes some explaining. In the middle of 1350 two groups came to York from Scotland, the first led by the king's cousin Thomas of Mar, the second an embassy of the king's friends. They both bear the signs of an initiative of David II rather than official embassies from the government. At York they held discussions with prominent northern lords. Shortly afterwards, William Douglas was released with proposals for David's ransom, which he took to Scotland. Douglas's captivity had been made more comfortable in early 1350.[10] He was now an agent of both David II and Edward III. The proposal centred on the recognition of Edward III's son, John of Gaunt, as heir to David II. Balliol was privy to these negotiations and was now kicking up a fuss.

The final terms were taken by Douglas to Scotland and debated in a general council chaired by the steward. They are composed of a ransom of £40,000 (after the first instalment Edward would release the castles and lands he controlled), restoration of the disinherited, and the promotion of a younger son of the English king to become David's heir if he died childless.

Edward wanted peace with Scotland, although not at any price, so he could continue the war with France. He was willing to forgo every English demand regarding homage and English overlordship, but he needed some compensation if he was to sell the agreement to the English public. England would guarantee Scottish independence under a Plantagenet king. John of Gaunt (David's nephew by marriage) would replace David's nephews by blood (the Steward and Sutherland) as heirs if David died childless. David has had a bad press ever since, but he was not being unpatriotic, Scotland would be served by saving the burden of a heavy ransom; the 'solution rose out of an appreciation ... that it protected the identity and separate standing of a Scottish kingdom whose territorial integrity had been restored'.[11] Besides, David was still a young man who hoped to have a son.

The two men who would lose under the treaty were Edward Balliol and David's heir, Robert the Steward. David had no qualms about disinheriting his nephew; he had not forgiven the Steward for his flight from Neville's Cross, a disgrace compounded by his self-serving inactivity regarding the king's release.

Both the Steward and Balliol sought help from France. The Steward kept in close contact with the French, sending an embassy to warn of the danger of a Plantagenet inheritance. Four of John II's replies survive. They indicate that the Steward presented John with a 'doomsday scenario' of the military defeat and expulsion of his Scottish allies. John offered a secure refuge and military aid in the event of an invasion. Edward Balliol had also reserved a French option; in an unholy anti-David alliance he was in contact with both the Scots and the French.

John offered Balliol the restoration of his lands in France if he made peace with the Scots.

Douglas returned to London in early March 1351 with details of the Scottish response. On the 7th, safe-conducts were granted for a Scottish embassy, including March, four bishops, and Erskine, to attend a conference at Hexham on 24 April—the location underscores the willingness of Edward to do everything he could to reach a settlement. Douglas would also attend, and the English representatives were named. One of Edward Balliol's closest companions, William Aldeburgh, received a safe-conduct to go to England in January. He was told of the agreement on 4 March and the next day Balliol was summoned to attend the Hexham conference. The Scottish embassy never came: it is likely that once Douglas had left it was blocked by the Steward.

In a bid to overrule the Steward's authority David called a parliament, which met in Dundee in May 1351. The parliament now appointed an embassy, four bishops, four earls and four knights, to go to Newcastle to enter negotiations. They completed their work in August, and on 4 September Edward announced that an agreement had been reached. The articles for the agreement are in two parts. The first are those demanded by the Scots: the restoration of occupied lands, waiving of any ransom for David II, a 1000-year truce (to save the English conceding Scottish independence, although the agreement provided that Scotland would be held 'without demanding anything of it'). The second part comprises the English demands: a military force to serve Edward, the restoration of the disinherited who would recompense the present holders, and finally the promotion of John of Gaunt as David's heir. The English moved some way on this point, promising that in the event of dissension the matter could be settled in Scotland.

In November 1351 David was given temporary release to go to Scotland and present the proposal to a Scottish parliament that met in February 1352. 'With one consent, in one voice', the parliament declared its willingness to pay a ransom but not to be subject to the king of England. Edward reserved a military option, based on an uprising of Scots loyal to David under the leadership of William Douglas and he told his Scottish supporters to be ready to assist him. The possibility of a war between the supporters of the Steward, backed by the French, and those of David II backed by Edward III was a real possibility in 1352. In the end David declined to win Edward's war for him, accepting his parliament's decision. By 16 May he was back in the tower. The project was abandoned in favour of a ransom. As a footnote, John of Gaunt's son, Henry Bolinbroke, who would have become king of Scots, usurped the English throne in 1399 to become Henry IV.

William Douglas of Liddesdale was released after his long captivity by allying himself with Edward III. He subsequently held Hermitage

Castle for Edward. In a kingdom riven with inter-noble feuds, an old ghost returned to haunt him. His godson, another William, son of Archibald Douglas, returned from France to claim the inheritance that William had usurped. The younger Douglas murdered Douglas of Liddesdale in Ettrick forest in August 1353. Douglas quickly asserted his authority in the west of Scotland and moved into Galloway where he won Duncan Macdouall back to Scottish allegiance.[1]

Negotiations resumed in 1353 along more traditional lines. In April 1354 English and French embassies concluded terms at Guînes that would result in John II renouncing the Franco-Scottish alliance. It was a hopelessly ambitious agreement which, if sealed, would have left Scotland isolated. It was under this threat that a draft treaty was made at Berwick in July 1354. David would be ransomed for 90,000 marks, paid over nine years, during which time there would be a truce. David was sent north in readiness for his release but the Scots prevaricated, delaying ratification until they knew the outcome of the talks at Avignon in January 1355 that would finalise the Guînes treaty. When the Avignon talks collapsed, the Steward scuppered the treaty in favour of military activity on behalf of the French.[13]

The steward was encouraged to re-open the conflict by King John II who commissioned 'Sire de Garencières' with 60 sturdy men-at-arms and 40,000 gold 'moutons' that would be distributed amongst the magnates on condition that they broke their truce with England.[14] The Scottish chronicler, John Fordun, describes the barons as 'led away, by lust for gold'. The money was left in Flanders until Garencières secured a promise that the Scots re-enter the war. It was handed over to a Scottish agent in Bruges in September.[15]

Fearing trouble in the north, Edward summoned an army to Newcastle in July and August. It was enough to secure a truce. He then lowered his guard, crossing the channel at the end of October with many northern magnates including the keeper of Berwick. It seems likely that the truce he secured with Earl Douglas was not acceptable to Patrick Dunbar. There was certainly antipathy between the two men; in April Douglas gave the earl of Northampton free reign to make forays into Dunbar's lands and in October Dunbar raided Norham. A counter-raid was ambushed. Few were killed but a French knight bought some of the English captives, led them away and had them beheaded in revenge for the death of his father in France. It was in this action that Thomas Gray of Heton, the author of the *Scalacronica*, was captured. He would spend his time in Edinburgh, 1355-7, as a prisoner compiling his chronicle.[16]

On 1 November Thomas Stewart, Dunbar and Garencières launched a raid on Berwick, landing from ships in the dead of night. At dawn William Towers scaled the walls at the Cowgate. They overcame fierce resistance from the town's garrison and took the Douglas Tower, part of the castle's defences, but could not take the castle itself where many of the English retreated.[17] John Copeland attempted to retake the town with a border force but was repelled. With this victory, Garencières returned to France.

Edward learnt of the capture of Berwick as he stepped ashore on his return from Calais and immediately began making preparations to take an army north. When the host reached Berwick, the citizens begged for mercy; there were too few men in the town to withstand a siege, while poor supplies and dissension amongst the magnates made relief unlikely.

Edward moved from Berwick to quarter at Roxburgh. On 20 January Edward Balliol appeared 'like a raging lion'. Balliol had paid little part in Scottish politics since Neville's Cross. Galloway was now mostly devastated or under Scottish control. In 1354 he had even lost his castle in Buittle, his 'last toe-hold in Scotland'. With an endearing sense of drama he lifted the crown from his head, took a handful of Scottish soil and handed them to Edward as formal resignation of his rights to the Scottish crown to the English king. He was too old and too dejected to continue a struggle that had been lost twenty years earlier. He resigned his rights to the kingdom to Edward in return for a gift of 5,000 marks and a generous pension of £2,000 a year. The chroniclers are completely silent over the character of the man who held centre stage for a brief time in the Anglo-Scottish conflict. After this, he all but disappears from the official record, making re-appearances as a serial poacher in Yorkshire. He died at Doncaster in 1364.[18]

The steward attempted to reopen negotiations, but Edward was determined on a show of strength.[19] Edward led what was to be his last military expedition in Scotland, a campaign known by the devastation his men caused as 'Burnt Candlemas'. He agreed a short truce to let the Lothian men decide whether to accept his lordship, but cancelled it when he found they were just using the time to remove their goods to safety. He crossed the Lammermuirs and spent ten days waiting for his supply fleet in Haddington, where the Franciscan friary was burnt. His ships disembarked men to pillage Whitekirk, but were prevented from entering the Forth by contrary winds. The king set off through Lothian in early February, burning anything that stood, reaching Edinburgh before making his way back to England.

A new truce was arranged between the English council and Douglas and William Ramsey, who later fought on the French side at Poitiers in 1356. The English victory at Poitiers and the capture of the French king proved decisive for Anglo-Scottish relations. Edward sent instructions to the Black Prince that the Scots were to be excluded from the negotiations with France.[20] The capture of the king of France triggered virtual anarchy in his kingdom. The Scots had no option but to sue for peace before Edward rekindled his ideas of overlordship in Scotland.

At the beginning of 1357 Robert the Steward presided over a full council at Perth that sent an embassy under Bishop Landallis of St Andrews. He was in London in May where an indenture, amounting to a draft treaty, was concluded.[21] Final negotiations took place in Berwick in late September, David arrived at the town on the 28th, and a treaty was sealed on 3 October 1357.[22] David was liberated for 100,000 marks, payable in ten annual instalments. A truce would exist until the final payment was made and would apply to Edward's allies, Edward Balliol and John of the Isles. Nine of the leading men of the realm, including the Steward, were named as hostages in the event of default, to go to England on a three-man rota.

The hostages were never demanded nor delivered. Two days later David ratified the treaty and was freed. David remained at peace with England for the rest of his reign. The treaty settled no points of issue between England and Scotland; it was merely the contract for the payment of a ransom, but it secured a truce that would last 27 years. Edward III would not renounce the claim to Scotland: he could not disinherit his descendants. The truce gave him money and freedom to manoeuvre in France and allowed him to reduce the border garrisons to a token force, releasing experienced soldiers for the continent.

The ransom was a heavy burden on a poor country. When the ransom had not been paid for two years, David went to London to renegotiate the terms of the treaty. He offered the restoration of the heirs of the disinherited, and named Edward, or one of his sons, as his heir if he died childless, with the proviso that England and Scotland would remain distinct realms. The Scottish estates met to discuss the proposals in March 1364 and threw them out, pointing out that they would rather pay the ransom. A new agreement was reached in May 1365, the obligation raised to £100,000 but in easier instalments of £4000 a year. By 1369 44,000 marks of the original 100,000 had been paid when David renegotiated the terms a second time. This time he was in a position of strength as the English were under pressure in France. The obligation was reduced to 56,000 marks, to reflect the sum already paid, at 4,000 marks a year.

David died suddenly in 1371, but the instalments continued to be made after the steward mounted the throne as Robert II. The last payment was made in the first summer of Richard II's kingship. The sum of 24,000 marks remained unpaid, but the truce was still kept until its expiry in 1384.

The pattern of hostility was now too entrenched on the borders for peace to last far beyond the latest truce. The defeat at Neville's Cross locked Scotland into a series of conflicts to regain the territories lost in 1347. The English made no great efforts to hold the lands they had won.

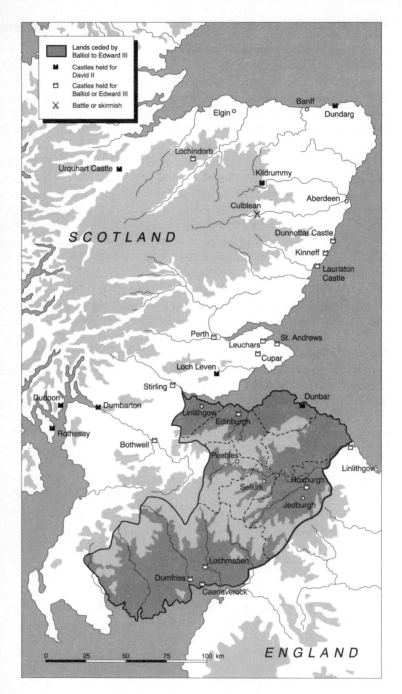

Lands ceded by
Balliol to Edward III

Castles held for
David II

Castles held for
Balliol or Edward III

Battle or skirmish

Banff
Elgin
Dundarg
Lochindorb
Urquhart Castle
Kildrummy
Aberdeen
Culblean
S C O T L A N D
Dunnottar Castle
Kinneff
Lauriston
Castle
Perth
St. Andrews
Leuchars
Cupar
Loch Leven
Stirling
Dunoon
Dunbar
Dumbarton
Linlithgow
Edinburgh
Rothesay
Peebles
Linlithgow
Bothwell
Selkirk
Roxburgh
Jedburgh
Lochmaben
Dumfries
Caerlaverock
0   25   50   75   100 km
E N G L A N D

The surrender of southern Scotland

When the Treaty of Berwick was signed in 1357 there had been no serious conflict for ten years, and no threat to Scottish independence since the failure to take Dunbar. English occupation slowly shrank. John Steward, the guardian's son and later king of Scotland styled Robert III, gathered an army and stayed in Annandale 'for as long as he needed until he brought all the people of that region' to Scottish allegiance in 1352.[23] Liddesdale was retrieved by the murder of Douglas by his namesake in 1353. The reversion of Macdouall lost the last of English territory in Galloway.

The long-term failure of England to recognise Scottish independence and Scottish alliance with France left the two countries in a cycle of long truces, interspersed with short wars as the Scots attempted to win back lost territories. Lochmaben did not fall to the Douglas clan until 1384 when war returned to the borders. English-held lands on the east survived longer. Jedburgh fell when war resumed again in 1409, a private operation of Teviotdale men; a hearth tax of 2d was levied to fund its demolition. Roxburgh did not fall until 1460, when James II was killed, standing too close to one of his precious guns. Berwick was surrendered in 1461 by Lancastrian forces seeking refuge after the defeat of Henry VI at Towton. It was retaken in 1482 as English forces supported the duke of Albany's claim to the Scottish throne. Berwick and the Isle of Man were the only long-term gains from the war, each retaining their own special status in Britain as expressions of a needless war between two neighbours.

NOTES

Chapter 1

1 Browning, 'The Problems of Edward I and the Scots', 203.
2 Norman Reid argues that the two men were not contesting the succession, but who was her heir if she should die. Reid, 'Margaret Maid of Norway,' 77.
3 Nicholson, *Scotland in the Middle Ages*, 28.
4 *Scotichronicon,* vi, 4-5.
5 Stevenson, *Documents,* i. 56.
6 Prestwich, 'Edward I and the Maid of Norway,' 134.
7 Fraser, *Bek* , 57.
8 Crawford, 'North Sea Kingdoms', 175-6.
9 Stones, *Anglo-Scottish Relations* no. 14.
10 Stones & Simpson, 7; 101-2.
11 The following relies on the work of E. L. G. Stones and Grant Simpson who collated the documents relating to the case in *Edward I and the Throne of Scotland*. This should be read with Duncan's reappraisal in , 'The Process of Norham, 1291,' and Barrow's *Robert Bruce*, chapter 3. The best discussion on the legal aspects of the case is Keeney, 'The Medieval idea of the State'.
12 Stones & Simpson i. 201n.
13 *Ibid*, 173; 139.
14 Prestwich, 'Edward I and the Maid of Norway', 134; Stones & Simpson, i. 138, ii. 385-7.
15 *Parl Writs,* i. 256.
16 Linehan, 'Scottish Narrative of 1321', 120.
17 Stones, *Anglo-Scottish Relations* no. 16.
18 Duncan, 'The Community of the Realm of Scotland', 192.
19 *CDS* ii, 497, Marshall, 'Two early English occupations in Scotland,' 20-40.
20 *CDS* ii. 508, Stones & Simpson, ii. 366-370.
21 Gerald of Wales, in Anderson, *Early Sources of Scottish History*, 400.
22 Stones & Simpson, i. 14.
23 It was Devorguilla who founded Balliol college Oxford together with three friaries, a Dominican at Wigtown, and Franciscan in Dundee and Dumfries and Sweetheart Abbey. She died in Buittle castle in 1290.
24 Stevenson, *Documents*, i. 318-21.
25 Stones, & Simpson, i. 180 25.
26 Barrow, *Robert Bruce*, 42.
27 *Foedera* i, 791.
28 Simpson, 'The claim of Florence, count of Holland,' 111-124.
29 Stones *Anglo-Scottish Relations* no. 19; Stones & Simpson, i. 21.
30 Powicke, *The Thirteenth Century*, 511.
31 Stones & Simpson, ii. 358-65, Prestwich, *Edward I,* 368.
32 Barrow, *Robert Bruce*, 51.
33 *Ibid,* 59.
34 Marshall, 'Two early English occupations in Scotland', 28.
35 *CDS* ii. 695.
36 Nicholson, 'The Franco-Scottish and Franco-Norwegian Treaties of 1295', 114-132.
37 Guisborough quoted in Barrow, *Robert Bruce*, 68.
38 Browning, 'The Problems of Edward I and the Scots', 205.

Chapter 2

1 Stevenson, *Documents*, ii. 25-32.
2 *Ibid*, ii. 19.
3 Lydon, 'An Irish Army in Scotland,' 184-190; Fraser, *Bek*, 66; Stevenson, *Documents*, ii. 38-39.
4 Not William de Ros of Ingmanthorpe, Robert de Ros's cousin; the barony was later forfeited to a third William de Ros, of Helmsley, in 1301 for services in Gascony: Hedley, *Northumberland Families*.
5 *Scalacronica*, iii. 18.
6 Stones, *Anglo-Scottish Relations* no. 8.
7 *Lanercost*, 156.
8 *Scalacronica*, iii. 18.
9 Rishanger, quoted by Prestwich, *Edward I*, 471.
10 Nicholas Mayhew, 'Alexander III—A Silver Age?', 56; Fox, *Historical Geography*, 79, 85.
11 Barron, *Scottish Wars*, 1.
12 *CDS* ii. 734.
13 'Let him pike, And let him dike, In scorne said they, He dikes and he pikes, In length as it pleases him.' *Langtoft*, 251.
14 Stevenson, *Documents*, ii. 37-38, 149-51, 152-6; *CDS* ii. 734.
15 Stones, *Anglo-Scottish Relations* no. 28.
16 *Lanercost*, 136; Barrow, *Robert Bruce*, 71n.
17 Fordun, ii. 318.
18 *CDS* ii. 742; *Langtoft*, 251.
19 *CDS* ii. 737.
20 *Bury St Edmunds*, 132.
21 *Lanercost*, 144.
22 Stones & Blount, 'The Surrender of King John'.
23 Stones, *Anglo-Scottish Relations*, no. 24.
24 *Langtoft*, 303.
25 Simpson, 'Toom Tabard', 169.
26 For which they claimed expenses of £428.3s 1 _d. *CDS* ii. 1027.
27 *CDS* ii. 854; 848.
28 Stones, *Anglo-Scottish Relations*, no. 27.
29 Young, *The Comyns*, 159-160.
30 Barrow, *Robert Bruce*, 72.
31 Prestwich, 'England and Scotland,' 189.
32 Stevenson, *Documents*, ii. 32-5.
33 Barrow, *Robert Bruce*, 76.
34 Nicholson, *Scotland: the Later Middle Ages*, 51.
35 Robert Bruce of Annandale's loyalty would later be rewarded with a far lesser prize when, for 'the good esteem he has for the good service of Robert de Brus', Edward ordered his exchequer to 'atterm', or postpone, his debts indefinitely. *CDS* ii. 852.
36 Watson, 'Edward I's peace in Scotland', 129.
37 Barrow, *Robert Bruce*, 61n.
38 'Non thesaurerium sed traytorarium regis', Guisborough quoted in Ramsey, *The Dawn of the Constitution*, 449.

Chapter 3

1 Trevelyan, *History of England*, 218.
2 Tout, *Chapters*, ii. 151.
3 Barron, *Scottish Wars*, 20.

4 *Scotichronicon*, vi. 83.

5 Fordun, ii. 321.

6 Guisborough, quoted by Fisher, *William Wallace*, 40.

7 *CDS* ii. 1689 (*Cal Inq Misc, 1219-1307* no. 1973).

8 Fordun, ii. 321.

9 *Scalacronica*, iii. 219.

10 Fordun, ii. 321.

11 Stevenson, *Documents*, ii. 217.

12 *CDS* ii. 922.

13 *Ibid*, v. 211.

14 Barrow, *Robert Bruce*, 84.

15 Norman Reid 'The Kingless Kingdom', 108; Duncan, 'The Community of the
     Realm of Scotland', 184-201.

16 Stevenson, *Documents*, ii. 183-184.

17 *Ibid*, 170.

18 The Percy's had been given land in Northumberland, but Alnwick, which was to
     become their principal residence and base, was not bought from the bishop of
     Durham until 1309.

19 *CDS* ii. 887, Stevenson, *Documents*, ii. 170, 200-201. June 4 not June 24. (*CPR
     1292-1301*, 251).

20 *CDS* ii. 894, 903-904, Stevenson, *Documents*, ii.177.

21 *Ibid*, 202.

22 *Ibid*, 198-200.

23 *Ibid*, 206-209.

24 *CDS* ii. 909, 910.

25 Stevenson, *Documents*, ii. 204-205, 207-208, *CDS* ii. 175.

26 Stevenson, *Documents*, ii. 200-203, 217 *CDS* ii. 916.

27 Stevenson, *Documents*, ii. 204-209, *CDS* ii. 918; 900.

28 Stevenson, *Documents*, ii. *CDS* ii. 933, 934, 936, 941.

29 Barron, *Scottish Wars*, 44, Stevenson, *Documents*, ii,175.

30 Barron, *Scottish Wars*, 46, *Rotuli Scotiae*, i. 41.

31 Stevenson, *Documents*, ii. 211-213.

32 *Ibid*, 227.

33 *Ibid*, 209-213, *CDS* ii. 923.

34 Barron, *Scottish Wars*, 56, Stevenson, *Documents*, ii. 226-227 .

35 *CDS* ii. 931.

36 Barron, *Scottish Wars*, 60, Stevenson, *Documents*, ii. 202.

37 *Ibid*, 216-219, 222-8; *CDS* ii. 933, 934, 935, 936, 941.

38 Lewis, The English Forces in Flanders', 313; *Langtoft*, 310.

39 Oman, *Art of War*, 563.

40 Guisborough quoted in Nicholson, *Scotland: The Later Middle Ages*, 54.

41 McNamee, 'William Wallace's Invasion of Northern England,' 42; *CDS* ii. 946;
     Scalacronica, iii. 220.

42 Stevenson, *Documents*, ii. 228-9.

43 Fraser, 'Edward I of England and the regallian franchise of Durham,' 329-342.

44 Stevenson, *Documents*, ii. 166-7.

45 *CDS* iii. 628.

46 Summerson, *Medieval Carlisle*, 2; McCarthy, 'Carlisle Castle', 133; McNamee,
     'William Wallace's Invasion of Northern England,' 49.

47 Fraser, 'Edward I of England and the regallian franchise of Durham,' 334-5.

48 *CDS* ii. 1021 (Oct 26); Stevenson, *Documents*, ii. 118-9.

49 Stevenson, *Documents*, ii. 237-9.

50 Gough, 70.

51 Guisbrorough, quoted by Barrow, *Robert Bruce*, 99.
52 *Parl Writs*, i. 317.

Chapter 4
1 Barrow, *Robert Bruce*, 105.
2 Stevenson, *Documents*, ii. 301-304, 431; *CDS* ii. 1978.
3 Ash, 'William Lamberton', 44-45.
4 Sayles, 'The Guardians of Scotland', 249.
5 *CDS* ii. 1014, 1015, 1022 (all c. Oct 17).
6 Stevenson *Documents*, ii. 333-5, *CDS* ii. 1028.
7 *CDS* ii. 1132.
8 *Ibid*, 1025; Stevenson, *Documents*, ii. 333-35.
9 *CDS* ii. 1036, *Parl Writs*, i. 320-15.
10 *Parl Writs*, i. 340-341.
11 *CDS* ii, 1220.
12 Boase, *Boniface VIII*, 206.
13 *CDS* ii. 1072.
14 Tout, *Political History*, 217.
15 *Parl Writs*, i, 321-325.
16 *Parl Writs*, i. 325-326; Tout, *Chapters*, ii. 139.
17 *CDS* ii. 1119.
18 Sayles, 'The Guardians of Scotland', 245-250.
19 *CDS* ii. 1101.
20 Prestwich, *Edward I*, 484. *Parl Writs*, i. 401.
21 Morris, *Welsh Wars of Edward I*, 300; Prestwich, *Edward I*, 484-5.
22 Prestwich, *War, Politics and Finance*, 64.
23 *CCR, 1296-1302*, 410, 402; *Caerlaverock*, 1.
24 *Langtoft*, 327.
25 Ramsey, *Dawn of the Constitution*, 473.
26 *CDS* ii.1147, 1148, 1159.
27 Rishanger 400-402.
28 *Langtoft*, 327.
29 Stones, *Anglo-Scottish Relations*, no. 28 .
30 Ramsey, *Dawn of the Constitution* 434-435; Graham, *Register of Robert Winchelsea*, 569-573.
31 Barrow, *Robert Bruce*, 114.
32 Tout, *Edward I*, 211; Powicke, *Thirteenth Century*, 704.
33 Stones & Simpson, i. 154-6.
34 Stones, *Anglo-Scottish Relations* no. 29.
35 Davies, *Domination and Conquest*, 4.
36 Stones, *Anglo-Scottish Relations*, no. 30.
36 E L G Stones, 'The Mission of Thomas Wale', 8-28.
38 Fordun, ii. 324 .
39 Goldstein, 'The Scottish Mission to Boniface VIII', 1-15.
40 Stones, *Anglo-Scottish Relations*, no. 31.
41 Powicke, *Thirteenth Century*, 704.
42 *Parl Writs*, i. 347-48; 358.
43 *Parl Writs*, i. 357-9; Prestwich, *War, Politics and Finance*, 96-7, Morris, *Welsh Wars*, 302.
44 Colvin, *HKW*, 412; Prestwich, *Edward I*, 493.
45 *CDS* ii. 1224, 1235, 1271, 1250; Stevenson, *Documents*, ii. 441-442, Colvin, *HKW*, 412.
46 *CDS* ii. 1215, 1219; Johnston, *Edward of Carnarvon*, 78.

47 McCarthy, 'Carlisle Castle', 133.
48 Oram, 'Bruce, Balliol and the Lordship of Galloway',37.
49 *Flores Historium*, iii.109; *Lanercost*, 172.
50 Stevenson, *Documents*, ii. 431-37. Stevenson mistranslated the number of ban-
    nerets.
51 Stevenson, *Documents*, ii. 433-35; *CDS* ii. 1230, 1236, 1293 (For Feb 21 read
    Mar 7).
52 *Parl Writs*, i. 54.
53 Stones, 'Mission of Wale', 14.
54 Colvin, *HKW*, 412, Taylor, 'Master James of St George', 433-57.
55 Tout, *Political History*, 221.
56 Duncan, 'The Community of the Realm of Scotland,' 184-201.
57 Stones, 'The submission of Robert Bruce,' 123-134; 1955 Duncan, 'The
    Community of the Realm of Scotland', 184-201; Barrow, *Robert Bruce*, 121-
    124.
58 *Flores Historium*, iii, 111, Johnston, *Edward of Carnarvon*, 83.
59 Sayles, 'Ancient Correspondence', 325-6.
60 *CDS* ii.1342.
61 Stevenson, *Documents*, ii. 448; *Langtoft*, 344-6; Fordun, ii. 326-8.
62 Stevenson, *Documents*, ii. 449-450.
63 Stones, 'An undelivered letter', 86-88.
64 Powicke, *Thirteenth Century*, 706.
65 Prestwich, *War, Politics and Finance*, 97-98; *Parl Writs*, i. 366-367.
66 Johnston, *Edward of Carnarvon*, 87-90.
67 *Scalacronica*, iii. 233.
68 *CDS* ii. 1375, Colvin, *HKW*, 416. Langtoft thought the bridges were never used
    as Edward found another crossing.
69 *CDS* ii.1374; Watson, 'Edward I's Peace in Scotland', 134.
70 *CDS* ii.1386.
71 *CDS* ii. 1412; Colvin, *HKW*, 417.
72 Fordun, ii. 328.
73 *CDS* ii. 1437; 1432.
74 Stevenson, *Documents*, ii. 486; *CDS* ii. 1393.
75 The surrender documents are in Palgrave, *Documents*, i. 278-291. For recent
    comment see Watson, 'Edward I's Peace in Scotland', 135-138; Young, *The
    Comyns*, 185-191.
76 *CDS* v. 346.
77 Stevenson, *Documents*, ii. 466-70.
78 Stevenson, *Documents*, ii. 471; *Langtoft*, 353; Stevenson, *Documents*, ii. 472-
    473.
79 Chaplais, 'Some private letters of Edward I.'
80 *CDS* ii. 1475, 1498, 1499 1500, 1519; Freeman, 'Wall-breakers and River-
    Bridgers', 13; Colvin, *HKW*, 417.
81 Taylor, 'Thomas de Houghton', 28-33; Stevenson, *Documents*, ii. 481; *CDS* ii.
    1502.
82 Taylor, 'Walter of Hereford', 44-6.
83 *Langtoft*, 357; Mathew of Westminster, 571.
84 Stevenson, *Documents*, ii. 479-80.
85 *CDS* ii.1489; *Langtoft*, 357.
86 *CDS* ii. 1560, 1599, 1668; Barrow, *Robert Bruce*, 129.
87 Stones, *Anglo-Scottish Relations*, no 33.
88 Barrow, *Robert Bruce*, 134.
89 Bellamy, *The Law of Treason*.

Chapter 5

1 Fordun, ii. 330-332.
2 Nicholson, *Scotland: the Later Middle Ages*, 70.
3 Barrow, *Robert Bruce*, 142.
4 Stones, *Anglo-Scottish Relations*, no. 33.
5 Duncan, 'The Community of the Realm of Scotland', 198-9.
6 Barrow, 'Lothian in the first War of Independence', 156-76.
7 (Ah! freedom is a noble thing|Freedom lets a man have pleasure,|Freedom all solace to man gives,|He lives at ease who freely lives.)
8 Stones, *Anglo-Scottish Relations*, no. 34.
9 *Scotichronicon*, vi. 320-321.
10 *CDS* ii. 1745.
11 Duncan, 'The War of the Scots', 125-151.
12 Prestwich, *Edward I*, 306.
13 This campaign may be confused with another conducted after his coronation.
14 Boyd was captured by 13th September by the prince of Wales. *CDS* ii. 1829.
15 *CDS* ii. 1753.
16 *CDS* v. 470.
17 Shortly after the ceremony the coronet 'fell' into the hands of Geoffrey de Coigners, who was pardoned for concealing it by the king of England. *CDS* ii, 1914.
18 *Scotichronicon*, vi. 317.
19 *Scalacronica*, iii. 329.
20 We should probably count Mathew Crambeth of Dunkeld amongst Bruce's earliest supporters, and John Kinninmouth of Brechin. Against these ecclessiasts were Henry Cheyne of Argyll, Thomas Dalton of Galloway, and Andrew of Argyll.
21 Stones, *Anglo-Scottish Relations*, no. 35; *CDS* iii. 50.
22 Neville, 'The Political Allegiance of the Earls of Strathearn', 133-153.
23 Barbour, ii. 188.
24 Duncan, 'The War of the Scots', 125-151.
25 *CDS* v. 492.
26 *Ibid*, ii. 1746-7.
27 *Parl Writs*, i. 409.
28 *CDS* ii. 1757.
29 *Ibid* ii. 1762, v. 420.
30 Duncan, 'The War of the Scots', 125-151.
31 This is the medieval idea of the dragon as a serpent and represents the devil. It meant that Valence was not to give quarter and to lay waste the country.
32 *CDS* ii. 1756.
33 *Ibid*, 1782, 1787, 1790.
34 *Ibid*, 1777, 1780, 1786, 1781; v. 446, 456. It was Geoffrey Moubray who brought the news of John Comyn's murder to Edward in February. *Ibid* v. 472.
35 *Ibid*, ii. 1807.
36 *Ibid*, 1803.
37 *Ibid*, 1769.
38 Johnston, *Edward of Carnarvon*, 113; *CCR, 1302-7*, 369-372, 399-400.
39 A total of eight destriers and thirteen runcins were lost at Methven, two destriers and eight runcins at Loch Tay. *CDS* v. 492.
40 *Ibid* ii. 1833, 4; iii. 502.
41 Knoydart, Moidart, Arisaig, Eigg, Uist, Barra, Gigha. She was the wife of Duncan of Mar, younger son of the earl of Mar.
42 Fordun, ii. 335.

43 *CDS* ii. 1811.
44 Wright, *Political Songs of England*, 216-8.
45 Prestwich, 'England and Scotland', 191, 193; Wright, *Political Songs*, 218-9.
46 McCarthy, 'Carlisle Castle', 134.
47 Moorman, 'Edward I at Lanercost Priory', 161-174.
48 Barbour, iv, 341.
49 *CDS* ii. 1771.
50 *Ibid* v. p. 215.
51 Duncan, 'The War of the Scots', 138.
52 Oram, 'Bruce, Balliol and the Lordship of Galloway', 29-47.
53 *CDS* ii. 1895.
54 *Ibid*, 1896.
55 *Ibid*, 1923.
56 Barbour, vii, 488-635; Duncan, 'The War of the Scots', 138.
57 *Ibid*, 138.
58 *CDS* ii. 1979.
59 *Ibid*, 1957.
60 *CDS* ii, 1926, with preference to Barrow's translation, *Robert Bruce*, 172-3.
61 *Scotichronicon*, vi. 331-333.
62 Prestwich, *Edward I*, preface to 1997 edition.

Chapter 6
1 *CDS* iii. 12.
2 *Parl Writs*, i. 369, 371.
3 McNamee, *Wars of the Bruces*, 46-7.
4 *Parl Writs*, i. 370.
5 *CDS* iii. 14.
6 *Lanercost*, 182.
7 *Parl Writs*, i. 370, *CDS* iii. 15.
8 Barnes, 'The Movements of Robert Bruce', 55.
9 Barrow, *Robert Bruce*, 179.
10 *Ibid*, 175.
11 Barbour, ix. 57-59.
12 Fordun, ii. 336.
13 *Parl Writs*, i. 372.
14 Barbour ix. 231-232.
15 *Ibid*. 294-300.
16 *CDS* v. 655.
17 *Lanercost*, 188.
18 It is possible that John of Lorn was stationed on the sea loch, Etive, although this would have meant that his view of the events would have been obscured by Ben Cruachan.
19 Douglas, 'War of the Scots', 142.
20 Barbour, IX, 311-324.
21 Barrow, *Robert Bruce*, p.175.
22 Douglas, 'War of the Scots', 143.
23 *Vita Edwardi*, 12-13.
24 *Ibid*, 1.
25 Johnston, *Edward of Carnarvon*, 131.
26 *Scalacronica*, iii. 457.
27 *Vita Edwardi*, 7.
28 Maddicott, *Thomas of Lancaster*, 69, 72.
29 *Parl Writs, i.* 373-5.

30 *Ibid*. 377.
31 *CDS* iii. 47 (For June read August 11).
32 *Foedera*, ii. 58, 70, 100, 106, *CDS* iii. 114, 138.
33 *Foedera*, ii. 63.
34 *Lanercost*, 189; *CCR 1307-1313*, 159; *Parl Writs, i.* 380, 381, 385, 389, 391.
35 *Foedera*, ii. 85, *CDS* iii. 101.
36 *Lanercost*, 190; *Rotuli Scotiae*, i. 80.
37 Barrow, *Robert Bruce*, 177.
38 *Ibid, Robert Bruce,* 183.
39 Duncan, 'The War of the Scots', 132.
40 Nicholson, *Scotland: The Middle Ages*, 81.
41 Stones, *Anglo-Scottish Relations*, no. 36.
42 Norman Reid, 'Crown and Community'.
43 *Foedera*, ii. 79.
44 *Vita Edwardi*, 11; *Foedera*, ii. 110,111.
45 *CDS* iii. 95, Maddicott, *Thomas of Lancaster*, 113.
46 Phillips, *Aymer de Valence*, 31.
47 Maddicott, *Thomas of Lancaster*, 113.
48 *Foedera*, ii. 114.
49 *Parl Writs*, II, i. 44-57.
50 *Ibid*, 400.
51 *Ibid*, 400-1.
52 *CDS* iii. 177 (the Chancellor to Valence).
53 *Vita Edwardi*, 12.
54 *Lanercost*, 191.
55 *Scalacronica*, iii. 457, *CDS* iii. 196.
56 *CDS* iii. 202.
57 Tout, *Edward II*, 17.
58 *CDS* iii. 203.
59 *CDS* iii. 216, v. 557-561, 563, 564, 532, 533, 536-539, 541.
60 Stanford-Reid, 'Sea-Power and the Anglo-Scottish War', 18.
61 *Parl Writs*, i. 408-411.
62 *Vita Edwardi*, 22.
63 Fordun, ii. 338.
64 *Lanercost*, 194-5.
65 *Rotuli Scotiae* I. 107-8.
66 *CDS* iii. 238; p. 427.
67 *CPR, 1307-1313*, 430.
68 *Rotuli Scotiae*, i. 108.
69 *CCR, 1307-1313*, 413; *CDS* iii, p. 401, *Rotuli Scotiae*, i. 109.
70 *RRS*, no. 18.
71 *CPR 1307-1313*, 456; *CCR 1307-1313*, 420-1.
72 Barrow, 'Lothian in the first Wars of Independence', 172.
73 *Lanercost*, 198.
74 McNamee, 'Buying off Robert Bruce,' 79.
75 *Lanercost*, 201-2.
76 Barbour, ix, 348-351.
77 *Ibid*, 390-400.
78 *Scotichronicon*, vi. 349; *CDS* iii. 339, v. 566, iii. 299; *Lanercost*, 202; Fordun, ii. 338.
79 Barbour, x. 137-258.
80 *CPR 1307-1313*, 559; *Foedera*, ii. 215-217, Maddicott, *Thomas of Lancaster*, 150.

81 *Lanercost*, 203.
82 Barrow, 'Lothian in the first Wars of Independence', 172.
83 *CDS* iii. 337.
84 *Lanercost*, 195.
85 *RRS*, v. 41.
86 Duncan, 'The War of the Scots', 131.
87 *Barbour*, x. 441-489, *Scalacronica*, iii. 458, *Lanercost*, 204.
88 *Scalacronica*, iii. 458.
89 Duncan, 'The War of the Scots', 149, *Parl Writs*, i. 421-3, 121-2.

Chapter 7
1 Since 685 when the Northumbrian King Ecgfrith was killed by Bridei at the battle of Nechtanesmere.
2 *Vita Edwardi*, 51.
3 Barbour, xi. 195-6.
4 *Vita Edwardi*, 50.
5 *Scotichronicon*, vi. 367-375.
6 Given-Wilson, '*Vita Edwardi Secundi*: Memoir or Journal,' 165-176,.
7 Becke, 'Battle of Bannockburn.'
8 *Vita Edwardi*, 50.
9 Ramsey, *Genesis of Lancaster*, 61.
10 Becke, 'Battle of Bannockburn.'
11 Maddicott, *Thomas of Lancaster*, 40.
12 *Vita Edwardi*, 49.
13 Phillips, *Aymer de Valance*, 73; Barrow, *Robert Bruce*, 206.
14 Barbour, xi, 101-106.
15 *Vita Edwardi*, 52-3. And repeats the charge twice for effect.
16 Phillips, *Aymer de Valence,* 73.
17 Morris, *Bannockburn*, 34-5.
18 Barrow, *Robert Bruce*, 208-9.
19 Ramsey, *Genesis of Lancaster* 59.
20 Barbour, xi. 107-106.
21 *Vita Edwardi*, 52; *Lanercost*, 207; *Scalcronica*, 460.
22 Mcdiarmid, i. 89. At the battle Walter is said to have been 'bot ane berdlas hyne.'
23 Four divisions was not unknown, see for example the well-documented Galloway campaign of 1300.
24 Oman, *The Art of War*, 84.
25 Tout, *Political History*, 260.
26 Barbour and the *Vita* name Sir Henry, the *Scalacronica* gives Peris de Mountfort. A Sir John de Mountfort was killed at Bannockburn, and appears before Bohun in the list of dead (6 and 7 respectively) printed in *Annales Londonienses*.
27 Barbour, xii. 50.
28 *Scalacronica*, Barbour disputes this, giving Clifford command of 800 men. (*The Bruce*, xii, 514-21).
29 A response to Mackenzie's thesis came from Maxwell, in 'The Battle of Bannockburn,' 233-51, and Morris, *Bannockburn*.
30 Barbour, xii, 388-406.
31 Barrow, *Robert Bruce*, 211-2.
32 *Scalacronica*, iii. 460.
33 *Lanercost*, 208.
34 Duncan, 'The Community of the Realm of Scotland', 199.

35 *Scalacronica*, iii. 460.
36 Tout, 'Bannockburn', 39.
37 Mackenzie, *The Battle of Bannockburn*; Miller, *The Site of the Battle of Bannockburn*; Christison, 'Bannockburn'.
38 Barrow, *Robert Bruce*, 211-5.
39 Mcdiarmid, i. 92.
40 *Lanercost,* 208.
41 'Many a mighty fierce dazing blow I Be rought there upon the other side I Where through the mail coat burst with blood I That went flowing freely to the earth.'
42 Yeoman, servants and labourers.
43 *Scalacronica*, iii. 460.
44 Edward asked his king of arms, Robert le Roy, who were the best three knights in Christendom, le Roy, whose own chronicle is lost and was possible the basis of much of Barbour, replied that the first was the Emperor Henry, the second Robert Bruce, the third Argentine.
45 *Scalacronica*, iii. 56.

Chapter 8
1 *Parl Writs,* i. 427-30.
2 McNamee, *Wars of the Bruces*, 72.
3 *Lanercost*, 210-211.
4 Morris, 'Cumberland and Westmoreland levies', 317-319; McCarthy, 'Carlisle Castle', 136.
5 *Foedera*, ii. 255, *Parl Writs*, i. 431-2.
6 Scammel, 'Robert Bruce & the North of England', 388-9; *CDS* iii. 543, 819.
7 Scammel, 'Robert Bruce & the North of England', 391.
8 *CDS* iii. 707, 858.
9 *Lanercost*, 216-7.
10 *CDS* iii. 384; v. 591, 596; *Parl Writs*, II, i. 433-4.
11 *CDS* iii. 397.
12 Fraser, 'Medieval Trading Restrictions', 140; See *AA* 381-3 for translation and comments.
13 Kershaw, 'The Great Famine', 1-50; Lucas 'The Great European Famine', 343-377.
14 *Vita Edwardi*, 70.
15 Maddicott, *Thomas of Lancaster* p. 161.
16 Tuck, 'Northumbrian Society', 29.
17 Galbraith, 'Extracts', 209.
18 *CDS* iii. 128.
19 Tuck, 'Northumbrian Society', 26-7.
20 Constable of Mitford 1316, *CPR 1313-1317*, 396.
21 Maddicott, *Thomas of Lancaster*, 159; *CDS* iii. 384, 458, 463.
22 *Parl Writs*, i. 126-7.
23 *CDS* v. 590, *Rotuli Scotiae*, i. 131, *RRS* no. 40, *Foedera*, ii. 255-6.
24 *CDS* iii. 402; *Lanercost*, 211.
25 *Foedera*, ii. 249.
26 APS, 464, quoted in Nicholson, *Scotland: the Later Middle Ages*, 91-2.
27 *Scotichronicon*, 377-381, *RRS*, 637-8, 652.
28 For the Bruce invasion of Ireland see Dunlop, 'Some notes on Barbour's Bruce,'; Frame, 'The Bruces in Ireland, 1315-1318'; Lydon, 'The Bruce Invasion of Ireland,' & 'The Impact of the Bruce Invasion 1315-27'; McNamee, *Wars of the Bruces*.

29 *Rotuli Scotiae* i. 122, 138.
30 Barbour, xiv. 221. A phrase he repeats for the battle of Connor (xv. 71).
31 *CDS* iii. 562.
32 Barbour, xiv. 4-6.
33 *CDS* v. 595, 8; *Parl Writs*, i. 435-6. McNamee, *Wars of the Bruces*, 78.
34 *Lanercost*, 212.
35 Including the bishops of Durham and Carlisle, the northern clergy and fifty-nine magnates to attend a council to consider the defence of marches.
36 Phillips, *Aymer de Valence*, 88-9.
37 *Lanercost*, 213.
38 *CDS* iii. 369.
39 McCarthy, 'Carlisle Castle', 396-7.
40 *Lanercost*, 213-215.
41 *Vita Edwardi*, 61-62; Lancaster, 170; *CCR 1313-18*, 433; *CDS* iii. 458.
42 Phillips, *Aymer de Valence*, 90, *Rotuli Scotiae* i. 150.
43 *Parl Writs*, i. 457-8 , 460, ii. 94-5; Maddicott, *Thomas of Lancaster*, 173-17.
44 *CDS* iii. 452.
45 *Ibid*, 486.
46 *Ibid*, 470.
47 *Ibid*.
48 *CCW 1244-1326*, 438-439.
49 *Rotuli Scotiae* I. 153, *CDS* iii. 474, *CCW 1244-1326*, 436.
50 *CPR 1313-17*, 450.
51 *CDS* iii. 486; *RRS* p. 138.
52 *CDS* iii. 486.
53 *CCW 1244-1326*, 436.
54 Powicke, *Military Obligation*, 142-144, *Parl Writs*, ii. 157, 461-3, 464.
55 *Parl Writs*, ii. 466-8.
56 Maddicott, *Thomas of Lancaster*, 185-7.
57 *Parl Writs*, ii. 461-3, 466-8, 476-8.
58 Powicke, *Military Obligation*, 144.
59 *RRS*, p. 139.
60 Macnamee, *Wars of the Bruces*, 149.
61 Barbour, xvi. 335-492 and note. The event is noticed by the *Scalacronica*, iii. 462. The chronicler's father lost a horse at the battle. *Achaeologia*, xxvi. 324.
62 *Scotichronicon*, vi. 383; *Archaeologia*, xxvi, 325.
63 *Scotichronicon*, vi. 383 and note; Barbour, xv. 319-425.
64 *Foedera* ii. 321, 327, 317.
65 For the Middleton affair see: Maddicott, *Thomas of Lancaster*, 203-5; Prestwich, 'Gilbert de Middleton', 179-194; Middleton, *Sir Gilbert de Middleton*.
66 Hailes, *Annals*, ii. 74. *RRS*, 140-143; Barrow, *Robert Bruce*, 245-247; *Foedera* ii. 351.
67 *CCW 1244-1326*, 458.
68 Duncan, *Nation of Scots*, 23-25.
69 *Parl Writs*, i. 487; *Vita Edwardi* 79-80.
70 *Archaeologia*, xxvi. 330.
71 *Rotuli Scotiae* i. 160-161, 169-170, *CPR 1313-17*, 322, 386-7, 390, 394, 400-1, 468-70, 484, 540, 543.
72 *CDS* iii. 554, 555, 558, 651; Barbour, xvii, 17-21.
73 *CDS* iii. 589.
74 *RRS* v. 144-5.
75 Barbour, xviii. 150-160. Duncan's translation. It was Galstone who brought

Douglas's body home from Spain. He died at the siege of Stirling in 1336.

76 *Lanercost*, 221. This is confirmed by another source, that says only those who resisted were killed. Barbour, p. 618n.

77 Barbour, note p. 626. *RRS*, v. 145, 150. For an award made on to Spalding, 1 May 1319.

78 Barbour, xvii. 239-254.

79 *RRS* v. 560.

80 *Scalacronica*, iii. 60.

81 *Taxatio Ecclesiastica*, 297-309. McNamee, *Wars of the Bruces*, 85-90 and Kershaw, 'Scots in the West Riding of Yorkshire', 231-239 have both drawn maps using this data.

82 Maddicott, *Thomas of Lancaster*, 172.

83 *Vita Edwardi*, 93-4.

84 *Parl Writs*, i. 501-7, 510-5; II. ii. 136; *Rotuli Scotiae* i. 194.

85 *Parl Writs*, i. 517-20; *Vita Edwardi*, 94, CDS iii. 663; Barbour, p. 630-1n; McNamee, *Wars of the Bruces*, 218-9.

86 CDS iii. 663, 4; *Anonimalle,* 96 quoted in Barbour, p. 632-4n.

87 *Lanercost* says that the town nearly fell with this first assault but he has almost certainly confused this with the second assault five days later.

88 *Flores Historium*, iii. 188.

89 Barbour, xvii. 794, 808-810.

90 Leadman, 'Battle of Mytton', 117-122.

91 Barbour, p. 630n.

92 Maddicott, *Thomas of Lancaster*, 249.

93 *Parl Writs*, i. 525, 7; Powicke, *Military Obligation*, 157; CDS iii. 667.

94 CDS v. 657; iii. 738-9.

95 *Brut*, 211.

96 Nicholson, *Scotland: the Later Middle Ages*, 101.

97 Barrow, *Robert Bruce*, 305.

98 Donaldson, 'The Pope's Reply', 119-120.

99 Stones, *Anglo-Scottish Relations*, no. 38.

100 Linehan, 'A Fourteenth Century History', 106-22.

101 Duncan, *Nation of Scots*, 31.

102 CDS iii. 746, 749.

103 *Lanercost*, 230-1.

104 CDS iii. 747, *Vita Edwardi*, 120-1.

105 *Parl Writs*, i. 559-560; 562-3, 5; 578.

106 Barbour, 678n, Fryde, *The Tyranny and Fall of Edward II*, 128.

107 *Lanercost*, 237-8.

108 CPR 1321-24, 102.

109 *Ibid*, 126.

110 Powicke, 'English Commons', 160.

112 CDS iii. 778, Barbour, xviii. 243-332.

113 CDS iii. 770. 772, 773; *Foedera*, ii. 506.

114 CDS iii. 783, 4.

115 *Lanercost*, 240.

116 Barbour, xviii. 559-569.

Chapter 9

1 *Parl Writs*, i. 612, 616, 620, 621-2.

2 *RRS* v 215, pp 480-85, 162; Stones, *Anglo-Scottish Relations* no. 39; Summerson, *Carlisle Castle*, 230-256.

3 CDS v. 691, *Lanercost* 242.

4 *Parl Writs*, i. 613, 280, 620-1, *Foedera*, ii. 500.

5 *Foedera*, ii. 500.

6 *CPR 1321-24*, 268.

7 *CPR 1321-24*, 288-9.

8 *RRS* v. 222.

9 Phillips, *Aymer de Valence*, 231.

10 *Foedera*, ii. 524.

11 *Foedera*, ii. 498, 508, 513.

12 *CPR 1321-24*, 277-9.

13 *CDS* v. 687; *Vita Edwardi* 131-2.

14 *CDS* v. 692.

15 *Ibid*.

16 Barrow, *Robert Bruce*, 251.

17 *Vita Edwardi*, 132; McNamee, *Wars of the Bruces*, 238.

18 *CDS* v. 694, 699.

19 Barrow, *Robert Bruce*, 251.

20 Grant, *Independence and Nationhood*, 33-34.

21 *CDS* iii. 817, 882-6, 848, 851, 852.

22 Fryde, *The Tyranny and Fall of Edward II*, 185.

23 Barbour, xix. 230-239.

24 *CDS* iii. 888, 889.

25 Nicholson, 'Edward Bruce's Invasion', 30-40.

26 Powicke, 'English Commons', 556-582.

27 *CPR 1324-7*, 180, 191.

28 Ormrod, *Reign of Edward III*, 4.

29 Fryde, *The Tyranny and Fall of Edward II*, 209.

30 *Foedera*, ii. 688, 9.

31 *CPR 1327-30*, 20; *Foedera*, ii. 696.

32 *CCR 1327-1330*, 118; Nicholson, 'Last Campaign', 236, *Rotuli Scotiae* i. 206, 208-9.

33 Stones, 'Anglo-Scottish Negotiations', 49-51.

34 *Brut*, 249; *CCR, 1327-1330*, 207, 216-7; Fordun 344.

35 Nicholson, 'Last Campaign', 237; Lucas, *Low Countries and the Hundred Years' War*, 64.

36 *Brut*, 250; *Foedera*, ii. 707.

37 Nicholson, *Edward III and the Scots*, 20.

38 *CDS* iii. 922.

39 Barbour, xix. 300.

40 Nicholson, *Edward III*, 22, *Scalacronica*, iv. 153.

41 Fordun, 344, *Rotuli Scotiae* i. 214; *CDS* iii. 920, 921.

42 Barrow, *Robert Bruce*, 252.

43 *Foedera*, ii. 709, 711.

44 *Foedera*, ii. 717.

45 *Scalacronica* iv, 29; Barrow, *Robert Bruce*, 252-3; Barbour, 287-291.

46 Le Bel, with preference to professor Duncan's translation in Barbour, 775.

47 Barrow, *Robert Bruce*, 373n and Mcdiarmid, vol. i, 106.

48 Barbour, xix. 742-758.

49 The younger brother of Walter Stewart, who died in 1326. He is styled earl of Angus after King Robert's death.

50 *Scalacronica*, iv. 155, who says the force numbered 5000 men; Barbour xix, 778-812, who says 10,000.

51 *Brut*, 251.

52 *CCR 1327-1330*, 216-7.

53 Fryde, *The Tyranny and Fall of Edward II*, 211.
54 *Foedera*, ii. 713.
55 *Historical Papers*, 347-8.
56 Barbour, xx. 3-4.
57 Nicholson, 'Last Campaign', 242.
58 Barbour, xx. 22-26; *RRS* v. 324.
59 Fordun, ii. 344; *Scalacronica*, iv. 30.
60 *Historical Papers*, 350-351.
61 Tout, *Political History*, p. 304.
62 Stones, 'Anglo-Scottish Negotiations', 49-51; trans. in Stones, *Anglo-Scottish Relations*, no. 40.
63 Stones, *Anglo-Scottish Relations*, no. 41.
64 Stones, 'English Mission to Edinburgh', 121-131.
65 *Foedera*, ii. 962.
66 Stones, 'Rotuli Scotiae', 23-51; *Anglo-Scottish Relations*, no. 42; *Foedera*, ii. 804, *Scalacronica*, iv. 30-31.
67 Stones, 'Rotuli Scotiae', 32-3; Mcdiarmid, i. 107.
68 *CDS* v. 799, 800; Stones, 'Allusion to the Black Rood of Scotland', 174-5.
69 Scammel, 'Robert Bruce & the North of England', 402; Stones *Anglo-Scottish Relations*, p. xxx.
70 Donaldson, *Scotland*, 169-170.
71 Nicholson, *Edward III and the Scots*, 55, quoting the *Scalacronica*, iv. 156; Baker, 40; and the *Brut*, 258.
72 Prince, 'Importance of the Campaign of 1327', 300.
73 Prestwich *Three Edwards*, 57; Tout, *Chapters*, iii. 56.
74 Tout, 'Boroughbridge', 711-5.
75 Morris, 'Mounted Infantry', 77-102.
76 Barrow, *Robert Bruce*, 322-3. Barbour, xx, 73-77.
77 Grant, 'Medieval Foundations', 4-24.
78 Barbour, 751-2n; Macdiarmid, i. 108.
79 Fordun, ii. 345-6.

Chapter 10
1 Barrow, *Robert Bruce*, 270-292.
2 *Scotichronicon*, vii. 73.
3 Fryde, *The Tyranny and Fall of Edward II*, 224-5.
4 Tout, *Political History*, 31.
5 Nicholson *Edward III and the Scots*, 70.
6 *CCR 1330-33*, 175; *CDS* iii. 1023, 1050.
7 *CDS* iii. 1022, 1024, 1034, 1035, 1036; *Foedera*, ii. 806, 824.
8 Balliol had already been given safe conducts to come to England in April and October 1330. *Foedera*, ii. 795, 799.
9 Reid, 'Edward de Balliol', 38-9.
10 Tout, *Political History*, 316.
11 *Foedera*, ii. 876; 833.
12 *Brut*, 275.
13 *CPR 1330-34*, 326, 482-3; *CDS* iii. 1057.
14 *Scotichronicon*, vii. 73.
15 *Scalacronica*, iv. 35.
16 Barbour, xx, 619-20 and note; *Scotichronicon*, vii. 63, 73.
17 Bridlington, *EHD*, iv. 54.
18 *Scotichronicon*, vii. 75.
19 Bridlington in *EHD*, iv. 55.

20 *Scotichronicon*, vii. 79, Wyntoun, v, 420-1; *Lanercost*, 270-71.
21 *Scotichronicon*, vii. 79 and note.
22 Nicholson *Edward III and the Scots*, 91-2.
23 The man implicated in the Soules plot.
24 *Lanercost*, 273-4.
25 *Foedera*, ii. 847-8.
26 *Ibid*, 847, 849.
27 *Rotuli Parliamentorum*, ii. 67.
28 *Lanercost*, 275; Brut, 281; *Scotichronicon*, vii. 83.
29 Nicholson *Edward III and the Scots*, 105-6.
30 Campbell, 'England, Scotland and the 100 Years War',
    184, quoting *Baker*, 50.
31 Nicholson, 'Siege of Berwick,' 23, 26.
32 *Foedera*, ii. 849, 860.
33 *Ibid*, 855-7.
34 Nicholson, 'Siege of Berwick', 27.
35 Brut, 281.
36 *CDS* iii. 1105.
37 Nicholson, 'Siege of Berwick', 29.
38 *CDS* iii. 1077.
39 Fordun, ii. 348, *Scotichronicon*, vii. 91; Brut, 282-3.
40 Bridlington in *EHD*, iv. 57.
41 Morris, 'Mounted Infantry', 92.
42 *Lanercost*, 279-80.
43 Frodun, 348.
44 Nicholson *Edward III and the Scots*, 142.
45 *Scotichronicon*, vii. 93; *CPR 1330-34*, 482-3.
46 *Scotichronicon*, vii. 97; *Scalacronica*, iv. 163; *CDS* iii. 1118, 9, 21.
47 *CDS* iii. 1094; *Rotuli Scotiae* i. 259; *Foedera*, ii. 870.
48 Nicholson *Edward III and the Scots*, 155.
49 *Foedera*, ii. 863, 888.
50 Nicholson *Edward III and the Scots*, 122.
51 *Foedera*, ii. 880-895.
52 Ormrod, *Reign of Edward III*, 9; Sumption, *Hundred Years War*, 132-137;
    Mckisack, *Fourteenth Century*, 117-118; Campbell, 'England, Scotland and
    the 100 Years War'.
53 Webster, 'Scotland without a King', 225.
54 *Scotichronicon*, vii. 103-7; Wyntoun vi, 40-45. Boardman, *Early Stewart Kings*, 4.
55 *Lanercost*, 287; Oram, *Dumfriesshire Transactions*, 43.
56 Fordun, ii. 349.
57 *Scotichronicon*, vii. 107.
58 Nicholson *Edward III and the Scots*, 170.
59 *Scalacronica*, iv. 188. The earl had rebelled by February 19 when his lands were
    forfeited to Henry Percy. *CDS* iii. 1145, 1146.
60 Nicholson *Edward III and the Scots*, 171.
61 Tout, *Chapters*, iv, 98-99.
62 Prince 'The Strength of English Armies', 354-7; Nicholson, *Scotland: the Later
    Middle Ages*, 131,.
63 *CDS* iii. 1138, 1161, 1164, *CPR 1334-38*, 45, 79.
64 *Scotichronicon*, vii. 109.
65 *Lanercost*, 291.
66 *Scotichronicon*, vii. 103, 109-111.
67 *Ibid*, 111.

68 *Lanercost*, 292-293, Nicholson, *Scotland: the Later Middle Ages*, 131, Namur paid a £4,000 ransom.
69 *CDS* iii. 1182, 1184.
70 Nicholson *Edward III and the Scots*, 222-3.
71 Webster, 'Scotland without a King', 228.
72 *Scotichronicon*, vii. 115.
73 Nicholson, *Scotland: the Later Middle Ages*, 132.
74 *Scotichronicon*, vii. 125.
75 CCR 1333-7, 414, 425.
76 CCR 1333-7, 507-8; *Foedera*, ii. 912.
77 Sumption, *Hundred Years War*, 152-3.
78 *Foedera*, ii. 923-933.
79 *Lanercost*, 297.
80 Sumption, *Hundred Years War*, 159-160.
81 Edward's itinerary is recorded in a contemporary diary. He reached Lochindorb on 15 July, Elgin 18th, and was at Aberdeen 22-23rd. Ellis, *Original Letters*, i. 33-39; Barrow, 'Wood of Stronkalter,' 77-79.
82 *Lanercost*, 299.
83 Fordun, ii. 353, *Scotichronicon*, vii. 123.
84 Sumption, *Hundred Years War*, 161-6.
85 Webster, 'Scotland without a King', 229.
86 Containime, *War in the Middle Ages*, 219.
87 *Scalacronica*, iv. 200.
88 *Scotichronicon*, vii. 127; 143-5. There is no confirmation of this migration of Scots to England.
89 Reid, 'Edward de Balliol', 43.
90 Tout, *Chapters*, iii. 82.
91 Tuck, 'Northern Nobility', 9-14.
92 Musgrove, *The North of England*, 118.
93 *CDS* iii. 1283.
94 Fordun, ii. 353; *Scotichronicon*, vii. 125-7.
95 Lewis, 'Recruitment and Organisation of a Contract Army', 4.
96 Scalacronica, iv. 192; .
97 *Lanercost*, 311, Fordun, ii. 354; *Scotichronicon*, vii. 127-9; Nicholson, *Scotland: the Later Middle Ages*, 137.
98 *Lanercost*, 312-4.
99 Fordun, ii. 355.
100 *CDS* v. 781.
101 *Scotichronicon*, vii. 141; Fordun, ii. 355-6; *CDS* iii. 1316. He was still paid as constable by the English 12 December 1339. *CDS* iii. 1321.
102 Campbell, 'England, Scotland and the 100 Years War', 191; *CDS* iii. 1386.
103 Nicholson, *Scotland: the Later Middle Ages*, 139, from Wyntoun, ii. 46. Ransom see *Foedera*, ii. 1140, *CDS* iii. 1350, 1364.
104 *Scotichronicon*, vii. 149. The negotiations for the exchange of Moray and Salisbury, agreed 26 October 1340 (*CDS* iii. 1343) were not complete until February 1342: its seems likely that both received their freedom before, anticipating a final agreement.
105 *CDS* iii. 1383.*Scotichronicon*, vii. 145-7.
106 *Scotichronicon*, vii. 243,.
107 *Lanercost*, 324.
108 Scalacronica, iv. 198.
109 Oram, 'Bruce, Balliol and the Lordship of Galloway', 45.
110 Fordun, ii. 357-8.

111 Nicholson, Scotland: the Middle Ages, 142-3.
112 Oram, 'Bruce, Balliol and the Lordship of Galloway', 45.
113 *Scotichronicon*, vii. 253, 7.
114 *Lanercost*, 326.
115 *Lanercost*, 331, CDS iii. 1610, 1670.
116 McCarthy, 'Carlisle Castle', 141; CDS v. 802-3.
117 Morris, 'Mounted Infantry', 98-99.

Chapter 11
1 *Scalacronica*, iv. 202.
2 *CDS* iii. 1479.
3 Nicholson, *Scotland: the Later Middle Ages*, 148.
4 *Scalacronica*, iv. 202.
5 *CDS* iii. 1507.
6 *CDS* v. 810; Nicholson, *Scotland: the Later Middle Ages*, 148.
7 *CPR 1345-8*, 226, 314, 552, CDS iii. 1482, 1495.
8 *Foedera*, iii. 108; CDS iii. 1486-7; v. 812. Fife was ransomed for £1000.
9 Duncan, *David II and Edward III*, 116-118; Balfour-Melville, 'David II's Appeal to the pope', 86.
10 *CDS* iii. 1549.
11 Nicholson, 'David II, the Historians and the chroniclers', 59-78; Duncan, *David II and Edward III*, 137.
12 *Scotichronicon*, vii. 296.
13 *Foedera*, iii. 281, 291; Campbell, 'England, Scotland and the 100 Years War', 198-9.
14 *Scotichronicon*, vii. 279; *Scalacronica*, iv. 197.
15 Campbell, 'England, Scotland and the 100 Years War', 200.
16 *Scalacronica*, iv. 203; CDS iii. 1607, *Foedera*, iii. 327; *Scotichronicon*, vii. 281.
17 *Scotichronicon*, vii. 281-3; CDS iv, 3, 21.
18 *CDS* iii. 1574, 1589, 1591-1605, 1622; *Foedera*, iii. 318-9.
19 *Foedera*, iii, 314.
20 Campbell, 'England, Scotland and the 100 Years War', 200.
21 Nicholson, *Scotland: the Later Middle Ages*, 162.
22 *EHD*, iv. 101.
23 *Scotichronicon*, vii. 297.

BIBLIOGRAPHY

Acts of the Parliaments of Scotland, ed. T. Thomson & C. Innes (Edinburgh, 1814-1875)

Anderson, A. O., *Early Sources of Scottish History* (Edinburgh, 1922)
Scottish Annals from English Chronicles, 500-1286 (London, 1908)
'Anglo-Scottish Relations from Constantine II to William,' *SHR* xlii (1963): 1-20

Anonimalle Chronicle, 1307-33, ed. W. R. Childs & J. Taylor (1991)

Ash, Marinell, 'William Lamberton, bishop of St Andrews, 1293-1308,' in *The Scottish Tradition*, ed. G. W. S. Barrow (Scottish Academic Press, 1974)

Ayton, Andrew, 'John Chaucer and the Weardale Campaign in 1327,' *Notes and Queries* xxxvi (1989): 9-10

Balfour-Melville, W. M., 'Two John Crabbs,' *SHR* xxxix (1960) 31-34
Edward III and David II (Historical Association, 1954)
'The Death of John Balliol,' *SHR* xxxv (1956) 82-3
'Papers relating to the Captivity and Release of David II,' *SHR misc* ix 1-56.
'David II's Appeal to the Pope,' *SHR* xli (1962): 86.

Barbour, J. *The Bruce*, ed. W. M. Mackenzie (London, 1909)
The Bruce, ed. M. P. McDiarmid & J. A. C. Stevenson 3 vols. (Scottish Texts Society, 1980-85)
The Bruce, ed. A. A. M. Duncan (Edinburgh, 1997)

Barnes P. M., & Barrow, G. W. S., 'The Movements of Robert Bruce between September 1307 and May 1308,' *SHR* xliv (1970): 47-59.

Barron, Evan, *The Scottish War of Independence*, 2nd ed. (Inverness, 1934)

Barrow, G. W. S., 'The Scottish Clergy in the War of Independence,' *SHR* xli (1962): 1-22
'The Anglo-Scottish Border,' *Northern History* i (1966): 21-42
'The Wood of Stronkalter,' *SHR* xlvi (1967): 77-79.
The Kingdom of the Scots (London, 1973)

'Lothian in the War of Independence,' *SHR* lv (1976): 151-171

'The Aftermath of War: Scotland and England in the Late Thirteenth and Fourteenth centuries,' *TRHS* 5th series xxvii (1978): 103-6

Robert Bruce and the Community of the Realm of Scotland, 3rd ed. (Edinburgh, 1988)

'The Army of Alexander III's Scotland,' in *Scotland in the Reign of Alexander III*, ed. Norman Reid (John Donald, 1990), 132-47

'A Kingdom in Crisis: Scotland and the Maid of Norway,' *SHR* lxix (1990): 120-141

Bates, Cadwallader, *The Border Holds of Northumberland* (Newcastle, 1591)

Bean, W. M., 'The Percies and their Estates in Scotland,' *AA* 4th series xxxv (1957): 91-99

Becke, F., 'The Battle of Bannockburn,' in *Complete Peerage*, vol. xi (1912), appendix b.

Bellamy, J. G. *The Law of Treason in the Later Middle Ages* (Nottingham University PhD thesis, 1966).

Blair, C. H. 'Knights of the March of Northumberland 1278 and 1324, *AA* 4th series xxvii (1949): 122-75

Boardman, Stephen, *The Early Stewart Kings* (Tuckwell, 1996)

Boase, S. R., *Boniface VIII* (London, 1933)

Bornstein, Diane, 'Military Manuals in Fifteenth Century England,' *Medieval Studies* xxxvii (1975): 469-477.

Bradbury, Jim, *The Medieval Siege* (Boydell, 1992)

Brown, R. A., Colvin, H. M., Taylor, A. J., *History of the King's Works*, (London , 1963)

Andrew Browning, 'The problems of Edward I and the Scots after the death of Alexander III,' in *Edward I and the Throne of Scotland*, E. L. G. Stones & Grant Simpson, vol. i (Oxford, 1978).

The Brut, ed. F. W. D. Brie, vol. i (Early English Text Society, 1906).

The Buik of the Croniclis of Scotland: A Metrical Version of the History of Hector Boerce by William Steward 3 vols. ed. W. B. Turnbull (Rolls Series, 1858)

Calendar of Chancery Rolls

Calendar of Documents Relating to Scotland (CDS), 5 vols. i-iv ed. Joseph Bain, (Edinburgh, 1881-4); v ed. G. G. Simpson & J. D. Galbraith (Scottish Record Office, 1988)

Calendar of Chancery Warrants

Calendar of Close Rolls

Calendar of Patent Rolls

Campbell, 'England, Scotland and the Hundred Years War in the Fourteenth Century,' in *Europe in the Late Middle Ages*, ed. J. Hale et al (London, 1965), 184-216.

Chaplais, Pierre, 'Some Private Letters of Edward I,' *EHR* lxxvii (1962): 79-86

Christison, General Sir P. 'Bannockburn, 23 and 24 June 1314. A Study in Military History,' *PSAS* xc (1959): 170-9

The Chronicle of Bury St Edmunds, ed. Antonia Grandson (London, 1964)

The Chronicle of Walter of Guisborough, ed. H. Rothwell (Camden 3rd series lxxxix, 1957)

The Chronicle of Lanercost, ed. & trans. H. Maxwell (Glasgow, 1913)

Chronicle of Pierre de Langtoft, vol. ii ed. T Wright (London, 1868)

Chronicon of Geoffrey le Baker, ed. E. M. Thompson (1889)

Contamine, Philippe, *War in the Middle Ages* (Oxford, 1984)

Cooper, M. 'The Numbers and Distribution of the Population of Medieval Scotland,' *SHR* xxvi (1947): 2-9.

Cotton, Bartholomew *Historia Anglica* (Rolls Series, 1859)

Crawford, Barbara, 'North Sea Kingdoms, North Sea Beaurocrat: A Royal Official who Transcended National Boundaries,' *SHR* lxix (1990): 175-84

Davies, I. M., *The Black Douglas* (London, 1974)

Davies, R. R., *Domination and Conquest: The Experience of Ireland, Scotland and Wales 1100-1300* (Cambridge, 1990)

'The People's of Britain and Ireland, 1100-1400, i. Identities', *THRS* sixth series iv (1994): 1-20; 'ii. Names Boundaries and Regnal Solidarities', v (1995): 1-20; 'iii. Laws and Customs', vi (1996): 1-25; 'iv. Language and Historical Mythology', vii (1997): 1-25

Dickinson, W. C., 'His Body Shall be Brought to the Lists,' *SHR* xlii (1963): 84-86

Scotland from the Earliest Times to 1603 (Edinburgh, 1961) rev. A. A. M. Duncan (1977)

Dixon, P. 'From Hall to Tower: The Change in Seigneurial Houses on the Anglo-Scottish Border after c. 1250', in *Thirteenth Century England IV* ed. P. R. Coss & S. D. Lloyd (Woodbridge, 1992)

Documents and Records Illustrating the History of Scotland, ed. F. Palgrave, (London, 1837)

Documents Illustrative of the History of Scotland, ed. J. Stevenson, 2 vols. (1870)

Donaldson, G. 'The Pope's reply to the Scottish barons in 1320,' *SHR* xxix (1950): 119-120

Duncan, A. A. M., 'The Earliest Scottish Charters', SHR xxxvii (1958): 103-135

'The community of the realm of Scotland and Robert Bruce: a review,' *SHR* xlv (1966): 184-201

The Nation of the Scots and the Declaration of Arbroath (Historical Association, 1970)

Scotland: The Making of the Kingdom (Edinburgh, 1975)

'*Honi soit qui mal y pense*: David II and Edward III, 1346-52', *SHR* lxvii (1988): 113-141

'The War of the Scots,' *TRHS* 6th series, ii (1992): 125-151

'The Process of Norham, 1291,' in *Thirteenth Century England*, ed. P. R. Coss & S. D. Lloyd, vol. v (Boydell Press, 1995)

Dunlop, R., 'Some notes on Barbour's Bruce,' in *Essays in Medieval History presented to T F Tout*, ed. A G Little & F M Powicke (Manchester, 1925)

Edwards, J. G., 'The Treason of Thomas Turbeville, 1295', *Studies in Medieval History Presented to F. M. Powicke*, ed. R. W. Hunt, W. A. Pantin, R. W. Southern (Oxford, 1948)

English Historical Documents (*EHD*), ed. A. R. Myers, vi ed. 1327-1485 (London, 1969)

Fisher, A., *William Wallace* (Edinburgh, 1986)

Flores Historiarum, ed. H. R. Luard (Rolls Series, 1890)

Foedera, Conventiones, Litterae e Cuiuscunque Generii Acta Publica, ed. T. Rymer

John of Fordun, *Chronicle of the Scottish Nation*, trans. William F Skene, (Edinburgh, 1872)

Fox, R. 'Urban Development, 1100-1700,' in *An Historical Geography of Scotland* ed. G. Whittington & I. D. White (London, 1983)

Frame, Robin, 'The Bruces in Ireland, 1315-1318,' *Irish Historical Studies* xix (1974): 3-37.

Fraser, Constance M., 'Edward I of England and the Regallian Franchise of Durham,' *Speculum* xxxi (1956): 329-342.

A History of Anthony Bek (Oxford, 1957)

'Medieval trading restrictions in the North-East,' *AA* xxxix (1961)

Freeman, A. Z., 'Wall-breakers and River-Bridgers: Military Engineers in the Scottish Wars of Edward I,' *Journal of British Studies* x (1971): 1-16

'The king's Penny: the Headquarters Paymasters under Edward I, 1295-1307', *Journal of British Studies*, vi, (1966): 1-22.

Fryde, Natalie, *The Tyranny and Fall of Edward II* (Cambridge, 1979)

Fergusson, J., *William Wallace, Guardian of Scotland* (London, 1938)

Galbraith, H. 'Extracts from the *Historia Aurea* and a French *"Brut"'*, *EHR* xliii (1928), 203-17

Given-Wilson, Chris, '*Vita Edwardi Secundi*: Memoir of Journal?' in *Thirteenth Century England*, ed. Michael Prestwich et al, vol. vi (Boydell, 1997), 165-176.

Goldstein, James, 'The Scottish Mission to Boniface VIII in 1301,' *SHR* lxx (1991): 1-15

Gough, Henry, *The Itinerary of Edward I: 1272-1307* (London, 1900)

Grant, Alexander, *Independence and Nationhood: Scotland 1306-1469* (London, 1984)

'To the Medieval Foundations,' *SHR* lxxiii (1994): 4-24.

Green, J. 'Anglo-Scottish Relations 1066-1174', in *England and Her Neighbours* ed. M. Jones & M Vale

Hadcock, N., 'A Map of Medieval Northumberland and Durham,' *AA* 4th series xvi (1939): 148-218

Historical Papers and Letters from the Northern Registers, ed. James Raine (Rolls Series, 1873)

Hedley, W. P., *Northumberland Families* (Newcastle, 1968)

Hewitt, H. J., *The Organisation of War under Edward III* (Manchester, 1966)

Higham, N. J., *The Kingdom of Northumbria: AD 350-1100* (Stroud, 1993)

Holt, J. C., *The Northerners* (Oxford, 1961)

Johnston, Hilda, *Edward of Caernarfon* (Manchester, 1946)

Keeney, B. C., 'The Medieval Idea of the State: the Great Cause, 1291-1292', *University of Toronto Law Journal* viii (1949): 48-71

'Military Service and the Development of Nationalism in England, 1272-1327,' *Speculum* xxii (1947): 534-49

Kershaw, I. 'The Great Famine and Agrarian crisis in England, 1315-1322.' *Past and Present* lix (1973) 3-50

'A Note on the Scots in the West Riding of Yorkshire, 1318-19,' *Northern History* xvii (1981): 231-239.

Leadman, Alex D. H., 'Battle of Mytton', *Yorkshire Archaeological and Topographical Journal*, viii (1884) 117-122

Lewis, N. B., 'The English Forces in Flanders, August-November 1297', in *Studies in Medieval History presented to F M Powicke*, ed. Hunt, R W et al (Oxford, 1948): 310-318

'The Organisation of Indentured Retinues in Fourteenth Century England' *THRS* 4th series xxvii (1945):29-39

'The Recruitment and Organization of a Contract Army, May to November 1337,' *BIHR* xxxvii (1964): 1-19

Linehan, A., 'A Fourteenth Century History of Anglo-Scottish Relations in a Spanish Manuscript', *BIHR* xlviii (1975): 106-22

Lucas, H. S., *The Low Countries and the Hundred Years' War, 1326-1347.* (1929)

'The Great European Famine of 1315, 1316, 1317.' *Speculum* v (1930) 343-377

'John Crabbe: Flemish Pirate, Merchant and Adventurer', *Speculum* xx (1945) 334-350

Lydon, J. F., 'The Bruce Invasion of Ireland,' in *Historical Studies*, ed. G A Hayes-McCoy, iv (1963), 111-25

'An Irish Army in Scotland in 1296,' *The Irish Sword* v (1962): 184-189.

Lynch, M., *Scotland: A New History* (London, 1991)

McCarthy, M. R. Summerson H. R. T. and Annis, R. G., 'The History of Carlisle Castle,' in *Carlisle Castle: A survey and documentary history*, ed. H R T Summerson (London, 1990)

Mackenzie, W. Mackay, *The Battle of Bannockburn a Study in Medieval Warfare* (1913)

McKisak, May, *The Fourteenth Century: 1307-1399* (Oxford, 1959)

McNamee, C. J., 'William Wallace's Invasion of Northern England in 1297,' *Northern History* xxvi (1990), 40-58

'Buying off Robert Bruce: an account of Monies Paid to the Scots by Cumberland Communities in 1313-14,' *TCWAAS*, xcii (1992): 77-89.

The Wars of the Bruces (East Lothian, 1997)

McNeil, P. & MacQueen, H., *Atlas of Scottish History to 1707*, (Edinburgh, 1996)

McNeil, P. & Nicholson, R., *An Historical Atlas of Scotland 400-1600*, (St Andrews, 1975)

Maddicot, J. R., *Thomas of Lancaster* (Oxford, 1970)

Marshall, D. W. H., 'Two Early English Occupations in Scotland: their Administrative Organization,' *SHR* xxv (1927): 20-40

Maxwell, H. R., 'The Battle of Bannockburn,' *SHR* xi (1914): 233-51

Mayhew, Nicholas, 'Alexander III-A Silver Age? An Essay in Scottish Medieval Economic History,' in *Scotland in the Reign of Alexander III* ed. Norman Reid (Edinburgh, 1990)

Middleton, A. E., *Sir Gilbert de Middleton* (Newcastle, 1918)

Miller, E. *War in the North: The Anglo-Scottish Wars of the Middle Ages* (Hull, 1960)

C Moor, *Knights of Edward I*, (Harl Soc, 1929) I (A-E)

Morris, J. E., *Welsh Wars of Edward I* (Oxford, 1901)

'Cumberland and Westmoreland Levies in the time of Edward I and Edward II,' *TCWAAS* iii (1903): 307-27

Bannockburn (1913)

'Mounted Infantry in Medieval Warfare,' *THRS* 3rd series, viii (1914): 77-102

Miller, T., *The Site of the Battle of Bannockburn*, (Historical Association, 1931)

Moorman, Rev J. R. H., 'Edward I at Lanercost Priory, 1306-7,' *EHR* lxvii (1952): 161-174.

Musgrove, F. *The North of England: a History from the Roman Times to the Present* (Oxford, 1990)

Neville, Cynthia J., 'The Political Allegiance of the Earls of Strathearn During the Wars of Independence,' *SHR* lxv (1986): 133-153

'Keeping the peace on the Northern Marches in the late Middle Ages', *EHR* cix (1994) 1-25.

Nicholson, Ranald, 'The Franco-Scottish and Franco-Norwegian Treaties of 1295', *SHR* xxxvii (1959), 114-132

'The Siege of Berwick,' *SHR* xl (1961): 19-42

'The Last Campaign of Robert Bruce,' *EHR* lxxvii (1962): 233-246

'A sequel to Edward Bruce's invasion of Ireland,' *SHR* xlii (1963): 30-40

Edward III and the Scots. (Oxford, 1965)

'David II, the Historians and the Chroniclers,' *SHR* xlv (1966): 59-78

Scotland: The Later Middle Ages (Edinburgh, 1974)

Nicolas, H. *The Siege of Caerlaverock* (London, 1828)

Oman, Sir Charles, *Art of War in the Middle Ages*, 2nd ed. (Oxford, 1924)

Oram, Richard D., 'Bruce, Balliol and the Lordship of Galloway: South-West Scotland and the Wars of Independence,' *Dumfriesshire Transactions* lxvii (1992): 29-47.

Original Letters Illustrative of English History, 3rd series, i, (London, 1848).

Ormrod, W. M.' *The Reign of Edward III: Crown and Political Society in England, 1327-77* (Yale, 1990)

Parliamentary Writs and Writs of Military Summons, ed. F. Palgrave (London, 1827-34)

Pevsner, N. *The Buildings of England, Northumberland*, (London Penguin, 1957)

Phillips, J. R. S., *Aymer de Valence Earl of Pembroke 1307-1324* (Oxford 1972)

Chistine de Pisan, *The Book of Fayttes of Armes and of Chyvalre* translated by *William Caxton from the French Original*, ed. A. T. P Byles (Early English Text Society, 1932)

Powicke, M., 'The English Commons in Scotland in 1322 and the Deposition of Edward II,' *Speculum* xxxv (1960): 556-582.

Military Obligation in Medieval England (Oxford, 1962)

The Thirteenth Century, 2nd ed. (Oxford, 1962)

Prestwich, Michael, 'Victualling estimates for English garrisons in Scotland during the early fourteenth century', *EHR* lxxxii (1967) 536-43

'The English Campaign of 1296 and the surrender of John Balliol: some supporting evidence,' *BIHR* xlix (1976)

'Cavalry Service in Early Fourteenth Century England', *War and Government in the Middle Ages*, ed. J. B. Gillingham and J. C Holt (Woodbridge 1984), 147-58

'Colonial Scotland: The English in Scotland under Edward I,' in *Scotland and England, 1286-1815* ed. R. A. Mason (Edinburgh, 1987)

War, Politics and Finance under Edward I (London, 1972)

The Three Edwards (London, 1980)

Edward I (London, 1988)

'England and Scotland during the Wars of Independence,' in *England and Her Neighbours, 1066-1453: Essays in honour of Pierre Chaplais* ed. M Jones & M Vale (London, 1989): 181-97

'Edward and the Maid of Norway,' *SHR* lxix (1990): 157-174

'Gilbert de Middleton and the Attack on the Cardinals, 1317,' in *Warriors and Churchmen in the High Middle Ages: Essays Presented to Karl Leyser*, ed. Timothy Reuter (London, 1992), 179-194

Armies and Warfare in the Middle Ages (Yale, 1996)

Prince, E., 'The Strength of English Armies in the Reign of Edward III', *EHR* xlvi (1931): 353-71

'The Importance of the Ccampaign of 1327,' *EHR* i (1935): 299-302.

'The Payment of Army Wages in the Middle Ages', *Speculum* xix (1944) 137-60.

Ramsey, Sir James, *The Dawn of the Constitution*, (London, 1908)

The Genesis of Lancaster, vol. 1 1307-1368 (Oxford, 1913)

'The Strength of English Armies in the Middle Ages', *EHR* xxix (1914) 221-7

Reid, Norman, 'The Kingless Kingdom, the Scottish Guardianships of 1286-1306', *SHR*, lxi (1982): 105-29

'Margaret 'Maid of Norway' and Scottish Queenship', *Reading Medieval Studies* viii (1982) p. 75-96

'Crown and Community under Robert I,' in *Medieval Scotland: Crown Lordship and Community. Essays presented to G W S Barrow*, ed. A Grant and K J Stringer (Edinburgh: 1993): 203-22

Reid, R. C., 'Edward de Balliol,' *Dumfriesshire Transactions* xxxv (1956-7): 38-63

Reid, W. Stanford, 'Trade, Traders and Scottish Independence,' *Speculum* xxix (1954): 210-22

'The Scots and the Staple Ordinance of 1313,' *Speculum* xxxiv (1959): 598-610.

'Sea-Power in the Anglo-Scottish War 1296-1327,' *The Mariner's Mirror* xlvi (1960): 7-23

Register of Robert Winchelsea ed. Rose Graham (Oxford, 1956)

Register Regum Scottorum vol. v ed. Archibald A M Duncan (1988)

Richardson, H. G. & Sayles, G. O., 'Scottish Parliaments of Edward I', *SHR* xxv, (1928): 300-17.

Reynolds, S., *Kingdoms and Communities in Western Europe, 900-1300* (Oxford, 1984)

Rotuli Scotiae, ed. D. Macpherson (London, 1814-19)

Sayles, G. O., 'Ancient Correspondence,' SHR xxiv (1927): 325-6

'The Guardians of Scotland and a Parliament at Rutherglen in 1300,' *SHR* xxiv (1927): 245-250

Scalacronica by Sir Thomas Gray of Heton, trans. Sir Herbert Maxwell (Glasgow, 1907), *SHR*, iii, iv

Scammel, Jean, 'Robert I and the North of England,' *EHR* lxxiii (1958): 385-403.

Scotichronicon by Walter Bower, ed. & trans. D. E. R. Watt vol. 6 (Aberdeen, 1991); vol. 7 (Aberdeen, 1996)

Scotland in 1298, ed. H. Gough (London, 1888)

Simpson, G. G., 'The claim of Florence, count of Holland, to the Scottish throne,' *SHR* xxxvi (1957): 111-124

'The Declaration of Arbroath, Revitalised', *SHR* lvi (1977): 11-33

'Why was John Balliol called "Toom Tabard"?' *SHR* xlvii (1968): 169-199

Simpson, D., 'The Campaign and Battle of Culblean, AD1335', *PSAS*, lxiv (1929-30), 201-11

Smallwood, T. M., 'An unpublished early account of Bruce's murder of the Comyn', *SHR* liv (1975): 1-10

Stones, E. L. G., 'The English mission to Edinburgh in 1928,' *SHR*, xxviii, (1949): 121-32

'An addition to the *Rotuli Scotiae*,' *SHR* xxix (1950): 23-51

'The Anglo-Scottish negotiations of 1327,' *SHR* xxx (1951): 49-54

'The Treaty of Northampton,' *History* xxxviii (1953): 54-61.

'The Submission of Robert Bruce to Edward I c. 1301-1302' *SHR* xxxiv (1955): 122-134

'Allusion to the Black Rood of Scotland,' *SHR* xxxviii (1959): 174-5.

Anglo-Scottish Relations, 1174-1328 (Oxford, 1965)

'An undelivered letter form Paris to London (1303),' *EHR* lxxx (1965): 86-88.

'The Mission of Thomas Wale and Thomas Delisle from Edward I to Pope Boniface in 1301,' *Nottingham Medieval Studies* xxvi (1982): 8-28.

Stones E. L. G. & Blount, M., 'The Surrender of King John of Scotland to Edward I in 1296: Some New Evidence,' *BIHR* xlviii (1975)

Stones, E. L. G. & Simpson, G., *Edward I and the Throne of Scotland*, 2 vols. (Oxford: 1978).

Stringer, K. J., *Earl David of Huntingdon: A Study in Anglo-Scottish History* (Edinburgh, 1985)

Summerson, Henry, *Medieval Carlisle: The City and the border from the later eleventh century to the mid-sixteenth century* (TCWAAS, 1993)

Sumption, Jonathan, *The Hundred Years War*, vol. 1, Trial by Combat (London: 1990)

Taxatio Ecclesiastica Angliae et Walliae Auctorite P Nicholai IV circa AD 1291, ed. J Topham (Record Commission, 1802)

Taylor, A. J., 'Master James of St George', *EHR*, lxv (1950), 433-57

'Thomas de Houghton: A royal carpenter of the late 13th century,' *Antiquaries Journal* xxx (1950): 28-33

'Walter of Hereford,' *SHR* xxxiv (1955): 44-6

Trevelyan, G. M., *History of England* (London, 1929)

Tout, T. F., *The Political History of England* (London, 1905),

'The Tactics of the Battles of Boroughbridge and Morlaix,' *EHR* xix (1906): 711-5.

'The Battle of Bannockburn', *History* v (1920): 37-40

Chapters in Medieval Administrative History, 6 vols. (Manchester, 1920-33)

The Place of the Reign of Edward II in English History, (Manchester, 1914)

Tuck, J. A. 'War and Society in the Medieval North,' *Northern History* xxi (1985): 33-52

'Northumbrian Society in the Fourteenth Century,' *Northern History* vi (1971): 22-39

'The Emergence of a Northern Nobility, 1250-1400,' *Northern History* xxii (1986): 1-17

Verbruggen, F. *The Art of Warfare in Western Europe During the Middle Ages* (Holland, 1977)

Vita Edwardi Secundi monachi cuiusdam Malmesberiensis: the Life of Edward II by the so-called Monk of Malmesbury ed. & trans. N Denholm-Young, (Nelson's Medieval Texts, 1957)

Watson, F. J., 'Settling the Stalemate: Edward I's Peace in Scotland, 1303-1305,' in *Thirteenth Century England*, ed. Michael Prestwich et al, vol. vi (Boydell, 1997), 127-144.

Webster, Bruce, 'David II and the Government of Fourteenth Century Scotland,' *THRS* 5th series xxi, 115-30.

'Scotland without a King, 1329-1341,' in *Medieval Scotland*, ed. Alexander Grant & Keith Stringer (Edinburgh, 1993), 223-238.

White, R. 'The Battle of Neville's Cross', *Archaeologia Aeliana*, new series i (1857): 271-303

Whittington, G. & White, I. D., *An Historical Geography of Scotland* (London, 1983)

Winter, P. M., *Newcastle upon Tyne* (Newcastle, 1989)

Wright, Thomas, *Political Songs of England*, ed. P Coss (Cambridge, 1996)

The Roll of Arms of the princes, barons and knights who attended king Edward I to the siege of Caerlaverock (London, 1864)

Young, A, 'Noble families and political factions in the reign of Alexander III,' in *Scotland in the Reign of Alexander III*, ed. Norman Reid (Edinburgh, 1990): 1-30

Robert the Bruce's Rivals: the Comyns, 1212-1314 (Tuckwell, 1997).

INDEX

Aberdeen, 53, 72, 73, 119, 134-5, 155, 157, 214, 252, 286
  archbishop of, see Alexander of Kinninmouth
  archdeacon of, see Barbour, John
  bishop of, 53, 72, 73, 224
Aberdeenshire, sheriff of, see Henry de Latham
Abernethy, 10
Abernethy, Alexander, 114, 117-18, 134, 136, 161, 165, 169
Abernethy, Lawrence, 275
Aboyne, 134
Acre, fall of, 36
Adam of Gashom, 119
Adam of Gordon, 122, 132, 138, 173-4, 210, 224
Agenais, 236-7, 274, 285, 288
Airdale, 220, 222
Airmyn, William, bishop of Norwich, 249
Airth, 280
Airth, William, 189
Alan of Galloway, 57
Alba, kingdom of, 9
Albanact, king of Scotland, 101
Albany, duke of, 309
Alcrum Moor, 229
Aldburgh, Ivo of, 240
Aldeburgh, William, 304
Aldstone Moor, 297
Alemouth, 120
Alexander II, 11, 30, 32, 55, 57, 185
Alexander III, 11, 15-19, 21, 35, 36, 37, 40, 57, 117, 144, 164, 203, 254
Alfonso XI of Castile, 255
Allerdale, 78, 208
Alnwick, 10, 77, 78, 107, 219, 229, 247, 282
Alphonse, son of Edward I (d. 1290), 32
Amory, Richard, captain of

Berwick, 221, 229
Ancrum, 70
Andrew de Rait, see Rait, Andrew
Anglesey, 205
Angus, 116, 291
  earl of, see Gilbert de Umfraville and Ingram de Umfraville and Robert de Umfraville and Thomas Stewart
Annan, 98, 265
Annandale, 32, 34, 44, 66, 80, 113, 132, 134, 161, 275, 277, 294
  lord of, see Bruce, Robert
Anthony de Lucy, 195, 200, 233, 235, 238, 243, 267, 278, 286, 292
Antrim, 140
Appeal of the Seven Earls, 23
Appleby, 95, 197, 242
Applegarth, 94
Aquitaine, Duchy of, 41, 112, 181, 208, 274, 288
Arbroath, abbot of, see Linton, Bernard
  see also Declaration of Arbroath
Archibald, bishop of Moray, 59
Argentine, see Giles d'Argentine
Argyll, 61, 152, 155
  barons of, 139
Arran, Isle of, 85, 106, 142
  lord of, see Mentieth, John
Artois, Robert of, 288
Arundel, earl of, see FitzAlan, Edmund and FitzAlan, Richard
Ashbridge, 24
Asnières-sur-Oise, treaty of, 108-10, 112
Athelstan, king of Wessex, 9
Atholl, earl of, see Campbell, John and Campbell, Neil and Strathbogie, David and

Strathbogie, John
Athy, John of, 205
Auchertool, 215
Audfinn, bishop of Bergen, 21-2
Audley, Hugh, earl of Gloucester, 107, 113, 292
Avignon, 139, 214, 236, 238, 305
Avoch, 64, 74
Award of Northam, 28
Aymer de Valence, earl of Pembroke, 73, 94, 103-4, 116, 136-9, 145-6, 149, 151, 154, 159-61, 168, 181-2, 194-5, 197, 200, 207-9, 211-12, 217-18, 225, 234
Ayr, 30, 68, 84, 106-7, 132-3, 140, 146, 155, 162, 165, 167, 170, 203, 206, 210
  constable of, see Leybourne, Robert and Montassieu de Noaillac
  sheriff of, see Percy, Henry

Badenoch, 54, 128
  lord of, see Comyn, John 'Red'
Badlesmere, Bartholomew, 165, 207-8, 211, 225, 227
Bailleul castle, 107
Baird, Robert, 96
Baker, Geoffrey, 266
Baldcock, Robert, 234
Balliol, Alexander, keeper of Selkirk, 90, 107, 111
Balliol, Bernard de, 31
Balliol, Devorguilla, 19, 31
Balliol, Edward (d. 1356), 39, 53, 54, 126, 237, 259-87, 290, 292-5, 300-7
Balliol, Eleanor, 31
Balliol, Henry, 265
Balliol, Hugh, 32
Balliol, John, king of Scotland, 18, 23, 24, 28,

29-30, 31-42, 48-50, 52-4, 57-8, 80, 86-7, 91, 95, 101, 107, 109, 112, 124, 129, 144, 163-4, 196
Balliol, John de, 31, 55
Balvenie castle, 154
Bamburgh, 40, 167, 201, 219, 221, 225-6, 229, 240-1, 269, 299
Bampton, 151
Ban, Donald, 10
Banf, 73, 135, 153, 162, 170
Bannockburn, battle of, 8, 148, 157, 171, 177-95, 196-7
Bar, see Joan de Bar
Barbour, John, archdeacon of Aberdeen, 127, 130, 135-6, 139, 140, 142, 144-6, 154, 171, 174, 177-80, 182, 184, 186-8, 192-4, 206, 218, 225, 246, 254
Barclay, David, 294, 296
Barnard Castle, 161, 200, 201, 219, 229, 243, 298
Barron, Evan, 8, 47, 76
Barrow, Prof., 55, 190
Bartholomew, Roger, 36-7
Barton, 261
Basset, Ralph of Drayton, 84, 148, 236-7
Bastenthwaite, Alexander, 151
Baston, Robert, 178
Bath and Wells, bishop of, see Burnell, Robert
Bayonne, 181
Beauchamp, Walter, 148
Beauchamp, William, 148
Beaumont, Ermengarde de, 11
Beauchamp, Guy, earl of Warwick, 39, 80, 94, 103, 114, 159, 160, 168, 174, 181, 200-1, 207, 259,
Beauchamp, Thomas, earl of Warwick, 278, 280-1, 291-2
Beaumont, Henry, earl of Buchan (d. 1340), 161, 172, 186-7, 194, 203, 209, 211, 212, 215-16, 223, 228, 235, 240, 250,

256, 258-61, 263, 265, 269, 272-3, 276-7, 280-1, 283, 287, 293
Beaumont, Katherine, 256, 283, 286
Beaumont, Louis, bishop of Durham (d. 1333), 212, 215-16, 229-30, 232, 238, 247
Bedewynde, Walter, 121
Bek, Anthony, bishop of Durham (d. 1311), 20-1, 23, 35, 40, 42, 45, 50, 52-4, 67, 73, 78, 81-4, 92, 158
Belford, 247
Bellegarde, battle of, 60
Ben, James of St Andrews, 263
Benedict Gaetani, see Pope Boniface VIII
Benedict, see Pope Benedict XI and XII
Benhol, Robert, 270
Benstead, John, controller of the wardrobe, 50, 116
Bentley, Henry, 199
Bergen, 21-2
Berkeley, Maurice, 182, 192, 210-11
Berkeley, Thomas, 280
Bermingham, John, earl of Louth, 205, 228-9
Bernard de Balliol, 31
Bernicia, kingdom of, 9
Bertrand de Got, see Pope Clement V
Berwick-upon-Tweed, attacked, 210-11, 216-17
bishop at, 133
Bishopthorpe truce, 240
captured by English, 45-50
ceded to Edward III, 271
controlling ships, 170
court hearings, 24-5, 30, 35
Cressingham at, 68
David and Joan marriage, 251
David II released, 307
demanded as surety, 40
Douglas imprisoned, 69
draft treaty of 1354, 305
as English sheriffdom,

282
Edward I at, 54, 57, 92, 93, 151-2, 166
Edward II at, 177, 196
English occupation 1298, 89
feudal demand from, 93-4
forces defending, 157, 170, 171, 277
Haliburton captures, 77
John Segrave at, 162
muster at, 103, 175
Neil Bruce executed, 141
parliament, 59
Percy at, 73, 277
population threatened, 201
prince of Wales at, 107
raid in 1312, 171
raid in 1314, 173
raid in 1355, 305-6
Rait at, 72
reclaimed by Balliol, 300
repairs in 1314
siege of, 220-1, 266-70
supplies redirected, 278
supply base, 108, 120
surrender in 1461, 309
treaty of Berwick, 8, 296, 309
treaty of Newcastle, 273
Valence sent to, 165
warden of, see Fitzroger, Roger
Warenne at, 70, 73-4, 77, 81
Beverley, 231
Biggar, 165
Bigod, Roger, earl of Norfolk, 61, 74, 80, 84-5, 99-100, 103, 165
Binnock, Matthew, 172
Birgham, 20-2
Birgham-Northampton, treaty of, 21, 24, 26, 37, 97, 116
Bishop Auckland, 243, 298
Bishopthorpe, 235, 237-8, 240, 256
Bisset, Baldred, 102, 118, 224
Bisset, Hugh, 140
Bisset, William, 71, 120
'Black Agnes', see Moray, countess of

Black Death, 301
'Black dog', see Warwick, earl of
Black Isle of Ross, 65, 154
Black Parliament, the, 225
Black Prince, 306
Black Rood, the, 250
Blackness, 119, 120
Blakehoumor, 230
Blanchland, 244
Blind Harry, 7, 63, 73, 76
Blunt, John, 123
Boharm, 64
Bohun, Edward (d. 1335), 269, 273, 276-7
Bohun, Henry de, 148, 186
Bohun, Humphrey, see Humphrey de Bohun
Bohun, William, 294
Bois, Thomas du, 117
Bolinbroke, Henry, 304
Bolton, 67
Boniface VIII, see Pope Boniface VIII
Bordeaux, 112, 138
    archbishop of, see Pope Clement V
Boroughbridge, 226-9, 253
Botetort, John, 110, 114, 119, 139, 145
Bothal castle, 302
Bothwell, 65, 119, 146, 157, 161, 170, 195, 288, 291
    baron of, see Aymer de Valence, earl of Pembroke
Boulogne, 153, 159
Bower, Walter, 7, 134, 148, 150, 172, 214, 256, 275, 288, 294
Bowes, 78
Bowness, 229
Boyd, Gilbert, 206
Boyd, Robert, 142, 155
Boyd, Roger, 132, 135
Boys, Humphrey, 267
Brabazon, Roger, 26, 35, 37
Brander, Pass of, 155
Brandons of Bute, 275
Braveheart, 7
Brechin, 113, 119, 133
Brechin, David, 154, 169-70, 225
Brian de Jay, 84

Bridlington, 230-1
Bristol, 96, 239
Brittany, 288
Brittany, John, see John of Brittany
Brodick, 142
Bromsgrove, Richard, 119, 120
Brotherton, Thomas, 239, 269
Brough, 197, 296
Brown, Richard, 225
Bruce, 178-9
Bruce, Alexander, earl of Carrick, 144, 262, 265, 271
Bruce, Christian, 142, 272, 282
Bruce, David, see David II
Bruce, Edward (d. 1318), 142, 155, 162, 163, 171, 175-6, 178, 183-6, 190, 197, 203-7, 220, 225
Bruce, Isabella, 34
Bruce, Joan, 285
Bruce, Marjorie, 69, 142, 202-3
Bruce, Mary, 141
Bruce, Neil, 139, 141
Bruce, Robert, lord of Annandale, 8, 12, 18-19, 22-3, 28, 29-36, 39, 43-4, 51, 54-5, 58, 66, 78, 84, 86-7, 93, 116, 118-19
Bruce, Robert II, lord of Annandale (d. 1142), 32
Bruce, Robert VII, lord of Annandale (d. 1304), 128
Bruce, Robert VIII, lord of Annandale, 34, 40
Bruce, Robert, bastard son of king Robert, 261, 263
Bruce, Robert, earl of Carrick, king of Scotland (d. 1329), 18, 27, 34, 54, 58, 65-6, 68-9, 73, 76, 80, 87-8, 93, 109, 113, 126-40, 142-58, 162-6, 168-75, 177, 179, 182-96, 201-9, 212-25, 228-37, 239-42, 247-50, 254-7
Bruce, 110
Brunton, 43

Buchan, countess of, 141
    earl of, see Beaumont, Henry and Comyn, John, earl of Buchan
Buittle, 19, 170, 172, 301, 306
Bullock, William, 291, 294, 296
Burgandy, 288
Burgh Muir, 280
Burgh, see Elizabeth de and Richard de and William de
Burghersh, Henry, bishop of Lincoln, 249
Burgh-on-Sands, 147
Burned Isle, 296
Burnell, Robert, bishop of Bath and Wells, 28
Burnt Candlemas campaign, 306
Burton-on-Trent, 227
Burtswick, 142
Bury St Edmunds, 60-1
Butler, Edmund, 204
Byland, 230-2
Bywell, 77, 200

Caddonlea, 40, 44
Caelaverock, 93-9, 155, 170, 172, 295
Caen, 296
Caernarfon, Edward, prince of Wales, see under Edward II, Caernarfon
Caillau, Raymond de, 210-11
Caithness, earl, 12, 134, 153
Calais, 297, 300-1
Camber, king of Wales, 101
Cambridge, 100
Cambuskenneth, 127, 189, 202
Campbell, John, earl of Atholl (d. 1333), 262, 271
Campbell, Neil, earl of Atholl (d. 1316), 139-40, 189-90
Campbell, Nigel, 71, 162
Canmore, Duncan, see Duncan II
Canmore, Edgar, 10
Canmore, Malcolm, see

Malcolm III
Canmore, Margaret, see Margaret, Maid of Norway
Canterbury, 91-2, 103
  archbishop of, 229
  see also Winchelsea, Robert
Cantilupe, Sir John, 54
Canute, king of Wessex, 9
Cardross, 254
Carham, battle of, 45
Carlisle, 10, 32, 40, 44-5, 49, 78, 79, 85, 95-8, 104-7, 138, 142, 145, 147, 150, 161-2, 169, 195, 197, 199-200, 208-9, 228-9, 233, 238, 243, 247, 265-6, 279, 297, 300
  bishop of, 292
  see also Halton, John
  earl of, see Harcla, Andrew
Carrick, 134, 140, 145, 286, 296
  earl of, see Bruce, Robert and Bruce, Alexander
Carrickfergus, 204-5
Carter Bar, 214
Castle Barnard, 57
Castleford, 222
Castleton, 297
Chandis, John, 148
Chapter of Myton, 222
Charles IV, king of France, 236, 288
Charles of Valois, 159, 236-7
Charter of the Forest, 99
Chester, 51, 65, 73, 139, 277
Chester, bishop of, 146
  justiciar of, see Grey, Reginald
Chester-le-Street, 208
Cheyne, Henry of Aberdeen, 59, 72
  see also Reginald le Cheyne, warden of Moray
Christian de Pisan, 55
Christine de Moubray, 43
Christison, General Sir P. 190
Cinque Ports, 38, 94, 228,

242, 273
Clackmannan, 84
Clare, see Gilbert de Clare and Margaret de Clare and Thomas de Clare
Clavering, John de, 200
Cleke, Christy, 290
Clement V, see Pope Clement V
Clement VI, see Pope Clement VI
Cleveland, 200, 227, 247
Clifford, Lady, 201
Clifford, Robert, 67-9, 80, 89-90, 114, 136, 144, 151, 154, 162, 166, 168, 181-2, 184, 186-9, 200, 265, 292
Clipstone, 24
Cobham, Ralph, 230
Coldingham, 51
Coldstream, 45, 56, 104, 210
  prior of, 56
Comyn, Alexander, 71, 88, 154, 202
Comyn, Alice, 203, 256
Comyn, Edward, 73, 113
Comyn, Joan, 256
Comyn, John 'Red', lord of Badenoch (d.1303), 18, 19, 21, 22, 29, 30, 31, 35, 53, 54, 55, 58, 71
Comyn, John 'Red', lord of Badenoch (the younger, d. 1306), 44, 49, 51, 58, 86-8, 93, 95, 112, 116-17, 126-9, 132, 136, 182, 256, 279
Comyn, John, earl of Buchan (d. 1289), 19
Comyn, John, earl of Buchan (d. 1308), 18, 31, 33, 37, 40, 44, 53, 54, 58, 71, 76, 78, 87-8, 92-3, 95-6, 106, 111, 113, 122, 122, 134, 153-4, 156, 161, 169, 202, 256
Comyn, Margaret, 202, 256
Comyn, Robert, 128
Comyn, Walter, 15, 265
Comyn, William, 87, 137
Connor, 204
Constantinople, 301

Copeland, 171, 208
Copeland, John, 299, 301, 306
Coquetdale, 292
Corbeil, treaty of, 238, 240, 248, 274
Corbridge, 77, 169, 171, 207, 243, 298
Córdoba, 226
Cork, 94
Corncarn, 153
Cornwall, earl of, 159, 280, 287
  see also Richard, earl of Cornwall
Coull castle, 153
Coupar, 137
Coupar-Angus, abbot of, 116, 122
Coupland, John, 298
Courtrai, battle of, 110, 111
Coventry, bishop of, 259
Cowick, 267
Coxet Hill, 183
Crabb, John, 263, 264, 267
Craig, John, 283
Crambeth, Matthew
  bishop of Dunkeld (d. 1309), 28, 39, 59, 60, 111, 122
Crawford, Reginald de, 71, 144-5
Crécy, battle of, 180, 250, 253, 297
Creighton, 228
Cressingham, see Hugh de Cressingham
Crichton, 292
Cromarty, 114
Cromwell, John, 162, 223
Cruachan, Ben, 155
Culblean, 283, 289
Culross, 228
Cumbria (Cumberland), 9-10, 78, 104, 151, 171, 173, 221, 227, 229, 290, 292, 297
  sheriff of, 67
Cumnock, campaign, 150-1
Cunningham, 264
Cunningham, Robert, 93, 146
Cupar, 133, 281, 283-5, 291, 293-4

Curthose, Robert, 10

d'Aimery, see Hugh
  d'Aimery
Dail Righ, see Dalry
Dalisle, James, 136, 146
Dalriada, kingdom of, 9
Dalry, 139-40
Dalswinton, 106, 126, 132,
  155, 170
Dalton, Thomas bishop of
  Whithorn, 59
Damme, 88
Darcy, John, 281
Darlington, 227, 244, 298
Dartmouth, 283
David ap Gryffydd, 124
David I, king of Scots (d.
  1153), 10, 32, 45, 78-9,
  122, 182
David II, king of Scots (d.
  1371), 203, 239, 248,
  250-1, 255, 258, 260,
  265, 272, 274, 279, 284-
  5, 287, 293-304, 307
David, earl of Huntingdon,
  31, 33
David of Inchmartin, 140
Dean, Forest of, 104, 277
Declaration of Arbroath,
  102, 129, 223-5, 254
Delilse, Thomas, 101, 102,
  107
Derby, earl of, 166
  see also Henry of
  Grosmont and Thomas
  of Lancaster
Derwent, 297
Desmond, earl of, see
  FitzThomas, Maurice
Despenser, see Hugh le
  Despenser (elder and
  younger)
Deyncourt, William, 187
Dieppe, 274
Dingwall, 163
Dirleton, 81, 200
disinherited, the, 256-99
Doddington, 282
Donald of Mar, see Mar,
  Donald, earl of (I and II)
Doncaster, 306
Donibristle, 214
Dornock, 267
Douglas, 62, 154, 172
Douglas, Alexander (d.

1333), 271
Douglas, Archibald, 232,
  242, 244-5, 263, 265,
  267-71, 289, 291
Douglas, James (d. 1330),
  142-4, 154-5, 174, 177,
  183, 184, 187-8, 194,
  208-11, 213-14, 216,
  218-19, 222-3, 226,
  228-30, 242, 247, 249-
  50, 255, 265, 267, 281,
  289
Douglas, James, son of
  Douglas of Lothian, 267
Douglas, William, first earl
  of Douglas, 296, 305
Douglas, William of
  Liddesdale, 302-5
Douglas, William, lord of
  Douglas (d. 1299), 47,
  64, 66, 68-9
Douglas, William of
  Lothian (d. 1353), 177,
  279-84, 286, 293-6,
  297-9, 305
Douglas Larder, 144, 155
Douglasdale, 144
Dover, 91, 246
Drip, 117
Drogheda, 94
Dryburgh, 45, 113
Dryman, 116
Dublin, 94, 203-5
Duèse, Jacques, see Pope
  John XXII
Duffes, 154
Dumbarton, 52, 133, 163,
  272, 274-5, 281-3, 293
Dumfries, 19, 89, 94, 98,
  126, 128, 132, 141, 150,
  155, 170, 172, 273, 275,
  282, 300
  sheriff of, see Maxwell,
  Eustace
Dun, Thomas, 48, 205
Dunaverty, 132-3, 139
Dunbar, 29, 49-52, 107,
  169, 194, 195, 292-3
  battle of, 49-52, 56, 58,
  65, 76
Dunbar, Patrick IV, earl of
  March (d. 1308), 18, 30,
  35, 43, 49, 50, 58, 83,
  90, 94, 104, 118, 122,
  134
Dunbar, Patrick V, earl of

March (d. 1368), 173,
  182, 202, 245, 249, 261-
  3, 267, 269, 272-3, 277,
  279-83, 291, 293, 299,
  305
Dunblane, 120
  bishop of, 249
Duncan II, king of Scots, 10
Duncan III, earl of Fife (d.
  1289), 9, 18, 19, 37, 59,
  133
Duncan IV, earl of Fife (d.
  1353), , 202, 249, 262-4,
  281, 291, 302
Duncan of Frendraught,
  147, 152, 153
Dundalk, 204-5
Dundarg, 276-7
Dundee, 135, 157, 162,
  166, 170, 214, 280, 304
  siege of, 73, 74, 77, 133-
  4, 169
Dunfermline, 112, 114,
  116, 254, 261
Dunkeld, bishops of, see
  Crambeth and Matthew
  and Sinclair, William
Dunnottar, 286, 291
Dunoon, 275
Dunotar, 285
Dunstaffnage, 152, 155
Dunstanburgh, 219, 227,
  229
Dupplin Moor, 253, 261,
  263, 289
Durham, 25, 78, 92, 171,
  197-8, 207-8, 215, 243,
  246-7, 250, 267, 297-8
  bishop of, see Beaumont,
  Louis and Bek, Anthony
  and Richard de Bury
Durisdeer, 132
Dyfford, William de, 296

Earl Warenne, see
  Warenne, John de
Ebchester, 298
Ecclefechan, 94
Edgar, king of England,
  101
Edinburgh, 9, 15, 52, 56,
  77, 81, 84, 87, 89-90,
  103, 107, 108, 113, 119,
  157, 170-1, 175, 178,
  229, 249, 273, 280-2,
  292-4, 300, 305

Edinburgh–Northampton treaty, 249, 255, 258, 260
Edmund Crouchback, second son of Henry III, 27, 38, 42, 60, 108
Edward I, 8, 11, 12-13, 15-21, 23-30, 32-62, 67-74, 76-8, 80-124, 127, 129, 132, 135-6, 138, 140-9, 158, 160, 164, 179-80, 200, 252
Edward II (d. 1327), 8, 22, 24, 138-9, 149, 150-3, 158-71, 174, 176, 177-82, 186-9, 192-4, 196-212, 215, 217- 221, 223, 227-37, 239-40, 252, 256
Caernarfon, prince of Wales, 19, 20, 32, 36, 37, 73, 80, 91, 94, 96, 98, 103-7, 116-17, 120, 138-9, 141-2, 147-50
Edward III, 8, 180, 198, 237, 239-48, 251, 255, 257-61, 264-91, 294-307
Edwin, king of Northumbria, 9
Elderslie, 62
Eleanor of Castile, 24, 26
Elgin, 54, 65, 72-3, 153-4, 286
sheriff of, see Wiseman, William
Elizabeth de Bohun, 136
Elizabeth de Burgh, queen of Scots (d. 1327), 128, 203
Ellis, a clerk, 214
Enzie, 72
Eric II, king of Norway, 17, 19, 20, 21, 30-1, 34-5, 140
Ermengarde de Beaumont, 11
Erskine, William, 244, 304
Esplechin, 294
Ettrick, 83, 300-1
Eu, count of, 286
Eure, see John de Eure
Evesham, abbot of, 25-6
battle of, 55-6

Falaise, treaty of, 10-11

Falkirk, 178
battle of, 55, 82-6, 89, 93, 157, 183
Falkland, 291
Faughart, 205, 220
Felton, Robert, 136
Felton, William, 287
Fergus of Ardrossan, 206
Ferriby, Richard, keeper of the wardrobe, 277
Ferry Bridge, 298
Fiennes, William de, 175
Fieschi, cardinal Luke, 215-16
Fife, earl of, see Duncan III and IV
sheriff of, 214
FitzAlan, Brian of Bedale, 29, 73
FitzAlan, Edmund, earl of Arundel (d. 1326), 80, 94, 103, 165, 181, 212-14
FitzAlan, Richard, earl of Arundel (d. 1376), 240, 280, 292
FitzAlan, Walter, 62
FitzHeyr, Hugh, 93
FitzMarmaduke, John, 81, 161
Fitzroger, Roger, warden of Berwick, 136
FitzThomas, Maurice earl of Desmond, 282
Fitzwarin, William, 65, 76-7
Flanders, 59, 68, 73-4, 78, 81, 91, 237, 241, 251-2, 288, 295
count of, see Guy of Dampierre
Fleming, Malcolm, earl of Wigtown, 272, 274, 295, 302
Flodden Field, battle of, 238
Florence, count of Holland, 31, 33, 35, 126
Fordun, John see John of Fordun
Forest of Dean, 104, 277
Forfar, 29, 134, 156, 157
Forres, 65, 72, 286
Forteviot, 261
Fortriu, kingdom of, 9
Fosse, master of Pelarym,

239
Francis, William, 175
Fraser, Andrew (d. 1333), 271
Fraser, James (d. 1333), 264, 271
Fraser, Simon (d. 1333), 87, 90, 106, 111, 113, 116, 118, 122, 124, 129, 137, 141, 264-5, 271
Fraser, William, bishop of St Andrews (d. 1297), 18, 19, 22-3, 33, 37, 39, 59, 60, 87
Frendraught, see Duncan of Frendraught
Frere, William, 102
Frescobaldi, bankers, 161, 167
Froissart, the chronicler, 299
Furness, 198, 212, 228
Fyvie, 154

Gaetani, Benedict see Pope Boniface VIII
Gaillard, château, 284
Galloway, 12, 15, 30, 55, 57, 59, 92, 95-9, 103-4, 113, 114, 123, 132-3, 142, 145, 151-2, 155, 166, 180, 250, 301, 309
bishop of, 249
see also Thomas of Galloway
Garencières, sire de, 305-6
Garioch, 33, 153
Gartnait of Mar, 72
Gascony, 37, 38-40, 41, 42, 44, 56, 60, 91, 108, 228, 233, 236-7, 288, 291
Gask, 262
Gateshead, 23
Gaucelin, cardinal John, 215-16
Gaveston, Piers, 98, 148, 151, 158-61, 166, 167-8, 174, 221
Geoffrey of Monmouth, 100
Geoffrey le Scrope, 233, 249, 265, 273
Germany, 252, 262
Gifford, bishop of Worcester, 20
Gilbert de Clare, earl of

Gloucester, 148, 160, 162, 165-6, 181-2, 184, 186, 192, 195
Gilbert of Glencarnie (the elder), 152
Gilbert of Glencarnie, commander of Elgin (the younger), 147, 153
Gilbert de la Hay, 137
Gilbert de Umfraville, earl of Angus (d. 1307), 29, 37, 43, 58, 90, 134
Gilbert de Umfraville, earl of Angus (d. 1381), 195, 200, 202, 211, 223, 257, 280-1, 292, 298
Gilbertson, Walter, 195
Giles d'Argentine, 139, 148, 194
Gilsland, 168, 200-1, 267
Glasgow, 59, 119, 123, 130, 280
  bishop of, 249
  see also Wishart, Robert
Glasrog, 68
Glen Trool, 145-7
Glencairn, 106
Glencarnie, see Gilbert of Glencarnie
Gloucester, 96, 227
  earl of, see Audley, Hugh and Gilbert de Clare and Monthermer, Ralph
Golightly, Patrick, 30, 35
Gordon, see Adam of Gordon
Goushill, Richard, 278
Graham, David, 87, 117, 122
Graham, James of Abercorne, 84
Graham, John, 299
Graham, Patrick, sheriff of Stirling, 50, 225
Grahamstown, 83
Granada, 255
Great Cause, the, 24, 26, 36, 101, 109, 126, 164, 226
Great Yarmouth, 228
Greenfield, William, archbishop of York, 207
Gretna Green, 44
Grey, Henry, 136
Grey, Reginald, justiciar of Chester, 73

Grey, Thomas, 63-4, 178, 182, 185, 187, 229, 300, 305
Gryffydd, David ap, 124
Guardians, the, 18-21, 23, 26, 27, 29-31, 36, 37, 87, 109
Guînes treaty, 305
Guisborough, 32, 75, 76, 77, 84
Guy, count of Namur, 280-1
Guy de Balliol, 31
Guy of Dampierre, count of Flanders, 39, 60, 91

Haakon of Norway, 86
Haddington, 76, 267, 273, 306
Haddon Laws, 295
Hadrian's Wall, 8
Haggerston, 167
Hailes, lord, 216
Hainault, count of, 239
  see also John of Hainault and Philippa of Hainault
Haliburton, see Henry de Haliburton and John de Haliburton
Halidon Hill, battle of, 253, 269-71, 273, 277, 289
Halton, John, bishop of Carlisle (d. 1324), 66, 69, 78, 89, 94, 225
Haltwhistle, 107, 168, 207, 244
Hambleton Hills, 230
Hamburg, 80
Hampyle, Hugh, 293
Happrew, 116, 117
Harbottle, 49, 168, 218, 219, 223
Harcla, Andrew, earl of Carlisle (d. 1323), 197, 209, 220-1, 227, 229-33, 253
Harrowby, 233
Hartlepool, 170, 208, 219, 227
Hastangs, Robert, 87, 90, 106-7
Hastings, Edmund, commander of Perth, 157, 161
Hastings, John of

Abergavenny, 31, 32-3, 34-5, 54, 142
Hatton, 46
Hawick, 296
Hay, Gilbert, 189
Haydon Bridge, 243
Helmsley, 230
Henry I, king of England, 11, 29
Henry II, king of England, 10, 25
Henry III, king of England, 11, 19, 20, 27, 76, 149
Henry IV, king of England, 304
Henry VI, king of England, 309
Henry, earl of Northumbria, 31
Henry, emperor of Luxembourg, 194
Henry de Bohun, 148, 186
Henry of Grosmont, earl of Derby (d. 1361), 295
Henry de Haliburton, 77
Henry de Latham, sheriff of Aberdeenshire (d. 1297), 73
Henry of Lancaster (d. 1345), 54, 94, 103, 114, 158, 159, 165, 196, 200-1, 209-10, 212, 215, 239, 280-1, 285-6
Henry Percy, see Percy, Henry II and III
Henry de Sully, 230, 233-4, 236
Herle, William de, 241
Hermitage castle, 295-6, 305
Heron, Robert, 123
Hertford, 54
Hesilrig, William, sheriff of Lanark, 63-4
Heston, 295-6, 301
Hexham, 49, 76, 78, 171, 198, 207, 298, 304
Historia Regnum Britanniae, 100-1
Holderness, 142
Holme Cultrum, 98, 228
Holy Island, 43, 228, 283
Holyhead, 205
Holyrood, 273
Holystone, 168
Horsely, Roger de, 201

Hotham, John de, 204
Houghton, Thomas, 119
Hugh d'Aimery, bishop, 284
Hugh de Cressingham, 59, 62, 67-70, 72-6, 80
Hugh le Despenser (the elder, d. 1326), 54, 114, 181, 194, 234, 239
Hugh le Despenser (the younger), 220-2, 226, 229, 234, 236-7, 239
Hugh du Puiset, bishop, 25
Hugh de Vere, 103
Hull, 261, 264
Humphrey de Bohun, earl of Hereford (d. 1298), 31, 50, 61, 74, 80, 84-5, 94, 96, 99-100,
Humphrey de Bohun, earl of Hereford (d. 1322), 100, 103, 136, 145, 148, 159, 161-2, 165, 184-6, 192, 195, 202, 209, 212, 227
Hundred Years War, 238, 278, 288, 300
Hungary, king of, 36
Huntercombe, Walter, 74, 90, 107
Huntingdon, earl of, see David, earl of Huntingdon
Huntley, 153
Hutton Moor, 77

Inchchonnell, 155
Inchkeith, 294
Inchmartin, 135
Inchture, 170
Inglewood, 151
Ingram de Umfraville, 39, 93, 96, 106, 122, 136, 162, 165-6, 181-2, 192, 195, 200, 202, 225
Inverbervie, 295
Inverkeithing, 119, 214
Inverkip, 104, 119, 132, 138
Inverlochy, Comyn of Badenoch's castle, 152
Inverness, 30, 64-5, 72-3, 135
Inverurie, 154, 156
Ireland, 203-8, 242
Ireys, John, 201

Irvine, 68, 69, 70, 72, 74
Isabel de Clare, 32
Isabel of Fife, countess of Buchan, 133
Isabel of Mar, 203
Isabella, queen of England, 153, 159, 237, 239-41, 247, 250-1, 257
Isabella of Mar, 278
Islandshire, 25
Islay, lord of, see Macdonald, Alexander
Isle of Bute, 139
Isle of Man, 21, 165, 172, 203-5, 273, 309
Isle of Wight, 119
Isobel of Huntingdon, 31
Ivo of Aldburgh, 240

James II, 309
James of St George, Master, 107-8, 119
James the Steward, see Steward, James the
Jardine, Humphrey, 267
Jay, Brian de, 84
Jean le Bel, 241, 243, 245, 254
Jean de Lamouilly, 120, 217
Jean de Valois, 39, 284
Jedburgh, 40, 45, 49, 52, 85, 113, 170, 213, 226, 273, 277, 293, 300, 309
Jedwood Forest, 214
Jettour, William, 170
Joan de Bar, 181
Joan of the Tower, sister of Edward III, 248, 250-1, 264
John, king of England, 11, 19, 26, 32
John I, king of France, 236
John II, king of France, 303-7
John, king of Scotland, see Balliol, John, king of Scotland
John of Aird, 72
John of Argyll, see Macdonald, John, earl of Argyll
John of Athy, 205
John de Balliol, 31, 55
John of Brittany, earl of Richmond (d. 1334), 94,

114, 122-3, 132, 151, 153, 160, 162, 200, 209, 223, 225-7, 230-1
John of Caen, 24
John of Cambo, 140
John de Clavering, 200
John le Despenser, 52
John of Eltham, 269, 279, 286-7
John de Eure, 200, 207, 215
John of Fordun, 7, 47, 51, 60, 63, 77, 101, 114, 126, 128, 140, 172, 271, 305
John of Galloway, 31
John of Gaunt, 303-4
John of Hainault, 239, 241-2
John de Haliburton, 137
John de Hotham, 204
John of the Isles, 280-1, 296, 307
John of Inchmartin, 122
John de Lilbourne, 201
John de Lindsay, 141
John of Lorn, see Macdougall, John of Lorn
John of Mentieth, 133
John of Ross, 203
John de Sandale, 123, 132
John de Soules, see Soules, John
John de St John (the elder), 35, 38, 60, 90, 92, 103-4, 109, 114, 136, 144, 145, 151, 161, 223
John de St John (the younger), 144
John de Stirling, see Stirling, John
John de Vescy, 23
John de Warenne, see Warenne, John de
John de Weston, see Weston, John
Joseph the Jew, see Aymer de Valence
Juliers, count, 280

Keith, Robert, 88, 95-6, 122, 132, 144, 177, 183-4, 193, 218, 264, 276, 299
Keith, William, 218, 255,

268-9, 284
Kellawe, bishop Richard,
198, 207, 212
Kelso, 45, 104
Kennedy, John, 296
Kent, 227
earl of, 237, 240, 242,
257
Kilbride, 113
Kildrummy, 129, 139, 141,
264, 272, 282-3
Kilkenny, 94
Kincardine, 53, 291
Kincardine-on-Spey, 286
Kinclaven castle, 116
Kinclevin, 291
King's Lynn, 285
Kinghorn, 261
Kingston, John, 87, 89-90,
92, 107, 119, 132
Kinloss, 114, 286
Kinneff, 286, 291
Kinninmouth, Alexander,
bishop of Aberdeen, 224,
253
Kintyre, 132, 142
lord of, see McQuillan,
Malcolm
Kirk, Alan, keeper of king's
tents, 278
Kirkcudbright, 95, 97, 139,
275
Kirkencliffe, battle of, 141
Kirkintilloch, 111, 133
Kirkoswald, 197
Kirkpatrick, 128
Knapdale, lord of, see
Mentieth, John
Knaresborough, 215, 220,
233
Kyle, 146, 264, 275

La Coruña, 255
Lacruarie, Lachlan, 88
Lacy, Henry, earl of Lincoln
(d. 1311), 42, 60, 84, 94,
103, 159, 165, 166-7,
220
Lady de Gynes, 265
Lamberton, William,
bishop of St Andrews (d.
1328), 69, 87-8, 93, 111-
12, 122, 127, 132, 133-
4, 137, 163, 170, 224,
234, 249
Lambley, 49

Lamouilly, Jean de, 120,
217
Lanark, 111
sheriff of, 60, 63, 123
Lancashire, 104, 212, 231
Lancaster, 73, 228
earl of, see Henry of
Lancaster and Thomas
of Lancaster
sheriff of, 67, 95
Landallis, William, bishop
of St Andrews (d. 1385),
307
Lanercost, 45, 47, 49, 51,
64, 66, 95, 106, 142,
145, 166, 171-2, 174,
178, 184, 188, 192, 196,
281, 294, 298
Langtoft, Peter, 95, 97, 120
Langton, Walter, 87, 158
Lardare, 198
Largs, battle of 1263, 12,
15, 55
Larne, 204, 242
Latimer, William, 90, 114,
136, 280
Lauder, Robert, 272
Lauderdale, 178
Laurence of Argyll, 59
Lauriston, 286, 291
le Bel, see Jean le Bel
Leake, 220
Leeds, 127
Leicester, 211
Leinster, 204
Leith, 178, 228
Lennox, 135, 189
countess of, 116
earl of, 163
see also Malcolm II
Lerebane, Patrick, 151
Leuchars, 22, 287, 291
Lewes, battle of, 55-6
Leybourne, Robert,
constable of Ayr, 146
Lichfield, bishop of, 239
Liddesdale, 250, 297
lord of, see Soulis, John
Liege, 241
Lilbourne, John de, 201
Limerick, 94, 205
Lincoln, 99-100, 103, 180,
199, 204, 209, 212, 231,
246
bishop of, see Burghersh,
Henry

earl of, see Lacy, Henry
and Thomas of
Lancaster
sheriff of, 170
Lindsay, Alexander, 69,
117, 122, 129, 155, 171
Lindsay, John, 264
Lindsay, Reginald, 171
Linlithgow, 52, 83, 103,
104, 107-8, 111, 114,
119-20, 144, 157, 166,
170, 172, 273, 276
Linstock, 171
Lintilee, 214
Linton, Bernard, abbot of
Arbroath, 224
Liverpool, 283
Livingston, 170
Livingston, Archibald,
constable of Linlithgow,
107
Loch Awe, 155
Loch Doon, 132-3, 141,
155, 170, 272
Loch Earn, 261
Loch Etive, 155
Loch Fyne, 275
Loch Ken, 296
Loch Leven, 272
Loch Linnhe, 152
Loch Lomond, 139
Loch Ness, 152
Loch Ryan, 104, 106, 145,
151
Loch Tay, 139
Loch Trool, 146
Lochabar, 276
Lochindorb, 65, 276, 283-
4, 286, 296
Lochmaben, 85, 91, 93-4,
106, 126, 128, 138, 155,
161, 170, 208, 232-3,
267, 276-7, 293-4, 309
Lockadale, 49
Locrine, king of England,
101
Logie, John, 225
London, 37, 51, 54, 56-7,
58, 61, 65, 67, 69, 74,
80, 99, 121-4, 150, 164-
5, 167, 199, 250, 278,
290, 301
Longridge, 209
Longshanks, Edward, see
Edward I
Lords Ordainers, 160, 164-

5, 167
Lorn, lord of, see
    Macdougall, Alexander
Lothian, 136, 166, 169
Loudon, 106
Loudoun Hill, 144, 145-7
Louis de Nevers, 235
Louis IX, king of France,
    27
Louis X, king of France,
    236
Louis of France, prince, 11
Louth, earl of, see
    Bermingham, John
Lovell, Richard, 136
Lowther, Robert, 284
Lubaud, Piers, 144, 175
Lubeck, 80
Lucy, see Anthony de Lucy
    and Thomas de Lucy
Luke de Wharton, 201
Lundie, Richard, 68, 75
Lundy, William, 64
Luxembourg, emperor of,
    see Henry, emperor of
    Luxembourg
Lyon, 110, 285

M'Ghie, Michael, 295
MacAlpine, Kenneth, king
    of Dalriada, 9
Macbeth, 9
MacCan, Donald, 68, 144,
    151, 155
MacCulloch, 144
Macdonald, Alexander,
    lord of Islay, 68
Macdonald, Angus Og,
    139

Macdouall, Duncan, 263,
    275, 295-6, 305
Macdouall, Dungal, 144-5,
    151, 155, 172, 208
Macdouall, Fergus, 295
Macdougall, Alexander,
    lord of Argyll and Lorn
    (d. 1310), 54, 68, 116,
    146, 149, 152,155, 156,
    203, 205
Macdougall, John of Argyll
    and Lorn ('John of Lorn'
    d. 1316), 139, 152, 155,
    156, 165
Macduff of Fife (d. 1298),
    37-8, 64, 69, 73, 84

MacGachan, Roland, 155
MacGoffrey, Duncan, 203
Mackenzie, W Mackay,
    179, 188, 190
MacRuairidh, Christiana
    of the Isles, 140
MacRuairidh, Ranald, 296
McQuillan, Malcolm, lord
    of Kintyre, 132, 144-5
Magna Carta, 99
Maid of Norway, see
    Margaret, Maid of
    Norway
Major, John, 7
Malcolm II, earl of Lennox
    (d. 1333), 9, 44, 75-6,
    80, 118, 120, 139-40,
    271
Malcolm III, Canmore,
    king of Scots (d. 1093),
    9-10, 29
Malcolm IV, king of Scots,
    31, 39
Malcolm of Wigtown, 299
Malestroit, 294, 296
Malherbe, Gilbert, sheriff
    of Stirling, 92, 225
Malise III, earl of
    Strathearn (d. 1313), 44,
    52, 58, 69, 73, 80, 90,
    114, 118, 120, 134-5,
    172
Malise IV, earl of
    Strathearn (d. c. 1329),
    172, 272
Mallore, Peter, justiciar of
    England, 123
Mandeville, see Roger de
    Mandeville
Manners, Robert, 247
Manton, Ralph, 111
Manx, Isle of, 21
Mar, 153
    earl of, see Mar, Donald I
    and II and Talbot,
    Richard
    see also Isabel of Mar
Mar, Donald I, earl of (d.
    1302), 22, 23, 33, 44,
    51, 53, 58, 72-3, 132
Mar, Donald II, earl of (d.
    1332), 202, 239-40,
    242-3, 249, 257, 261-3,
    289
March, earl of, see Dunbar,
    Patrick IV and V

Margaret, daughter of
    Henry III, 19
Margaret, Maid of
    Norway, queen of Scots,
    17, 19-23, 29, 30, 36,
    37, 40
Margaret, queen of
    England, 148
Margaret, sister of Edward
    I, 24
Margaret de Clare, 159
Mark, bishop of Sodor and
    Man, 59
Marmaduke, Richard, 211
Marseilles, 285
Matthew of Westminster,
    118
Maubuisson, Odard de,
    224
Maule, Thomas, 114
Maxwell, Eustace, sheriff
    of Dumfries, 225, 263,
    278, 295
Maxwell, John, 301
Mazun, John, 37
Meath, 204
Melrose, 45, 113, 211,
    229, 255, 295
    abbot of, 122, 213
Melton, William,
    archbishop of York, 219,
    222, 232, 246-7, 260
Menteith, 117
    earl of, 281, 302
    see also Murdoch and
    Stewart, Alexander
Mentieth, John, lord of
    Arran and Knapdale,
    139-40, 162-3
Mere (Wiltshire), 137
Merrington, 298
Methven, 137-9
    battle of, 133, 135, 147,
    163
Michael de Miggel, 63
Middleton, Gilbert, 173,
    215-16, 217
Miller, Revd T, 190
Mitford, 80, 200, 208,
    215-16, 219
Moffat, 265, 292
Moigne, Marjorie, 36-7
Monmouth, Geoffrey of,
    100
Montagu, admiral Simon,
    94, 140, 165, 172

Montagu, William, earl of Salisbury, 268, 272-3, 282-3, 286-7, 291-3, 294

Montassieu de Noaillac, constable of Ayr, 106

Montfichet, William, 169-70, 234

Montfort, Simon de, 27

Montgomery, Owen of, 119

Monthermer, Ralph, earl of Gloucester, 32, 80, 94, 103, 127, 145, 146

Montreuil-sur-Mer, 91-2, 159

Montrose, 53, 113

Moorholm, 265

Moray, 9, 64, 71, 135, 156
bishop of, see Murray, David
countess of ('Black Agnes'), 292-3
earl of, see Randolph, John and Randolph, Thomas
warden of, see Reginald le Cheyne

Moray, Andrew, see Andrew de Moray

Moray, Maurice, earl of Strathearn, 293, 299

Moreham, Herbert, 92, 141

Morpeth, 196, 269

Morris, John, 93

Mortimer, Roger, earl of March (d. 1330), 148, 204-5, 237, 240, 242, 247, 251, 255, 257

Moubray, Alexander, 276, 279

Moubray, Geoffrey, 160

Moubray, John, 113, 118, 122, 135-6, 153-4, 156, 161, 265, 276, 280

Moubray, Philip, 175, 186, 194, 206

Moubray, Roger, 225, 258

Mowat, William, 247

Mowbray, Philip, 206

Muckhart, 170

Munster, 205

Murdoch, earl of Mentieth, 249, 262-3

Murimath, 271

Murray, Andrew (d. 1297), 13, 64-5, 70-6

Murray, Andrew, justiciar of Scotland (d. 1298) 64-6, 84, 104

Murray, Andrew (d. 1338), 263-4, 272, 279, 282-4, 286, 289, 291-3

Murray, Andrew of Tullibardine, 262

Murray, David, bishop of Moray (d. 1326), 97, 134, 224, 249

Murray of Duffes, 72

Musselburgh, 228, 261

Myton, 222

Nairn, 65, 71, 72, 152

Namur, count of, Guy, 280-1

Narve, bishop of Bergen, 22

Navarre, king of, 173

Neath abbey, 239

Neville, Ralph, keeper of the March, 229, 272-3, 275-7, 279-81, 291-2, 298-9, 300, 302

Neville, Robert, 'Peacock of the North', 111, 211

Neville's Cross, battle of, 238, 250, 253, 299, 303

Newark, Henry, 21

Newburn, 197

Newcastle, 10, 37, 40, 43, 78-9, 89, 95, 120, 134, 141-2, 168-9, 196, 199, 202, 209-10, 212, 217, 220-1, 228-9, 241-4, 248, 273, 278-80, 304-5
treaty of, 273

Newminster, 179

Newton, Adam, 217

Nicholas IV, see Pope Nicholas IV

Nicholas de Soules, 30, 35

Nicholson, Ranald, 57-8

Nithsdale, 106, 145, 206, 292

Noccasini, Niccolò, see Pope Benedict XI

Norfolk, earl of, 181
see also Bigod, Roger, earl of Norfolk

Norham, 25, 26-7, 35, 45, 166, 170-1, 197, 229, 239-40, 247-8, 305
Award of, 28, 36

Normandy, 274, 288, 296

Northallerton, 219, 222, 230

Northampton, 21, 160, 165, 199, 221, 249, 287
earl of, 305

Northburgh, Roger, 194

Northumberland (Northumbria), 9-10, 22, 25, 48-9, 79, 90, 103, 108, 136, 151, 171, 173, 197-8, 200, 219, 223, 229, 243, 247, 267, 290

Norway, 17, 20-2, 30, 34, 39-40
see also Eric II, king of Norway

Norwich, bishop of, see Airmyn, William
see also Walter de Norwich

Nottingham, 96, 222, 255, 293

Ò Néill, Domnall, king of Tyrone, 206

O'Brien, Donough, 205

O'Brien, Murtough, 205

Oban, 155

Odard de Maubuisson, 224

Old Cambus, 217

Oldmeldrum, 154

Oliphant, William, 117, 118-19, 121, 124, 172

Ordainers, see Lord's Ordainers

Orkney, 12, 15, 21, 141, 161

Ormande, at Rothesay castle, 282

Ormesby, William, 57, 62, 64

Orygynale Cronykil of Scotland, 7

Ospringe, 71

Owen of Montgomery, 119

Oxford, 100
earl of, 278, 280

Oxnam, 266

Paisley, abbot of, 130

Paris, Treaty of, 11, 111-12, 236

Park of Duns, 212
Patrick of Dunbar, see
    Dunbar, Patrick IV and V
Patrick of Ireland, 48
Payne, Thomas, 136
Peebles, 87, 104, 111, 273,
    278, 300
Pembroke, earl of, see
    Aymer de Valence
Pennersax, 197
Penrith, 21
Percy, Henry II (d. 1314),
    46, 59, 67-9, 73-4, 78,
    80, 116, 136, 139, 144-
    5, 160, 161, 166, 168
Percy, Henry III (d. 1352),
    200, 238, 240, 242, 246-
    50, 260, 271-3, 275-7,
    279, 280, 291-2, 298-9,
    300
Perth, 21, 22, 30, 52, 63,
    84, 113, 114-17, 119,
    120, 122, 136-7, 139,
    156, 162, 166, 169-72,
    261, 263-4, 272, 279-82,
    285-7, 289, 291, 293,
    297
Pessagno, Antonio, 167
Petty, 64
Philip III, king of France,
    288
Philip IV, king of France,
    36, 38, 39-40, 48, 49,
    61, 73, 84, 86-8, 91, 98,
    103, 107, 109-10, 111,
    151, 163-4, 173
Philip V, king of France,
    236
Philip VI, king of France,
    273-5, 283-5, 287-8,
    294-7
Philip, count of Valois, 288
Philippa of Hainault, 239
Picardy, 54, 107, 196
Pickering, Robert, 207
Pilche, Alexander, 65
Pinkeny, Robert, 31, 35
Pius, Antoninus, 8
Poitiers, battle of, 253, 306
Poitou, 110
Pontefract, 181, 212, 217-
    18
Pope Benedict XI (Niccolò
    Noccasini), 110
Pope Benedict XII (Jacques
    Fournier) 284-5, 287

Pope Boniface VIII
    (Benedict Gaetani) 61,
    88, 91, 97, 100-2, 108-
    10
Pope Clement V (Bertrand
    de Got), 110, 130, 163
Pope Clement VI (Pierre
    Roger) 302
Pope John XXII (Jacques
    Duèse), 206, 214-15,
    224-6, 253
Pope Nicholas IV (Jerome
    of Ascoli), 20
Porchester castle, 137
Prescott, John, 7
Preston, 43, 228
Prestwich, Michael, 56
Prudhoe, 200

Ragman Roll, 57, 59, 64,
    124
Rait, Andrew, 71-2
Ramsey, Alexander (d.
    1342), 289, 294-6
Ramsey, John of
    Auchterhouse, 206
Ramsay, William, 302, 306
Randolph, John, earl of
    Moray (d. 1346), 265,
    271, 274-5, 278-81, 283,
    289, 293-4, 297-9
Randolph, Thomas II, earl
    of Moray (d. 1332), 28,
    138, 142, 154, 163, 175,
    183-5, 187-9, 192, 197,
    201-7, 213, 215, 218-20,
    222-3, 226-8, 230, 234-
    6, 238, 242-3, 246-7,
    255, 260-3, 265, 289
Rathlin, 140
Ravenser, 261
Raymond de Caillau, 210-
    11
Red Comyn, see Comyn,
    John 'Red'
Redesdale, 49, 169, 200,
    257, 292
Reginald, master, 119
Reginald le Cheyne,
    warden of Moray, 65,
    72-3, 147, 154, 156
Reginald de Crawford, 71,
    144-5
Reid, Norman, 66
Renfrew, 166
Ribblesdale, 220

Richard de Burgh, earl of
    Ulster (d. 1326), 18, 21,
    42, 54, 104, 113, 114,
    116-17, 142, 162, 165,
    204-5, 242
Richard de Bury, bishop of
    Durham, 273, 287
Richard I, king of England
    (d. 1199), 10, 32, 102,
    159, 274
Richard, earl of Cornwall
    (d. 1272), 46-7, 165
Richard of Cornwall (d.
    1296), 46
Richmond, 197, 212, 219,
    247, 298
    earl of, see John of
    Brittany
    see also Thomas de
    Richmond
Rickerby, 44
Rievaulx, 132, 230
    abbot of, 240
Ripon, 198, 219
Rishanger, 95, 118
Robert I, 272
Robert II, see Robert the
    Steward
Robert III, king of Scots,
    309
Robert of Annandale, see
    Bruce, Robert, lord of
    Annandale
Robert d'Arcy, 139
Robert of Artois, 288
Robert of Bedford, master,
    119
Robert de Béthune, 235
Robert de Clifford, see
    Clifford, Robert
Robert de Kethose, 50
Robert de Ros, 43
Robert de Sapy, 215
Robert the Steward
    (Robert II, king of Scots),
    184, 203, 225, 265, 272,
    275, 281-2, 285, 293-4,
    299-300, 303, 307
Robert de Tilliol, 91
Robert de Ufford, earl of
    Suffolk, 291
Robert de Umfraville, earl
    of Angus, 161, 173, 200
Rochester, 74
Roger de Horsely, 201
Roger de Mandeville, 30,

35

Rokeby, Thomas, 244, 296, 298-9

Roland, Sir, see MacGachan, Roland

Ros, Robert de, 43

Ros, William, 161

Ros, William of Kendal, 43

Rose castle, 98, 171, 228, 292

Roslyn, battle of, 110-11, 112

Rosport, 94

Ross, bishop of, 249
    earl of, see Ross, Hugh and Ross, William

Ross, Effie, countess of, 65, 72

Ross, Godfrey, 276

Ross, Hugh, earl of Ross (d. 1333), 72, 116, 134, 141, 163, 249, 271

Ross, Walter, 195

Ross, William, earl of Ross (d. 1310s), 49, 51, 58, 61, 65, 72, 152-4, 156, 163

Rosslyn, Thomas, 282, 285

Rothes, 54

Rothesay, 132-3, 272, 275, 282

Roulston Scar, 230

Roxburgh, 40, 43, 52, 54, 69, 70, 77, 81, 87-9, 94, 107, 112, 141, 157, 165-6, 170-1, 173, 174-5, 229, 264, 272-3, 278, 282, 287, 293, 295-6, 300, 306, 309
    sheriff of, 276

Rufus, William, 10, 31

Rushen castle, 172

Rutherglen, 92-3, 162

Ryton, 79, 298

St Andrews, 30, 84, 114, 119, 163, 287, 291
    bishop of, see Fraser, William and Lamberton, William and Landallis, William

St Duthac, 141

St John of Beverly, 43

St Margaret, 250

St Sabina, cardinal of, 137

Saint Sardos, 236-7, 288

Salisbury, 19-20, 61
    earl of, 166
    see also Montagu, William and Thomas of Lancaster
    treaty of 1290, 20

Sampson, John, 92

Sandale, John, 134, 211

Sanquhar, 43

Sapy, Robert de, 215

Scalacronica, 127, 134, 158, 178, 184, 187-8, 216, 305

Scandinavia, 252

Scarborough, 168

Scawton Moor, 230

Scimus, fili, 97-102

Scone, 17, 35, 56-7, 64, 133, 225
    abbot of, 137

Scot, Michael, 20

Scotichronicon, 7, 150

Scrymgeour, Alexander, 77, 140

Scrymgeour, Nicholas, 247

Segrave, John, lieutenant of Scotland, 80, 90, 94, 110, 112, 114, 119, 121, 123, 162, 195

Segrave, Nicholas, 165, 202

Segrave, Stephen, 197

Selby, Walter, 297

Selkirk, 44, 50, 69, 70, 74, 83, 88, 90, 107-8, 110, 161, 165-6, 273, 300
    keeper of, see Balliol, Alexander

Seton, Alexander, 189, 216, 225, 234, 261, 266, 268, 285

Seton, Christian, 141, 202

Seton, Christopher, 128

Seton, Thomas, 268-9

Seton, William, 268

Severus, Septimus, 8

Sherburn, 226

Shetland, 15

Sicily, 24, 27

Siloch, 153

Simon de Montfort, 27

Sinclair, Henry, 144

Sinclair, William, bishop of Dunkeld (d. 1337), 214, 224, 249, 263

Siward, earl of

Northumbria, 9

Siward, Richard, commander of Dunbar castle, 49, 114, 132

Skaithmuir, 210

Skelbo, 154

Skerries, battle of, 204

Skinburness, 94, 132, 139, 140, 161

Sodor and Man, Mark, bishop of, 59

Soules, John, guardian of Scotland (d. 1310), 39, 88, 101, 106-7, 109, 111, 117-18, 122, 128

Soules, Nicholas de, 30, 35

Soules, William, 225

Soulis, John, lord of Liddesdale, 206

Spalding, 210

Spalding, Piers, 218-19

Spennymoor, 198

Spott, battle of, 50-1

Stafford, Ralph, 262

Stainmoor, 78, 197

Stamford, 160, 162

Standard, battle of, 10, 183

Stanhope Park, 245-6

Stanhouses, 106

Stapledon, Walter, 234

Stephen, king, 10, 159

Steward, James the (d. 1309), 18, 62, 66-8, 68, 73, 75-6, 88, 93, 111, 117, 122, 163, 213

Steward, Robert, see Robert the Steward

Steward, Walter the, 183-4, 206, 219, 221, 230

Stewart, Alan, 296

Stewart, Alexander, earl of Mentieth (d. 1306), 44, 49, 51, 58, 71, 88, 118, 120, 122-3, 154

Stewart, James of Durisdeer, 242

Stewart, John, 206, 245, 309

Stewart, John of Bunkle, 257

Stewart, John of Mentieth, 123

Stewart, Thomas, 305

Stirling, 30, 34, 39, 50, 52, 74-6, 84, 90, 92, 93, 112-22, 157, 166, 170-1,

174, 177-8, 185, 194, 287, 291, 294, 296
Stirling, John, 276, 285, 287, 292-3
Stirling Bridge, battle of, 7, 70-1, 74-7, 79, 80, 95, 99
Stirling campaign, 115-22
Stone of Scone, 133, 250
Stratford, chancellor, 266
Stratford, John, bishop of Winchester, 236, 275-6, 287
Strathbogie, David, earl of Atholl, (d. 1326), 134, 169, 170-1, 223
Strathbogie, David, titular earl of Atholl (d. 1335), 257, 265, 267, 272-3, 275, 277, 279, 281-2
Strathbogie, John, earl of Atholl (d. 1306), 22, 44, 49, 51, 58, 73, 93, 114, 116, 121, 133-6, 139, 141, 153, 202
Strathclyde, kingdom of, 9, 12, 22
Strathearn, 116-17, 272
countess of, 225
earl of, see Malise III and IV and Moray, Maurice
Stronkalter, 289
Suffolk, 239
earl of, see Robert de Ufford
Sully, see Henry de Sully
Sunderland Bridge, 298
Surrey, earl of, see Warenne, John de
Sutherland, Kenneth, earl of (d. 1333), 12, 134, 153-4, 163, 271
Sutton, abbot Thomas, 20
Sutton Bank, 230
Sverre, king, 19
Swaledale, 197, 212
Sweetheart Abbey, 98
Swinburn, Adam, 216

Talbot, Richard, earl of Mar, 272, 276-7
Tange, Edward, 24
Tarbert castle, 280
Tarradale, 154
Teba de Ardules, 255
Templars, 163

Teviotdale, 247, 292, 294
Thomas, 144-5
Thomas, bishop of Whitehorn, 95, 163
Thomas, master, king's engineer, 119
Thomas du Bois, 117
Thomas de Clare, 18, 148
Thomas of Galloway, 57
Thomas, of earl Lancaster (d. 1322), 54, 94, 160, 166-8, 174, 181-2, 207, 211, 215-22, 226-8, 239, 242-3, 252, 257
Thomas de Lucy, 296
Thomas of Mar, 303
Thomas de Richmond, 214
Tibbers castle, 155, 170
Tickhall, William, 287
Tilliol, John, keeper of Lochmaben, 106
Tinwald, 94
Tiptoft, Payn, 148
Torwood, 185
Tournai, 81
Treaty, 91
Towers, William, 306
Towton, 309
Traquair, 104
Tudhoe, 243
Turbeville, Thomas, 39
Turnberry, 18, 106-7, 109, 133, 145, 155
Turnbull the Scot, 270
Tweedmouth, 165, 240, 267-8
Tweng, Marmeduke, 74-7, 195
Twynham, Master Walter, 234
Twynholm, 95
Tyndrum, 139
Tynedale, 21, 168, 200, 212
Tynemouth, 168, 235
Tynham, Walter, 285
Tyrone, king of, see Ò Néill, Domnall

Ughtred, Thomas, 230, 287, 291, 294
Ulster, 204-5, 242
earl of, see Richard de Burgh and William de Burgh
Umfraville, earl of Angus,

see Gilbert de and Ingram de
see also Robert de and Roger de
Upsettlington, 25, 29, 258
Urquhart, 65, 71, 114, 152, 272

Valence, William de, 20
see also Aymer de Valence and
Valentinian, Emperor, 55
Valois, see Charles of Valois and Philip, count of Valois
Vaux, lords of Gilsland, 200
Vegetius, 55-6
Vienne, 163
Vipont, Alan, 272
Vipont, William, 195
Votadini, 45

Wake, baron of, 80
Wake, Thomas, 240, 250, 257-8, 261, 292, 297
Wale, Thomas, 101, 102, 107
Wales, prince of, see under Edward II, Caernarfon rebellion, 39, 56, 212
Wallace, Malcolm, 64, 87
Wallace, William, 13, 18, 47, 54-5, 60, 62-4, 66-7, 69-70, 73-80, 83-4, 86-8, 112-13, 116-18, 121-5, 128, 141, 169
Walsingham, 84
Walter of Amersham, 59
Walter of Guisborough, 7, 23, 63, 64, 66, 112, 125
Walter of Hereford, master, 120
Walter de Manny, 264
Walter de Norwich, treasurer to Edward II, 211
Warenne, John de, earl of Surrey (d. 1304), 20, 21, 31, 40, 42, 50, 53, 59, 62, 67, 69-70, 73-7, 79-81, 94, 96, 103, 159, 165-6, 168, 181
Warenne, John de, earl of Surrey (d. 1347), 209, 229, 259, 272, 280

Wark, 43, 56, 111, 165-6, 170, 177, 179, 218, 219
Warkworth, 229, 247
Warwick, earl of, see Beauchamp, Guy, and Beauchamp, Thomas
Waterford, 94
Weardale, 246, 248, 251, 253
Welbek, 20
Wellington, duke of, 183
Wemyss, Michael, 20, 137
Wensleydale, 219
Wessex, kingdom of, 9, 12
Westminster, abbot of, 250 see also London
Westmoreland, 104, 151, 171, 208, 227, 265, 290, 292
sheriff of, 67
Weston, John, chamberlain of Scotland, 174, 210
Wharfedale, 220, 222
Wharton, see Luke de Wharton
Whitby, 217, 239
Whitehorn, bishop of, see Thomas, bishop of Whitehorn
Whitekirk, 306
Wigtown, 19, 97, 275
earl of, see Fleming, Malcolm
William I, king of England, 102
William de Bevercotes, 123
William de Burgh, earl of Ulster (d. 1333), 242
William de Durham, 106
William de Dyfford, 296
William of Eaglesham, 102
William of Ferrers, constable of Linlithgow, 108
William de Fiennes, 175
William of Gainsborough, 101, 102
William de Herle, 241
William the Lion, king of Scots, 10-11, 26, 30-1
William de Ros, 30, 35, 44
William of Sardinia, 100, 102
William, earl of Sutherland, 299
William de Valence, 20

William de Vescy, 30, 35
William de la Zouche, archbishop of York, 298
William La Zouche of Ashby, 136, 249, 250
Winchelsea, 205
Winchelsea, Robert, archbishop of Canterbury, 61, 97-8, 100, 158-9
Winchester, 135, 137
bishop of, see Stratford, John
Windsor, 168
Wiseman, William, sheriff of Elgin, 154
Wishart, Robert, bishop of Glasgow (d. 1316), 18, 19, 21, 27, 28, 33, 34, 59, 66-9, 73, 88, 110, 117-18, 127, 130, 133-4, 137, 163, 202
Wogan, John, 104
Worcester, bishop of, 225
Wyntoun, Andrew, 7, 275, 283

Yolande, Queen, 17-19
York, 11, 12, 40, 59, 80-1, 95, 121, 150, 160, 164, 197, 199, 201-2, 207-8, 212, 216-17, 220, 222-3, 228, 230, 233, 237, 241-2, 247-8, 265-6, 273, 278, 279, 290
archbishop of, see Grenfield, William and Melton, William and William de la Zouche
Yorkshire, 136, 197, 212, 218, 231, 234